The
DOG CARE
Question and Answer Book

The
DOG CARE
Question and Answer Book

Barry Bush BVSc PhD FRCVS

BLACK CAT

The photograph on page 7
was supplied by Equinox

First published in Great Britain by
Orbis Publishing Limited, London 1982
Reprinted 1988 by Macdonald & Co
(Publishers) Ltd under the Black Cat
imprint

Macdonald & Co (Publishers) Ltd,
3rd Floor, Greater London House,
Hampstead Road, London NW1 7QX

a member of Maxwell Pergamon Publishing
Organisation plc

ISBN 0-7481-0186-1
Printed in Hungary

Contents

Introduction

In the twenty years since I began to practise as a veterinary surgeon there has been a tremendous, and accelerating, increase in all aspects of our knowledge about dogs. Much more is now known about their behaviour, nutrition and diseases than ever before. Many of our most highly prized veterinary drugs were introduced during this period, including drugs to remove major parasites effectively and safely, eliminate stubborn infections and control the heat period in bitches. Even an entirely new, and often fatal, disease — parvovirus infection — appeared, requiring the production of a new vaccine to protect against it.

Coincidentally, dog owners began to ask for more information about how to care for what has long been the world's most popular companion animal. (In Britain a quarter of all homes contain a dog and in some countries, such as France and the United States, the proportion is even higher.) Faced with differing opinions about such matters as the value of commercial diets and how to train their animals, owners turned increasingly to the impartial advice of their local veterinarian. Unfortunately, because so much information has become available in recent years, the type of wide-ranging discussion that most people would like to arrange with their vets would be prohibitively time-consuming. With a busy practice to run it is shortage of time that makes vets keep their consultations brief.

It was this problem in communication that prompted me to present in book form a type of extended 'consultation' that would make it possible to answer fully those questions about dogs which are asked most frequently, and to discuss other topics of general interest. Like many of my colleagues, whose main concern is the teaching of veterinary undergraduates, I believe that the best and quickest way to raise the standard of care of pet animals is to disseminate accurate information as widely as possible. And I feel sure that the one thing we would all agree about is the need to look after our animals to the best of our ability.

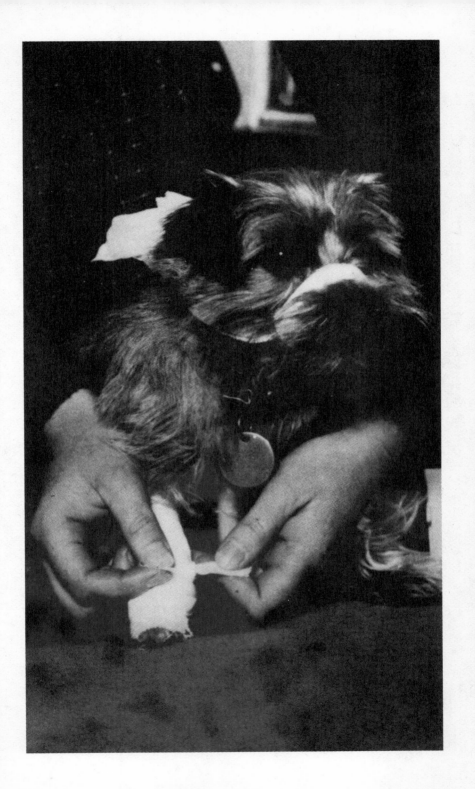

1
Helping Your Vet

Q *How can I be sure that a vet is knowledgeable about dogs?*

A All veterinary surgeons receive the same basic training so that they are competent to deal with all domesticated species. These are chiefly the meat-producing animals (cattle, sheep and pigs) and the companion animals (horses, dogs and cats). Cats and dogs, together with other smaller pet animals such as rabbits, guinea pigs and hamsters, are referred to professionally as 'small animals', while the other species are known as 'large animals'. Poultry, exotic animals (i.e. zoo animals) and fish are also dealt with in veterinary training, but less extensively.

After qualification, some vets feel that they would prefer to treat all these species of animals in order to utilize all that they have learned, and consequently they take employment in a 'mixed practice' (i.e. one treating both large and small animals). Others prefer to deal solely with either small or large animals and therefore may establish, or find employment in, a practice which concentrates on that particular group. Alternatively, they may work with other veterinarians in a mixed practice but take responsibility for just the small or large animal patients.

Increasingly there is a tendency for vets to concentrate on just one species; this is particularly so in the large animal field and there are, for example, a number of specialist equine practices. In general, small animal practices will treat both cats and dogs, although in some parts of North America there is a trend towards greater specialization. Some veterinary surgeons devote themselves to dealing with particular groups of dogs (e.g. racing Greyhounds or guard dogs being trained by the police, army or government departments). At the present time in Great Britain the governing body of the veterinary profession, the Royal College of Veterinary Surgeons, is still formulating its ideas about specialization, and currently no British vet is able to describe himself as a specialist in any particular field, even though this may be so.

However, a telephone call to your local veterinary practice will usually establish whether one or more of the veterinarians has a particular interest in small animals. If so, this interest is almost certain to be largely or primarily in dogs because solely feline specialists are few and far between. (There are also some animal welfare societies whose names suggest that they are chiefly concerned with dogs.)

Veterinary practices in urban areas are invariably predominantly concerned with treating small animals, and in both North America and Great Britain many such practices are described as 'hospitals'. This term implies the provision of certain facilities over and above those of a routine practice.

The recommendation of other dog owners (e. g. friends, neighbours or fellow members of a breed society or dog training club) is valuable in choosing a veterinary surgeon to treat your pet. Certainly, once you have found a veterinary surgeon that you find helpful and sympathetic, and in whom you have confidence, you should take his advice.

Q *Is it worthwhile taking an apparently healthy dog for a regular check-up?*

A Certainly it is advisable for all dogs to be vaccinated against certain diseases and, in order for them to maintain a high level of immunity, re-vaccination should be carried out every one or two years. The interval should depend on the type of vaccine used (see page 190). At the time of each vaccination, the dog will be routinely examined by a vet to ensure that it is clinically healthy. If there is any evidence that the dog is currently combating an infection (e. g. an abnormally high temperature), the vaccination is best delayed. Otherwise, the body's immune responses may be engaged in fighting the infection to the extent that they cannot respond fully to the stimulus of the vaccine.

It is doubtful whether any other check-up is required, provided the dog remains apparently healthy, unless it is in response to a particular problem. For example it may be desirable to check a dog for evidence of an infectious disease if it has been in contact with another dog known to be infected, or to check whether it is affected with ringworm if a cat in the household develops this disease. However, such examinations may involve specific tests which would not normally form part of a routine check-up.

It has been suggested that there might be merit in a routine examination of blood samples from dogs, say every one to two years, to determine the numbers of the different cell types and the levels of certain blood constituents. Such testing might reveal evidence of some developing, and as yet unsuspected, disorder, but it has also been argued that it would provide a record of the normal values for that individual animal. If the dog subsequently developed signs of disease and the blood was re-examined, knowledge of the previous 'normal' values would permit any relatively small change to be detected, thereby assisting diagnosis of the condition. Unfortunately, tests have shown that the concentration of some cells and substances in the blood can fluctuate considerably from day to day in an individual, thus making it difficult to use information in this way. It is also debatable whether, at least in some dogs, the benefits of such routine blood sampling would outweigh the difficulties of collection.

Q *My dog has been behaving strangely and he must be ill. How can I best help my vet to find out what is wrong?*

A Most human patients will be able to answer questions about their illness but clearly dogs are unable to do this. So it is important that whoever consults the veterinary surgeon should be able to express exactly what it is that they are worried about; in other words the nature of the problem. The person who is present when the dog is examined should be prepared to supply information about both recent and past events; this is known as the 'history' of the case. Usually questions will be asked about the animal's diet, appetite and thirst, its temperament and willingness to play or exercise, the passage of urine and motions, past illnesses and injuries, how long it has been owned, whether it has been neutered and, in the case of entire (i. e. unspayed) females, the date of birth of any litters and whether the animal has been in heat recently. You will also be asked for details of any abnormal signs that have been observed. Where abnormalities have been noted, it is important to be able to say, at least approximately, how long they have been present (for months, weeks, or days) and whether they have been present continuously or intermittently. If it is possible to give exact dates, so much the better.

Some owners keep a diary, or at least make notes about the sequence of events in an illness, and certainly, whenever the succession of events becomes complex and therefore difficult to remember, it is useful to have a written record of the salient points. Most vets are very busy and therefore won't relish the idea of ploughing through page after page of unimportant details, but all of them will welcome an accurate and concise step-by-step account of what has occurred. Whenever you have additional documentation (e. g. the dog's pedigree or vaccination certificates), these should be made available, especially when you are consulting a particular veterinary surgeon for the first time.

In situations where the dog's thirst is greatly increased, it is also very helpful if you are able to measure the total amount drunk in twenty-four hours. If you know that the dog normally drinks two to three bowlsful a day, measure how much the bowl holds; the capacities of dog bowls are, like the lengths of pieces of string, very variable. Or even better, measure the total amount provided during twenty-four hours and subtract the amount remaining undrunk at the end of that period.

From what has already been stated, most owners will appreciate the problems that are created for the vet, and therefore for the patient, if the person present with the animal knows little or nothing of the background to the illness. This is frequently so when children or helpful neighbours bring a sick dog to the consulting room. Wherever possible therefore, the owner, or whoever normally looks after the dog, should be available. When this isn't possible, the best substitute is a written record of the facts together with a telephone number at which the owner can be contacted — in case further details are required, or if it is necessary to obtain their consent for anaesthesia or other procedures to be performed.

Q *Is it a nuisance if I telephone my veterinary surgeon for advice?*

A Whenever there is a real emergency it is always preferable to make a telephone call before taking your dog to the vet's premises, particularly when it occurs outside normal surgery hours. This is because the practice/hospital can make arrangements to receive and treat the dog as soon as possible (maybe even at home), as well as offering advice on how to proceed in the meantime. Of course, a telephone call will also enable you to inquire about consultation times or to arrange an appointment, as well as checking on the arrangements for, and costs of, such routine procedures as vaccinations and spay operations.

However, most vets are unwilling to spend a long time on the telephone while you relate what has happened to a dog which they may never have attended, and then to be asked questions about what should be done. Even if the animal has been seen before, the veterinarian will not usually have the dog's notes to hand to refer to. And, of course, it will not be possible to examine the animal to establish a diagnosis, nor to hand out drugs or a prescription for treatment. Since it is also unlikely that the vet will be able to recall the details of the conversation later, it is usually better to make an appointment for a proper consultation at the outset. Telephone calls like this can block the line for a long time preventing other more urgent calls from being received. And perhaps you should not be surprised if your vet appears reluctant to give out advice for nothing; after all, he also has a living to make.

It is of course a different matter if, while the animal is on a course of treatment, it develops signs which you find worrying; often a telephone call will then establish whether there is anything to be concerned about. Indeed, often you may be asked to telephone and report the dog's progress. Also, if your dog is hospitalized, it is reasonable that you should telephone and inquire about his condition. However, if you have been asked to telephone at a particular time, it is always much appreciated if you can keep to that arrangement. It may be that the vet dealing with your dog knows that he will only be available at that time and wishes to speak to you personally about what is happening. Co-operation is always appreciated and helps to cement good relationships to ensure the best possible treatment for your animal.

Q *Why is veterinary treatment sometimes thought to be expensive?*

A The establishment and running of a private small animal practice or hospital is a private business venture just like any other. The veterinary surgeon(s) involved will have to raise sufficient capital initially to build, buy or lease the premises, and to pay for highly specialized equipment and instruments without any preferential loan or subsidy from the government or any other organization. Subsequently the business must generate sufficient money to pay all the expenses — charges for water, electricity, telephones, insurance, rates and probably the interest on mortgage or bank loans, the cost of drugs and replacement equipment — in addition to providing the salaries of the veterinary surgeon(s) and the other staff required to run the practice efficiently.

Obviously, if the return on the money put into the enterprise is not at least comparable to that which could be provided by other forms of investment, there will be no incentive to undertake all the hard work required, a lot of it during unsocial hours. However, when the cost of veterinary attention is compared with that of other services such as routine car maintenance, taxi journeys or simply getting a repair man to call and examine the washing machine, it is usually found to be low, bearing in mind the level of skill which is demanded.

In North America pet owners are well aware of the high cost of private medical attention for themselves and their families. In Great Britain the way in which the National Health Service is financed disguises the true cost of medical care and many people are unaware that modern drugs and vaccines are extremely expensive. Consequently, owners are sometimes very surprised when they discover the real cost of drugs and may perhaps resent paying so much for their animals' treatment.

There are of course pet insurance policies available which provide some degree of protection against having to pay really hefty bills for operations and treatment, although it is important to read the exclusion clauses carefully before deciding whether what is offered is adequate and fair.

If you are genuinely unable to afford the fees of a veterinarian, assistance can usually be obtained from one of the animal welfare societies, although it should be borne in mind that these charitable organizations have limited resources and should not be asked to help unless you really cannot afford normal veterinary fees.

Q *The vet has told me he would like to do some 'diagnostic tests' on my dog. What does this mean?*

A Often the history of events combined with a clinical examination of the dog are sufficient for your vet to diagnose what is wrong and to recommend a course of treatment. However, this information may be inadequate for a precise diagnosis to be made so the vet may advise that one or more diagnostic tests should be performed. This may involve collecting samples of blood, urine or motions for laboratory examination. In fact, you might be asked to collect some urine or motion samples yourself and to deliver them to the vet's premises. Sometimes other types of sample may be collected for laboratory tests, such as bacterial swabs or fluid from the abdomen. Radiographic examination may be recommended and occasionally the performance of an electrocardiograph (E. C. G.) or electro-encephalograph (E. E. G.), which record the electrical signals coming from the heart and brain respectively. At times, investigatory surgery may be advised, and usually this takes the form of an exploratory laparotomy (opening the abdomen and examining the organs within) or a biopsy (taking a small piece of tissue for microscopic examination).

Some of these procedures must always be performed under a general anaesthetic to avoid pain (e. g. surgery) or prevent the risk of damage arising from sudden movement (e. g. collection of cerebrospinal fluid); at other times anaesthesia is useful to keep the animal still (e. g. during radiography) or simply because the animal's temperament makes it difficult to handle otherwise. If there is a possibility that anaesthesia might be required, it is important for the dog not to have been fed for at least eight hours beforehand. This can also help with blood tests which are best performed on 'fasted' animals.

It is important for the owner's family to have discussed the situation and to have decided whether to consent to anaesthesia and/or surgery. Whoever presents the animal should have the authority to make a decision about what is to happen next: whether the animal should be investigated further (if necessary under general anaesthesia), whether it should be hospitalized for tests and/or observation, or whether surgery can be undertaken immediately to treat the condition. Most veterinary surgeons will be pleased to explain precisely what the problems are, what possible conditions the tests may help to confirm or eliminate, and the purpose of any treatment. It is helpful if this is matched by a clear decision on the owner's part as to what should happen to his pet.

Q *Under what circumstances would my dog have to stay in hospital?*

A In the treatment of many canine conditions it is usually not necessary to hospitalize the animal. But there are circumstances in which hospitalization of a dog is desirable to ensure efficient diagnosis and therapy, and in some situations it is essential to increase the animal's chances of survival.

A critically ill animal, suffering from such conditions as massive blood loss, severe shock, difficulty in breathing or maintaining normal heart action, unconsciousness, extensive injuries or acute pain, is obviously best hospitalized because of its need for continuing expert treatment and nursing. This may involve blood transfusions or intravenous fluid therapy, the administration of oxygen, the use of special heating devices and heart monitors, and of course the injection of drugs including painkillers. This type of intensive care simply could not be provided at home.

It is also imperative that animals receiving general anaesthesia should be hospitalized until they are sufficiently recovered to be allowed home. Animals requiring general anaesthesia prior to radiography or the performance of some comparatively straightforward procedure can often be discharged later the same day, or on the following day. Those that have undergone major surgical operations should stay in hospital until they are sufficiently improved and this period can vary from a few days upwards, depending upon the animal's response.

Hospitalization may also be required for the performance of specialized diagnostic tests. Where the owner has difficulty in collecting routine urine or motion samples, again it may be preferable to hospitalize the dog to obtain them. Certain types of treatment are difficult for owners to deal with, such as the stabilization of a diabetic dog, the administration of an enema or at times even the combing out of a dog that is difficult to handle.

Finally, hospitalization may be advisable so that the veterinary surgeon can observe the animal for an extended period, particularly where neurological disturbances are suspected.

In all instances where admission to hospital is advised, owners will naturally be upset at being separated from their pet. In fact, in many cases the owners are probably more upset than the dogs, most of whom adapt very quickly to their new surroundings. Owners can rest assured that a veterinary surgeon will not want to prolong the period of hospitalization unnecessarily, but on the other hand there is no sense in discharging the dog before diagnosis or treatment is completed or, following an emergency admission, recovery is assured.

Q *If my dog is hospitalized should I visit it?*

A It is better not to visit your dog if the period of hospitalization is going to be comparatively short. An animal is usually very pleased to see its owner again and naturally believes that they will be permanently reunited. Consequently, when the owner leaves again after only a few minutes, the dog feels rejected.

Fortunately, the feelings of most pet animals seem to be more objective than subjective and whilst the owner is absent they usually do not pine or fret as the owners anticipate, particularly if there is a certain amount of activity in the hospital to occupy their attention.

On the other hand, if hospitalization is unduly prolonged for whatever reason, then the question of the advisability of visiting should be discussed with the vet in charge of the case.

Q *Should I continue giving my dog his course of tablets now that he looks so much better?*

A When treatment of an illness is in progress, the vet's instructions should always be carefully followed. Most owners will do this to the best of their ability but there are some who vary the treatment as they see fit and may discontinue a course of tablets if they feel the animal has improved sufficiently, not realizing that by so doing they risk the animal relapsing. On the other hand, if the animal has entirely recovered from a condition and the vet has advised stopping treatment, it could be harmful to prolong drug therapy. Some owners even obtain drugs from other sources and give them indiscriminately, thereby damaging the health of their pet.

Q *Do vets ever get bitten by the dogs they treat?*

A Yes, occasionally they may get bitten when, in an unguarded moment, a dog snaps because it resents being handled, or a painful area is touched. Fortunately, most vets have sufficient experience, and common sense, to avoid injury from the few really vicious dogs which can inflict quite horrifying damage. Such animals are often mentally deranged, and most are much worse in their own territory; another reason why vets prefer to treat animals at their practice premises.

If you know that your dog is difficult to handle, the nurses and vets would appreciate learning this fact beforehand so that they can take any necessary precautions in dealing with it.

2
Choosing and Living with a Dog

Q *What factors should we consider when choosing a dog?*

A Well, the first thing to be absolutely sure about is that everybody in the family (or household) really does want a dog. The care and disciplining of a dog are frequent causes of disputes, and certainly its presence is going to mean more work for whoever is in charge of the normal day-to-day running of the household; in most families that will be the wife and mother. There are almost certainly going to be some muddy footprints on the kitchen floor and hair on the carpets and in general having a dog around means more wear and tear on your garden and on your furniture. You will obviously have to provide somewhere for the dog to sleep; often a corner of the kitchen or utility room is used. The animal will need regular feeding, exercising and grooming, and may restrict your freedom to go away for weekend visits or holidays. If the dog is not able to accompany you on holiday, alternative arrangements have to be made for it to be looked after.

Although children often request a dog, and love to play with it, they may quickly tire of the novelty of feeding, training and exercising it. This means that children cannot be put in sole charge of the animal's care, especially a child under seven or eight years old. An adult must assume responsibility for the dog's welfare, supervising and guiding the child.

The proper training and exercising of a dog will be time consuming; it is not enough simply to turn it loose in the garden, although for all dogs possession of a garden in which they can roam at will is very desirable. However, make sure that any area to which they have access is escape-proof, i. e. that gates are fastened securely and that fences are sound and both high enough and low enough (some dogs are particularly good at tunnelling) to keep them in.

You should also appreciate that a dog will normally live for between ten and fourteen years, perhaps longer, so that if a puppy is bought for children it is likely still to be around when they have left home.

If you are a tenant, a vital step is to establish whether there is any

16

restriction on owning a dog. In France every citizen has the legal right to keep a dog or cat, provided that it is not a public nuisance, whereas in Britain 60 % of local authorities either ban or restrict the keeping of pets in public housing administered by them; though sometimes only by requiring permission to be obtained beforehand.

You will also need to consider whether you can afford to keep a dog. After the initial purchase, costs will include feeding, buying bowls, a bed, collar, lead etc., vaccination, insurance and/or vet's fees for possible illness or accident, and also boarding fees if you intend to board the dog when you go away.

You will also have to decide whether to get a pedigree or non-pedigree dog and what size of animal is most suitable. In general a medium-sized dog is best for a family. Large dogs need more space (indoors, outdoors and in the car), more exercise and more food. Because their coats, leads and bowls need to be bigger they are more expensive, and since the dose of most drugs is related to body weight, drug treatment also costs more. The presence of a large dog may deter potential attackers or intruders and make the owner feel more secure but a big dog may frighten young children and may, accidentally, knock them over. Ideally, large dogs should have a sizable outdoor area where they can spend most of the day, but bear in mind that they can also jump higher to escape. They are not necessarily best kept in the country; often large towns have more open spaces where a dog can be exercised.

Small dogs usually don't fit in with very young children, because the children tend to be rather rough and clumsy and can cause the animal pain and actual damage, such as broken bones. As a result, a little dog may become very frightened and snappy. These 'lap dogs' are best confined to adults and older children and, with those limitations, they are ideal in small apartments. Also, of course, they can be easily picked up and carried and are generally much easier to transport.

If you intend to buy a puppy or dog as a present for someone else, *do* make sure beforehand that they genuinely want it and are capable of looking after it. Bear in mind that someone in that family might not like dogs, or might be allergic to them, or they might not have enough money to feed a pet — for example, if the breadwinner has been made redundant. Also, never buy a pet for a child without the parents' consent, because they will have to assume responsibility for it and will often end up looking after it.

Q *Should we buy a pedigree dog? Surely mongrels get fewer illnesses?*

A One advantage of a pedigree animal is that you know more or less what to expect; for example, how big a puppy will grow and what type of temperament and other characteristics it will possess. Secondly, by buying directly from a breeder you can reduce the likelihood of a puppy contracting some disease. And if you want to show your dog, or breed from it professionally, only a pedigree animal will do.

About half the dog population of Britain is composed of pedigree animals, and there are around 200 breeds to choose from. If you are not aware of the range of breeds available, it is a good idea to look through a book which illustrates and describes various dog breeds (often to be found in the Public Library) before making a decision. In addition, there are books devoted to each of the most popular breeds, though you must allow for each author's exuberance in describing his or her own favourite breed as the best possible choice.

Sometimes there is so much variation between individual dogs within a breed, that the breed is not officially recognized as a separate entity; instead, these animals are referred to as 'typed dogs'; for example in Britain the Jack Russell Terrier and the Lurcher. With cross-bred dogs, which result from a mating between pedigree dogs of two different breeds, there is more scope for variation, although the influence of the parents is discernible.

Mongrels (animals of mixed breeding) are the result of totally random mating, usually for several generations, and such animals may have strongly developed roaming instincts. Many people believe that mongrels are hardier and have better resistance to disease, but there is no real evidence for this view, apart from the fact that they are unlikely to suffer from those conditions that affect certain breeds as a result of in-breeding.

If someone in the family is allergic to dog hair you could consider buying a Poodle, Bedlington Terrier, or Kerry Blue Terrier which don't moult, though it would be wise checking their effect on the allergy-sufferer before committing yourself to purchase. Apart from the rare hairless breeds (Mexican Hairless or Chinese Crested), all the other breeds will shed hair to some extent, and in centrally heated homes this often occurs all the year round, though it is worse in spring and autumn. In general, dark hairs show up less, and long hairs often prove easier to remove from soft furnishings.

A long-haired breed of dog will require more frequent grooming and its coat is more difficult to dry if it gets wet as the result of swimming, crawling in ditches or through wet undergrowth, or having had a bath. Also their long hair can more easily pick up grass seeds (see page 295). Those breeds which don't moult will require regular clipping (every four to six weeks) to keep them looking their best. Spaniels and the wiry-coated terriers also require clipping, or stripping (i.e. removal of dead hair), roughly every three months. You might also prefer to acquire a breed that does not, according to the dictates of fashion and breed standards, need to be docked in order to be shown.

Q *Does temperament vary much between breeds of dog? We were wondering whether certain breeds might be better with children than others.*

A Over the years, different breeds of dogs were developed to perform specific tasks (e.g. guarding, hunting, herding), and consequently, as well as developing a characteristic appearance, they also developed variations in temperament.

The gundog breeds (retrievers and setters), although inclined to be boisterous, are essentially good-natured and easy to train. The majority of guide dogs for the blind (seeing-eye dogs) are Labrador Retrievers. Also very even tempered are the smaller spaniels (King Charles, known in North America as the English Toy Spaniel, and Cavalier King Charles), and, while rather playful and slow at learning, most Beagles have an easy-going disposition. The large streamlined dogs which hunt by sight (Afghan Hound, Saluki, Borzoi and Greyhound), often prove difficult to control, particularly if allowed off the lead. Collies develop a strong loyalty to members of the family and are rather wary of strangers. Border Collies have a strong herding instinct and, with nothing to occupy them, they can become frustrated to the point of hysteria. Given the opportunity, they will chase sheep and even try to herd people. Probably better for a family would be the smaller breeds of these two types, the Whippet and Shetland Sheepdog. Both are very good with children if not handled too roughly.

The Bulldog is a placid breed but its habits of slobbering and snoring can be tiresome and many people would prefer the Bull Terrier or Staffordshire Bull Terrier. These breeds are not to be trusted with strange dogs, which they will usually want to fight, though they are very affectionate towards people, including children, and make first-class family pets.

In general, the smaller breeds are less easy-going, more on the defensive and inclined to be snappy with children. In Corgis, in particular, this tendency needs to be firmly curbed early in life. As a rule the small terriers are tough, wiry and inquisitive, and certain breeds (e.g. Border Terrier and Boston Terrier) tolerate children much better than others (e.g. the Scottish and Yorkshire Terriers). Both the Dachshund and Chihuahua are inclined to bark a lot if unchecked, which may lead to complaints from neighbours, and the latter is particularly likely to be bad-tempered with children and strangers.

The German Shepherd Dog (Alsatian) is the most popular breed in the world and an excellent working dog, but some individuals are very shy and apprehensive and become aggressive through fear. The Boxer is usually a friendly exuberant dog which remains playful for several years, though some animals develop unstable temperaments.

Dogs bred primarily for their guarding ability (such as the Dobermann Pinscher and Rottweiler) have forceful, dominant personalities, especially the German strains, and should always be well trained and strictly controlled. They are really not suitable as family pets. Great Danes are like young colts, rather skittish and inclined to crash into things; not the best choice for a young family. Indeed, because of their size and strength, the larger breeds do not make good family pets, particularly as nowadays some members of these breeds have very unstable personalities. Particular strains of certain breeds exhibit very strange behaviour. For instance, some Dobermanns will happily suck the skin of their flank for long periods, and some extremely nervous pointers will 'freeze' at the approach of a human or any loud noise.

Regrettably, the temperament of many breeds has suffered through the years as a result of their breeding. Two factors are responsible. First, the breed standards, i.e. the ideal characteristics for each breed which have been established by each particular Breed Society, have concentrated almost exclusively on the animals' appearance and paid little attention to temperament. As a result of trying to produce what they regard as an ideal physical type, breeders may have unwittingly developed strains which are mentally unstable. Secondly, tempted by easy profits, some dog breeders have bred from animals that were clearly physically or mentally unsound, in order to satisfy the enormous public demand for the currently 'fashionable' breeds. Over the years, Cocker Spaniels, Toy and Miniature Poodles and German Shepherd Dogs (Alsatians) have been harmed in this way.

As a result of this state of affairs, there are nowadays some members of almost all breeds that suffer from inherent behavioural defects which cannot be corrected by training. Such dogs are politely described as highly strung; a euphemism for neurotic and snappy. Some of these are unpredictable, and will show vicious unprovoked aggression (idiopathic viciousness or rage syndrome) during which they will attack adults and children indiscriminately. At such times these animals develop a glazed look in their eyes and do not recognize anyone, including their owner. In Britain this behaviour is well recognized in some of the most popular breeds, especially Cocker Spaniels, German Shepherd Dogs (Alsatians) and Labradors. In the Netherlands the same problem is seen in St Bernards and in the United States is not uncommon in Dobermanns and in Bernese Mountain Dogs. Investigation has shown that all the affected British Cocker Spaniels have the same four champion ancestors, and there seems little doubt that in this and other breeds the temperamental defects have a genetic origin. The best way to try and avoid purchasing an animal from one of the known affected strains is to consult your local vet who will usually be familiar with the quality of the dogs produced by local breeders. Any dog which becomes so mentally unstable as to make unprovoked attacks is clearly best put to sleep without delay, particularly if children are at risk.

Q *Are some breeds of dog more prone to certain illnesses?*

A Unfortunately, most canine breeds are likely to suffer from one or more specific types of disorder, some of which are definitely known to be inherited. If dogs suffering from these genetic defects are used for breeding, the problem can be expected to recur in following generations. In many cases, the defects have arisen through excessive inbreeding, particularly in the more exotic breeds which have been established from relatively few individuals.

Sometimes the breed standards have deliberately encouraged the selection of animals showing undesirable features, such as excessive skin folds in the Bloodhound which interfere with its sight, a massive skull in the Bulldog which causes difficulty in giving birth, small eyes (micro-ophthalmia) in Chow Chows and the diamond eye of the Bloodhound, which causes abnormal exposure of the haw, or third eyelid. In Britain meetings have been held between representatives of the dog registration body, the Kennel Club, and the British Veterinary Association to persuade certain breed societies to amend their breed standards and thereby eliminate the worst excesses. However, many of the inherited abnormalities are not connected with breed standards at all.

Inherited eye diseases, of various types, affect a number of breeds. Hereditary cataract (opacity of the lens) can occur in such breeds as the Boston Terrier, American Cocker Spaniel, Miniature Schnauzer and Old English Sheepdog, ultimately resulting in complete loss of vision. Of course, cataracts can be also due to a number of other causes such as injury and some generalized diseases. Some breeds are particularly likely to suffer from progressive degeneration of the light-sensitive part of the eye, the retina (progressive retinal atrophy), causing slowly worsening vision. In many working breeds (for example the Border and Rough Collies, Shetland Sheepdogs and Labrador and Golden Retrievers) the centre of the retina is affected first, which means that although dogs can see moving objects they may bump into quite large obstacles that are straight in front of them, and their vision is worse in bright light. In Miniature and Toy Poodles, Irish Setters and Elkhounds, however, a generalized retinal degeneration occurs which results in their sight being worse at twilight, and also sometimes in tunnel vision (seeing objects better if they are directly in front). The Cardigan Corgi may suffer from either type.

Collie eye anomaly is another inherited defect of the Collie breed which causes poor vision. It may result in, for example, inability to catch a ball, and in extreme cases it ends in blindness. At one time 80–90% of Collies may have been affected. In Britain, the Kennel Club and the British Veterinary Association have organized a scheme whereby dogs can be examined for progressive retinal degeneration (PRA) and Collie eye anomaly, and if found to be free will be issued with a certificate to that effect.

Some of the small terriers (Fox Terriers, Jack Russells and Sealyhams) are more inclined to suffer from sudden displacement of the lens of the eye (lens luxation) causing considerable pain and loss of vision. Another painful inherited eye condition is glaucoma, an increase in the fluid pressure within the eyeball, which is particularly common in Cocker Spaniels and Basset Hounds. At times the eyelashes may rub on the front of the eye, producing severe irritation; this can be due to the edge of the eyelid turning inward (entropion, e.g. in Chow Chows), or a double row of eyelashes (distichiasis, e.g. in Pekingese) or an abnormal direction of eyelash growth (trichiasis, e.g. in Poodles).

Hip dysplasia is a developmental disease of the hip joints which can occur in all breeds but affects more than 20% of dogs in some of them, including German Shepherd Dogs and retrievers. The socket of the joint is too shallow and because the bones can pull apart they wear abnormally. There is a wide range of severity so that some dogs may show only slight lameness as they get older, whereas in others the joint dislocates so easily that, without surgery, the dog would be permanently crippled. In Britain a scheme exists to examine dogs radiographically and then to issue a certificate if they are found to be free from hip dysplasia. Other inherited disorders of the bones and joints include patellar luxation (slipping of the knee cap) which is particularly common in small breeds like the Miniature Poodle, intervertebral disc protrusion ('slipped disc'), common in long-backed breeds such as the Dachshund and Corgi and responsible for pain and paralysis, and a deformity of the neck vertebrae which results in pressure on the spinal cord in large dogs (e.g. Great Dane), causing the affected animals to stagger, prance or drag their feet, and therefore known as the 'wobbler syndrome'.

In dogs which have a short nose and flat face (brachycephalic breeds) such as the Boxer and Pug the soft palate can easily obstruct the entrance to the larynx (voice box) resulting in difficulty in breathing. On the other hand, the longer-nosed dogs are more inclined to suffer from nasal diseases, including nasal tumours. Miniature breeds with dome-shaped heads, such as the Chihuahua, may suffer from hydrocephalus due to an excess of cerebral fluid, popularly known as 'water on the brain'. In some breeds (Bull Terriers, Dalmatians and Sealyhams) deafness is commonly found in dogs with a white coat or predominantly white markings.

Some breeds, particularly the Dachshund, are especially prone to suffer from diabetes mellitus ('sugar diabetes') and the Boxer is particularly likely to be affected by neoplasia (tumour-formation), which if malignant is known as cancer. Persistent diarrhoea is generally associated with one of the larger breeds of dog, especially German Shepherds.

Some diseases appear to be confined to a single breed. Examples include Scottie cramp, a type of muscle spasticity following strenuous exercise, shown by Scottish Terriers, the presence of dermoid sinuses (one or more thick walled tubes opening on to the skin's surface) in Rhodesian Ridgebacks, deficiency of an enzyme, (pyruvate kinase) which produces a progressive type of anaemia in the Basenji breed, and a chronic inflammatory liver disease (hepatitis) associated with increased storage of copper in the liver, which occurs only in Bedlington Terriers.

Unfortunately, many books about dog breeds are concerned almost exclusively with the good points of each breed and fail to mention the subject of breed-related illnesses. Understandably, breeders usually also avoid this topic, unless asked direct questions, so that probably the only person likely to be both knowledgeable and unbiased in his/her advice will be your local veterinarian.

Q *Are some breeds much more subject to inherited diseases than others?*

A Quite definitely this is so. There are seven breeds which it is known can each suffer from twenty or more different disorders of genetic origin: the American Cocker Spaniel, Beagle, Boston Terrier, Boxer, Bulldog and the Toy and Miniature Poodles. A further ten breeds are each subject to at least ten separate inherited diseases: the Chihuahua, the Collie breeds, Dachshund, Fox Terrier, German Shepherd Dog (Alsatian), Great Dane, Labrador Retriever, Pekingese, St Bernard and the Shetland Sheepdog.

In fairness, it must be pointed out that these breeds are some of the most popular, so that much more is known about them compared with many of the rarer breeds. In fact it is this very popularity which has contributed to the appearance of these defects, by encouraging indiscriminate breeding to satisfy public demand. In the case of some diseases, for example progressive axonopathy in Boxers (a degenerative nervous disorder), the condition is rare and limited to dogs bred in one country, in this instance, Britain. With co-operation between breeders and the breed society, the family lines which have produced affected dogs can be identified, so that by avoiding matings with these families it may be possible to prevent the birth of further individuals suffering from the disorder.

Q *What is the most unusual breed of dog?*

A Amongst the great variety of breeds which have developed there are a number with unusual characteristics. But probably two breeds of dog would tie for the title of the most unusual: the Mexican Hairless (Xoloitzcuintli) and the Basenji.

The Mexican Hairless is an extremely rare, indeed almost extinct, breed thought to have originated in Asia. It stands about 18 inches (45 cm) high at the shoulder and apart from a short growth of coarse hairs on the top of the head it is indeed quite hairless. It also differs from other breeds in having no premolar teeth, a much higher body temperature of 105 °F (40.5 °C) and by making a crying noise in place of the conventional bark.

The Basenji (or Congo Dog) from Central Africa, which is of similar size, is also reputed not to bark and is frequently described as voiceless. However, when very frightened these dogs will make a few, low-pitched barking sounds. It is more common for them to make a sort of yowling or yodelling noise, and they can also growl and whine. Like wild species of dog, but unlike other domesticated breeds, Basenji bitches generally come into heat only once a year, during the autumn; although in recent years much more variation has been seen in the timing of heat periods than formerly. The Basenji is known to metabolize iodine much faster than the European breeds, it is much better at climbing than other dogs, and it uses its paws to 'wash' its face in the same way that the cat does. It is a formidable hunting dog and forms a very strong attachment to its owner, from whom it dislikes being separated. However, since all the Basenjis in Europe and North America have a common genetic base of only about twelve dogs it is perhaps not surprising that they suffer from a number of inherited disorders. These can produce haemolytic anaemia, opacity of the lens in the eye, malabsorption of food, umbilical hernia and certain renal defects (Fanconi syndrome) which progress to kidney failure.

Q *Should I get a puppy, or would an older dog who needed a home eventually fit into our family?*

A As a general rule it is better to take on a puppy rather than an older dog. Bear in mind that the existing owners of an older dog usually want to find it a new home because of some defect in its temperament or behaviour, which could constitute a risk to children. Even when you know that there is a good reason for its needing to be re-housed (e.g. because the owner has died, or has moved abroad or into accommodation where dogs are not permitted), it may still have habits that you dislike and find difficult to eradicate. Older dogs take longer than puppies to accept new premises as their home (two or three months as a rule) and during that time they may make determined efforts to escape and return to their previous quarters.

Dogs that end up in dogs' homes or animal shelters are often confirmed wanderers, or else dogs that have been abandoned because of some behavioural defect, e.g. aggression or being dirty in the house. Many of them will not have mixed adequately with humans during the important 'socialization period' (four to twelve weeks of age) so that they shrink from human contact. Some will have been neglected or ill-treated as puppies, and for this reason can be fearful of humans and even aggressive. If they have been kennelled for long periods, animal shelter inmates will often have got into the habits of barking and jumping up to attract attention. Also many of these abandoned animals will not have been vaccinated and may be incubating an infectious disease.

Retired racing Greyhounds usually become available at four or five years old (sometimes earlier if they have not been successful track animals), but again, having been used to kennelling, will not transfer easily to a house. To summarize, it would probably be fair to say that the training of an older dog requires more effort than that of a puppy, and that disappointments are more frequent.

Q *Is it better to get a puppy from a recognized breeder?*

A Wherever possible a puppy should be bought directly from the breeder — it will not cost any more, and avoids many of the problems that can affect animals bought from shops, dealers or 'puppy supermarkets'. Where puppies from different sources are brought together for sale on the same premises, there will inevitably be an exchange of the bacteria and viruses which all of them will be carrying. As a result, they can easily encounter organisms new to them, against which they have not acquired any immunity from their mother. Puppies which have had to travel long distances in crates from the breeders to the pet store may suffer from stress due to cold and poor feeding which lowers their resistance to infection and thus increases their chances of becoming ill.

Another important reason for direct purchase is that a single change of home and diet before the age of three months is enough for any puppy; further changes only serve to confuse it and may even disturb its growth. Having said this, it is only fair to point out that there are many well-run pet shops who do the best they can for the animals they sell, and that some of these will even help you contact breeders directly. But never buy from an unclean or badly run pet store or, worse still, from street traders, no matter how sorry you may feel for the puppies; you will simply be buying trouble.

To locate a breeder of the particular breed in which you are interested you might:

1 Consult your local veterinary surgeon, who may know of a breeder in your area. In any case, he can certainly offer advice about your choice of breed.

2 Look at advertisements in the specialist dog breeding journals and newspapers (in Britain these are *Dog World* and *Our Dogs*, and in North America *Dog World* and *Popular Dogs*. Another useful source in Britain is *The Dog Directory*, published annually).

3 Contact your dog registration society (in Britain this is the Kennel Club and in the United States the American Kennel Club) or dog-owning societies such as the National Dog Owners Association in Britain.

Remember that a breeder is unlikely to have puppies available for sale all year round and may even have a waiting list. Even so, most breeders will welcome you visiting their premises to discuss a future purchase. This will allow you to judge the suitability of the breed for your circumstances (if you were previously unsure) and to assess the quality and temperament of the bitch which is likely to be reflected in the puppies. At the outset it is as well to realize that properly reared pedigree dogs are not cheap, particularly in the case of the rarer breeds and those that only have small litters, such as the small terriers. Breeders may, however, sell a less than perfect specimen, useless for show purposes, more cheaply, simply as a pet.

A pedigree puppy should of course be accompanied by its pedigree, a form giving the details of all its ancestors for four or five generations, at least back to its great-great-grandparents. If there are champions (prefixed on the pedigree by 'Ch.') in recent generations, the puppy might do well at shows. However, if you specifically want a dog for showing, and not just as a pet, it is as well to make this clear to the breeder, and you must expect to pay rather more for a better animal. Always try to arrange for a puppy to be checked by a veterinary surgeon, either your own or the breeder's, before committing yourself to a purchase. Be suspicious if this is strongly resisted.

Mongrel puppies may become available, at little or no cost, from friends and neighbours whose bitch has whelped. If you know, or can see the mother you can at least make some assessment of the puppy's physical type and temperament. As always, it is best to see the puppies personally to make your choice; don't allow yourself to be blackmailed into taking a puppy that you don't really want. Mongrel puppies can of course also be obtained from welfare societies and pet shops, although with the same risks of infection.

Q *What points should I look for when buying a puppy?*

A First of all, resist the temptation to choose the poorest-looking specimen (the runt of the litter) just because you feel sorry for it. Such an animal begins life less well nourished and with less immunity to disease than average, and because of the treatment it has received from its littermates it may grow up to be excessively timid, or in some cases very aggressive. Any puppy that has little or no contact with other dogs during the important socialization phase of its life (an orphaned puppy, a single puppy or one which has been kept alone for a long period in a pet store cage) will respond abnormally to other dogs. For example, it will usually be very nervous of them and refuse to mate with them, and often it will fight dogs at the least provocation.

Choose a friendly, alert puppy which is neither the most extrovert and pugnacious in the litter, biting all its littermates, or the most timid, which shrinks from human contact. Ideally, it should play happily with its littermates, show an interest in what is happening around it and not be unduly distressed (struggling and crying) when it is picked up and examined. Nervous individuals will be very upset, even panicky, if turned on their back or stared at, or if they hear a sudden noise. Dominant animals, that can prove very difficult to control later in life, will show their resentment at being handled by continually struggling and biting. A well-balanced future pet will tolerate most handling, after only a momentary struggle, without any undue alarm or aggression. If you are able to observe the litter at feeding time it will be easier to spot the most dominant and the most submissive members.

The testing of an animal's response to noise, to being handled and to an unfamiliar plaything, like a ball of paper, is best carried out in a separate room where there are no other dogs to distract it. These tests, which no reasonable dog breeder would object to, will allow you to make a fair assessment of the puppy's future personality; indeed the probable success of guide dogs (seeing-eye dogs) can be predicted with·fair accuracy by studying their behaviour as puppies.

If you are buying from a breeder, a good time to pay a visit to assess the puppies' characters is around five weeks old. If you are not sure of your own ability, it is a good idea to ask a more knowledgeable friend to accompany you. However, your chosen puppy should not leave its mother for a further two or three weeks, that is, until it is properly weaned at about eight weeks old.

The social development of a puppy takes place between the ages of three and fourteen weeks, and primarily between four and twelve weeks old. During this period a puppy learns to relate to other animals, including humans, and its experiences at this time determine its behaviour throughout the rest of its life. Around eight weeks is a particularly impressionable age when fear responses develop and an unpleasant event at this time can have a psychologically damaging effect on a puppy. The ideal age for a puppy to begin relating to humans is between six and eight weeks old. If it is removed from its mother much earlier than this, it may be unable to relate to other dogs, as mentioned above. On the other hand, a puppy which remains with its mother beyond twelve weeks of age and has little human contact, tends always to be apprehensive of people and difficult to train; this has been confirmed in the training of guide dogs.

A puppy should appear adequately nourished; neither abnormally thin, with prominent backbone and ribs, nor potbellied, and it must be able to move freely. Its eyes should be clear and bright, and both the ears and eyes should be free from any discharges. The pup's coat should be clean and well groomed, with no obvious hair loss or any yellow staining of diarrhoea beneath the tail. The skin should be soft and pliable without obvious lesions or signs of parasites (see page 157), the presence of which often causes continual scratching.

It is best not to take young children to visit breeders' premises because they are likely to fall in love with any puppy that they see, and this may make it difficult for you to leave without making a commitment to purchase.

Q *Would a puppy make a good Christmas present?*

A No, Christmas is not a good time to bring a puppy into the household. It is probable that everyone will be too busy and distracted to concentrate fully on looking after the animal, and the general excitement and disordered routine is not conducive to a quiet settling-in. There is also the danger that children may regard it as simply another plaything.

Soon after Christmas would be a more suitable time to purchase a puppy, although probably even better would be later in the year, which would allow the puppy to spend a lot of time in the garden without getting cold, wet or muddy. However, the time of purchase should be related to your summer holiday, assuming that you intend taking one and that the animal cannot accompany you. Putting a puppy into kennels within six months of moving to a new home will have a very unsettling effect on it and in particular will upset its training. In any case, few boarding kennels will accept dogs under six months of age.

Veterinarians and animal welfare societies are dismayed by the large and increasing number of animals that they are asked to destroy humanely immediately after Christmas (having been bought on impulse as Christmas presents) and during the summer months (because they would inconvenience the taking of a holiday).

Q *Is a bitch a better companion than a dog?*

A In general a bitch will fit in with normal family life better than a male dog. Bitches are rather more affectionate and easier to control, and although often gentler with children are equally good as guard dogs. Male dogs, whatever their breed, tend to be more dominant than females of the same breed, more inclined to get into fights and more likely to attempt to dominate children. In general, therefore, male dogs need firmer handling.

Males also have an instinctive urge to escape and wander away from home for a period ranging from an hour or so to several days, or even weeks. In particular, if he should detect a bitch that is in heat, he may attempt to remain nearby during the whole of her heat period. This roaming instinct increases the male dog's chance of being involved in a road accident.

Sometimes a very dominant male dog, even though previously house-trained, will begin to urinate in the house in order to scent-mark his territory and affirm his dominant status. Training may help these problems, but where they prove intractable an improvement can only be produced by removing the effect of male sex hormone (testosterone) produced by the testicles. This can be achieved either by castration (i.e. surgical removal of the testicles) or, for short-term effects, administration of a drug such as female sex hormone (oestrogen), a progestagen, or a specific anti-androgenic drug.

Q *Is a bitch more trouble than a dog?*

A The problems associated with keeping a bitch relate primarily to her 'heat' periods and the possibility of her having unwanted puppies. The majority of bitches come into heat approximately twice a year for a period of around three weeks (see page 226). At these times the bitch will be rather more excitable, and because she has an urge to mate she will generally try to escape. Also she will produce a discharge (initially blood-stained) that will be deposited wherever she sits or lies, although many bitches lick this up after themselves. And, of course, the presence of a bitch on heat will attract the local males whenever she goes out, and they may assemble near the house.

The discharge of 'heat' can be kept off carpets and furniture by insisting that she lies on an old blanket, or by confining her to a room with an easily-washed floor. The problem of escape followed by unwanted mating can be countered by confining her indoors during her heat, or if she is allowed into the garden making sure that the area is securely fenced to a height of at least 6 feet (2 metres) and that male dogs cannot get in. Of course she should not be let off the lead in a public place. Her attractiveness to male dogs can be reduced by applying one of a number of proprietary liquids or sprays (e.g. 'Veterinary Amplex' or 'Bitter Apple') to her hindquarters in order to mask the attractive scent particles (pheromones), particularly before she is taken outdoors.

Following the heat period some bitches, although not mated, will show a so-called 'false pregnancy' (see page 229), with usually either increased affection with some abdominal enlargement, and occasionally milk production, three to four weeks later, or more pronounced lactation (sometimes accompanied by all the signs indicative of giving birth) nine weeks later. This particular problem, together with all the others of a sexual nature, can be avoided if the bitch is spayed or if she is given contraceptive treatment regularly (see page 231). Sometimes it is suggested that a bitch be sent to a boarding kennel during her heat period, but of course accidental matings are also possible there.

Q *We are considering having our dog neutered. What would be the effects of this operation?*

A The term 'neutering' means, in the female, spaying (i.e. the removal of the uterus and the ovaries) and, in the male, castration (i.e. removal of the testicles). In both sexes neutering is performed under a general anaesthetic. These operations not only make it impossible for the dog to be the sire, or the dam, of a litter of puppies, but by eliminating the production of sex hormones by the gonads (ovaries or testicles) they also cause behavioural changes.

In the bitch the main change is that the typical behaviour shown during 'heat', and its possible sequel — a 'false pregnancy', will not occur. Nor will the bitch produce a discharge, or prove attractive to males. Otherwise the bitch appears unchanged. In the male the effects may be more marked. Castration reduces roaming in about 90% of male dogs, in about two-thirds it stops aggression between males, and in about 50% it stops urine-marking in the house. In about half of the cases where these improvements occur they do so fairly rapidly (within two to three weeks), and more slowly in the others. Despite castration, if a male dog has already had sexual experience he may continue to show mating behaviour. Since the most common reason for having these neutering operations performed (certainly in males) is to produce these changes in behaviour, there is no advantage in substituting an operation which would merely prevent reproduction without stopping sex hormone production, i.e. tying-off the Fallopian tubes in the bitch or performing vasectomy in the male.

If it is intended from the outset that neutering should be performed (for example if a bitch and a male are to be kept together) this is best done when the animal is old enough to withstand the operation and for the anatomical structures to be clearly seen, but before puberty when breeding becomes possible and the characteristic sexual behaviour develops. However, neutering is often carried out to correct behaviour which does not become apparent until *after* puberty. Many veterinary surgeons are against neutering dogs, especially males, unless it appears really necessary.

There is a belief that the character of a dog develops more fully if it is allowed to reach puberty before being neutered, but there is little evidence that this is in fact so. Certainly letting the bitch have one litter before spaying confers no special benefit; indeed, if anything it slightly increases the possibility of problems occurring. There could be difficulties during the pregnancy and during the time of the birth, and, because the uterus (womb) and its blood supply are now better developed, marginally more risk is associated with the spay operation. A bitch is best not spayed whilst she is producing milk because by altering the hormonal balance at a critical time the period of lactation will be unduly prolonged. Of course at times there may be medical reasons for spaying (e.g. bacterial infection of the uterus — known as pyometra) or castration (e.g. a tumour of the testicles).

There is no evidence that neutering causes a dog (male or female) to be less active (most guide dogs are neutered), or reduces its prowess as a guard dog. There may be a greater tendency for a neutered animal to gain weight but this can be checked by reducing its food intake. Spayed bitches may develop urinary incontinence later, either because of the lack of oestrogen or because of a change in the position of the bladder following surgery which interferes with closure of the bladder sphincter. Surveys suggest that as many as 10% of spayed bitches may become incontinent.

Q *How serious an operation is neutering?*

A In the male it is a relatively minor operation; castration (orchidectomy) involves removing the testicles of the anaesthetized dog through a small incision into the scrotum. The surgical wound requires two or three sutures and heals quickly.

In the bitch, spaying (ovario-hysterectomy) is a little more serious because it involves opening into the abdomen. Usually the incision is made on the underside of the abdomen, although some veterinary surgeons prefer an incision on the side, i.e. the flank. Depending on the type of stitches used, between four and eight are usually required to close the wound. Immediately following this operation the bitch should not be allowed to indulge in vigorous exercise such as running, jumping or walking long distances. It is advisable for a few days to take her outdoors (on a lead) only long enough for her to pass urine and motions. If her appetite is impaired afterwards it will usually only be for two or three days.

In both sexes the sutures which have been inserted to keep the edges of the wound together should be taken out by your veterinarian after seven to ten days, when healing is complete. Very rarely complications are seen such as infection of the operation site and/or breakdown of the wound (i.e. the edges beginning to come apart). If anything untoward *is* seen your vet should be contacted as soon as possible. Dogs should be prevented from licking, or otherwise interfering unduly with the wound; if this becomes a problem in a bitch it may be necessary to fit a many-tailed bandage (see page 265).

Q *I have been offered a mongrel puppy but am concerned about how big it may grow. How can I judge this?*

A The guide often given is to look at the feet of the puppy; big feet denote that it is going to grow into a big dog.

Probably more scientific is the observation that most breeds of dog have reached approximately half of their adult body weight by the age of fourteen weeks, and two-thirds of their adult height (measured at the top of the shoulders, directly above the front legs) by the age of sixteen weeks.

At birth there is much less variation in the weight of puppies of different breeds than there is later in life. For instance at birth the average weight of a Great Dane puppy is only five times that of a Pomeranian puppy (23 oz (650 g) and $4^{1}/_{2}$ oz (130 g) respectively), whereas when both are fully grown the Great Dane will weigh over twenty-five times more (130 lb (59 kg) and 5 lb (2.2 kg) respectively).

Because the differences in body weight are much less at an early age, and because growth rates are not identical for all individuals, predictions of adult size based on measurements made earlier in life than fourteen weeks tend to be less accurate than those based on later measurements. It may also prove difficult to measure the height and weight of a young puppy sufficiently accurately. Nevertheless, as a general rule most puppies at eight weeks old will be about a quarter of their adult weight. The really large breeds, however, will eventually weigh slightly more, and the very small breeds slightly less, than this calculated weight.

Q *Would buying a puppy help my son to overcome his fear of dogs?*

A If the purchase of a puppy is specifically intended to help a child get rid of a fear of dogs it would be better first of all if arrangements were made for the child to visit, and handle, a good-tempered older dog on a number of occasions. In this way the child could gradually gain confidence before the puppy entered the household. The playful behaviour of a puppy might upset the child, and, because at the outset the puppy will be uncertain of its own position in the family 'pecking order' (see page 69), it might try to dominate a child that it perceives is wary of it.

If a child is *extremely* afraid of dogs it is recommended that to start with he or she should simply be allowed to see a friendly dog, and that the best times for this to take place are the child's mealtimes. The reason for this is that eating is an activity which tends to reduce anxiety, so that less stress would be associated with the experience. On subsequent occasions the length of the dog's visit, and its proximity to the child, should be increased.

Q *Will my new dog get along happily with the existing pets in the house?*

A This rather depends on their individual temperaments and the age at which they are introduced to each other. A puppy is socialized, i.e. has his relationship to humans and other animals established, between four and twelve weeks of age. Consequently, two puppies reared together from that time will usually get on well together; in fact they may be less trouble than a single puppy because they are more likely to play with each other instead of wanting to play with you, or chewing the furniture. Similarly, where a puppy and a kitten, or any other young animal, are raised together they tend to accept each other as equals and live together harmoniously.

When a young puppy is introduced into a home where an older dog is already in residence a problem *can* occur, but whether it does depends largely on the owner's handling of the situation. This is because wherever there are two (or more) dogs in a household a definite hierarchy of dominance is created (see page 68). The resident dog will almost certainly regard himself as dominant, since he already occupies the territory, and in general the puppy will accept this and adopt a submissive role.

33

However the owner may unwittingly upset the relationship between the two dogs by lavishing much more affection on the puppy. In this situation the existing dog may feel that the newcomer is being raised in status by the owner's attention, and that consequently he is compelled to assert himself to defend his superior position. Therefore he will threaten, and may even attack, the puppy to demonstrate that he is in fact the top dog. The owner can avoid this conflict by giving more affection to the resident, and dominant, dog thereby confirming the hierarchy and stabilizing the relationship.

When an *older* dog is introduced into a home where another dog is already present the newcomer may not automatically accept the role of underdog, so that the order of dominance has then to be determined, usually with fights over territory (who sleeps where), food and favourite toys. It may all be settled with a single fight or the power struggle may go on for some time before being resolved. Again, the owner can help by accepting the final outcome and *not* favouring the underdog, as tends to be human nature. Instead he should give more attention to the dominant partner, who will regard it as his due. Both dogs will be much happier if the owner can accept the situation. Whenever the owner upsets things by making a fuss of the underdog the dominant animal will feel his position threatened and be impelled to attack the other dog for his insubordinate behaviour, even though he probably realizes that by doing so in the owner's presence he risks the owner's displeasure. It is suggested that acceptance of one dog by another may be helped if at the outset they are introduced on 'neutral' territory, such as a local park or open space.

Once established, the hierarchy may not persist unchanged. As a younger dog grows up he may make a bid for the top position, particularly if the formerly dominant dog becomes weaker as he grows older, or develops an illness. A struggle for superiority may then ensue, ending either with the confirmation of the existing order or with a reversal of roles. Once the two dogs have determined their relative social position, however, they can be very happy together; indeed an ageing dog can often be rejuvenated by a new companion (although at times a young puppy always wanting to play may irritate a very old dog). Probably the most harmonious relationship between dogs of different ages exists between two bitches, one of which is the offspring of the other.

Introduction of a dog into a household where there is already a cat may result in behavioural problems on the part of the cat (e.g. breakdown of toilet training in the house, sulking and failure to eat or groom). But if affection is lavished on the cat, and the two pets are fed quite separately, i.e. either in different rooms, or at opposite ends of the same room, they will in most instances gradually come to tolerate each other. Within six to eight weeks the two animals should be getting along amicably.

Q *As dog owners are there likely to be any problems if later on we have a baby?*

A In general there are no problems and the dog accepts the child as a member of the 'pack' (i.e. the family group) to which they both belong. Jealousy can develop, however, when a newly arrived baby causes a dog to feel neglected and rejected. This is most likely to occur where an animal that was previously the centre of attention finds affection being lavished on the newcomer and himself ignored. To avoid this situation developing it is very important for the dog to continue to receive a considerable amount of attention and affection and this should occur particularly when the baby is *present*. This will ensure that the baby comes to represent, for the dog, the signal that it is going to receive extra attention. If the dog only receives attention from its owner when the baby is in another room, and this ceases whenever the baby appears, it may foster a true rivalry and encourage a hostile reaction from the dog. (The same situation can arise when grandparents enthuse over a new grand-child and their dog feels ignored.)

If you choose a large, energetic breed soon after getting married bear in mind that it might be difficult to provide it with sufficient exercise when there are babies and toddlers around. Another problem with children under two years old is that they have a natural tendency suddenly to grab at objects and animals, which a dog might find alarming and cause it to snap. Also bear in mind that the disease visceral larva migrans can be transmitted by a dog, and children are particularly at risk because of their habit of putting fingers, and objects, in their mouths. Dogs and children should not be permitted to eat each other's food and the dog should be stopped from licking the child's face. After stroking the dog a child's hands should be washed, and until that happens it should not be allowed to put its fingers into its mouth.

In general, dogs and children have happy relationships, as shown by the fact that the level of dog ownership in households with children is approximately twice that of households where no children are present.

Q *If I am out all day is it fair to keep a dog?*

A If there is no one at home to look after a dog for most of the day then it really wouldn't be fair to keep one. The dog, unlike the cat, is by nature a very sociable animal and fond of company, and young dogs in particular become extremely lonely and bored when left alone. They may resort to destructive behaviour, or continuous barking or howling, when there is no one around to stop them.

It may be more acceptable to keep a dog if it only has to be left alone for a short period on a regular basis (for example if you have a part-time job), or for a longer period occasionally, particularly if the dog is of a placid temperament and familiar with its surroundings. In this case, one of the less energetic breeds should be chosen. If you have two dogs to act as companions for each other, they will probably be less bored.

If you acquire a puppy and spend a good deal of time away from home you will be unable to house-train it. If you acquire an older dog which is left on its own for long periods it may lead to a breakdown in house-training and other behavioural problems.

The same type of problems can occur with dogs left alone in cars all the time that their owners are at work. Here there is an additional danger that if the sun beats down on an unventilated car any animal inside may quickly develop heatstroke (see page 291).

Q *My mother was recently widowed. Would a dog be a good companion for her?*

A It might be thought that having to look after a dog could prove a burden for an elderly person, but there is no doubt that a dog provides a single, elderly person with companionship, interest value and protection, as well as giving them something to care for, i.e. satisfying the need to be needed. In particular, they may come to rely on a pet for companionship at times of death, divorce or other causes of grief. There is also growing evidence that companion animals can have a beneficial effect on their owner's health. Not only can they decrease depression by distracting attention from other worries and stimulate the taking of exercise, but in itself the physical contact obtained by touching and stroking an animal may actually lower blood pressure. One study showed that one year after their hospitalization in a coronary unit, the survival rate amongst pet owners was significantly higher than amongst those without a pet.

The choice of dog needs to be carefully considered. An elderly person may have insufficient strength to control a large breed; the dog may knock them over if it jumps up or, if on a lead, pull them to the ground. On the other hand, they may be unable to bend down to pick up a small dog, and if, because of poor eyesight, they cannot see it they may trip over it. A puppy which is lively and destructive, and which will require training, may be too much for an old person to cope with. Similarly, breeds requiring large amounts of exercise are best avoided. Probably the best choice is a placid-natured, older dog from a known stable background that has had to be rehoused.

Unfortunately, in Britain, over half the sheltered housing provided by local authorities for the elderly has a ban on keeping any kind of pet.

3

Understanding Your Dog's Body

Q *Why are all the breeds of dogs so physically different?*

A Charles Darwin considered that the great variety of dog breeds must be the result of interbreeding between the various wild members of the dog family (Canidae) including the wolf, jackal and coyote. The contemporary view is that the wolf is probably the sole ancestor of today's dogs, but that at least four main races of wolf, which vary considerably in their appearance and behaviour, were involved. It is believed that in the 10,000 years or so since domestication took place only ten or twenty major mutations would have been required to give rise to the huge variety of breeds that exists at present. These mutations would have affected the colour, length and texture of the coat, body size, and the structure of the body (for example short legs, pendulous ears and flattened faces), as well as the animal's behaviour. Different groups of humans would have selected certain characteristics as most suitable for their particular requirements (guarding, hunting, herding, etc.) and bred from the most desirable specimens. As a result of this selective breeding various specific types of dog evolved in different parts of the world, and the independent development of dogs in a number of isolated communities laid the foundation for the major breed differences. Since domestication there have been around 4000 generations of dogs (compared with only 400 in man) so the effects of selection have had more opportunity to appear. Man has also tended to protect and nurture some of the more extreme examples of selective breeding which could never have hoped to survive in the wild. Of course this process of selection still continues and the present-day members of some breeds show significant differences from their breed ancestors of only a hundred years ago. Several breeds or varieties of dog that once existed are now extinct. Many of these were hunting and coursing dogs, including a number of small terriers (for example the Elterwater, Cowley and Roseneath Terriers), but there were also curiosities such as the Indian Tailless Dog, toy dogs (the Toy Bulldog and Toy Bull Terrier) and such ancient British breeds as the Blue Paul, Ban Dog,

Tie Dog and Alaunt. Some of these disappeared completely; others gradually evolved into the breeds we know today.

In the breeding of dogs certain characteristics are dominant and others are recessive. For example the offspring of a flat-faced dog and a long-nosed dog will all have long noses, and crossing a black Poodle with any other colour will produce black puppies. However, some of the offspring will 'carry' the recessive character and if two individuals carrying the same recessive are mated, that characteristic will probably reappear in some of *their* offspring. (Similarly the gene for short hair is dominant over that for long hair, and the gene for a rough coat dominant over that for a silky coat.)

Amongst the great diversity of present-day breeds are some with particularly interesting and unusual features. For instance, dogs such as the Newfoundland and Otterhound that were bred to work in water not only have an oily, waterproof coat but webbed feet as well. This 'web' on the foot reaches only to the second bone of the toes in most dogs, whereas in the Newfoundland and Otterhound it extends all the way down. The Chow Chow is the only breed with a bluish-black tongue (due to the pigment melanin), though some small bears also have this characteristic.

Some peculiarities are not visible: the male Scottish Terrier has a prostate gland which in relation to its size is four times larger than that of other dogs, and the Greyhound has distinctive variations in its eosinophilic blood cells, a much higher concentration of red blood cells in its blood, a comparatively larger heart and, in addition, an almost complete absence of body fat which means that it takes much longer to recover from the injectable barbiturate anaesthetic, thiopentone. This anaesthetic, widely used by vets, normally acts for only a short period because it is quickly withdrawn from the circulation into fat, but in a dog having little fat its effect lasts considerably longer. German Shepherd (Alsatian) bitches, on the other hand, require a proportionately much larger dose of the heat-suppressant drug mibolerone than any other breed.

The curious features of certain breeds are discussed elsewhere in this book, but mention might be made here of an unusual dog that has recently been saved from extinction. The Shar-Pei or Chinese Fighting Dog, once described by the *Guinness Book of Records* as the rarest breed in the world, has a distinctive harsh coat on a skin that appears several sizes too large, and which hangs in loose folds from its massive body. The interest of breeders in the USA has resulted in a marked upturn in its numbers and increasingly the breed is appearing in Europe.

Q *What use is a dog's tail?*

A In a dog the tail is used to indicate the animal's emotional state. It also serves as a rudder for a dog that is swimming, and helps to keep the balance of a dog that is running fast, especially when cornering. It does not, however, appear to be used as it is in the cat in helping to maintain balance when walking along narrow surfaces, such as planks or the top of walls. In wild dogs it may also help protect the vulnerable hind parts from attack.

In a relaxed and confident dog the tail is generally carried high and gently moved from side to side as the animal walks along, though while it is concentrating on eating or sniffing a scent the tail is usually lowered and kept still. This lower position is generally adopted most of the time in the long, sleek breeds, such as the Greyhound.

When interacting with other dogs, or with people, a dog that is feeling confident will hold its tail upright and this occurs both in aggression and when it is playing. An aggressive dog holds its tail either vertically upwards or curved forwards over its back, and the tail then remains motionless except for its tip which is often flicked rapidly from side to side. A friendly dog on the other hand will raise its tail and wag the entire length of it quite vigorously. (A playful dog may also bite, or tug at, the tail of another to attract its attention and encourage it to play, although the other dog may not always respond favourably to this approach!) The degree of movement is thought to reflect the degree of excitement that the dog experiences, usually most marked in play or in greeting a friend. By the age of one month old 50 % of puppies have begun to show tail-wagging behaviour.

A dog that feels insecure will hold its tail down, firmly tucked between its legs, and keep it stationary. This is seen, for example, when a dog has just lost a fight, or is being threatened. It is also seen when a dog is approaching an animal or person which it considers superior to itself and with whom it wishes to be on good terms. Then the dog will sidle up in a typical posture of submission and appeasement, which consists of crouching down, almost on its belly, with ears flattened back along the head, lips drawn right back in a so-called 'submissive grin', its tongue flicking in and out, its eyes narrowed and its gaze deflected to one side. At such a time the tail *may* be wagged, though often it appears motionless and instead the hindquarters appear to be wagged from side to side. The dog may even raise a forepaw which is a preliminary to rolling on its side in total submission (see page 58).

Of course in the development of some breeds of dog, animals have been selected that carry their tails in a characteristic position, such as the high plumed tail of the Pekingese and Japanese Chin, the twist of the Pug, and

39

the permanently curled tail of the Spitz breeds (e.g. Elkhound, Samoyed and Keeshond). This obviously limits the visual signals that these breeds are able to convey to other dogs.

Other breeds have their tails deliberately docked (i.e. cut short to a greater or lesser extent) and in doing so the tendons of the tail muscles may be shortened in some breeds to keep the stump permanently erect as in the Airedale, Wirehaired Fox Terrier and Kerry Blue Terrier. Again this must interfere with the animal's ability to express its moods, although even in breeds with the shortest possible stump some movement (rudimentary wagging) will be detectable when the dog becomes excited.

Incidentally, a bitch that is in heat shows a characteristic deflection of her tail to one side when she is mounted by a male (or sometimes just sniffed at), or when her lower back is stroked by the owner. This behaviour is obviously designed to facilitate mating.

Q *What is the purpose of tail docking?*

A The original stated purpose of tail docking was to prevent the tails of breeds used for hunting getting caught up in undergrowth such as briars and gorse and so being damaged. However, docking is now performed routinely for so-called aesthetic reasons; in other words it has become accepted practice in certain breeds and the dog registration authorities generally require it to have been performed if a dog is to satisfy the relevant breed standards and become a champion. Since the livelihood of breeders is linked to the ability of their dogs to win championships it is hardly surprising that the practice continues. It should be made clear, however, that there is no *need* for routine docking and there is absolutely no advantage in performing the operation in crossbred or mongrel dogs. There are no truly tailless breeds of dog (i.e. the equivalent of the Manx cat) and therefore all the dogs you see with stumpy tails are the result of docking.

If docking is carried out before a puppy's eyes are open, the operation is said to be relatively painless; though not if judged by the noise the puppy makes. In Britain if the operation is performed after the eyes are opened a general anaesthetic is required by law. Nevertheless, as long ago as 1969 the British Veterinary Association declared itself opposed to this operation, and all other unnecessary mutilations. In fact, amputation is really only needed if the tail suffers irreparable damage, such as being shut in a car door, or has some defect which affects the dog's well-being, such as the screw tail of Bulldogs which can interfere with defecation.

At least forty-five breeds are docked for show purposes, and the proportion of the original tail that should be left in the case of each breed is specified, and varies considerably. In the Irish Terrier and Airedale Terrier three-quarters of the tail is left, but in the Rottweiler and Pembroke Corgi only one of the tail bones (vertebrae) should remain. In fact in the case of the Welsh Corgis the rules appear quite arbitrary; the Pembroke Corgi has virtually all of its tail removed, whereas the Cardigan Corgi, which looks almost identical, must be left undocked. In the case of the Affenpinscher (Monkey Terrier) and the Cavalier King Charles Spaniel, docking is optional; the tail can either stay its natural length or be docked.

Q *Why don't dogs draw in their claws like cats do?*

A In both dogs and cats the claws protect the ends of the toes and they are also used to increase the animal's grip, for example when running (especially in the dog) and climbing (chiefly in the cat) and for attack and defence (again, mainly in the cat). In the dog the claws are stronger; in the cat they are sharper. It would appear that it is to keep the claws sharp, and to assist in the mechanics of climbing, that the cat is able to retract them into a protective sheath. The dog is unable to do this.

In both species there are four main toes, or digits, on each foot, and each toe consists of three bones (the phalanges) with joints between them. The horny claw (the equivalent of a human fingernail or toenail) is attached to the third of these, the last and smallest bone in the chain. Two strong elastic ligaments run between the second and third bones. In the cat there is a small recess on the outer face of the second bone at its front end so that at rest the third bone is pulled by these ligaments right the way back to lie alongside the second bone; when the bone is in this position the claw is back inside its sheath. In the dog there is no such recess, so the pull of the ligaments does not cause retraction of the claw.

On the underside of each toe runs a strong muscle tendon (the deep flexor tendon) which is attached to the third bone. A pull on the tendon moves this bone forwards and downwards in both species, but in the cat, where much more movement is possible, this results in the claw being unsheathed.

If the tracks of dogs and cats are examined it can be seen that the dog leaves claw marks in front of its digital pads, whereas there are no claw marks left by the cat because its claws are retracted while walking. Incidentally, the tracks of a dog can be distinguished from the similar tracks of a fox because its pads are larger and closer together and because the front edge of the outer pads extends beyond the back edge of the central pads (see the diagram on page 42).

Paws and claws

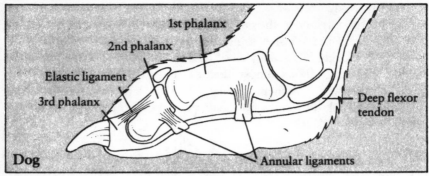

The claw at the end of each toe is attached to the last bone (third phalanx) in a chain of three. Two elastic ligaments (one either side) hold this bone against the one behind, but the limited backward movement prevents retraction of the claw.

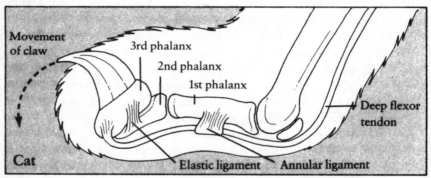

In the cat a recess on the outer face of the second phalanx allows the bone bearing the claw to be drawn right back by similar ligaments, thereby retracting the claw. A pull on the deep flexor tendon moves the bone forwards and unsheaths the claw.

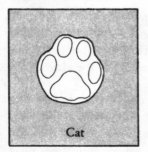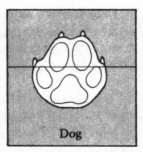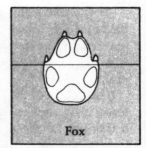

The tracks of dogs and cats of similar size can readily be distinguished because the cat's claws, being retracted, leave no marks. Both the dog and fox leave claw marks, but the fox's outer pads don't extend forward beyond the central pads.

Q *What is the purpose of the dew-claws? Should they be removed?*

A The fifth, or innermost digits (the equivalent of human thumbs and big toes) are very poorly developed in the dog and when the dog is standing they do not come into contact with the ground. The claws associated with these digits are known as dew-claws, and do not serve any useful function.

Dew-claws occur on the forelegs of all dogs but on the hind legs of only about a quarter. In many instances the hind dew-claws have no attachment to the skeleton but are merely fixed to the skin and can be moved about quite freely. There *is* a good case for removing these hind dew-claws, three or four days after birth, because often they get caught (on undergrowth or wire netting), causing tears in the skin. The Pyrenean Mountain Dog (Great Pyrenees), Briard and Beauceron are exceptions, however, as they usually have *double* dew-claws on their hind legs, and for show purposes these must be retained. The front claws should not be removed; they usually have a firm attachment and seldom cause problems.

Like other claws, dew-claws continue to grow and because they receive no wear they will eventually grow round in a circle and begin to re-enter the skin, producing pain and lameness. From time to time they should be checked and if necessary trimmed (see page 147).

Q *My dog is always having to have his anal glands squeezed out. What purpose do they serve?*

A What are popularly termed the anal glands of dogs, but should strictly be called the anal sacs, are two small pouches situated on either side of, and a little below, the anus (i.e. at about the four o'clock and eight o'clock positions). They vary in size from a pea to a walnut, though in a medium-sized dog they are about $^2/_5$ inch (1 cm) across. A small duct, or tube, leads from each to open at the anus. In their walls are numerous glands producing a secretion (very pungent and unpleasant smelling to us) that is stored in the sacs. This secretion is a thick, greyish liquid which acts as a scent marker. When the dog passes a motion some of this liquid is squeezed out of the sacs to be deposited on the stool so that other dogs will be able to identify it — an important aspect of inter-canine communication (see page 70). Some dogs will also evacuate the sacs when frightened.

Unfortunately in many domesticated dogs the sacs fail to empty properly (often because the duct becomes blocked) so that the secretion accumulates and distends the sacs causing them to press on adjacent structures. The dog shows evidence of discomfort, frequently rubbing its rear end on the floor or trying to lick or bite around its anus to relieve the irritation.

It is to remove this accumulated material that the sacs are squeezed. It can be done either by gently squeezing both sacs together into a pad of cotton wool held over the anus, or, with a hand covered by a plastic glove, inserting a finger through the anus and squeezing out each sac in turn. If the secretion has solidified it may be necessary to flush the sac out while the dog is anaesthetized.

If untreated the impacted secretion may become infected, giving rise to a painful abscess alongside the anus; this is often so painful that the dog tries not to defecate. Ultimately this will burst open on to the surface, though your vet may lance it to save the dog further suffering and permit drainage. The opened abscess is then treated (see page 259).

Many dogs, especially of the smaller breeds, may require to have their anal sacs emptied at frequent intervals and may even be subjected to repeated abscesses. If so, your vet may recommend surgical removal of the anal sacs as an effective and permanent solution to the problem.

Q *When dogs race are all four of their feet ever off the ground at the same time?*

A Yes, as long ago as 1887 the photographs of Edward Muybridge showed that this is so. The extent to which it happens depends on the exertion of the animal, but when a Greyhound is moving rapidly (in the so-called light lateral or rotary gallop) it occurs twice during each cycle of movements. The first occasion is when the thrust of the hind limbs pushes the dog forwards in a great bound, so that its front legs are stretched forwards and its hind legs extended backwards, just like a horse clearing a fence. The second time comes after the dog has landed again on its front legs and uses them to push itself forwards. Then front and hind legs are crossed for an instant, with all of the feet clear of the ground; hind legs pointing forwards and forelegs in between them pointing backwards.

The great flexibility of the spine of the Greyhound (and similar breeds such as the Whippet) allow these movements to be more exaggerated than in other dogs, so that the length of each stride is markedly increased. This enables racing Greyhounds to achieve speeds of 40 mph (64 km/h) over short distances. The forces acting on the skeleton at such a speed are considerable but the properties of bone (85 % of the tensile strength of cast iron for only a third of its weight) enable it to withstand them.

Q *Is it true that dogs only have sweat glands on their pads?*

A No, there are sweat glands over the entire skin surface with the exception of the skin of the nose which is completely free of glands. This misconception probably arises because the sweat glands are of two types, eccrine sweat glands found only in the pads of the feet, and apocrine sweat glands found everywhere else.

The apocrine glands produce a secretion which is broken down by the bacteria normally present on the skin into substances that are responsible for the dog's characteristic body odour. The mammary glands are also apocrine glands but specially modified to produce milk.

In man, the eccrine glands are important as the source of sweat, which in a hot environment cools the body as it evaporates. In this way the glands assist in maintaining a constant body temperature. But in the dog, where these glands are confined to the pads, they are of little importance in temperature regulation. Nevertheless, on a hot day it is noticeable that the dog leaves wet footprints behind it. These glands are also activated by emotional stimuli, just like the glands on the palms of the hand in man which cause 'sweaty palms' at times of anxiety. Consequently, a frightened dog (e.g. one being examined by the vet) can also be seen to leave damp footprints, which are particularly obvious on a dark surface.

In human skin there is also a network of small blood vessels close to the surface which facilitates heat loss by radiation and conduction; there is no such network in the dog.

These facts have led to the conclusion that although in man the skin is important in cooling the body in hot weather or after exercise, in the dog the skin and haircoat serve primarily as insulation.

Q *If dogs can't lose heat from the skin, how do they cool down?*

A When he is overheated a dog pants with his mouth open — a sight familiar to most dog owners. This is to permit the evaporation of moisture which has the same effect as the evaporation of sweat from human skin, namely that a certain amount of heat (the latent heat of evaporation) is withdrawn from the moist surface each time some of the liquid evaporates.

However, the moisture being evaporated is not primarily saliva from the lining of the mouth and the surface of the tongue, as is popularly supposed, but moisture from the lining of the nasal cavities. The large quantity of water required for evaporation is produced by the lateral nasal gland on each side (a gland not present in humans, see page 155) and ducted to within $3/4$ inch (2 cm) of the opening of the nostrils.

When only moderately overheated a dog often pants with his mouth closed so that both breathing in (inspiration) and breathing out (expiration) take place through the nose. But with a great excess of heat to dissipate the dog opens his mouth and then breathes *in* through his nose (during which most evaporation takes place) and *out* through his mouth; a one-way system which provides the most efficient evaporation and therefore heat loss. Tests have established that as the air temperature increases so the secretion of the lateral nasal gland rises accordingly.

Q *Is it correct that a dog cannot drink if its tongue becomes paralysed?*

A Dogs and cats normally drink by lapping. The muscles which comprise the bulk of the tongue form the organ into the shape of a ladle (i.e. with its tip curved round to form a trough), which is able to pick up liquid. Then with a rapid flick the liquid is thrown to the back of the throat and swallowed. This procedure is repeated several times a minute.

If the nerves which activate these muscles are damaged the tongue will be paralysed, often hanging from one side of the mouth, and lapping is no longer possible. Nevertheless if such animals are provided with a water bowl deep enough for them to submerge their mouth they can learn to take in water by sucking it up, which is the normal method adopted by horses and farm animals.

As a matter of interest, it is the tip of the dog's tongue which is particularly sensitive to the taste of water. Sweetness is detected by taste buds on the tip and sides of the tongue, saltiness at the sides and back, and sour tastes affect taste buds over the tongue's entire upper surface.

Q *You said earlier that it is unusual for Basenjis to bark. Why is this?*

A The sounds which constitute the 'voice' of an animal are produced by the unimpeded vibration of the vocal cords within the larynx (voice box) as air passes over them. The larynx is part of the respiratory tract along which air passes to and from the lungs, and is constructed of five main pieces of cartilage, held together by ligaments and muscles, and lined by membrane. The membrane is in fact arranged into two folds on either side, one of which is the vocal cord and the other (in front) the vestibular fold or false vocal cord. Between the two folds is a slit-like recess which opens out into a small cavity, the laryngeal saccule.

Careful examination has shown that in the Basenji the recess between the folds is markedly shallower than usual, which limits the vibration of the vocal cord, and in addition the laryngeal saccule is either absent or greatly reduced in size, which similarly reduces vibration of the vestibular fold. As a result of these differences in its larynx the Basenji is incapable of producing a sound which has either the character or intensity of the normal canine bark.

Two other breeds suffer, though not invariably, from specific disorders involving the larynx. In the Bouvier, a breed very popular in the Netherlands, an inherited defect can result in paralysis of the laryngeal muscles so that affected dogs are unable to part their right and left vocal cords. As a result the airflow through the larynx is disturbed causing great difficulty in breathing. Among Chow Chows some individuals suffer from episodes of generalized muscular spasm, most apparent after a long rest, termed hereditary myotonia. If the laryngeal muscles are involved greater tension than usual is placed upon the vocal cords producing both obstruction of the airway and an abnormally high-pitched bark.

Q *Do dogs see as we do? Can they see in colour?*

A In good lighting conditions the eye of the dog is unable to distinguish details as clearly as the human eye can, and stationary objects or people only a short distance away are often not perceived at all. Anything which is moving however is readily detected and the hopping of a rabbit may be closely observed from a mile away.

The eye of the dog really comes into its own in dim lighting conditions – sometimes so dim that to human eyes it may appear as almost complete darkness. Then the dog is much better able than ourselves to detect any movement in the surroundings. There are two main reasons for this:

1 In the retina there are two types of nerve endings which are named, according to their shape, as rods and cones. The cones are most strongly stimulated by bright light and these nerve endings are responsible for colour vision in man and for the perception of fine details. The rods, on the other hand, are stimulated by light of lower intensity but are not capable of producing such sharp images. Night vision, or more correctly, twilight vision, in all animals is due to the functioning of the rods. The eye of the dog contains a much higher proportion of rods to cones (approximately 20:1) than the human eye (approximately 4:1).

2 The dog, in common with many other domesticated animals but unlike man, has a reflecting layer (tapetum lucidum) situated just behind the retina. The effect of this is that light rays which have entered the eye and penetrated the retina, thereby stimulating the nerve endings, are immediately reflected back on to exactly the same nerve endings. Consequently each ray of light produces double stimulation of a particular nerve ending giving a type of image intensification. The presence of the tapetum also accounts for the typical 'cat's eyes' effect when a beam of light (e.g. from car headlights) is shone into the eyes in the dark. The light is reflected back from the greenish-yellow tapetum so that the eyes appear to glow yellow or green in the dark.

The low proportion of cones in the dog's retina led to the belief that dogs, like most domesticated animals, were colour blind and saw things merely in black, white and shades of grey — like the picture on a black and white television set. Now it is believed that although the number of cones is limited they do provide some degree of colour vision, though the dog's ability to discriminate different shades of colour is clearly inferior to that of man.

The eyes of the dog are placed slightly further to the side of the head than in man, which means that the dog has a total field of vision which is greater than that of humans. Dogs can detect movement within an arc of 250° – 290° (approximately three-quarters of a circle) depending on the breed, whereas in humans the comparable arc is about 180° – 200° (approximately half a circle). Because the central part of the total field of vision is seen by both eyes (i.e. the views from the eyes overlap) the brain is able to superimpose these images to produce a stereoscopic effect and obtain a three-dimensional impression of the area ahead. This phenomenon is known as binocular vision. In man the overlap is greater (120° – 140° compared with 60° – 80° in dogs) so that humans have a better appreciation of distance over a wider area.

Q *How old are puppies when their eyes open?*

A At birth the edges of the upper and lower eyelids of a puppy are firmly united because final development of the eyes is still taking place. The cornea, the retina and the tapetum are not yet fully mature. Separation of the eyelids usually occurs between ten and fourteen days later and the eyes then open. If the lids continue to remain united after that time it is considered abnormal. Sometimes the eyelids appear simply to be gummed together and gentle bathing with warm water frees them (see page 257). However, if the eyes of a puppy are not open after two and a half weeks, or if pus is seen between the lids, a veterinary surgeon should be consulted. On the other hand premature separation results in severe inflammation of the eye.

Initially the puppy's eyesight is poor but it rapidly develops so that by around four weeks of age its vision is almost the equal of an adult dog's, though its interpretation of what it sees is not as good.

Q *Is it really true that dogs can be fitted with contact lenses?*

A Yes, and cats as well, although this is done not to improve their sight but to protect the front of the eyeball, after injury or surgery, while healing takes place (see page 221). Visual acuity is difficult to measure accurately and short-sightedness is not recognized as a major problem in dogs. The important eye disorders from which dogs suffer would be little affected by contact lenses, or spectacles.

The contact lenses that have been used are not specifically made for dogs but are those intended for human use, trimmed to size where necessary.

Q *If my dog injures his eye in a fight, could he manage with one?*

A An eye may sometimes have to be removed following severe injury. Then, the eyelids would be sewn together so as not to leave a gaping wound. Such one-eyed dogs manage perfectly well in most circumstances although obviously they are at some disadvantage in hunting or fighting. There will be a loss of vision on the affected side, and a loss of stereoscopic vision (the superimposition of images from both eyes which gives a feeling of depth). Nevertheless, the animal quickly compensates for these deficiencies and essentially behaves as any other dog.

Q *If my dog should go blind in old age, would it be kinder to have him put to sleep?*

A There would be no necessity for that; many dogs that are partially or totally blind manage very successfully in familiar surroundings, particularly if their senses of hearing and smell are still adequate. They know from experience the position of doorways, steps, furniture and so on, but it is obviously important not to leave unexpected obstacles in their path or to alter the position of furniture in a room.

Dogs adapt well to this handicap, particularly if blindness comes on slowly, and if among people they know and like they will be quite content. Similarly, with dogs that become totally deaf, if you appreciate that they cannot come when called or respond to other verbal commands, and you take care that they are well under control near traffic, they can still lead an active and happy life.

However, care should be taken not to suddenly approach or handle blind or deaf animals; if they receive no warning beforehand they may be startled and react defensively by growling or snapping. Always let a deaf dog see you, and speak to a blind dog before touching it.

Q *Do you ever get cross-eyed dogs?*

A Yes, this can occur though very seldom. A squint (strabismus) arises from a failure to coordinate the movements of those muscles which alter the direction of each eyeball. As a result the eyeballs point in different directions at the same time.

In the dog this may be due to a congenital defect (i.e. one the dog is born with) or arise from damage to one of the cranial nerves controlling the muscles or to the muscles themselves.

Q *Is it true that white dogs are always deaf?*

A No, white dogs are not *always* deaf but in some breeds, especially Bull Terriers, Sealyhams and Dalmatians, white animals, or those with a predominance of white markings, frequently have this defect. The exact mode of inheritance is probably different in each breed but essentially the gene responsible for white coat colour appears often to be linked to a gene responsible for malformation of that part of the inner ear (cochlea) sensitive to sound waves. Certainly in Dalmatians varying degrees of deafness can occur, involving one or both ears.

In some breeds deafness, and blindness, occurs in an individual that inherits the dominant gene for a 'spotted' coat from both parents (merle Collies, harlequin Great Danes and dappled Dachshunds). Dogs that inherit this gene from only one parent have an identical coat without deafness but are often 'wall eyed', the iris of the eye appearing part blue and part white.

In other breeds deafness can also be inherited though it appears not to be linked to coat colour, for example the Fox Terrier, Foxhound and Scottish Terrier.

Hearing can be difficult to evaluate, especially in puppies. In an isolated area one should observe the animal's reaction to sudden noises, whistles of different pitch, rustling sounds and spoken words, but to rule out other factors, take care to do this out of the animal's sight. For example stand behind it, but not so close that it might react to any movement of the air. Stamping on the floor is unsatisfactory because the dog will feel the vibration even if it hears no sound. Movement of the ear flaps will usually be absent, or less marked, in a deaf dog. Bear in mind that puppies are born deaf because their ear canals are closed, although this condition is corrected at the end of their third week.

Q *While feeling the beats of my dog's heart over its chest I noticed that they regularly speeded up and then slowed down. Is this normal?*

A Yes, this phenomenon, known as sinus arrhythmia, is *normal* in resting dogs after the first month of life. In general the heart rate speeds up when the dog is breathing in and slows down when he breathes out, though occasionally it happens the other way around. A number of physiological mechanisms contribute to this link between respiratory and cardiac activity. However, this repeated acceleration and deceleration of the heartbeat disappears if the dog is exercised or becomes exited. It also disappears in diseased hearts and may be replaced by another, more significant, irregularity.

Q *If my dog badly injures one leg, could he manage with three? Would it be kinder to have him put down?*

A Amputation of a limb may be necessary if it has been extensively injured or, less commonly, if it is diseased (e.g. affected with gangrene or a malignant tumour, i.e. cancer). If the animal is otherwise relatively healthy, the continued presence of the limb could jeopardize its future because the complications which would ensue would eventually involve the rest of its body.

Successful amputation is relatively straightforward and after a brief period of adjustment the dog will again be doing all the things it did before. Obviously the fact that dogs normally walk on four legs makes it easier, compared to ourselves, to compensate after losing one. They may have difficulty jumping but in general will not attempt anything outside their capabilities.

It is usually the owners who wish the dog to be put to sleep rather than to have an amputation performed because they 'don't like the look of the dog' with only three legs. The dog, however, in common with other domestic animals, is more objective. Almost certainly, such animals spend little time thinking that they used to have four legs or that other dogs still have four legs, but rather they get on with living their lives and making the best of them.

Q *Why do some dogs become locked together during sexual intercourse?*

A First of all we should be clear that in dogs this locking together during mating is *not* an exceptional feature; it occurs in almost all instances, and it is those individuals in which it does not take place (especially those of certain breeds, such as the Chow Chow) that should be regarded as unusual.

After mounting the bitch (during which he clasps her in front of the hips with his front legs) the male dog introduces his penis into her vagina and commences a series of pelvic thrusts. During this behaviour the end of the penis, the bulb, becomes considerably enlarged, and the contraction of the constrictor muscles of the vagina around the penis holds the male firmly in position, preventing withdrawal, in the so-called 'tie' or 'lock'.

The ejaculation of sperm takes place early on, when pelvic thrusting stops. Soon afterwards the male, still locked to the female, will drop down on to his forefeet at the side of the bitch, and raise one hind leg over her back which brings their rear ends together and their heads facing in opposite directions. This position both affords the male some rest and also makes the united pair less vulnerable to attack.

They usually remain in the tie for between twenty and twenty-five minutes, though it can range from as little as five minutes to as long as one hour fifteen minutes; in general it does not last more than forty-five minutes. During the time that they remain locked together fluid from the prostate gland of the male is slowly ejaculated, and therefore it may be that the purpose of this behaviour is to flush the sperms through the female reproductive tract and thereby increase the chance of a fertile mating. However, it would appear that the tie is not absolutely essential, since animals in which it does not occur breed quite successfully.

Occasionally the bitch will attempt to pull against the tie, with suffi-cient force at times to upset the balance of the male, though the tie will still be maintained. This is all perfectly normal and an attempt should *not* be made to separate the animals (i.e. by pulling them apart or pouring cold water over them) because such attempts can result in serious and permanent injury. Even if the mating is unwanted it should be allowed to be completed naturally. As the tie relaxes, the male and female can part and both will normally lick their genitals for a while afterwards.

Q *Is it true that there is a bone in the penis of the dog?*

A Yes, there is a well-developed penile bone (the os penis or baculum) inside the dog's penis. It is a narrow, tapered bone, about 4 inches (10 cm) long in a large dog, and just under $^1/_2$ inch (1 cm) wide. It lies surrounded by expandable spongy tissue and on its lower surface there is a groove in which runs the urethra (the tube which conveys urine to the exterior). Being surrounded by bone on three sides means that the urethra cannot distend very much in this region. Consequently this is one of the two sites where small stones (calculi) which have formed in the bladder, and then been flushed out in the flow of urine, become arrested (the other is the point where the urethra has to make a tight turn around the rear edge of the pelvic bone).

It is believed that the purpose of the os penis is to provide increased rigidity during mating. The dog and cat are the only domesticated mammals with an os penis though many wild mammals have this struc-ture and in some carnivores the female possesses a comparable bone in the clitoris.

Q *At what age should a male puppy's testicles descend?*

A The testicles of the male dog (like the ovaries of the bitch) develop inside the abdomen, but in contrast to the ovaries they normally descend through the inguinal canal to lie in the scrotum — a pouch of skin between the thighs. This is because for the testicles to produce sperm (i.e. for the dog to be fertile) they must be kept at a slightly lower temperature than that of the abdomen.

This descent is very gradual but in the majority of dogs the testicles are in the scrotum either at birth or within the next ten days. In some dogs they descend later, but if descent is going to take place it is always *before* six months old and usually the testicles are in the scrotum by three and a half months old. However, there are dogs in which up to nine or ten months old one testicle can readily be withdrawn from, and returned to, the scrotum. In early life the small size of the testicles may make detection difficult; however they can usually be felt by two months old, although sometimes not before they begin to enlarge (prior to puberty) at about four months of age.

The failure of one or both testicles to descend is known as cryptorchidism and in the USA probably occurs in about 10 % of dogs, especially Yorkshire Terriers, Pomeranians and Poodles. The right testicle is almost twice as likely to be retained as the left. There is no truth in the belief that cryptorchid dogs are more likely to be vicious. An undescended testicle is able to produce male sex hormone (testosterone), though not sperm, and is much more likely (more than twelve times) to develop a tumour in later life.

Where neither testicle has ever left the abdominal cavity there has clearly been arrested development and many affected animals are male pseudohermaphrodites (i.e. their external genital organs resemble, in varying degrees, those of a bitch).

There is no medical treatment which will cause the testicles to descend. Although it is possible to breed from a male with only one retained testicle this is inadvisable since the condition is inherited. For this reason cryptorchids are disqualified from official shows. Surgery to bring an undescended testicle into the scrotum should *not* be undertaken because it will not correct the underlying genetic defect; it is far preferable for both testicles to be removed (i.e. for the dog to be castrated) to *prevent* breeding taking place.

The total failure of one, or both testicles, to develop at all is possible, but extremely rare.

Q *Is it true that one year of a dog's life equals seven of a human's?*

A This comparison is based on the assumption that on average people live three score years and ten (i.e. seventy years) whereas a dog only lives for ten. In reality there is considerably more variation.

Most dogs will live for between ten and thirteen years if well looked after, and the small breeds survive longer than the large. Great Danes, Mastiffs, St Bernards and Irish Wolfhounds do not usually reach ten years old, and Boxers will not normally live much beyond that age. Bulldogs usually do not last more than seven or eight years. On the other hand Pekingese, toy breeds and the small terriers often live for between fourteen and seventeen years.

Naturally enough it is always the exceptionally long-lived dogs that one hears about, but these animals, living between twenty and twenty-five years or more, should not be regarded as typical. There is even a report of a dog living to the age of thirty-four.

Unspayed bitches usually come into heat until the end of their lives, though generally less frequently (there is no canine equivalent of the menopause), and male dogs may still be capable of siring a litter at sixteen years old.

Q *Is it possible to tell a dog's age from its teeth?*

A Like other mammals the dog has two consecutive sets of teeth; first the twenty-eight deciduous or milk teeth, followed by the permanent teeth of which there are forty-two. The number of teeth is almost always the same regardless of the breed, though in dogs with short noses the teeth may be rather crowded. These flat-faced (brachycephalic) breeds are the ones most likely to have fewer teeth and if some are absent they are usually molars or premolars of the lower jaw.

The ages at which teeth in different positions (in both jaws) erupt is fairly constant. Therefore in the dog's early life, by observing which of the teeth are already present, and whether they are deciduous or permanent, it is possible to state the age with reasonable certainty. However, by seven months of age all the permanent teeth are present, so that after that date estimates of age are made chiefly by reference to the degree of wear on the incisor (front) teeth. However, dogs that are in the habit of chewing stones or other hard objects will show an excessive amount of wear for their age. Dental wear will also appear abnormal with dogs with an overshot jaw (where the upper jaw projects further forward than the lower) and an undershot jaw (where the reverse is the case).

When they first erupt, the incisor teeth have prominent projections (cusps or tubercles) which gradually wear down, and by observing which of the teeth have lost them, and later still by noting the shape of the wearing surfaces and the tooth length, it is possible to form a fair estimate of a dog's age up to about ten years old. After that age it is progressively more difficult to form an estimate, although in general at sixteen years old the incisors have all disappeared and at twenty years of age even the canines (the large 'fang-like' teeth) have been shed.

Up to the age of seventeen weeks old the tooth enamel (the outer white covering of the teeth) is still soft enough to be scraped off with a metal instrument, though it is destined to become the hardest material in the body. Dogs which have extra teeth, or never have teeth, or grow a third set of teeth, are encountered only occasionally.

Q *How will my dog's body change as it gets older?*

A The aged dog is less active and less adaptable than formerly. The reduction in the amount of muscle on its frame means that it has less strength and stamina; it moves more slowly and is less agile. Arthritis often produces stiffness in moving, especially on rising. Like old people elderly dogs acquire grey hairs, and because of decreased exercise may develop overgrown claws (requiring regular trimming) and sometimes constipation. The latter may be corrected by giving between one and four dessertspoonsful of liquid paraffin (known in North America as mineral oil), although this should *not* be repeated regularly as it will impair the absorption of fat-soluble vitamins and ultimately give rise to the seepage of oil (smelling of faeces) from the anus, which can impregnate carpets and furnishings.

It is best to provide exercise more often but for shorter periods, and one should consider the use of a coat in cold weather. Any severe loss of fluid (e.g. due to vomiting or diarrhoea) takes longer to correct, and temperature regulation is less efficient so that exposure to cold can easily result in hypothermia (abnormally low body temperature). This is a particular hazard for old dogs kept in outdoor kennels during the winter. The healing of damaged tissue takes longer and the senses of smell, taste, sight and hearing are all impaired to some extent. The older dog often shows an opacity of the lens of the eye due solely to age changes (and erroneously referred to as senile cataract) which does *not* impair its vision. Because its metabolic rate is slower the old dog needs less food and so, if it is not to become overweight, its food consumption should be reduced.

The elderly dog is also less interested in what is happening around it, preferring to remain inactive for longer periods. It resents alterations to its daily routine and will not readily accept changes in its surroundings or type of food.

Diseases of the kidneys, heart and teeth, and the occurrence of growths (tumours) are all more common in old dogs, and some are unable to control the sphincters of the bladder or anus resulting in incontinence. The skin is less elastic and, because the dog is less interested in grooming, discharges from the eye and ear can accumulate and have to be cleaned away by the owner.

Old age, however, should not be regarded as a disease but merely as a state in which, unfortunately, the dog has decreased powers of survival and of adjustment to change.

Q *Do dogs chew their food? Can my dog survive without his teeth when he is old?*

A Dogs do not chew their food as we do. The natural function of their teeth is to serve as a means of killing their prey and of cutting it up into pieces small enough to swallow.

The large canine teeth ('fangs') are used to kill the prey. Then the premolar and molar teeth along the sides of the jaw are used to cut up the prey into pieces or strips which can be swallowed. Especially important are the largest of these teeth (the carnassials) which have a scissor-like action as the jaws close. The small incisor teeth at the front of the jaws can be used for pulling flesh off bones as well as for carrying objects. And, of course, all the teeth, but especially the canine teeth, are used for attack and defence.

Dogs fed on canned or home-cooked diets, or even on raw meat which has been well cut up into tiny pieces, have no need to use their teeth at all. As a result of this lack of wear, tartar accumulates on the teeth initiating a dental disorder (see page 144) which may end in the teeth loosening and dropping out, or having to be removed. It is not unusual for Yorkshire or Maltese Terriers to have their teeth loosen or fall out before five years old. But of course if the dog needs only to swallow the same precooked, soft food, it will certainly not require its teeth, and indeed there are some old dogs who have lost all their teeth and yet eat normally and remain quite healthy. So the presence of teeth is not essential and digestion will proceed normally with or without them, although of course a dog without teeth is not so well-equipped to defend itself.

Obviously, it is *preferable* to prevent the dog from losing its teeth. This may be achieved by cleaning the teeth and by feeding it dry foods, or by giving some large, hard biscuits or a hide chew (available at pet shops in various shapes). All of these will provide good dental exercise and reduce the possibility of dental disorders developing later.

4

Understanding Your Dog's Behaviour

Q *How does my dog indicate his moods?*

A A dog is able to communicate its moods to other animals, and to humans, by the posture and movement of its body (in particular the position of its tail and ears), the directness of its gaze and the sounds that it makes. The visual signals, however, are the most important in determining how a dog is feeling and how it is likely to react.

When the interest of a dog is aroused by what it sees or hears it will appear alert; remaining still, with its muscles tense and its ears pricked (i.e. erect, or at least as erect as is possible for certain breeds). If it is listening intently it will move its ears slightly to change the direction of the opening and thereby collect the sound waves most efficiently. When the dog is watching something nearby, particularly the approach of another animal, it will stand with its tail raised and usually with one forefoot lifted, the typical 'aroused position'. Unless it immediately shows hostility towards the newcomer the dog will usually move forward to investigate.

Two dogs that are strangers will generally approach each other rather warily, with both showing the characteristic submissive signs, i.e. ears back along the head, tails between their legs and careful avoidance of eye to eye contact. They will sniff at each other to determine each other's scent, first of all nose to nose and then sniffing at the inguinal region (between the hind legs). When confronted with a strange human the dog will first sniff at the leg, simply because the face is too high to reach.

If the dog recognizes an individual (canine or human) that it likes, either immediately or after investigation, it will show what is termed 'greeting behaviour' in which its tail is raised and wagged from side to side and its mouth is slightly opened with its corners drawn upwards, to produce what is sometimes referred to as a 'greeting smile'. In 'play soliciting' behaviour the dog will, in addition, lower the front part of its body but keep its hind legs raised (the 'play bow'). It will lift weight from one front leg to another and often jump about barking to encourage the participation of the other animal or person in a game. This behaviour is usually best seen when you are throwing a stick or ball for a dog. Often at this time, to encourage play, a dog may run off with the ball, thereby inviting pursuit, or it may put the ball down just in front of itself, only to pick it up and run away again should you attempt to take it.

Some dogs adopt a submissive posture at the approach of another dog or person. This consists of crouching down with the tail between the legs (page 39) and the ears drawn back along the head. A very submissive dog will roll over on one side and raise its uppermost hind and forelegs to show its underside, just as a puppy would to its mother. (It may also pass a small amount of urine, just as a puppy would; a sign of total deference.) However, to encourage a smaller dog to play, a larger, dominant one will often adopt this submissive posture, as if to indicate that it means no harm.

An aggressive dog will hold its tail high and stare intently at its opponent, with its ears erect and pointed forwards (a sign of confidence), its neck extending forwards, its mouth partly open and the upper lips curled up to bare the teeth in a snarl. If it is near enough it may even place a forepaw on the other dog to indicate dominance. Its hackles rise (i.e. the hairs along the centre of the back, particularly the shoulders and rump, stand up) and it stands stiffly, almost on tiptoe — both of which make it look larger and more menacing.

Confronted with this display a subordinate dog will turn away. On the other hand, an equally aggressive individual will stand its ground, so that ultimately the situation will only be resolved by a fight. The two dogs will slowly circle around trying to force each other to retreat. If any sudden movement is made, both dogs will immediately snap at their opponent's neck.

A dog that is nervous, and may bite out of fear, shows some signs of aggression (raised hackles, lips curled and teeth showing) combined with some signs of submission (ears flattened back along the head, and tail between the legs). These animals require gentle reassurance and a very cautious approach by humans to gain their confidence and permit handling.

Q *If my dog should get into a fight, how should I deal with it?*

A When wild dogs fight they seldom inflict serious injuries on each other. A heavy dog usually has the advantage because it may more easily unbalance its adversary. Eventually the weaker dog has to let go of its grip and adopts the submissive posture, whereupon the winner withdraws. But domestic breeds of dog which have been selected for their aggressive tendencies often continue to fight beyond this point. A terrier, for example, although technically defeated, may sometimes continue to fight almost to the death. Unlike the situation in the wild, the winning dog will sometimes continue to fight although the other dog has already surrendered.

The best way for an owner to break up a dog fight is to walk away and call his dog from a distance. This has the effect of withdrawing the owner's 'support' for the dog, thus weakening his confidence and therefore his aggression. As a result the dog often decides to withdraw from the contest. However, onlookers may react unfavourably to this apparently cowardly approach. Attempts to separate the dogs physically may simply intensify the fighting. A dog receiving a blow, or feeling itself being seized, will probably assume that the other dog is responsible and respond with added ferocity. It is better to throw a bucket of cold water over the combatants, which may produce a lull in the fighting during which they can be seized and separated.

Q *How do dogs communicate using sounds?*

A In addition to body posture, vocalization is another means of canine communication, with a certain amount of variation between breeds. Some breeds, for instance the Dachshund, tend to be very vocal, whereas others such as the Greyhound and Saluki bark much less frequently.

Apart from warning growls and snarls of aggression, dogs will also whimper, whine, bark, howl and yelp. In domesticated dogs barking may occur in any situation where the animal gets excited and wants to draw attention to itself; for example when playing, being fed, greeting its owners and generally responding to other sights or noises. The typical canine bark consists of a single syllable lasting no longer than one second. While barking is obviously valuable in drawing attention to intruders, if allowed to go unchecked the behaviour can be extremely tiresome for owners, neighbours, and in fact anyone who comes within earshot. Some small dogs are such frequent and persistent barkers that they suffer from permanent tonsillitis, pharyngitis and laryngitis because of the continual damage which they inflict upon their throats. In most breeds barking begins at around three weeks of age. There is some evidence that the continued administration of female sex hormone gradually reduces the amount of barking by male dogs.

Whining and whimpering are considered to be extensions of the 'mewing' noise that a puppy makes to its mother when it is cold, hungry or in pain. (It has, however, been established that the mother will not respond to these sounds unless she can also *see* the puppy.) Under natural conditions these noises occur most frequently between four and nine days old and cease at four to five weeks of age. Beyond this age whining is generally made to encourage a sympathetic response from the owner, such as giving food or opening the door. Just as with barking, careful training is needed to discourage indiscriminate whining, because once the dog has realized that its whining has elicited the desired behaviour from the owner it will be conditioned to whine again. In the absence of humans, adult dogs seldom whine to each other.

The yelp is a response to sudden pain, such as a kick, cut or wasp sting. Howling, fortunately, is not common in dogs, except those in hunt kennels and in such northern breeds as Eskimo Dogs (formerly called Huskies) and Alaskan Malamutes. Analysis has shown that howling is a complex sound which can be triggered by a number of factors, including loneliness and the scent of the chase ('the baying of hounds'); it is always performed standing still, never whilst moving. It is also a communal activity and once one dog starts howling others will join in; this behaviour in the wild will allow a dog to relocate his pack. It might also explain why the singing of certain people will cause the family pet to howl!

Q *Why do male dogs lift their legs to urinate?*

A Urine, like other bodily excretions, contains highly individual scent chemicals called pheromones, and is used by dogs to scent-mark the area in which they live or through which they roam; what might be termed their territory. This is done both to inform other dogs of their presence and to provide reassurance for themselves by giving a familiar odour to the surroundings. The need to emphasize their presence is much stronger in adult males and it is possible that they are able to control, at least partially, the addition of scent secretion to their urine specifically for this purpose. Also by fully raising one hind leg a male dog is able to direct his urine on to any prominent vertical surface (e.g. a tree, lamp-post, fence etc.) so that it will be distributed more widely and therefore be more obvious to other passing dogs. Most males will raise whichever leg is nearest the 'target'; others seem to favour one leg and will alter their position accordingly. Adult males, however, may also urinate on the ground, presumably simply to relieve themselves, and when they do this a hind leg is only partially elevated.

A male dog urinates about three times as often as a bitch, so that left to his own devices his progress on a walk is continually being interrupted by the investigation of urinary scent-marks left by other dogs, followed by the addition of his own. Even when his bladder is empty the behaviour will persist because the instinct is so strong. The strongest stimulant to scent-mark is the odour of another male, but the scent of a bitch in heat, and sometimes other strong-smelling substances, such as tobacco, will elicit the same behaviour.

After passing urine male dogs will sometimes scratch at the earth, not, as in the case of a cat, to cover up the excretion, but to reinforce his urine scent with scent from the sweat glands on the pads, and also to leave a visual signal. Such behaviour is most likely to take place near the territory of another male, or if other dogs are watching. Urine marking in the house may be shown by previously housetrained male animals trying to establish their dominance, for example following the introduction of another adult male into the household (see page 117).

Incidentally, some members of the dog family that scarcely meet each other outside the breeding season, such as foxes, produce a much more strongly scented urine than the domestic dog.

Q *Do very young male dogs also lift their legs in this way?*

A No, males do not begin to show this typical leg-raising behaviour until near the age of puberty; in fact it usually begins between five and eight months old. Between five to seven weeks of age and puberty male dogs adopt a posture in which they stand with all four legs on the ground and with their hind limbs slightly extended backwards − giving the impression of leaning forwards. This posture is not the same, however, as the squatting position adopted by bitches when urinating.

The changeover from one urination posture to the other around the time of puberty is undoubtedly due to the influence of male sex hormone (testosterone). But the change appears not to be due to any hormone actually produced *at* puberty, and in fact all the evidence indicates that it is a delayed effect of that testosterone which is produced by the developing puppy before it has even been born. Consequently dogs castrated before puberty still develop the typical leg-lifting behaviour at the usual age (around five months old). Also, dogs castrated after puberty continue to leg-lift. Furthermore, the administration of either testosterone or the female sex hormone (oestrogen) to male dogs produces no change in the position they adopt to urinate, regardless of whether they are entire (uncastrated) or castrated, either before or after puberty. (The only obvious effect that giving these hormones produces is to increase the *frequency* of urination.) On the other hand dogs that have both their testicles undescended, plus a poorly developed penis and low libido (features which suggest minimal testosterone production at all times, even as a foetus) never adopt the adult male posture.

Grossly obese male dogs and males suffering from severe cystitis tend to adopt the juvenile posture of urinating, or even to squat, rather than leg-lift. In the former instance this is because of physical difficulty and in the latter because of the pain and discomfort which it produces.

Throughout their life bitches usually squat to pass urine, although it is quite normal for one hind limb to be slightly lifted between one and six inches (2.5 – 15 cm) off the ground, and even for the normal raised leg posture of the male to be adopted on up to 10% of occasions. Leg-lifting is more likely to occur around the time of heat, and certainly at that time bitches are more interested in investigating urine scents and in leaving their own marks. Interestingly, if bitches are given testosterone early in their development, either before birth (i.e. when it is given to their mothers) or soon afterwards, they will adopt the typical male posture for urinating almost every time. However, testosterone given to bitches later in life produces no change in the normal urination posture. These observations support the view that the development of the male pattern of behaviour depends upon the presence of male sex hormone at a very early age.

Q *I have heard that some dogs eat their own motions. Why do they do that?*

A Firstly there may be a medical explanation for this behaviour (coprophagia). Some dogs suffer from an inability to digest or absorb completely all the food they eat (see page 164). This means that only a proportion of the nutrients in their food will take the normal routes out of the digestive tract into the bloodstream. As a result such dogs remain hungry, lose weight and have an excessive appetite; and furthermore their motions still contain a considerable amount of the original nutrients. Naturally enough, these seem attractive to many such dogs and consequently may be eaten. Following the correct diagnosis and treatment of these cases (e.g. with pancreatic enzymes or drugs appropriate to the particular type of malabsorption) the behaviour usually ceases.

This behaviour is not confined to dogs that are clearly undernourished, however, but can occur in apparently normal healthy animals. To some extent it might be considered normal canine behaviour, although obviously aesthetically displeasing to dog owners. Some behaviourists consider that it is particularly likely in bitches, arising out of their natural instinct to eat the droppings of their young puppies.

It has been suggested that animals may eat their droppings to acquire adequate vitamin K or vitamin B, and therefore that administration of an extra supply of these vitamins (for example by adding raw liver to the diet) will break the habit. Alternatively it may arise from boredom, particularly in confined dogs. And of course very young dogs, like young children, will explore the taste of all sorts of unusual materials, e.g. soil, coal, wood, etc. It may be that by eating their mother's motions, which is common in three-week-old pups, young dogs obtain the particular types of bacteria that normally inhabit the canine intestine.

In cases where there is no evidence of a medical disorder, discovering the true underlying cause may be virtually impossible, and in these circumstances treatment is directed towards stopping the behaviour. Recommendations to remove the faeces as soon as they are passed, or to put some unpleasant tasting substance on to them (e.g. cayenne pepper or paraffin (kerosene)) really require the owner to be present each time motions are passed. A simpler technique is to administer to the dog a drug that will inevitably make his motions taste foul; for example the oral anti-flea drug cythioate, although there is a limit as to how often this can be given.

Even more effective is to teach the dog that eating motions can have unpleasant consequences. A nausea-provoking drug (such as apomorphine) is administered to the dog under veterinary supervision, shortly after it has eaten a motion. Within ten minutes or so it will begin to feel unwell. This feeling of sickness the dog associates with the last substance to have been consumed (the motion) and as a result 'learns' (i.e. is conditioned) not to eat faecal material again. The dog recovers completely from the drug's effect in two or three hours. Such a technique may need to be applied a second time in some cases, but seldom fails.

Some dogs will also eat the faeces of other species, such as cattle and horses. In this way they might take in the eggs of worms which commonly inhabit the digestive tract of the particular species concerned but not the intestine of the dog. Consequently finding the eggs of these parasites in the dog's motion confirms that this behaviour is taking place. Access to other animal's faeces should be restricted, for instance on country walks, by training the dog to return to you immediately when called or if necessary keeping it on a short lead. In the home the contents of the cat's litter tray should be disposed of promptly.

Q *Why does my dog turn around several times before he lies down in his bed?*

A In doing this the dog is curving its spine to allow it to sleep tightly curled up, a position which conserves body heat. However, in hot weather the dog will lie completely stretched out, preferably on a cool surface, such as stone or vinyl tiles, or somewhere shady, even under a bed.

It may also be that in the wild this behaviour was intended to enable the dog to feel with the paws for a smooth area on which to rest, or alternatively to flatten down vegetation to make a bed before lying down.

Q *Why do dogs bury bones?*

A A dog may in fact bury any food which is surplus to its immediate needs; so that it has a sort of store cupboard. Presumably bones are frequently chosen because often they are not completely consumed at once, and are easy to handle.

The dog chooses a spot where the soil is soft, and as a rule close to where it lives, for instance in the garden. It then digs a hole with the front paws, usually while holding the bone or other food in its mouth. Once the hole is dug the bone is dropped into it. Finally the dog covers the food by pushing the loose soil forwards into the hole with its nose.

Quite often the dog then seems to forget all about the hidden bone, as many gardeners can testify. When they are eventually unearthed the bones are often found to be in a putrefying state, and to allow a dog to eat them then carries the risk that the products of decay will cause vomiting and/or diarrhoea.

Q *What does it mean if my dog twitches and makes running movements when asleep? Is he having a fit?*

A No, he is certainly not having a fit. This behaviour is quite normal and occurs during periods of deep sleep. It is now recognized that, as in humans, the dog has periods of light sleep and deep sleep. After an initial ten- to thirty-minute period of light sleep in which there is incomplete muscular relaxation, there occurs a short session of deep sleep when the muscles are fully relaxed. At this time, although the eyes are closed, there are bursts of rapid eye movements (REM sleep) together with sounds such as growls and whimpers, and obvious movements of the limbs, paws, tail, ears and whiskers, particularly running movements. At times male dogs may even ejaculate.

In humans dreaming occurs during this type of sleep, which is believed to be a state in which the brain is 'programmed' with information about recent events; the information is being transferred from a temporary memory store to the main banks of data. This would explain why the young puppy, with so much new information to store, experiences only this type of sleep ('dreaming' or 'activated' sleep) for the first months of its life. From then on it gradually develops the adult sleeping pattern, in which a long session of sleeping will contain a number of short periods of deep sleep.

Q *Is a dog's sense of hearing more developed than ours?*

A Like cats, dogs have much more acute hearing than humans, so that they can detect sounds at very much greater distances, can discriminate between sources of noise that are very close together, and are also able to detect ultrasonic sounds. The human ear can detect sounds with wavelengths up to about 20 kHz; wavelengths greater than that are said to be ultrasonic. The dog can certainly detect ultrasonic sounds to a frequency of 35 kHz, and possibly even as high as 100 kHz. This allows dogs to detect the high-pitched squeals of small rodents (useful in hunting), and of bats, and also the sounds of electronic devices, all of which are inaudible to humans. Remote-control units for television sets which produce an ultrasonic signal can distress some dogs (though nowadays most units work by transmitting an infra-red beam to the set). They can of course also hear and respond to so-called 'silent' dog whistles, which again produce a frequency (about 30 kHz) well above the range of the human ear. However the lower limit of audible frequencies seems to be very similar in both dogs and humans; about 20 Hz.

The dog is also able to move its ear flaps (pinnae) to collect sound waves more efficiently than man, and this enables it to pinpoint the source of any sound very accurately. Sounds that a human can detect from 100 yards can be heard by a dog a quarter of a mile away. The dog's greater powers of sound discrimination permit it to distinguish familiar sounds (the noise of its owner's car or footsteps, or a familiar key in the door) from other sounds, and to do this from a long way away. However, as might be expected, breeds with pendulous ears have less acute hearing.

The excellent hearing of the dog has been put to good use in the USA since 1975 in the training of 'hearing dogs' to assist deaf people to lead fuller lives. These dogs are able, for instance, to tell their owners when the door bell, telephone, oven timer or alarm clock rings, when the baby cries, or if a fire or smoke alarm sounds. They wear a distinctive orange collar and leash as identification, just as a guide dog (seeing-eye) wears a white harness, and like guide dogs they are allowed into areas where dogs are generally prohibited. A similar scheme has now been started in Britain.

Unfortunately, as with all species, the acuity of canine hearing diminishes with age, and some old dogs may be almost totally deaf.

Q *Can my dog understand what I say to him?*

A Certainly a dog is capable of understanding a number of simple command words (such as 'Sit', 'Stay', 'Come', 'No' and so on) and of learning the appropriate behaviour that is required when these are spoken. However, his brain isn't sufficiently well developed to appreciate the meaning of complete sentences; a man has a body of similar size to a St Bernard but his brain is seven times larger.

A dog's apparent understanding of sentences is based upon his ability to recognize key words (such as walk, biscuit, bed, car etc.) in those sentences. Since, by experience, he has learned to associate the word with certain events he will make an appropriate response, for instance anticipating receiving a biscuit or waiting near the door in expectation of a car ride. Essentially, therefore, dogs do *not* have the command of language.

Even though what you say may not be understood, your dog will be very receptive to the *tone of voice* in which words are spoken. This tells him whether you are pleased or angry with him and he will respond accordingly. Unpleasant words spoken in a soothing voice to the accompaniment of stroking will give him pleasure; kind words spoken in a harsh voice whilst staring hard at him will elicit a worried and submissive response.

Q *Whenever anyone talks to my bitch she rolls on to her back and passes a small amount of urine. Why does she do this?*

A This behaviour is a marked submissive response, and happens whenever very submissive dogs greet a human or a more dominant dog. It is believed to be derived from the infant puppy's habit of urinating when stimulated by the licking of its mother.

Punishing such a dog for this act will be of no value at all. The animal is already being as deferential and self-effacing as possible. What is required is increased praise and affection for all behaviour that meets with your approval, including praising the dog for *not* showing this submissive urination. The behaviour is not confined to bitches, but does seem to occur in them much more often than in males.

Q *Why does my dog persist in rolling in other animals' droppings and other foul-smelling material?*

A There appear to be two points of view concerning this behaviour. One is that it was developed by wild dogs to disguise their natural canine scent when hunting. The second view considers this to be a dog's attempt to reinforce his own natural scent, so that his body odour will be stronger, thereby enhancing his status amongst other dogs. This would explain why a dog that has recently been bathed will often indulge in this behaviour if given the opportunity. The bathing effectively de-odorizes him, depriving him of his social status, and covering himself with some strong-smelling substance is his attempt to retain his position in a species where scent is all important.

Q *Do dogs sometimes pretend to be ill to gain attention?*

A There are quite definitely some dogs that will do this. All dogs, of course, crave the attention and affection of their owners, and following illness or accident (even simply having a paw trodden on) some animals learn that to exhibit a sign such as lameness will produce a sympathetic response. Consequently, this 'sympathy lameness' tends to reappear whenever the dog wishes to obtain additional attention, and particularly when it feels that it is in competition with other members of the household for that affection. Accordingly, such behaviour tends to be most common where there is more than one dog in the family, although, contrary to what might be expected, it is usually shown by the animal which is already receiving the lion's share of the owner's attention.

Dogs have also been reported to cough, mutilate their own legs or tails by chewing, drink large amounts of water, or even vomit, to attract the owner's notice. Some indulge in other types of attention-getting behaviour, unrelated to illness, such as chasing imaginary mice, or chewing the furniture. In the latter cases, far from obtaining a sympathetic reaction the dog may be threatened or even chastised by the owner. However, from the dog's standpoint its objective, which is to be noticed, has been achieved. 'Love me or hate me, but do not ignore me,' seems to be the watchword.

In the absence of an obvious cause for the dog's behaviour the possibility of an illness being simulated should be borne in mind. One of the things that frequently gives the game away is that the particular sign is not present consistently. It may only become evident when other animals are receiving attention, or it may only be shown in the presence of a person whom the dog judges to be especially sympathetic. Because of this, it can be very illuminating to watch the dog when it believes that it cannot be seen. Very often the signs will disappear altogether when the dog is transferred to a totally different environment, such as boarding kennels or a veterinary hospital.

The best way to handle the problem is to completely ignore the dog's 'illness' behaviour, even to leave the room when it starts. Praise and affection should be reserved for desirable behaviour, especially responding promptly to commands.

Q *Why does my dog sometimes hold up a front paw? Is he trying to shake hands?*

A The raising of a forepaw by a dog has nothing to do with the human habit of shaking hands, although it may in fact occur when the animal meets a stranger. Essentially it is a submissive gesture which is learned in infancy (as early as three to four weeks of age) as a response to the licking of the bitch. It is classed as care-soliciting behaviour and in most dogs it disappears with maturity. However, nervous and submissive dogs often continue to show it when they are anxious, such as when confronted with a stranger. The disadvantage of encouraging paw-raising is that the dog may begin to follow it with other submissive behaviour such as rolling on to its side and urinating.

Another submissive gesture which originates in puppyhood is 'nudging' which a dog will perform with its nose to attract its owner's attention. This action is derived from that used instinctively by puppies when suckling.

Q *My puppy chases his tail a lot. Does this mean that he has worms?*

A No, there is no reason to suppose that a puppy always behaves like this *because* it is suffering from worms, even though this activity and the presence of worms are both common. This behaviour frequently occurs in normal healthy pups; a puppy sees the end of his tail and turns to bite it, but finds that as soon as he turns, so does the tail. He then gives chase, and ends up twisting round and round, until eventually he gets dizzy and may fall over. Such behaviour may also occur in extremely bored dogs as a means of passing the time, or sometimes as a method of securing the owner's attention, and become established as a habit.

The association with worm infection probably derives from the fact that when large numbers of segments of tapeworms are shed and pass out through the anus (see page 204) they can cause irritation. As a result the animal turns and licks and even bites at its anus or, if it cannot reach there, its hind leg, back or tail. Tapeworms are uncommon in puppies, however. Far more common causes of irritation in this region, responsible for similar licking and biting, are flea infestation or a blockage of the anal sacs (popularly called the anal glands), although tail chasing is not generally a feature of these conditions either.

Q *What makes some dogs so aggressive?*

A Essentially the dog is a pack animal with a strongly developed sense of its own position within the pack. It regards some individuals as superior to itself, and others it considers inferior. The social rank of any individual is determined by 'dominance conflicts', i.e. confrontations between dogs. As a result of this *dominance aggression* one animal will emerge as dominant to another. This may involve a fight, but often the loser will back down before this stage is reached. The dog which has lived in the household longer is often dominant, although generally large dogs dominate small, adults dominate puppies and males dominate females.

In the domestic situation the dog's 'pack' may only consist of the owner and itself, or there may be a large family which includes a number of other pets. In most instances the dog will regard its owner as the pack leader, but some dogs clearly consider themselves better suited for this position and will show dominance aggression to anyone who attempts to thwart them. Such a dog will disobey the owner's commands and will reserve the right to sit and sleep where it likes. Any attempts to force it to do something will be met with threatening behaviour. Obviously this type of display should be countered when it first appears (for example by holding a puppy firmly by its scruff and shaking it), because considerably more training will be required to correct it at a later date. Sometimes a dog will readily accept the owner as pack leader, but will consider one or more members of the family as inferior to itself and will show dominance aggression towards them alone.

Regardless of the 'pack' size a dog will take a keen interest in protecting not only its own personal territory (its kennel or sleeping area), but the entire territory of the pack; i.e. the owner's home and garden. When the owner, who is dominant, is present, the dog will accept the entry of visitors because it sees that the owner permits it without showing aggression. But when the owner is absent many dogs will guard the territory very assiduously and threaten any intruder. The dog's barking alone may prove a sufficient deterrent; indeed it is suggested that any household in London without a dog is three times more likely to be broken into. Dogs become encouraged by the apparent success of their *territorial aggression* and therefore visitors who appear to the dog to be easily frightened away, because they soon depart again (such as the postman and delivery men), are more likely to be attacked. However, visitors whom the dog perceives are bringing food, such as the baker and butcher, are much more likely to be tolerated. If the visitor stands his ground the dog often becomes perplexed at the failure of its threat and may retire in confusion.

Other forms of aggression shown by dogs are as follows:

Maternal aggression — shown by a bitch towards any animal or person she feels might harm her puppies. The bitch may attack *without* any preceding threat such as growling.

Intermale aggression (see page 30) — the innate tendency for a male to fight other males. The tendency of some Greyhounds to bite other competitors during a race is a variant of this type of aggression.

Fear-induced aggression — shown by a dog who is afraid of how a stranger may behave. Fear-biting usually only occurs when a dog is being approached and reached for. Consequently the extended hand is most often bitten. In particular a dog raised in a home without children may be afraid of them, because their behaviour (sudden movements and noise) is unlike that of adult humans. In New York half of all dog bites are inflicted on persons under twenty years old. This type of behaviour can be reinforced both by the dog learning that when it behaves in this way people back off, which is what the dog wants, and by the owner's presence and attempts at reassurance. Whilst the owner is really attempting to calm the animal's fears, thereby stopping the aggression, by stroking and talking to the dog, the dog interprets the owner's behaviour as support for what it is doing. As a consequence this type of behaviour is likely to be even worse if the animal feels itself particularly protected, for instance when it can retreat behind the owner's legs, or in the case of a small dog, when it is being carried.

Pain-induced aggression — any dog receiving a sufficiently painful stimulus will respond aggressively. Therefore attempts to break up a dog fight by hitting the combatants, or using a shock collar (page 123) which involves causing pain, may simply increase the aggression and intensify the fighting. Likewise dogs with painful injuries may respond aggressively when the damaged part is handled.

Also a dog will learn to associate the pain with the situation in which it was experienced. When placed in a similar situation the dog will respond aggressively. A dog injured in a road accident may respond aggressively whenever it encounters a motorbike, or after experiencing a painful injection a dog may be aggressive on subsequent visits to a veterinary surgeon. If the dog has been ill-treated earlier in life it may have an inherent distrust of the same type of person, e.g. a dislike of children or of men.

Predatory aggression — the dog's natural instinct to catch and kill prey, which is usually small mammals, especially rodents, but sometimes may include cats, chickens or even sheep.

Learned aggression — this is the type of aggression which police dogs and other security dogs are trained to show. Owners of those large breeds with a well developed guarding instinct should avoid encouraging an exaggerated aggressive response in case they are subsequently unable to control the animal.

Q *How is it possible for dogs to follow tracks and find hidden substances?*

A This is because, compared to ourselves, the dog has a sense of smell which is well over a hundred times more sensitive. It is certainly the dog's most highly developed sense. In common with all mammals, except man and certain other primates, the dog has a special pair of organs, the vomeronasal organs (or Jacobson's organs) which lead off the roof of the mouth and contain cells sensitive to odours. The total number of scent-detecting cells (olfactory cells), both in these organs and at the back of the nasal cavities, is forty times greater in the dog than in man. When a dog wishes to concentrate on an odour it can dilate its nostrils and sniff up a greater than usual volume of air, which is directed particularly on to those parts where the olfactory cells are most numerous. Furthermore, that part of the brain which interprets the signal coming from these cells, the rhinecephalon, is comparatively much larger than it is in humans.

This increased sensitivity allows the dog not only to detect minute amounts of substances, but to distinguish them from all the other surrounding odours. For instance the dog can detect the organic acids in human sweat when only four-billionths of a gram of sweat is present (of which 99 % is water!), and a good tracking dog can distinguish the trail left by a particular person from that of several others. Even when the urine of a bitch in heat has been highly diluted male dogs can distinguish it from the urine of a bitch that is not in heat.

This extraordinary ability of the dog has been harnessed by man, and over the years dogs have been trained to track down a wide variety of items, ranging from criminals and missing persons (including those buried under snow or wreckage), to illegal drugs, gas leaks, ammunition and explosives, moonshine whisky, various types of game and, of course, truffles, the much-sought-after underground edible fungi. Some breeds have a well deserved reputation for their powers of scent discrimination, particularly Bloodhounds, Basset Hounds and St Bernards, to which list should nowadays be added Labrador Retrievers.

It has been shown that fasting will enhance a dog's sense of smell (up to three times) and, conversely, eating only a small amount of animal fat (containing as little as one gram of fatty acids) will markedly decrease its ability. Strangely, newborn pups appear to have a poorly developed sense of smell, such that they cannot even detect the odour of their own mothers from more than a short distance away. Hearing and sight are also poorly developed, although not their taste or the tactile sensations of pressure, pain and cold.

Q *Are dogs attracted to the smell of aniseed?*

A Oil of aniseed (essentially anethole) is derived from the seeds of the plant *Pimpinella anisum*. It has a strong and distinctive smell, so powerful that it tends to obliterate other scents and consequently has been used by criminals to hide their trails from tracker dogs, and by opponents of fox hunting to obliterate the scent of the fox and confuse Foxhounds.

Being so distinctive the scent of aniseed is easily followed and in the sports of drag-hunting and hound trail racing it is one ingredient used in laying a trail across the countryside. Dogs are then let loose to follow the trail and the winner is the first at the finishing point, where they are fed. Therefore it may not be the scent that is particularly attractive, but the expectation of a pleasurable experience (feeding and praise from the owner) which results from following it. This view is supported by tests on day-old puppies in which their mother's nipples were smeared with aniseed oil. When the puppies were hungry they were attracted by the smell of aniseed in the expectation of a feed. On the other hand puppies that had not previously encountered this scent were repelled by it.

Q *Do dogs ever suffer from psychosomatic illnesses?*

A Certainly, there is evidence that the onset, or persistence, of certain types of illnesses in dogs may be influenced by emotional factors. Animals of an anxious and apprehensive disposition may respond to emotional stress by developing diarrhoea ('psychogenic diarrhoea') or becoming prone to attacks of colitis (inflammation of the colon) in exactly the same way as humans of similar temperament. The sudden and uncontrollable onset of very short periods of muscle relaxation and sleep during the daytime (narcolepsy) has been reported in the dog, as well as in man, to be the result of emotional stimulation. On rare occasions even hair loss has been associated with a stressful situation.

Although investigation of this subject is in its infancy, it would appear that, just like people, some dogs may react to stress with behavioural changes and others with functional disturbances.

Q *Why do dogs like to fetch sticks?*

A Almost all dogs have a natural instinct to retrieve objects — sticks, balls, and of course prey animals — which is related to their hunting instincts. Young animals also often play together with a stick, having a tug-of-war with it and chasing after each other to gain possession of it. This carrying behaviour develops around four to five weeks of age. The fetching of a stick thrown by the owner may be considered as a similar play activity.

This type of play, like others, contributes to a dog developing the skills of hunting, prey-chasing, killing and retrieving, which in the wild would be of great importance in ensuring its survival. With proper training this desire to retrieve can be used to teach dogs to bring back game-birds to their hunter masters, and in obedience training to retrieve objects bearing the owner's scent. Perhaps of greater practical value to most owners would be training to fetch their slippers or newspaper, or even to retrieve lost golf balls.

5

Feeding
and Feeding Problems

Q *What sort of food is needed by my dog?*

A Although the dog possesses the typical features of a carnivore, namely teeth adapted for the tearing and shearing of flesh and a large stomach which will permit the intermittent intake of large meals ('gorge feeding'), it is in fact one of the least carnivorous of the *Carnivora*. Nowadays the dog is regarded instead as an omnivore (i. e. an animal that can eat foods of both animal and plant origin) that has a preference for meat. This is in direct contrast to the cat which is indisputably carnivorous and has a definite *need* for food derived from animal sources.

As a result the dog is very adaptable in its feeding habits and can be fed quite satisfactorily on a wide variety of diets, which may be either home-prepared or manufactured commercially. Just so long as the diet you choose satisfies the nutritional requirements of the dog, your animal will thrive.

The basic principles of nutrition are quite straightforward. Food is required by any animal for two main purposes, one is to build new tissue and the other to provide energy.

The production of new tissue cells is obviously essential in a young animal, because it can only grow if it produces more cells. However, adult animals also need to make new cells, though at a slower rate, to replace those which are continually wearing out and being broken down. Since the main component of the body's tissues (apart from water which accounts for about two-thirds of a dog's total body weight) is protein, protein must be provided in the diet to build new tissues. It can be provided either from animal sources (e. g. meat, fish, eggs) or from plants (e. g. soya beans).

Energy is constantly required by cells in all parts of the body to enable them to perform their various functions, such as the movements of the heart and skeletal muscles, the secretion by glands and the production of heat to maintain the body temperature. This energy is obtained from the breakdown of foodstuffs in the diet. Any of the three major classes of nutrients — proteins, fats and carbohydrates — can be used for this purpose but, because proteins are more difficult to digest, energy is obtained most efficiently from fats or carbohydrates. Weight for weight fat will yield twice as much energy as the other two. Some fat is also essential in the diet, to supply the body with the essential fatty acids needed in making new cells and in synthesizing prostaglandins (prostaglandins are vitally concerned in a number of body functions including blood clotting and reproduction). Fats also serve to 'carry' the fat-soluble vitamins.

In summary, then, protein is essential (for growth and tissue repair) and some fat is also essential, but carbohydrates (e. g. starchy and sugary foods) are not. However, provided that the starches are pre-cooked (e. g. biscuits, bread, potatoes, rice), carbohydrate foods can be used as an energy source and are cheaper to supply than either protein or fat. Consequently most canine diets contain a significant proportion of carbohydrate.

If the amount of water in the diet is excluded from the calculation (simply because the proportion can vary considerably with the type of diet) the requirements of a normal household pet dog can be expressed as a proportion of the actual 'dry matter' in the diet. On this basis protein should account for at least 18 %, though ideally 22 % (to allow for stress situations) and fat 5 %. Also (included in the fat requirement) a minimum of 1 % of the total 'dry matter' should consist of the essential fatty acid, linoleic acid. It should be emphasized that these are minimum requirements. If a greater proportion of the diet is made up of protein and fat this won't be harmful but neither will it be beneficial; they will simply be broken down to provide energy.

Also essential in the diet, though only required in minute amounts, are vitamins and minerals. A small amount (approximately 2–5 %) of roughage (or fibre — referring chiefly to the cellulose components of plants which dogs, like humans, can't readily digest) is valuable in the diet. It provides 'bulk' which assists in the movement of food through the intestines (peristalsis) and it gives a slightly firmer consistency to the motion. If necessary it can be provided in the form of bran, readily available from health food shops.

When it comes to the question of exactly what to feed, you may decide to prepare the dog's meals yourself, from basic foodstuffs bought at the butcher's, fishmonger's or pet store, *or* to buy ready-prepared dog foods. In either case you can economize by including a certain amount, up to a quarter of the total, of 'household scraps', (i. e. left over from what the human members of the household eat), provided that you avoid highly spiced foods such as curry.

Many dogs appear to be quite content to consume the same familiar diet day after day, and so long as it is nutritionally adequate they will remain fit and healthy. However, feeding trials indicate that dogs appreciate a variety of tastes and aromas in their diet, at least until they get older and less adaptable, and some even have a liking for unusual foods such as oranges and bananas. Certainly, by feeding a variety of diets you are less likely to create a deficiency of some essential nutrient. Any marked change from one type of diet to another should preferably occur gradually (over a period of three days) to allow the digestive system time to adjust.

Q *Are commercial pet foods good for my dog?*

A There is often a feeling that proprietary foods are in some ways inferior to those prepared at home. However, there is no evidence to support this view, and therefore no reason to feel guilty about feeding them. The pet food industry is now a multi-million pound/dollar business with plenty of competition, and no reputable manufacturer would dare risk losing his share of the market by selling substandard products.

There are three main types of proprietary dog food: canned 'wet' diets with a moisture content of around 75–83 %; semi-moist ('soft-moist') foods in sealed, plastic pouches containing 25 % water; and dry foods containing 8–10 % water. Each type can be obtained 'balanced', that is containing protein, fat and carbohydrate in the correct proportions needed by the dog, plus the necessary vitamins and minerals. Obviously, the less water there is in the diet the less of it needs to be eaten to satisfy the protein and energy requirements. Always follow the manufacturer's directions about the manner of feeding and if you intend to feed it to pregnant or lactating females, or to growing puppies, check that it is recommended for that purpose. In the United States any dog diet described as 'balanced' (or alternatively 'complete' or 'scientific') has by law to be nutritionally adequate for the feeding of all weaned dogs, but this is not yet the case in Britain. Pet food manufacturers often advise feeding biscuit with their all-meat canned products (i. e. those not containing cereal) to avoid the expensive protein being used as an energy source.

The larger manufacturers conduct a lot of research, both into basic nutrition and into the quality of their products, and they take great pains to ensure that pet foods advertised as balanced diets do in fact contain all the nutrients known to be required and in the optimum amounts. In contrast, diets prepared at home are in some cases very unbalanced, despite the additional expense and all the work that goes into their preparation. Commercial diets intended for feeding to cats have a higher protein content than commercial dog foods, and although not intended for the feeding of dogs are quite suitable for this purpose.

(The converse, though, is not true, i.e. commercial dog foods are not adequate for the nutrition of cats.)

Q *Apart from the fact that they are 'balanced', are there any particular advantages or disadvantages in feeding commercially prepared diets?*

A All have the advantage that unopened they will keep for long periods and can therefore be kept as a 'standby' for when other food is unavailable. Canned foods can be stored for up to a year, whereas dry or semi-moist products should be used within three to four months. Even after the pack is opened, the dry 'complete' foods will keep satisfactorily for long periods and this makes them very suitable for self-feeding (see page 82). Like other dry foods (such as dog biscuits), their palatability is low but is improved by coating the particles with fat, which is stabilized to prevent it going rancid. Dry foods are comparatively cheaper (since you are not paying for water) and they also give 'exercise' to the teeth, reducing the deposition of tartar. Dogs fed on dry diets compensate for their low water content by drinking correspondingly more water (usually immediately after feeding), unlike cats which take in less water overall when fed dry foods than on 'wet' diets. Of course dry foods don't necessarily have to be fed dry; they can be moistened to whatever consistency is most acceptable to your dog.

Semi-moist foods (having a softer texture, like marzipan) also keep well after opening (though eventually they will dry out) because they contain humectants to keep them moist — including a large quantity of sugar which also prevents bacterial growth. The presence of sugar makes these foods much more palatable but renders them unsuitable for diabetic dogs. Because they are so concentrated they are particularly useful in situations where a dog needs increased nutrition (e.g. rapidly growing puppies and lactating bitches), though dogs that overeat will gain weight quickly.

Canned 'wet' foods are the most palatable; and those containing cereal have a stiffer 'meat-loaf' consistency than those which are almost all-meat diets composed of chunks in a gravy or jelly. The small cans of special variety foods ('speciality' or 'gourmet' diets) are highly palatable but are not intended to be balanced and should therefore not be fed exclusively day after day, even if the dog expresses a clear preference for them. They can either be used as a special reward, e.g. for good behaviour in training, or be fed mixed with a balanced diet, so long as they don't exceed 10% of the total food intake.

Q *If I decide not to feed a proprietary diet what food should I provide?*

A The major problem facing owners preparing pet diets at home is to ensure that they are balanced, i. e. that they contain adequate amounts of all essential nutrients, including vitamins and minerals. Although tables are available which list the composition of different foodstuffs, making it possible to calculate precisely the composition of any particular diet, most owners are unwilling to do this. In practice therefore the best way of ensuring that all the necessary nutrients are provided is to vary the type of foods being fed from day to day. In this way problems which can arise from nutritional deficiencies in particular foodstuffs are avoided.

As was mentioned earlier a dog requires adequate amounts of readily digestible protein and fat, with vitamins and minerals, plus additional energy which is usually provided in the form of carbohydrate. The traditional protein foods are meat, offal (liver, hearts, melts, lights, tripe, etc.) and fish, although eggs and cheese are also highly nutritious and usually well liked. Protein foods are graded in terms of their biological value. A protein of high biological value (high-quality protein or first-class protein) is one which contains, in the ideal proportions for the dog's needs, the ten essential 'amino acids' (the basic components required to build new tissue). The protein food with the highest biological value (100), in other words the one most efficient at meeting the dog's requirements, is in fact whole egg. Almost as good are chicken, beef, fish (both white and oily) and liver. But a lot of raw liver, though palatable, should be avoided because the bile salts it contains have a laxative effect; it also contains exceptionally high amounts of vitamins A, B and D. Most other offal has a lower, though reasonable biological value, but contains little fat. Vegetable protein, from peas, beans and cereals (and therefore present in bread and biscuits) is cheaper and a useful additional source, though of low biological value and on its own not very palatable.

Since the cheaper cuts of muscle meat are invariably the most fatty, 'scrap' meat from butchers (often supplied ready-minced) usually has a high content of fat (and often of gristle as well). Rabbit and chicken are frequently of comparable price and much less fatty.

If a *variety* of animal protein foods are fed, sufficient fat will usually be provided from their tissues. Those which contain most fat are minced beef for pets (25%), cheese (33%), and eggs (10%); most offal, milk, and dog biscuits and meal (which have beef dripping added for increased palatability) contain 4–5%. A varied diet, particularly one containing some liver, cheese and eggs, will also supply adequate vitamins and minerals. Incidentally, most brands of dog biscuits and biscuit meals intended for feeding with meat products are enriched with those vitamins and minerals in which both meat and offal are deficient. Biscuit meals

77

can be either coarse or fine to suit different sizes of dogs and can be soaked if necessary (e. g. in hot water or gravy) before feeding to improve their flavour and make them easier for old dogs to eat.

As a general rule for a household dog half the daily diet should consist of these protein foods (though slightly more than half if a low protein offal like tripe, lights or melts is fed) and the remainder should be a carbohydrate food (such as dog biscuits, dog meal, bread, pasta, potatoes or rice). This 50:50 combination compensates for the higher water content of most protein foods (50–75 %) compared with biscuits (10 %) and bread (40 %). Household scraps, which may also be either mainly protein or carbohydrate, can of course be substituted when available.

Q *Surely a diet consisting solely of meat would be best for any dog?*

A No, it wouldn't. A diet composed solely of meat, as well as being unnecessarily expensive, especially if you insist on feeding best-quality butcher's meat, is also likely to give many dogs diarrhoea. In addition the dog will have to break down much of this expensive meat protein in order to obtain energy, which could be provided far more cheaply by feeding some carbohydrate. Muscle meat is also deficient in vitamins A, D and E and in iodine which is required for the formation of thyroid hormone (although any signs of iodine deficiency would take a very long time to appear).

Furthermore, feeding an 'all-meat' diet to young dogs between three and twelve months old will result in defective bone formation because the proportions of calcium and phosphate in muscle meat and offals are far from ideal (containing relatively too little calcium and too much phosphate). Affected animals, suffering from what is termed nutritional secondary hyperparathyroidism, are lame, indeed reluctant to walk at all, and their bones are weak and more liable to fracture. However, feeding meat does *not* make a dog vicious, nor does a high-protein diet damage the kidneys as is sometimes stated. Problems only arise if a dog already suffers from renal failure; then the waste products derived from the breakdown of protein foods accumulate and cause the typical signs of illness (see page 213).

Q *I thought that potatoes were bad for dogs. Isn't this the case?*

A No, there is no truth in this belief, provided that the potatoes have been cooked to gelatinize the raw starch which they contain, and the same applies to all other starch-containing foodstuffs, such as maize, wheat, pearl barley and oats. If the starch is uncooked it is much less digestible and the residue will be fermented by bacteria in the intestine.

In large quantities it can give rise to diarrhoea and flatulence. For the same reason undercooked commercial pellets and mashes can have a laxative effect.

If cooked, potatoes are a valuable and palatable source of energy for dogs. Indeed, in the rare cases where dogs are sensitive to the protein gluten, present in foods containing wheat or rye flours (bread and biscuits), the cheapest alternative sources of carbohydrate are potatoes and rice.

Q *If I feed my dog bread, is brown bread better than white?*

A In general, no it isn't, if only because, at least in Britain, most mass-produced brown, or wheatmeal, bread is simply white bread dyed brown with caramel and contains only a minute amount of extra fibre (0.6%). Genuine wholemeal bread, containing 96–100% of the wheat grain, is more expensive and contains more fibre and wheatgerm but less calcium, which is deliberately added (in the form of chalk) to white and brown bread in Britain.

The feeling against white bread is probably derived from the fact that during and between the two world wars flour in Britain was bleached, both to make it whiter and also to cause more rapid ageing (so as to reduce the storage period before satisfactory bread could be made from it), using a chemical named accordingly agene (nitrogen trichloride). In 1945 it was discovered that this bleaching agent was responsible for causing convulsions in dogs which were fed on dog biscuits made using bleached flour. Soon afterwards, largely because of concern about its possible effects on the human population, the use of agene was banned. However, except in certain countries such as France which totally prohibits the practice, the bleaching of flour with other agents continues.

Some owners prefer to dry the bread in the oven (so-called baking or toasting) before feeding. This isn't necessary, but the dried crust, like biscuits, does help to prevent the accumulation of tartar on the teeth.

Q *Would it be valuable to include some green vegetables in my dog's diet?*

A Green vegetables, like root vegetables, are not necessary in a dog's diet because normal healthy dogs can produce sufficient vitamin C for their needs within their body. In fact, large quantities of vegetables are difficult for them to digest and give rise to flatulence. Many dogs like raw carrots, probably due to their sweet taste, and it may be possible to use them as 'treats' (i.e. rewards for good behaviour) which are much healthier than chocolate drops.

Although they contain useful amounts of carotene, which dogs can convert to vitamin A, the main value of cooked green vegetables such as cabbage is to add bulk to the slimming diet of an obese dog. Since they consist mainly of roughage and water with a little protein they will make the dog feel that it has eaten a sizeable meal without adding to its weight problem.

Q *Is it all right to feed my dog the special pet meat I can buy at the pet shop or frozen food store?*

A Frozen pet meat is quite acceptable but it should be allowed to thaw out before being cooked lightly (i.e. boiled for fifteen minutes) to allow the heat to penetrate all the meat. *Never* feed foods that are still frozen because this reduces the digestibility of the food and increases intestinal motility, resulting in digestive upsets. (In the dog, food normally takes at least five to ten hours to pass from the mouth to the anus but in cases of extreme intestinal motility, e. g. food poisoning, it can take as little as twenty to thirty minutes.)

In addition there are a number of pet meat preparations in which the meat is mixed, compressed and presented in the form of a large slab or large sausage. Many of these foods contain a chemical preservative to discourage the growth of bacteria and moulds, though they have a short shelf-life and to avoid bacterial contamination should be kept refrigerated. Recently there has been a move towards the production of vacuum-sealed cooked brawn products.

Dehydrated foods, such as fish and meat meals, and dried fish, may also be available at pet stores. Their nutritional quality ranges from very good to very poor depending upon the quality of the processing. Again, the feeding of these poorly processed, indigestible products causes diarrhoea.

Q *We are a committed vegetarian family. Can we feed our dog a vegetarian diet without harming her?*

A Yes, this is possible, although because vegetable proteins are generally of lower biological value and less digestible than animal proteins it will be necessary to feed rather more of them, and ideally from a variety of sources, to provide an adequate amount of all the essential amino acids. Soya protein, however, is of higher quality than other plant proteins, and dogs are able to use it fairly efficiently and to maintain good health whilst fed on it, though more than loz per 12 lb (5 g per kg) body weight may give rise to diarrhoea. (In contrast to the cat, the dog has no need of the amino acid taurine, found only in animal tissues, in its diet because it is able to synthesise taurine from other sources.)

Provided it is supplied with sufficient linoleic acid, the essential fatty acid widely present in vegetable oils, a dog, unlike a cat, can itself manufacture the two other essential fatty acids (linolenic and arachidonic) which it requires and which are found ready-made only in animal tissues. Adequate linoleic acid can be readily provided by feeding a teaspoonful (5 ml) of corn oil per day for each 18 lb (8 kg) body weight. However, if *all* the fat requirement is to come from this source, two and a half times as much should be fed; alternatively nuts, eggs or hard cheese (such as Cheddar) could supply some of the total fat. There is obviously no problem providing other *energy* foods of plant origin, in the form of bread, potatoes, breakfast cereals, peas, beans and so on.

Although vitamin A is only found pre-formed in animal tissues, including eggs, the dog, but not the cat, is able to synthesize it from the carotene available in many vegetables, especially carrots. Other vitamins and minerals can also be provided from plant materials, and cheese and milk are good sources of vitamin D and calcium; alternatively, white bread or even calcium lactate tablets can be supplied. Yeast tablets or extract (e.g. Marmite) will improve the flavour of the diet, as well as providing additional vitamin B (though cheese, eggs, milk and peas already contain adequate amounts).

In summary therefore, it is certainly possible to prepare a nutritionally adequate vegetarian diet for a dog but whether the dog finds it acceptable is largely a matter of training and habit. An animal fed from weaning on such a diet will accept it as a matter of course and, indeed, studies show that the dog will prefer it to any other. But a dog that is already accustomed to a diet of animal protein may well prove reluctant to abandon it altogether.

Q *Some dogs seem to like drinking milk, tea and beer. Are these good for them?*

A Of the three you mention only milk is of any real nutritional value, being a useful source of calcium and other nutrients, and many dogs clearly prefer the taste of milk to that of water. However this doesn't mean that there is any *need* to provide it. Milk consists mainly of water and it supplies nothing that cannot be obtained more cheaply from other foods. A dog receiving a good balanced diet has no nutritional requirement for milk, so that if it is provided at all it should be given as a treat *after* the normal ration has been eaten.

In fact, most adult dogs are intolerant of a large quantity of milk because they have a relative deficiency of the enzyme lactase needed to digest the milk sugar (lactose). As a consequence, if more than 1 gram of lactose is consumed at a time the surplus remains undigested and is later fermented by bacteria producing lactic acid which gives rise to diarrhoea. (There is, however, no truth in the statement that milk encourages worms.) In practice, the main use for milk is simply as a supplement for pregnant and nursing bitches, puppies and convalescent dogs. Incidentally, cheese has virtually no lactose in it since it is practically all removed in the whey.

Dogs are probably attracted to tea by the taste of the milk and sugar in it and, in fact, are much better able to digest sucrose (cane sugar) than lactose.

As a general rule it is inadvisable to give alcohol to dogs (since it can make them difficult to control, sleepy and obese) but beer is so dilute that if a dog is one of the few that has acquired a taste for it (and most don't care for its bitter flavour), there is no great harm in giving a little from time to time. But any stronger alcoholic drink should be avoided; some dogs can develop a craving for it and even 'steal' it.

In essence, then, all these beverages could be given in moderation though none of them is essential. Whether they are provided or not, a bowl of fresh water should always be available so that the dog can satisfy its normal water requirements.

Q *How often should I feed my dog?*

A The conventional recommendation has been to feed adult dogs (i. e. from nine months old onwards) one meal a day, mainly in the evening at about six o'clock, or to split the daily ration into two meals, a small one at mid-day and the main meal again in the evening (especially for the smaller breeds because they are more prone to lose body heat). Surveys reveal that three-quarters of owners do indeed feed their pet dogs one meal a day. About 20% of owners give two meals and very few provide more (i.e. three or four per day).

Recently, however, this conventional advice has been called into question. Dogs allowed free access to food in feeding trials generally eat a much larger number of small meals over a twenty-four-hour period, i. e. there is more of a 'nibbling' pattern of food consumption, although there is considerable variation between breeds and even between individuals. Basenjis fed a dry diet take most of their meals during two periods of the day (between 9 a.m. to 1 p.m. and 3 p.m. to 7 p.m.), whereas Beagles on the same diet eat at intervals of two to four hours throughout both the day and night. When Beagles are switched to a semi-moist diet (with a greater concentration of nutrients) the interval between meals becomes longer. Toy Poodles seldom eat at night, and are most stimulated to feed by contact with people.

These findings suggest that there is no need for every dog to be fed in the same way; rather that it is preferable for owner and pet to develop their own mutually satisfactory feeding programme, and to feed when it is most convenient, provided that the minimum ration to satisfy nutritional requirements is supplied each day. Feeding should not take place too late in the day because it stimulates intestinal movements (peristalsis) and creates the urge to drink afterwards, so that it is likely that the animal will need to relieve itself within the following three to four hours. An opportunity should be provided for it to do this, otherwise it may do so when you are asleep. It might be suitable for the dog to be fed at the same time, or possibly just before, the rest of the household; even to be fed *ad libitum*, i. e. to have food down all the time so that it can eat whenever it chooses. The latter regimen is ideal if someone cannot be present to feed the dog at regular times, and it cuts out barking and begging, but under normal domestic conditions only dry, expanded complete foods can be fed this way. Semi-moist and 'wet' foods (i. e. canned or prepared at home) are not suitable for *ad lib* feeding because they are much more likely to be overeaten and deteriorate quickly if left down; they become stale, allow food-poisoning organisms to grow and attract flies. In general, if these more moist foods are not consumed within twenty to thirty minutes of being offered they should be removed and no more presented until the next mealtime, and then in a smaller amount.

Whatever feeding regimen is adopted, it should be adhered to as far as possible. Dogs appreciate a routine and feeding times are amongst the highlights of a dog's day; psychological tensions can be created by an animal never knowing what to expect from day to day. Varying the type of food or the pattern of feeding should be done as infrequently as possible and as slowly as possible.

Some owners advocate starving a dog completely one day a week to simulate the intermittent feeding that might occur in the wild state, though in fact wild members of the dog family tend to eat their prey at intervals after making the kill. There is no evidence that this weekly fast is beneficial, and some dogs suffer from behavioural and digestive upsets as a result.

If dry food *is* fed *ad lib*, a widespread practice in the United States, the feeding bowl should be replenished as necessary to keep the dish full, by placing the uneaten food on top of the new food in the bowl so that it is eaten in rotation. Although most dogs will only eat enough to satisfy their energy requirements, i. e. they regulate their intake according to the Calorie content of the food, about 10 % of dogs fed this way will overeat and become obese (though this is no higher percentage than those fed 'regular meals'). These individuals must revert to being fed set amounts at regular times. A number of dogs when first changed to *ad lib* feeding will overeat for a while, then only eat as much as they need. It is recommended that *ad lib* feeding shouldn't start until a dog is 80% fully grown.

Other factors may influence the number and timing of meals. Because most animals tend to sleep after feeding, working dogs are usually fed in the evening, except for guard dogs working at night which are fed in the morning. However, more frequent feeding is preferable since some dogs may be too fatigued to eat an adequate amount after work, and at least a light meal before work begins is advisable. Greyhounds are fed twice daily, though when racing in the evening their second, and main, meal of the day is delayed until the race is over.

Bitches that are feeding puppies (lactating bitches) require three times as much food, and puppies that are just weaned require just over twice as much food, as normal adult dogs on a body weight basis. This increased quantity simply could not be consumed at one time and therefore it must be divided into a number of meals per day, usually a minimum of three. Unless *ad lib* feeding is to be adopted the number of meals for a growing puppy can gradually be reduced to a minimum of two a day at four to five months of age, and possibly to one a day at six to nine months.

Frequent feeding throughout the day is valuable if animals show a tendency to vomit soon after eating, sometimes through eating too rapidly. It is also employed if they appear to be frequently hungry, a situation which can occur when dogs suffer from difficulty in digesting or absorbing food in the alimentary tract, or when they are having to be dieted to reduce weight. Frequent feeding in these situations helps to some extent to appease the animal's appetite.

Q *How much food does my dog need each day?*

A First of all, if you are feeding a commercial product always follow the manufacturer's advice about quantities and note whether the product is intended to be mixed with other foodstuffs. These instructions will have been formulated on the basis of the diet's precise composition.

As a guide, feeding the amounts suggested below, of different types of diet, should provide adequate nutrition for normal adult dogs.

1 oz of *dry food* for every $3\frac{1}{2}$ lb body weight (i.e. $^2/_7$ oz/lb or 18 g/kg).

1 oz of *semi-moist food* (soft-moist food) for every 3 lb body weight (i.e. $^1/_3$ oz/lb or 21 g/kg).

1 oz of a balanced diet, consisting of *equal weights* (not volumes) *of wet meat or fish* (canned or home-prepared) *and dog biscuit or biscuit meal* for every 2 lb body weight (i.e. $^1/_2$ oz/lb or 31 g/kg).

1 oz of a *balanced* canned or preserved '*meat-loaf*'-*type* diet (i.e.

containing cereal as well as meat) for every 1 lb body weight (63 g/kg). In relation to this guide the following points should be noted:

1 The recommendations given above are based on a medium-sized dog of about 40 lb (18 kg) body weight such as a Welsh Springer Spaniel, Schnauzer or Keeshond. However, energy requirements are more directly related to a dog's surface area (which is comparatively greater for lighter animals) than to its body weight. This means that smaller dogs need more food in relation to their weight, and vice versa. In other words, smaller dogs should be fed relatively more than would be calculated (e. g. a 10 lb (4.5 kg) dog needs an extra half of the calculated amount adding on) and larger dogs fed relatively less (e.g. a 100 lb (45 kg) dog needs 20 % of the calculated amount to be subtracted). Intermediate weights should be fed correspondingly larger or smaller quantities.

However, recent surveys on the giant breeds (above 100 lb (45 kg)) have shown that their requirements for energy are different to the majority of dogs, and that they need more food than might be expected. For example, Newfoundlands should be fed at exactly the rates stated earlier, *without* any reduction for their greater size, and Great Danes should be fed at those rates *plus an extra 10 %* (i. e. a rate which is *higher* than that for the 40 lb (18 kg) dog).

2 These quantities should only be regarded as a guide, because there is considerable variation in the amount of food required by adult dogs of the same weight, even from the same litter, related particularly to how active they are. The simplest way to establish whether you are under- or overfeeding is to monitor the dog's weight. To keep the weight constant may involve an upward or downward revision of the amount fed.

3 Its age and physiological state also influences the dog's nutritional requirements. In the last three weeks of pregnancy (though not earlier, see page 236) a bitch needs an extra 50 % of the normal ration for her weight, and puppies between weaning and being half-grown (i. e. half their adult weight) require just over twice as much as an adult of the same size. Growth requires protein for the new tissues as well as energy for the process itself. (Great Dane puppies have to gain an average of over 5 oz a day for their first three months of life.) A bitch with a large litter at the peak of her milk production (i. e. just before the puppies commence weaning) needs three-and-a-half times more food than usual.

In old age, on the other hand, dogs require between 10 and 20 % less food for their weight if they are not to become obese, and cope best if this is fed in at least two meals per day.

4 It is recommended that, to produce a balanced diet, 'wet' meats or fish (either canned 'whole meat' products or cooked at home) should be mixed with an equal weight and *not* an equal volume of dog biscuit or biscuit meal. A large 14 oz (400 g) empty dog food can holds about 7 oz

(200 g) of fine biscuit meal, $6^{1}/_{2}$ oz (180 g) of small biscuits and 5 oz (140 g) of an expanded meal.

5 Compared with meat or fish, a slightly greater weight of offal (all except liver) should be fed to compensate for its lower protein content. Similarly, compared with biscuit or biscuit meal twice as much *un-toasted* bread and four times as much potato should be fed to compensate for their higher water content (and therefore lower energy content).

6 The weights of manufacturers' packs vary considerably but of the three commonly used can sizes for 'meat-loaf' balanced diets the small size holds approximately 7 oz (200 g), the large (the most popular) holds approximately 14 oz (400 g) and the giant size contains approximately 28 oz (800 g). The weight of 'all-meat' products is *slightly less* for each size.

7 When weighing dog foods on the kitchen scales, cover the scale pan with a piece of plastic (e. g. a polythene bag) first. This makes the food easier to handle and minimizes contamination. Always wash the scale pan well afterwards, using hot water.

Q *How much more food do working dogs need than pet dogs?*

A Because of their greater activity, working dogs such as sheepdogs and patrolling police dogs need twice as much food on work days as a pet dog of the same weight. Greyhounds require 50% more on race days.

The requirement is only for more energy and it can be met most economically by giving extra fat. Contrary to the situation with human athletes, giving a carbohydrate-rich diet does not improve performance but actually reduces it. To keep the nutrients balanced, every 4% increase in fat must be accompanied by a 1% increase in protein content. A concentrated diet is preferable in order to supply sufficient energy without exceeding the dog's eating capacity.

As a rule a light meal should be fed before work and the major portion of the ration afterwards, but snacks of food and water during long work periods will overcome the problem of weakness due to hypoglycaemia (low blood-sugar levels).

Extra energy will also be required in cold weather to maintain the normal body temperature, for example in dogs which sleep outdoors. Eskimo Dogs (Huskies) pulling sleds in temperatures well below freezing point combine both of these increased requirements, and their food intake must be two-and-a-half times that of a pet dog of similar weight kept in a temperate climate.

Q *Should I let my dog drink as much water as he wants?*

A The short answer is yes — unless he is vomiting.

In every case except one (a rare psychological disorder) dogs drink to replace water which has already been lost from the body. If you do not allow them to make up for the loss, whether it has arisen normally or as a result of disease (e. g. vomiting and diarrhoea), they will become dehydrated. When less moisture is available from the food, as when a dry or semi-moist diet is being fed, a dog will drink correspondingly more. A total lack of water will cause problems (even death) much more rapidly than a lack of any other component of the diet such as protein or fat. Therefore a bowl of clean water must *always* be available. As far as possible, discourage drinking from other sources (the sink, toilet bowl, puddles) which could assist in the transmission of disease.

Normal dogs fed a 'wet' diet drink $1^1/_2$–$1^3/_4$ fl oz (40–50 ml) of water for every $2^1/_4$ lb (1 kg) of their body weight each day. This means that a 26 lb (12 kg) dog such as a Cocker Spaniel should drink about a pint ($^1/_2$ litre) a day, and more in hot weather or after exercise. Providing free access to water for working dogs increases their work output by about 80 %.

Animals which continuously have an excessive thirst are almost certainly suffering from some disorder that should be investigated by your vet. A number of disease conditions, listed in Table I on page 150, might be responsible. In these disorders the body loses water more rapidly than usual, i. e. cannot retain it, so that the dog produces more urine than usual. The dog often has difficulty in holding all this urine in its bladder over a long period of time, e. g. overnight, so that when indoors it either wakes its owner up to go out or makes a puddle. Some owners mistakenly think that the answer to this problem is to withhold water from the dog, not realizing that they will prevent the animal making good the heavy losses which have occurred and provoke the onset of dehydration, thereby making the illness worse. If the dog has an increased thirst always take it for veterinary attention.

Only withhold water from an animal if it vomits. Vomiting is most often due to some irritation of the lining of the stomach which causes the stomach contents to be rejected. The loss of water and salts in the vomit makes the animal very thirsty so that it *wants* to drink, but the presence of water in the stomach provokes further vomiting. In this way a cycle of drinking and vomiting can develop which may lead to severe dehydration and collapse.

Therefore, after vomiting occurs, withhold all liquids and food for at least two hours. Then give a small amount of water, e. g. a saucerful. If this is not followed by vomiting soon after, further small amounts can be given at hourly intervals, but if vomiting occurs wait a longer period (eight to twelve hours) before giving any liquids or food. If in the meantime further vomiting occurs, seek veterinary advice.

Q *Is it ever necessary deliberately to stimulate a dog's thirst?*

A Yes, when a dog has previously suffered from the development of bladder stones (urinary calculi) requiring surgical removal, it is advisable to minimize the possibility of further stones forming. Although other factors may need attention, the single most effective measure to prevent recurrence is to double the dog's water intake by adding table salt to its diet. This dilutes the mineral salts in the urine and reduces the likelihood of them precipitating out and forming calculi again.

The same technique of salting the food is valuable in treating cases of bacterial cystitis (urinary tract infection), to dilute the bacteria and their toxins. In addition, affected animals should be encouraged to urinate frequently in order to void the bacteria and prevent them multiplying to high numbers (one organism can give rise to over a million within five hours under optimum conditions).

Q *Will I know if I am not giving my dog enough food?*

A If a dog fails to receive sufficient food it will usually ask, even pester, you for more. However, a more reliable sign is evidence of the dog's gradually decreasing weight. This is also more accurate than relying on appearance; there may be no obvious change in the early stages of weight loss, especially in long-haired dogs, and some breeds normally appear lean, e. g. Irish Setters and Salukis. Regular weighing, say once a month as a routine but more fequently if an abnormality is suspected, will allow you to recognize a problem and correct it, if necessary with your veterinarian's help. Obviously, the effects of overfeeding can also be detected by routine weighing.

The weight that adults of different breeds are expected to attain is known, largely from breed society standards, and to allow for some degree of individual variation these are expressed as a range. As a rule bitches are slightly lighter than male dogs.

If a dog is consistently underfed it will fail to attain both normal weight and size. In particular, the skeleton is very sensitive to a lack of food and so the dog's growth will slow down and, in severe cases, may even stop. If underfeeding has occurred over a long period, even though it is subsequently corrected, it is unlikely that the lack of growth will ever be made up. The affected animal will stop growing at the usual age for the breed, and if it is undersized it will remain stunted. There are growth tables available showing the expected range of weight at different ages.

Adult dogs that are seriously underfed, in addition to losing weight, have less energy and stamina, show a lifeless, dull coat and may be unable to mate and breed successfully. Extreme cases appear emaciated, especially in the flank (just in front of the hind limbs) with an evident loss of muscle mass from the head and the hind legs. The ribs, hip bones, backbone and nuchal crest (the central ridge along the skull) all appear, or can be felt to be, unduly prominent. Poorly nourished animals of any age also have reduced resistance to infection from both micro-organisms, such as bacteria and viruses, and from the larger parasites, that is to say the worm and skin parasites.

Weight loss can occur on diets where the concentration of nutrients is low (such as dry food low in fat and rich in fibre, or those mixed with plenty of water) so that the dog becomes 'full' before its energy needs are satisfied. Reducing the water content or feeding a high-fat diet (or adding suet or vegetable oil to the existing one) may solve the problem. Small breeds in particular prefer a more concentrated formula which is easier to eat.

But increases in appetite associated with a below-average body weight, despite the feeding of a considerable amount of good-quality food, and particularly where weight continues to be lost, should be investigated by your vet. In adult dogs such cases are hardly ever due to intestinal worms (though popularly believed responsible) but may be due to some impairment of digestion or absorption, or to some metabolic disorder (e. g. diabetes mellitus or hyperthyroidism due to thyroid cancer).

Q *Why do dogs go off their food?*

A A complete loss (anorexia) or partial loss (inappetence) of appetite usually occurs in association with illness. In conditions where waste products accumulate in the blood, such as renal failure and pyometra (pus in the womb), and where the body temperature is raised (e. g. with the fever of infectious diseases, and in heatstroke) the appetite centre in the brain is directly affected.

Pain in the mouth or throat (for example due to loose teeth or ulcers) or pain elsewhere in the body (for example following a road accident) may discourage the animal from eating. With such disorders as meningitis and a 'slipped disc' in the neck region, the animal experiences great pain if it attempts to lower its head to eat. In these cases raising the food bowl to chin height will greatly assist feeding. At times the masticatory muscles, i. e. those which move the jaws, may be acutely inflamed and painful, especially in German Shepherd Dogs (Alsatians), or severely wasted or even paralysed following facial nerve damage, and consequently the animal is either reluctant, or unable, to feed.

In a few dogs the appetite may be lost, although usually only temporarily, following some psychological shock, such as being hospitalized or boarded, or during the absence of some member of the household, or when strangers (to the dog) come to visit. This is generally associated with very strong emotional bonds between dog and owner, i.e. where the dog has become a child substitute.

Sometimes apparent inappetance occurs in a dog that is allowed to roam, because it is being fed by a neighbour or is scavenging food; confining the dog to its own territory for a few days will allow you to check this. Where dogs are fed in a group the dominant members may prevent one or two individuals getting their fair share, and, of course, male dogs may fail to eat whilst there is a bitch in heat nearby.

Q *Should I give my dog bones to chew?*

A Opinions tend to be divided on this matter. If a dog is receiving a balanced commercial diet, or a bone-meal supplement with a home-prepared diet, it will already be receiving adequate calcium and therefore will not actually *need* to consume bones. There is no doubt, however, that most dogs enjoy chewing bones, and the exercise it provides for the teeth is valuable in preventing a build-up of tartar which may lead to periodontal disease, particularly if the animal receives a 'wet' diet.

However, the benefits of bones can be provided in other ways; bone meal is an alternative source of calcium, and dental exercise can be provided by chewing at a hard biscuit, a rawhide 'chew' or a nylon meat-flavoured 'bone', or by the regular feeding of a dry diet.

If a bone is given it should be a large, raw marrow bone (e.g. part of a limb bone) and when it starts to look ragged and the dog can easily chew off bone spicules it should be removed and later on replaced with a new bone. Fragments of bone can both irritate the stomach lining, provoking vomiting, and, in large numbers, recombine to form a concrete-like mass in the intestines, resulting in severe constipation.

Cooking makes bones brittle and liable to splinter; warnings are usually given about poultry and rabbit bones penetrating the wall of the digestive tract, though in fact a more common hazard is that irregular bones, like chop bones, get wedged in the oesophagus just above the heart. To extract this 'foreign body' involves removing one of the dog's own ribs first of all, in order to gain entry to the chest. It is also not uncommon for small bones to become wedged in the mouth, causing frantic pawing and rubbing (see page 296).

Dogs can be very possessive about bones and so it is sensible to train them from a very early age to allow you to take bones, food or playthings away from them if you feel it is necessary.

Q *Should my dog's food be fed raw or cooked?*

A It is not advisable to feed dogs on raw meat foods because this is a major route by which they become infected with the protozoal parasite *Toxoplasma gondii* which produces the disease toxoplasmosis. As well as destroying this parasite, cooking will also destroy any disease-producing micro-organisms and also any toxins formed by food-poisoning organisms multiplying on the food.

There is, however, no truth in the stories that raw meat makes dogs aggressive or that it makes them have fits. Food starches (found in biscuits, rice and potatoes) are rendered more digestible by being cooked, and so are soya-bean products. Eggs are a valuable source of first-class protein and also provide calcium and phosphorus, but raw egg whites contain avidin which is antagonistic to biotin (a member of the vitamin B complex) and also a substance (trypsin inhibitor) which interferes with protein digestion. Light cooking destroys both of these substances. (In addition, heating foods responsible for allergies appears considerably to reduce their potency.)

Cooking also improves the flavour of most foods. Gentle cooking is all that is required — boiling for a quarter of an hour, for example. This will have no harmful effect upon proteins and there will be little change in most vitamins. Manufacturers of canned foods often add extra vitamin B to their products to ensure that a controlled amount survives the autoclaving stage, a sterilizing process similar to pressure cooking but with the food already contained in the can.

Q *Should my dog's food be served warm?*

A We all know that foods served warm have more flavour than when they are cold and that there are also improvements in texture; the food is softer and fats are smoother. Certainly for the dog the acceptability of canned food increases with its temperature, up to blood heat (around 104 °F or 40 °C) and the food temperature can be critical in persuading a sick or convalescent animal to eat. Further increases in temperature beyond this point result in a sharp reduction in acceptability, and dogs are reluctant to tackle hot foods.

Q *How can I tempt my dog to eat when he has been ill?*

A Animals may have to be coaxed to eat after a severe illness or if, for medical reasons, they have to be fed a special diet which is not very palatable. In particular, those suffering from respiratory disorders need to be tempted with foods having strong, distinctive flavours and odours because otherwise they are unable to smell or taste their food. In general, the following should be tried:

1 Feed foods with a strong taste and odour such as sardines, kippers, herrings, pilchards, liver, salmon (tinned or smoked), tuna fish, cheese, chicken fat, chicken livers, cooked rabbit and fried fish. Milk puddings (e. g. canned) and sweet foods often prove irresistible. Any discharge round the nose should be wiped away to enable the animal to smell the foodstuff. If necessary, an inhalant can be used to help clear the nasal passages.

2 Add to an existing diet such flavouring agents as the oil from a can of sardines, meat extract (e. g. Bovril), yeast extract (e. g. Marmite), dairy cream, the juices from roast meat, gravies and meat soups. If the dog will not consume these voluntarily, smearing a little on the nose or teeth usually causes the animal to lick it off, thereby providing a first taste which stimulates him to take more. The addition of a pinch of salt to many dishes, including canned foods, will often enhance the flavour and stimulate the appetite.

3 Feed foodstuffs at blood heat rather than cold. All foods have more flavour when heated. In addition, your vet can provide special convalescent diets which are rich in nutrients and highly palatable. Make sure that the feeding dishes are rinsed clean with absolutely no residue of stale food, disinfectant or detergent which could give an unpleasant taste or odour, and feed only a little food at a time.

Such foods as proprietary invalid diets, baby foods and chicken, although nutritionally excellent and therefore ideal for the feeding of sick or convalescent animals, have a relatively bland or insipid taste and it may prove difficult to persuade dogs to eat them. Competition with another animal may sometimes provide the incentive to eat, though care should be taken to see that a weaker animal is not prevented from eating by a more dominant one. If the dog cannot be tempted to eat, so-called 'force-feeding' or artificial feeding (artificial alimentation) may be required, as described on page 254.

Q *My dog seems very fond of eating grass. Is this because I am feeding her the wrong things?*

A It seems that at times dogs may eat grass to provide fibrous bulk lacking in the diet (possibly to avoid constipation), just as wild dogs consume the vegetable material in the stomachs of herbivores which they kill. It seems unlikely, though, that grass provides any other nutritional benefit.

Furthermore, dogs suffering from alimentary disturbances will often consume a lot of grass, usually of the coarsest varieties, and vomit afterwards, i. e. they use grass as a natural emetic. Presumably they do this because they feel nauseous and wish to provoke vomiting in order to obtain some relief; for instance, puppies have been seen to vomit up roundworms after grass-eating. Some dogs may consume other materials, such as wood shavings or gravel, for the same purpose.

Consequently there would not appear to be any reason for preventing your dog eating grass, unless of course the grass has previously been treated with a toxic herbicide.

Q *Is it cruel to pin back a Spaniel's ears with a clothes peg before he eats?*

A Provided that the peg doesn't have a strong spring, thereby inflicting pain, this is a simple way of fastening the ears together above the head to prevent them dangling in the food bowl. Alternatively, a piece of adhesive tape can be used for this purpose, or the ears can be tucked inside a mob-cap, snood or hood to keep them out of the way when eating. Certainly this last-named method is common in long-haired dogs like Afghan Hounds that have to be fed *after* being specially groomed for a show (and a bib may also be worn).

Sometimes owners feed these breeds using a deep bowl with a narrow opening so that the ears hang on either side of the dish rather than into it, though they are less effective at stopping some soiling of the hair. It is always a good idea to check the dog's ears and mouth after feeding (and to sponge away any residues and then dry the hair) rather than to allow food to dry and mat up the hair.

Q *Should I put a block of sulphur into my dog's water to purify his blood?*

A No — this really *is* an old wives' tale! Powdered sulphur was used in the past as a purgative (known as brimstone and mixed with treacle) because it is converted in the intestines to highly irritant sulphides which initiate diarrhoea. Nowadays there are far more pleasant and acceptable drugs available for this purpose. But since sulphur is insoluble in water the dog is hardly likely to be receiving any appreciable amount anyway. Even if it did, it would not have any 'purifying' effect (whatever that means) or any other beneficial effect on the blood, or indeed on *any* part of the body.

Similarly, other supposed 'tonics' and 'conditioners', including a variety of herbal remedies, powdered seaweed, rhubarb and raspberry tablets etc. are of doubtful efficacy. If your dog is being fed a balanced diet and is apparently healthy they are a waste of money; if the dog is clearly unwell it would be better to consult your vet first rather than to delay matters to find out if any of these products actually work.

Q *Are dogs ever allergic to certain foods?*

A True allergic responses to foods are uncommon in dogs, although they are often suspected. Many reactions to foods are caused not by an allergy but by an inability to digest or absorb a particular food, so that in large amounts the food produces diarrhoea or sickness. However, in the case of a *true* allergy, even small amounts of that particular food will be sufficient to trigger the allergy, provided that a minimum of ten to four-teen days has elapsed from the time that type of food was first consumed by the dog. This is necessary for the dog's body to produce sufficient antibody to give a reaction. Food allergies are *not* present at birth, al-though they may develop as early as puppyhood. Most dogs show in-creased salivation and vomiting, either immediately after eating the particular food or within two hours, followed soon afterwards by diar-rhoea which is often blood-stained. Frequently there is also skin ir-ritation, and in rare cases a type of asthma attack occurs. Any type of food may be involved, including meat, fish, egg, milk, fruit, chocolate, cereals, and so on. At other times the apparent food allergy is in fact a reaction to some disease-producing organism or to a drug. (Some dogs can even become allergic to contact with plastic feeding bowls.)

Discovering the food responsible for an allergic reaction involves feeding a variety of different meals and noting the response. This can be a tedious process but when the causal foodstuff is absent an improvement is usually noted within three to five days.

Q *Are 'treats' or chocolate drops harmful to dogs?*

A No, not if given in moderation in training, or as a reward for good behaviour. Too many chocolate drops, being rich in fat, and sweets (candies) rich in sugar, may contribute to obesity, to tooth decay and to the dog not eating sufficient of its normal meals. If the animal begins to reduce its protein or vitamin intake as a result, other problems could follow.

Dogs have a very sweet tooth but feeding more than $1/8$ oz per lb (6–8 g per kg) body weight of cane sugar can lead to diarrhoea. Although dogs have an aversion to saccharin (and will drink plain water in pre-ference to a saccharin solution) it is believed that it is their liking for sweet-tasting substances that encourages the consumption of such poi-sonous materials as ethylene glycol (anti-freeze) and lead-based paint.

Yeast tablets (vitamin B) and pieces of carrot are nutritionally more acceptable, though if any treat is frequently offered the dog may come always to expect them and begin to pester you. For this reason, unless intended as a special reward, it is unwise to give dogs titbits of food between meals. Feeding titbits from the table should particularly be avoided as it can result in dogs begging throughout your mealtime and may encourage the stealing of food when the dog is unsupervised. If the habit of begging for titbits at the table has already become established you can only break it by ignoring the dog totally or (usually better) excluding it from the room during meals.

Q *How can I stop my dog from being a finicky eater?*

A Quite healthy dogs may have a poor appetite for a number of reasons:
1 They may have been fed so many highly palatable 'treats' and titbits that their appetite is jaded.
2 They may relish the attention that an anxious owner bestows on them if they refuse to eat immediately.
3 They may have learned that their owners will bring out the highly prized, more appetizing (and more expensive) foods if they fail to eat their 'regular' diet.

The solution in each of these instances is obvious: stop *all* feeding between meals and feed only at regular times, and if the food is not eaten within twenty minutes remove it and give no more until the next meal-time, i. e. don't provide a 'few biscuits' in case the dog gets hungry in the meantime. Don't worry if no food is eaten for one or two days; this shows it has become a battle of wills and dogs have got enough sense not to starve themselves to death.

At other times dogs may fail to eat because they are physically ill and need treatment. The important distinguishing feature is that here the dog seems genuinely disinterested in everything, including going for exercise, and simply wants to rest quietly all day.

Between these two extremes are genuine 'poor feeders', eating well one day and poorly the next, and often just picking at their food. These are twice as likely to be males as females. In these cases check that the food is both palatable and providing sufficient energy. The combination of smell ('nose appeal'), taste, and texture ('mouth feel') is important: some dogs prefer dry, crunchy food, others food soaked in gravy.

The strongest taste preferences of dogs are for meat (beef, pork, lamb, chicken and horsemeat) and sugar. The presence of fat, salt, and liver (even garlic and onion) contributes to palatability, and so does warming the food and wetting a dry diet. Dogs are sufficiently discerning to be able to distinguish between diets containing natural foodstuffs and those artificially flavoured with beef, chicken and liver. (The colour of the food is of little importance to the dog although it can influence the owner's choice, and it is for this reason alone that colourings are often added to commercial foods.) Ensure, though, that the diet is nutritionally sound; unfortunately the palatability of food is *not* a reliable indicator of its nutritional value.

The appetite may improve if a higher-energy food is offered, e. g. changing to a semi-moist food, or adding oil or suet to a home-prepared diet; and the presence of a 'competitor' will often stimulate a dog's appetite. Make sure clean water is always available, remove any uneaten food after twenty minutes, and, if the dog appears lively and healthy, *don't worry*.

In exceptional cases, where a dog doesn't eat because of emotional stress, coaxing and hand-feeding may work, though at times drugs (progestagens) have been employed.

Q *The vet has said that my dog is overweight and should be slimmed. How should I do this and how will I know when she is slim enough?*

A Obesity, the most common nutritional disorder, is defined as the condition in which the body weight is 10 % or more above normal. It almost always arises because an animal consumes more food than is needed to supply it with energy, and the surplus food is then stored as fat, especially just beneath the skin. In general, if you cannot feel a dog's ribs it is overweight. At times hormonal and neurological disturbances will give rise to obesity but these are relatively uncommon.

Obese dogs live shorter lives than normal because they are more likely to suffer from sugar diabetes, arthritis and heart and respiratory disorders. They are also more prone to heat exhaustion, skin problems and difficulty in giving birth; they are often more irritable, have diminished immunity, and also represent poorer anaesthetic risks.

In Britain and other developed countries, about a third of all dogs are obese. The condition is more common in bitches, and is perhaps related to the fact that the body of a bitch normally contains about 16 % more fat than that of a male dog. After the neutering of both males and females the incidence of obesity rises even further, affecting two-thirds of all spayed bitches. It has been found that only two months after spaying, food intake will be higher, if permitted, resulting in a thicker layer of fat around the ribs.

As in humans, the incidence of obesity in dogs rises with the onset of middle age, approximately doubling in females and trebling in males. Interestingly, middle-aged and elderly people are more likely to own a dog that is obese, especially if they are themselves overweight. Obese owners are also more liable to judge that their obese dog is of normal weight.

Offering an excessive amount of a highly palatable diet encourages dogs to eat more, though the extra amount consumed will vary between individuals, even those of the same breed. Dogs fed mainly on table scraps or on a home-prepared diet are more likely to become obese. Cocker Spaniels, Labrador Retrievers, Beagles and Collies show a much greater tendency to gain weight excessively.

In theory the treatment of obesity is simple. If less energy foods are provided than the dog needs to satisfy its energy requirements, then it will begin to reduce its fat store. This body fat is used to supply the energy which is deficient in the diet. It is possible to provide less energy by restricting the animal's consumption, *or* offering unpalatable food (so that it voluntarily eats less) *or* offering palatable but low-energy food. If the last option is chosen, specially prepared obesity diets are available from veterinarians. These contain no special reducing ingredients but simply less energy and more roughage than other diets. Although exercise can contribute to reducing body weight, forced exercise may make diseases of the heart and joints very much worse.

To slim a dog, *ad lib* feeding, if practised, must be stopped. There must be no giving of titbits, and other sources of food (e. g. from neighbours) should be eliminated. Appetite suppressants have been tried in dogs, without success.

A 'target' weight should be established, either the normal body weight for the breed or, in the case of those dogs that are not purebred, based on the degree of obesity. The dog should then be fed each day an amount of food which will provide 60 % of the energy requirement of a normal dog of that target weight. Either a relatively unpalatable commercial diet (and ideally one to which the dog is unaccustomed) may be fed, in which case you would feed 60 % of the normal recommended amount, *or* a special obesity diet, as referred to above, following the veterinary surgeon's instructions. Drinking water should be the only other nutrient provided. The food is best fed as three to four small meals per day and the dog should be isolated from the preparation and consumption of meals by the family. Regular weekly weighing and weight recording are advisable to assess progress. Dogs of less than 20 lb (9 kg) body weight can be expected to lose about $^1/_2$ lb ($^1/_4$ kg) per week and those over 40 lb (18 kg) about $1^1/_2$ lb ($^3/_4$ kg) per week. When the dog reaches the target weight (and this usually takes around three months) the daily energy intake should be increased by a fifth (20 %) for the weight to be maintained. This daily ration of food can then be fed continuously, probably for the rest of the animal's life, unless it becomes ill or pregnant or shows any further marked weight change.

Q *Can crash dieting be practised?*

A Total caloric restriction (complete starvation) is sometimes employed in cases where it is imperative to reduce weight quickly, e. g. in severe cardiac or joint diseases, where exercise is inadvisable or impossible.

Because the majority of owners would be unable to harden their hearts sufficiently this procedure almost always requires the dog to be hospitalized. It is a quick and effective method (the dog being provided only with water) and is not complicated, as it is in humans on 'crash diets', by the onset of acidosis. Dogs on this regimen remain in good health. Although seemingly cruel, in practice this appears to be a more humane method of dieting than consistent underfeeding. This is because after a few days of total starvation hunger seems to disappear, whereas dogs that are always being underfed apparently always remain hungry.

Q *Will my dog's diet require supplementing with extra vitamins and minerals?*

A Both vitamins and minerals are essential for the correct functioning of the body, but they are needed only in relatively small amounts. The term minerals refers to certain inorganic chemical elements and the term vitamins denotes certain vital organic compounds.

A balanced commercial diet will, by definition, contain adequate amounts of vitamins and minerals and *no* supplementation of the diet is advisable. However, in respect of home-prepared diets this may not be the case. Meat and offal are deficient in vitamins A, D and E and in calcium, and consequently many brands of biscuit meal come ready-supplemented with these by the manufacturer, so that when the combined meat plus biscuit diet is fed it will be nutritionally adequate.

However, if the biscuit meal has *not* been supplemented (refer to the label) or if wholemeal bread is fed, a vitamin/mineral concentrate (such as Canovel or Stress) should be added in the quantity recommended by the maker. Alternatively to each 8 oz (225 g) of the total diet add one level 5 ml teaspoonful of sterilized bone flour (*not* the unsterilized product intended for gardening) and a quarter of a 5 ml teaspoonful of cod liver oil. Do *not* add more as this could be harmful; indeed, if the dog's diet includes liver twice a week this cod liver oil supplement will be unnecessary and should *not* be given.

The major vitamins are considered to be A, B, C, D, E and K, but the normal, healthy dog is able to synthesize adequate amounts of vitamin C and K within its body so that these do not need to be present in its diet. In addition, the action of sunlight on the skin probably permits the production of sufficient vitamin D, at least during the summer months.

There is a general feeling among pet owners that the more vitamins and minerals that are consumed the better will be the health of the recipient. But this is not so; once the essential requirements have been met, there is *no* advantage in providing more. Additional supplementation of the diet will be at best a waste of money and at the worst can lead to damage to the body which may be permanent. Unfortunately, such dietary excesses are nowadays more common than deficiencies.

Cod liver oil is a convenient source of the fat-soluble vitamins A, D and E, but because these vitamins are stored, i. e. accumulate in the body, too much can create problems. An excess of vitamin A (hypervitaminosis A) causes a loss of appetite and a thinning and weakening of the 'walls' of the limb bones with pain in the limbs. Excess vitamin D can retard growth, cause malformed teeth and jaws and lead to changes in other organs. Disorders due to excesses of vitamins E and K are rare but greatly excessive quantities of vitamin E may impair blood clotting and too much vitamin K can cause jaundice. However, there appear to be no ill-effects from giving excessive amounts of the water-soluble vitamins, vitamin B (e. g. in yeast extract or tablets) and vitamin C.

Bone flour is a simple way of supplying calcium and phosphate but in excess it can cause a variety of skeletal abnormalities and joint problems with lameness, especially in growing animals. Also there is no need for routine iron supplementation, because anaemia due to iron deficiency is extremely rare in dogs.

Q *If my dog had a serious illness would he need a different diet?*

A Yes, the successful control of a number of illnesses involves important dietary changes. It is particularly important in chronic renal failure where the kidneys' inability to excrete substances derived from the breakdown of proteins results in their accumulation in the blood. High levels of these products are toxic, causing loss of appetite, vomiting and ulceration of the mouth. Feeding a diet containing minimal protein of high biological value plus more calories, vitamin B and salt than usual is an essential part of managing the disorder, and the dog should be encouraged to eat those foods usually regarded as unsuitable for pets (chocolate, ice cream, cake, chips, jam and honey) rather than meat products.

Heart failure requires a low salt diet, intestinal disturbances a bland and easily digested diet and diabetes mellitus (sugar diabetes) a diet low in fat and carbohydrate.

In the convalescent stage of debilitating illnesses a readily digestible diet containing additional high-quality protein is extremely valuable in speeding the animal's recovery. A few pet food manufacturers produce specialized canned or packet diets (available from your veterinary surgeon) to assist in treating some of the above conditions.

6
Handling a Dog

Q *What is the best way to pick up and put down a dog?*

A At times it may be necessary to lift a dog, for example to place it on a table to be examined, or to lift it into a car. Many large dogs that are too heavy to pick up easily will co-operate by jumping up if the height is not too great, or at least will be able to get their front legs up and wait for you to lift their hindquarters. If this is not possible a dog will usually manage to climb on to a table if a chair is provided as an intermediate step.

How to lift your dog

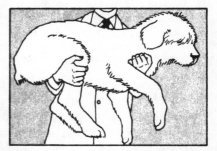

A small or medium-sized dog *is readily lifted by placing one arm beneath the dog's chest and the other at the back of its hindquarters, holding it firmly.*

A large dog *is better supported with a hand placed in front of both shoulders rather than underneath its chest. Extra help is needed to lift very heavy dogs.*

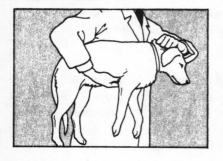

A dog of uncertain temperament *is best restrained by grasping its scruff (its collar may be loose or suddenly snap) before lifting it with a hand beneath the breastbone (sternum). The lifting arm should pass over the dog so that by closing the elbow towards your side the dog is securely held. Avoid excessive pressure on the abdomen, especially in pregnancy.*

If you are able to lift the dog, always raise and lower it gently, supporting it firmly from underneath. If too much strain is put on one part of its body when it is picked up and carried, the dog will find it uncomfortable, even painful. Both the forequarters and hindquarters need support. A medium-sized or small dog can be lifted by placing one arm beneath the animal's chest (just behind its forelegs) and the other hand or arm (depending on the dog's size) behind its hindquarters to lift and support its rear. Hold the dog closely to you, with your arm(s) around it; this method will allow you to cradle it in a sitting position and if necessary to carry it some distance.

With a larger dog better support is obtained if, before lifting, your arms are positioned so that one is in front of the dog's shoulders, the other behind its upper thighs. It is better to avoid picking up a dog with an arm beneath its abdomen, particularly a pregnant animal as this will put pressure on the developing foetuses.

An alternative method of lifting a dog, particularly one of uncertain temperament, is first to grasp its collar in one hand (or better still its scruff: collars can slip off or break) to restrain it securely, and then pass your other arm over and around the dog, bringing your hand up underneath its chest. As you lift with this hand press the animal close to you by bringing your elbow in towards your side. Your arm will then help to support the dog's rear end. With a very heavy dog, additional assistance will be required to raise its hindquarters, for instance someone behind the dog grasping a thigh in each hand.

Q *Should I pick a puppy up by the scruff of its neck?*

A Although a bitch will, if necessary, retrieve a puppy by picking it up and carrying it by its scruff (the loose skin at the back of the neck) in the first week of life, dangling an older puppy by the scruff puts undue strain on the neck muscles. In fact a bitch most commonly retrieves a stray pup by licking its face, because the pup reacts by crawling in the direction from which it was touched (and incidentally, it is the sight of the straying puppy rather than its cries which stimulates the bitch to retrieve it).

It is much better to pick up a puppy in a similar way to a small adult dog, i. e. to take the weight of the pup on the upturned palm of one hand, and to use the fingers of the other to hold it, if need be by the scruff, to limit the amount of wriggling. Hold the puppy close against you, its hind legs resting on your arm, so that it feels secure.

Although puppies benefit from plenty of handling at an early age, to encourage socialization with humans, it is unwise to allow very young children to be alone with a puppy, until they have been taught the correct way to handle it; unsupervised, they may pick it up solely by the scruff, or by the front or hind legs alone, or by putting their hands around the abdomen (the soft 'middle' of the pup, behind its chest). Even older children need instruction: ideally they should be in a sitting position before being allowed to handle a puppy because if it begins to wriggle or playfully bite they may otherwise let go and drop it.

Q *What is the best way of approaching a strange dog?*

A When handling all animals it is best to be firm yet gentle, and to have a confident approach. Avoid making a sudden grab at a dog, especially a strange one, because it will instinctively defend itself from what it believes is an attack and you may be bitten. Even a hand extended to stroke a dog can appear menacing to the animal itself. Approach the dog cautiously and quietly while talking to it in a friendly, reassuring voice. With elderly animals particularly, make sure that they can both see and hear you coming; suddenly finding you nearby can cause panic. Always keep your eye on the dog but avoid obvious staring, which dogs interpret as a threatening sign.

Signs of friendliness include coming to greet you, wagging the tail and licking you. Obvious unfriendly signs include lifting and curling the lips to expose the teeth, raising the hairs along the back, and showing the whites of the eyes. If you need to back off do so slowly, walking backwards; turning your back often encourages small dogs (e. g. Corgis) to bite at your heels or legs. Running away invites a dog to chase you.

Many dogs, however, are merely nervous and apprehensive and require extra reassurance before they will approach you or allow you to approach them. Such animals will usually show the tell-tale signs of trembling, licking the lips, being unable to look at you steadily and wagging the tail but backing away when approached. With these dogs it is advisable to stop still three feet (1 m) or so away from them, and then to bend or crouch down, continuing to talk encouragingly until the animal gains confidence and approaches to sniff at you, or alternatively permits you slowly to approach it. When you hold out a hand to pat the dog, do so with your fingers clenched into a fist, not extended, as they may be bitten, and allow the dog to sniff the hand if it wants to, to get your scent.

Q *Is any breed of dog more likely to bite than any other?*

A Statistics from the United States indicate that more people are bitten by German Shepherd Dogs (Alsatians), Chow Chows und Poodles than by other breeds. Since both German Shepherd Dogs and Poodles are amongst the five most popular breeds, the inference may be drawn that in relation to their numbers Chow Chows are the dogs most likely to bite, and this confirms an opinion long held by many veterinarians.

Q *How should a dog be approached after a road accident?*

A Following its involvement in a road accident a dog, if still conscious, will be disturbed and frightened and will often run away blindly in an attempt to escape from the scene. The animal does not understand what has happened to it and reverts to defensive behaviour. Even when approached by its owner, it may prove aggressive and resent handling.

The approach to such a dog should be calm, quiet and yet purposeful. It is useful to have the help of two or three sensible people, and noisy and hysterical onlookers should be asked to leave. Be very cautious if the animal is on a wall or projection above ground level, or if it is cornered, because it may try to attack. By talking to the animal in a quiet, reassuring voice, you may be able to get close enough to restrain it, at least temporarily. If the dog has a lead attached to its collar or harness, attempt to get hold of that first; often it helps to put your foot on the end of the lead before picking it up, to prevent the animal moving away. Collars and leads are not always securely attached, however, and so, whether you have managed to secure the lead or not, the next step is carefully to make a few preliminary stroking movements and then to take a firm grasp of the dog's scruff. Keep your hands away from the animal's mouth and avoid touching any obviously injured part. Be prepared for the animal to struggle, and don't let go unless you absolutely have to because second attempts are usually much less successful. Watch the animal all the time.

If you find you are unable to gain the animal's confidence sufficiently to allow you to do this, you might be able to apply a 'slip noose'. You can make this from a strong, flexible dog lead, by passing the end with the clip through the looped end. The slip noose should be dangled in front of the animal's head, and slowly and gradually manipulated into position around its neck. A quick pull will then tighten it. Hold the lead high to prevent the animal biting through it. A similar slip noose can be made by running a narrow trouser belt or dress belt through the buckle, or even by using a piece of thick cord after first tying one end to form a small loop through which the other end can be passed.

If all attempts fail, you will need to telephone for professional assistance, e. g. from an animal welfare society, veterinary surgeon, police or, in some countries, a professional dog catcher. Devices specially developed for catching stray animals will probably have to be used.

Of course, it is the less seriously injured dog, and sometimes the totally uninjured but very frightened dog, that presents the greatest problem.

How to catch a dog with a slip noose

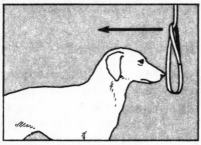

A 'slip noose', made by passing the clip-end of a flexible dog lead through its loop, is dangled in front of the dog, until it can be passed over the head.

The 'slip noose' is then tightened round the neck by a quick pull on the lead. Keep the lead held high to prevent the dog from biting at or even through it.

The seriously injured animal is unlikely to be aware of or to care much about your presence; indeed, it may be unconscious. Some of the things not to do in this situation include chasing the dog (this will simply increase its fear), trying to tempt it with food or drink (after an accident eating and drinking are far from its mind), shouting and making sudden movements. When the injured animal is securely held and led to safety it should, as soon as possible, receive veterinary attention.

Q *Is it ever necessary to muzzle a dog?*

A Yes, at times a leather muzzle, obtainable from a pet store, is necessary to prevent a dog interfering with a dressing (page 266) or to prevent an aggressive animal from attacking other dogs or people. Whatever type is obtained, the muzzle should be a good fit that prevents the dog from opening its jaws.

The application of a 'tape-muzzle' allows you to handle, examine and treat a dog without risk of being bitten. It is a sensible precaution when dealing with dogs known to be or suspected of being bad-tempered, and those that are nervous or injured. A tape-muzzle can be made from a 3–4 foot (1–1.25 m) length of gauze bandage or tape 2–3 in (5–7.5 cm) wide, or in an emergency from a tie or dress belt. Make a half-hitch in the tape (the first stage in tying an ordinary knot or bow) so as to form a loop. Usually it is best to apply the tape-muzzle with the dog standing on the floor, with the scruff of its neck firmly held so as to keep its nose pointing directly ahead (*not* downwards). Often it helps if the person holding the scruff can place a leg on either side of the dog's body to prevent the animal moving from side to side. The dog should not be allowed to jump up.

Holding the tape by its ends, place the loop over the animal's nose to

How to apply a tape-muzzle

1. *Firstly tie a half-hitch in a length of gauze bandage or strong tape, keeping the ends fairly long. In an emergency a man's tie or a dress belt can be used.*

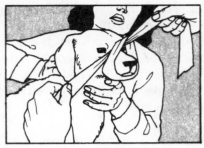

2. *Then, with the dog firmly restrained, place the loop of tape around the dog's nose. By pulling the ends sideways draw the loop tight, closing the dog's jaws.*

3. *Immediately bring the ends downwards and cross the right to left and left to right underneath the lower jaw. Keep the tape tight and draw the ends backwards.*

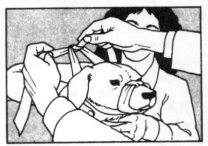

4. *Finally, tie a tight bow at the back of the dog's head, making sure that the knot is in front of the dog's collar. Check that the tape-muzzle is secure.*

include both the top and bottom jaws. Draw the loop tight to close the jaws by pulling on the ends; it is best to pull them sideways. This will form a knot on top of the dog's nose. Immediately, and without allowing any slack to form in the tape, bring each end down on either side of the dog's mouth and then cross the two ends over underneath the lower jaw. Bring the ends up behind the ears and tie a tight bow on the upper part of the neck, in front of any collar the dog may be wearing.

The position of the tape-muzzle is important: if it is too near the tip of the nose it will easily come off, and if it is too far back the dog may still be able to open its mouth. Since the animal does not normally breathe through its mouth there is no reason to be afraid of tightening the tape-muzzle, as it will not prevent the animal breathing. Be careful, however, not to clamp the tongue between the teeth, and also be careful if the animal is having difficulty in breathing, or is bleeding from the nose or mouth, or has any damage to its jaws or skull.

A slack tape-muzzle is useless and you should have no confidence in it. If, because the animal is struggling, you have had difficulty in putting on the tape-muzzle tightly, apply a second tape-muzzle on top of the first, making sure that this time it is tight. Don't remove the first tape to apply the second. Having applied a tape-muzzle, always keep the dog's head up and its front legs down; if necessary these should be held by a helper. Small dogs in particular are very successful at using their forefeet to push a tape-muzzle off.

Q *I have heard that the eyes of a Pekingese can drop out if it is grasped too tightly around the neck. Is this so?*

A Yes, it is. If the scruff is firmly held it increases the pressure behind the eyeballs, and in the flat-nosed breeds such as the Pug and Pekingese whose eyes are protruberant, the eyeballs may be dislodged (prolapsed) forwards from the shallow eye sockets. Because it is difficult to apply a tape-muzzle to these breeds, they are best restrained by a hand-towel twisted into a spiral and passed under the chin and around the neck, the two ends of the towel being held securely above and behind the dog's head. The towel thus acts as a very thick 'collar' around the neck and makes head movements difficult.

If a prolapse of the eyeball should occur, do *not* attempt to replace the eye yourself; as it will be swollen and inflamed this won't be possible. Keep the eyeball supported with a pad of clean lint, cotton wool or cloth soaked in cold water (never dry) and obtain veterinary assistance as soon as possible.

Q *Is it better to get a collar and lead or a harness for my dog?*

A Guide dogs for the blind wear harnesses, but most pet dogs are better controlled wearing a collar, especially as any training will almost certainly be carried out using a check (choke) chain around the neck (page 120). Harnesses are best reserved for small dogs that frequently need to be picked up, e. g. on public transport and in shops (they can be lifted by the harness if it is secure), and animals with neck injuries such as skin wounds or cervical 'slipped discs'.

As soon as you acquire a puppy, after it is eight weeks old, it should be fitted with a collar for a few minutes each day so that it gets used to the idea of wearing one. Initially the pup's reaction will be to scratch it off, but gradually it will accept the collar. You can then leave it on permanently, which means not only that you avoid having to fasten and unfasten the buckle every time the dog is taken out, but that it is convenient for restraining the dog and, if a name tag is fitted, means that it can be identified if it escapes from the home or garden. Later, a lead can be clipped on to the puppy's collar so that the puppy can grow accustomed to its presence in the same way.

Always invest in a good-quality, sturdy leather collar that has the buckle and ring firmly stitched in place. Those made of plastic with a fabric lining, and those with thin rivets and staples, may look fashionable but are apt to break if any force has to be applied suddenly. Collars that are too wide or too narrow are uncomfortable to wear, and only large dogs should wear chain collars. Ensure that the collar is fastened securely, and is neither too tight (it should be possible to slip a finger between the collar and the neck) nor too loose (and not, as some owners have it, so that the collar easily slides over the dog's head if the lead is pulled). You will probably have to buy a larger collar as the dog grows. The collar of an old dog should also be checked from time to time because it may become so worn, especially where the buckle is fastened, that it snaps in an emergency.

In Britain the law requires every dog in a public place to wear a collar with the owner's name and address permanently attached to it (e. g. on an engraved name tag), and in other countries special tags have to be worn to show that the dog is currently licensed and/or has undergone rabies vaccination.

For attachment to a check chain or directly to the collar, a lead (leash) is required. Again, a good-quality leather lead is to be preferred — about 40 inches (1 m) long for a medium-sized dog, fitted with a hand loop at one end and preferably a bolt clip (see page 297) at the other to fasten to the collar. Specialized types of lead are also available, including short chain or leather leads for use with tall dogs in towns, nylon slip or show leads and long training leads or ropes (including the 'Flexi' extending lead which winds and unwinds from the handle like a spring tape-measure and which allows you to stop your dog at any distance). Chain leads have the advantage that a frustrated or bored dog is unlikely to chew through them, but they are uncomfortable to wind around your hand.

When presenting your dog for veterinary examination, *don't* remove his collar and lead unless the vet specifically asks you to do so, because you may then be unable to control him.

Q *Does my dog need a coat?*

A In general coats are unnecessary for dogs, although they are valuable in very cold or wet weather for:
1 Short-haired dogs, especially of the small breeds which tend to lose body heat comparatively quickly. Greyhounds and Whippets usually wear a coat at cold evening meetings (in addition to the numbered racing jacket) except when actually racing.

2 Dogs that have lost a lot of hair, as the result of clipping or a skin disorder, or (in rare cases) those that are naturally hairless. The owners of dogs suffering from diseases which produce baldness (alopecia; page 202) are often so embarrassed by the appearance of their pet that they prefer to hide the problem under a coat.

3 Very ill or elderly dogs.

If the temperature falls extremely low, coats are advisable for *any* dog sleeping outdoors. A showerproof or waterproof finish to the coat is preferable, to prevent it being soaked with rain and to make it easier to dry and wipe clean. Poodles' 'trouser macs' are also available, and these cover not only the chest and abdomen but also the legs.

Q *My dog is difficult to handle. Can the vet give him a 'whiff' of something to control him?*

A Admittedly some dogs are very difficult to handle, sometimes almost impossible, but the miraculous 'whiff of something', like other forms of magic wand, just doesn't exist. Anaesthetizing gases or vapours (inhalation anaesthetics) all have to be brought into close contact with the animal before sufficient will be inhaled to be effective. Any attempt to blow these at an unrestrained animal from a distance results in them being considerably diluted by the air; the dog simply moves away in the meantime to avoid the unpleasant smell. Other problems are that some of these vapours are explosive and inflammable, others can produce delayed toxicity, and others are extremely expensive; and all of them will affect humans as well as dogs. Also, if you administer an inhalation anaesthetic on its own, a stage of excitement occurs before the individual becomes relaxed, and this adds to the problem. When inhalation anaesthetics are used in the operating theatre, a premedicant drug is injected beforehand to control this excitement phase, but of course to do this means that the animal needs to be restrained already.

In short, therefore, some form of *physical* restraint is always required first of all. Once the dog is securely restrained, it becomes feasible to use some form of tranquillizer or anaesthetic which will permit the vet to examine and treat it. Some drugs can simply be injected into the hind leg muscles if the dog won't permit an intravenous injection.

The practical difficulty is that a sick animal will usually need repeated handling, to give medication, to bathe wounds or to change dressings, and if an anaesthetic has to be given on *every* occasion obviously the procedure becomes increasingly distressing, and hazardous, for the dog, and the owner may then decide that it is preferable for the dog to be put to sleep. Clearly it is far preferable to prevent this situation developing by training the dog to allow handling from the outset.

Q *You say that I should weigh my dog regularly. What's the best way to do this?*

A In the early stages of puppyhood the kitchen scales may be used, provided the scale pan is well washed afterwards; it should be protected with a couple of paper towels in case of accidents which won't alter the reading significantly. Later the bathroom scales can be used, preferably with the puppy inside a cat basket or laundry basket, or even a cardboard box, to prevent him from jumping or falling off. Weigh this container without the animal first, and find the puppy's weight by subtracting this figure from the weight of the puppy and container together.

This method may be used with small breeds throughout life, but with larger breeds the best technique is to weigh yourself, first holding the dog and then alone, and find the dog's weight by difference. (It is usually necessary to have someone else to read the dial of the bathroom scales when you have your arms full.) It is impossible for most adult dogs to sit on the small platform of the bathroom scales, and even if they can, it usually isn't for long enough for you to be able to read it accurately. Use the same scales each time if possible, so that any error in the weighings will be consistent, allowing a meaningful comparison.

More difficult problems arise if you either cannot lift your dog or if your combined weight exceeds the capacity of the scales. Then, unless you want to buy special scales with a wide platform, it is usually necessary to have your dog weighed either by your veterinary surgeon, assuming he has such scales, or at a depot which handles produce, parcels or freight.

Q *Do I need to make any special arrangements to take my dog for a car ride?*

A Most dogs enjoy car travel, at least for short distances – probably because they have learned to associate the journey with an opportunity to exercise and explore new ground when the car stops. They regard the car as an additional piece of personal territory and will guard it from strangers. During a journey the dog should be kept under control because accidents can be caused if it ceaselessly yaps or leaps over the seats, distracting the driver's attention and getting beneath the driver's feet so that the pedals cannot be operated. And if it becomes necessary to stop or swerve suddenly the dog may suffer severe impact injuries.

Five options are available when transporting dogs by car:
1 The dog can be trained to sit or lie quietly on the back seat or the floor of the car. It often helps to define the permitted area by laying down the dog's own blanket.
2 In estate cars (station wagons) a tubular steel grille (dog guard) can

be fitted above or behind the rear seat to confine the dog(s) to the rear of the vehicle. Grilles are readily obtainable from both pet shops and motor accessory stores and are easily fitted.

3 A small dog can be carried in a passenger's arms, but this is only appropriate for very short journeys. Certainly don't try to carry the dog yourself if you are driving.

4 An unruly dog can be tethered by its lead to some projection, such as the tubular legs of the front passenger's seat, preferably behind it.

5 You can carry the dog in a proper carrying cage or crate, made of either wire mesh, fibreglass or plastic. These are most often used for small dogs, although suitable sizes are available for large breeds. Put a blanket or woolly garment in the bottom of the crate. If you have to leave the dog in the car alone it is wise to remove it from the crate to allow the dog to have more air and to move into a shadier area if necessary. Park out of direct sunlight and leave the window a little way open (see page 291).

When the vehicle is in motion don't let the dog stick its head out of the window; not only is there a risk of it being hit by some projection (e. g. another vehicle or the branches of a tree) but the continuous stream of cold air may severely inflame the eyes, causing conjunctivitis, and particles of grit may also enter the eyes. Occasionally dogs have jumped through open windows, with disastrous consequences.

Adequate fresh air can be supplied without the risk of the dog sticking its head outside by fitting a 'car ventilator', a trellis-work arrangement, between the top of the window glass when it is partially wound down and the frame of the door.

Q *Should my dog have a sedative before he travels?*

A Not as a general rule. Sedatives are best reserved for dogs that become distressed by travelling, but even then only when they have to undertake a long journey. Most dogs will accept travelling by car or public transport without problems arising, though some become hysterical with excitement while others are clearly afraid of the experience. Fearful dogs become very upset, show dilated (i. e. wide-open) pupils and salivate. Excessive salivation and panting are in fact features of both extreme anxiety and true travel sickness.

To minimize the fear of travel make sure that a puppy's first experiences are favourable; for example, don't make his first car ride one to the vet, where he may experience the pain of a vaccination injection. A nervous animal (i. e. one that is unwilling to get into the car and tries desperately to get out again) can be trained to accept travelling in a car by first being played with near to, and then inside, the vehicle and then being rewarded with titbits for sitting in the car for short periods with all the doors open, or even fed its regular meals inside it. Gradually the dog progresses to sitting in the stationary car with the doors closed, then with the engine running, then moving a few yards and eventually to short journeys. A dog that has been involved in a car accident as a passenger may be very reluctant to travel again and might well require this type of de-sensitization.

Travel sickness is a response to the motion of a moving vehicle (car, bus, plane or boat) which continually stimulates the organs of balance in the animal's inner ears and which in turn stimulates that part of the brain known as the vomiting centre. It most commonly affects young adults rather than puppies or older dogs, and the majority of them grow out of it, just as children generally do. A dog showing travel sickness is initially very quiet, and then may salivate, retch and finally vomit. Fortunately, recovery takes only a few minutes after movement ceases.

To minimize the occurrence of travel sickness, don't give any food for six to eight hours before a journey, and no liquid for one or two hours beforehand. Make sure that the dog receives adequate ventilation, i. e. don't let the vehicle become hot and stuffy. Allow the dog to urinate and defecate before starting and to have frequent breaks during the journey. As a general rule, it is inadvisable to give food and drink on a journey of less than twelve hours, although small drinks are permissible for animals that don't become travel sick.

Many more dogs become hysterically excited during car journeys (as shown by a willingness to get into the car, followed by barking and screaming with the tail wagging, and by continual leaping about) although their owners may wrongly attribute this behaviour to anxiety. Such animals need to be either strongly dominated to make them conform or for the owner to behave in a manner which fails to reward the dog. As the dog will be keen to get to the journey's end in order to exercise, if its failure to respond to its owner's orders leads to the car being stopped and the owner disappearing for a while, the dog will eventually learn to sit still and remain quiet. Often this fact isn't appreciated, and owners usually react to their dog's behaviour by driving faster (to put an end to the noise) and/or making a fuss of the dog, which the dog regards as a reward. Therefore this type of response effectively reinforces the dog's behaviour and causes it to continue and even intensify.

Sedatives given by mouth as tablets, to control anxiety, excitement or motion sickness, begin to exert their maximum effect within one or two hours. When injected, they are effective within twenty to thirty minutes, though faster if given intravenously. Their effect lasts for around six hours, but some degree of sedation, with a reduced ability to respond to stimuli, lasts for at least twenty-four hours.

7
Housing and Training

Q *What basic behaviour should I expect from a properly trained dog?*

A By the time a dog is adult it should have been trained:
1 To be clean in the house and to ask to go outdoors to urinate and defecate when necessary.
2 To sleep in its own bed.
3 To come in response to its name being called.
4 To walk to heel when on a lead and to sit when you stop, and to stay when instructed.
5 Not to damage furnishings, clothing or other articles in the home whether you are present or not.
6 Not to jump on to chairs or beds, or leap around in the car.
7 To permit you to take food, a bone or a toy away from it, if you feel this action is necessary.
8 Not to be aggressive with members of the family, other pets or invited guests, but ideally to be defensive against intruders.
9 Not to indulge in other types of antisocial behaviour, such as fouling the footpaths and other people's gardens, jumping up, excessive barking, chasing sheep or chickens, stealing food etc.
10 To be obedient immediately, not merely to respond when it feels like it.

Being a pack animal the dog will look to you, as its pack leader, to be told how it must behave; in other words it is expecting discipline. If you don't provide it not only will you have an unruly dog but it may assume that you regard yourself as an inferior, and may begin to adopt a dominant role.

Q *What should I remember when training a dog?*

A In training your dog you have to be fair, you have to be firm and you have to be consistent. It is no good letting the animal indulge in a certain type of behaviour today (for example jumping up at you, or sitting on the sofa) and tomorrow trying to stop it. Habits that you don't want to continue and develop must be eradicated as soon as they appear. If you are consistent in your approach, the dog will realize exactly what is expected of it; if not it will simply become confused and anxious. Also you must correct its behaviour *at the time* it does wrong, not later. Dogs have child-like minds and poor memories for events so you should chastise it *when* you see it chewing the furniture, or making a puddle on the floor, but not later when you have only just found the evidence. Naturally enough the dog will adopt a submissive posture whenever you shout at it, but this is not necessarily because it understands what it has done wrong.

Remember that it will be trying to please you, so that it is important to reward it for good behaviour with praise and affection (e. g. stroking). As a general rule don't reprimand the dog simply for failing to obey a command during obedience training because it will tend to associate the 'punishment' with the command and behave poorly in future. In essence, reward good behaviour and ignore its failures.

As soon as you acquire a puppy you should start elementary training. Choose a simple and distinctive name and use it to call the puppy to you, using a friendly voice. Reward it with praise, plus in the early stages a little food, when it arrives. But don't allow everyone in the family to call the name incessantly, otherwise the puppy will attach no significance to the sound and will just ignore it.

Keep any command words that you use simple (e. g. 'No' when you want its present behaviour to stop, 'Heel', 'Sit', etc.). Make each command sound different by using a different tone of voice, and when you speak these words use the same tone each time so as not to confuse the dog.

Usually stern words, reinforced by a smack if necessary, are all that is required to indicate your displeasure. Whacking with a rolled-up newspaper is not an effective punishment and is usually either treated as a game or encourages the dog to be aggressive. But *never* give food or praise soon after a dog has behaved badly; you will appear to be rewarding it for its bad behaviour and it will be encouraged to repeat it.

Q *How can I house-train my puppy?*

A First let us consider a puppy's natural behaviour, to see how it can be harnessed for successful training. In the period of their life soon after birth puppies are stimulated to pass motions and urine by the licking of their mother's tongue, and the bitch will continue to lick them until

113

these excretions are completely cleaned away. By three weeks of age the pups are able to walk away from their bed to defecate and urinate, although they do not yet use specific spots, just somewhere close by. But by eight and a half weeks old (the age at which many puppies enter their new home) they will quite naturally start to use definite, fixed places for these purposes, usually somewhere as far away from their feeding bowl as possible.

Before using its chosen area a puppy will sniff around the spot, and the odours of previous eliminations encourage further use of the site. This is a key point in training, so you should help your puppy establish an area for the passing of motions and urine. Ideally the area chosen should be outdoors because ultimately that is where you will want these matters to take place. Try to choose a place close to the house so that it can be reached quickly, not too muddy (to reduce muddy footprints) and not part of your prize lawn, unless you are resigned to the grass being killed (dog urine is sufficiently acid to do this very effectively). Ideally use an area covered with gravel or clinker which will allow the urine to soak away and make it easy to collect the motions for disposal.

Get into the habit of instructing the dog to perform when you take it outside, preferably choosing a command word or phrase that you will not be embarrassed to have overheard; for example 'Outside', 'Good boy', 'Busy', 'Hurry up', or whatever. Then stay with the puppy until it performs, repeat the word while it does so, and afterwards praise it extravagantly for its good behaviour. Unfortunately young pups do not have great powers of concentration and yours may begin to play as soon as it gets outdoors. Nevertheless stay with it, if necessary replacing it in the correct spot, and wait until the job is done. Then praise it and bring it back indoors. This can be a very irksome chore late at night, especially if it is raining, but if you try to leave the puppy outdoors on its own it will simply come to the door and whine to get back in with you. There are no short cuts; it has to be done like this every time.

If using a place outdoors presents real problems, for example if you are a flat-dweller and it would be impossible to reach the ground floor before an accident occurred, or if it is mid-winter with very inclement weather, you may be obliged to choose a spot indoors *to start with*. Cover a small area of a floor that is easily cleaned with newspaper, or alternatively supply a large version of a cat's litter box, containing soil, peat or cat litter, and let the puppy use that. When the weather improves, or when it is old enough to control itself better, you should transfer to a site outdoors. When the transfer is made it will help to place a piece of the newspaper, or alternatively the litter box, at the outdoor site for a day or two, to encourage the puppy's use of the area.

Whether indoors or outdoors do not clean the area with strong disinfectants or other deodorizers because it will remove the scents which trigger the puppy's behaviour, although of course you will, inevitably, have to wash the floor occasionally. Conversely, an area where an 'accident' has occurred indoors *should* be deodorized to discourage its further use. White vinegar, or diluted bleach (if the floor covering will withstand it), are ideal to remove the odours, as are some commercial preparations (e.g. 'No Stain Carpet Cleaner' by St Aubrey). Ammonia, smelling like stale urine, may actually encourage further urination, and some pine disinfectants are reported to have the same effect.

Puppies at eight and a half weeks old will not willingly soil their sleeping area and can sleep for long periods, even overnight, without urinating and defecating. However, when awake and active they may need to do so every one to two hours, particularly after eating. The arrival of new food in the stomach stimulates a reflex movement of material through the bowel (the gastro-colic reflex). Consequently, it is necessary to place your puppy on to the chosen spot *immediately* it has been fed, and also as soon as it has woken up, and to leave it there until it has performed. It also helps not to give much to drink last thing at night. Activity and cold will also stimulate urination and defecation. At other times when indoors the puppy should be confined to a room (preferably uncarpeted) where someone can watch it. As soon as it begins to show the typical behaviour preparatory to eliminating (i.e. sniffing the floor whilst circling around), it should be picked up and taken to its correct spot. To allow a puppy of this age the run of the house *without* supervision is to invite problems. Ideally take it outside for five minutes each hour in the early stages of training.

If the animal does urinate or defecate indoors and, as should happen, you catch it straight away, show it where it has misbehaved and, speaking in a stern voice, smack it and take it to its correct spot. (Rubbing its nose in the mess, however, is unkind and not effective.) But if you find the evidence later it will be too late for punishment; you must simply clear it up and deodorize the area.

By four or five months old the intervals between the dog wanting to eliminate will be longer, and often the dog will be able to signal that it wants to go out, for example by going to the door. By eight months old most puppies will be fully housetrained. By then just giving the command word when the dog is let out should be sufficient to encourage it to empty bladder and bowel. This word-association training is very important as it can be used when away from home to overcome the reluctance of some bitches to relieve themselves in unfamiliar surroundings. (In North America the term house-breaking is sometimes used for this type of training, although in Britain this term has an entirely different meaning, denoting the illegal entry of premises.)

It is possible to install a 'dog door' in one of the external doors of the house to allow the dog free entry and exit to relieve himself. The device is hinged at the top and can be pushed open from either side, but is normally held closed by a magnet to prevent draughts, and can be locked shut when required. A number of sizes are available, though unfortunately the largest opening, 12 inches by 15 inches (30 cm × 40 cm), would be sufficient for a child or small adult to enter uninvited.

Q *Recently there has been a lot of public debate about the toilet habits of dogs and the fouling of pavements and parks. How should I train my dog to behave in this respect?*

A The enormous amount of excrement deposited in public places every day by dogs, especially in urban areas, appears to be the major reason why an anti-dog attitude has developed in recent years. Having to pick your way along a pavement covered in droppings is obviously distasteful, and, quite naturally, many people resent not being able to let their young children play freely in a public park in case their shoes or hands or footballs become daubed with faeces. When this happens it is not only unpleasant, but may be a health risk, as several diseases are spread by canine faeces, especially parvovirus infection in dogs and that caused by the roundworm *Toxocara canis* in humans. The provision of specific fenced-off zones in public areas, in which dogs can defecate and from which motions can be easily cleared ('dog loos'), has not unfortunately resulted in them being widely used, and increasingly there is a call for local authorities to employ dog wardens to enforce existing legislation against fouling parks and footpaths.

Dogs should be trained from an early age to pass urine and motions on a fixed area of their owner's garden from which the motions can easily be removed (see page 114). A normal healthy dog will only need to pass motions once or twice a day, and can be trained to do so at specific times in response to a command word. Its bladder will need to be emptied rather more often, although a normal dog should be able to hold its urine for at least four to six hours, and also overnight (urine is formed more slowly when asleep). It should always be let out first thing in the morning and last thing at night.

Droppings should be removed every day, and ideally should always be burned to prevent the spread of parasites. Since they are not intrinsically flammable the motions will need to be added to an existing fire. Other methods of disposal will not necessarily destroy the infective stages of parasites, merely transfer them elsewhere. The eggs of *Toxocara* (see page 207) are very resistant to disinfectants and other chemicals and therefore it is unlikely that they will be killed by chemical treatment before or after disposal. Therefore, if the incineration of refuse is customary in your locality, place the faeces in a plastic bag, seal it and dispose of it with your other rubbish.

If incineration is difficult to arrange this material can be flushed down a toilet. Some local authorities dump their treated sewage at sea so that environmental contamination is minimal; others spread it on the land, however, thereby encouraging widespread contamination with the infective stages of these parasites. It is advisable *not* to place the collected motions on a compost heap. Garden 'dog loos' are also available for the disposal of droppings. Looking like a plastic dustbin (trash can) with holes, the container is sunk into a hole dug in the ground, so that its top is level with the ground surface. Liquid 'enzyme' chemicals are added to dissolve the waste matter, though again it seems probable that *Toxocara canis* eggs would survive this treatment.

If special areas for elimination are available in parks and streets they should obviously be used. If not (and especially if you are a flat-dweller with no garden) the dog should be trained to use the gutter. It is also strongly recommended that when on a walk, owners should take with them a small plastic scoop, or child's spade, and a stout plastic bag so that any droppings the dog should pass can instantly be removed from public areas and taken away for hygienic, safe disposal.

Q *My dog seemed perfectly house-trained but recently he has been soiling indoors. Why has he forgotten his training?*

A First of all it would be necessary to check with your vet that there is nothing medically wrong with the dog which might be affecting its control of bowels or bladder. Indications that this *might* be so include:

1 A change in the consistency of the motions (from formed to soft or liquid), and/or a markedly increased amount of them.

2 An increase in the total quantity of urine being formed (and resulting in a corresponding increase in the amount of water drunk), so that the volume of urine might exceed the capacity of the dog's bladder (see page 87).

3 The dog having to pass motions and urine much more frequently.

4 The dog apparently being unaware that urine, or sometimes even liquid faeces, are leaking away from it. This is often associated with a soiled coat.

Even so, many dogs that are obliged to eliminate more frequently are still aware of the fact and will inform the owner, if he or she is present, when they need to go outdoors.

You should also consider whether the breakdown in training coincides with anything which might have given rise to a feeling of insecurity in the dog, particularly the arrival of another animal (sometimes another person) in the household. The feeling that he was being supplanted in your affections by the newcomer could force him to emphasize his rank by urine-marking indoors. In this situation the urine is not passed as a large puddle on the floor, as would be the case if the animal was simply needing to empty its bladder, but as a number of 'marks' on vertical surfaces. Also the urine usually has a much more pungent smell. Removing the newcomer from the home, or showing the resident dog more affection, could solve the problem. If not, treatment of the dog with progestagens, or even castration, could be required to produce an improvement.

If none of these explanations applies, or if the behaviour began with a medical problem and has persisted despite successful treatment of it, it would indeed appear to indicate a real breakdown in training. It should be handled by confining the animal to the room in which it is usually fed, or even, by fastening the dog to a lead, confining it to just a small part of the room (containing its bed, and food and water bowls). Then at regular intervals (initially as short as one hour) the dog should be taken outdoors for a few minutes and instructed to eliminate, just as a young puppy would be. Lavish praise and even titbits of food should be given if, and when, the dog performs. Any mess-making indoors should not be punished, simply ignored, and the area cleaned up and deodorized. Gradually as the dog's toilet habits improve the intervals between being taken outdoors can be lengthened and the area to which it has access can be enlarged, until eventually it is again allowed into other rooms in the house.

Q *How much exercise does my dog need?*

A Obviously this will depend upon the size and breed of dog, and its age and state of health. What is important is that a dog receives at least some exercise each day rather than a marathon session occasionally, for example at the weekends.

The total length of walks that a dog requires each day can range from 10 miles (16 km) in the case of the larger, faster breeds, such as the hounds and gundogs, down to half a mile ($^3/_4$ km) for the small toy breeds, which can probably be achieved simply by a run around the garden. However, regular exercise is important not only in helping to keep a dog fit but to provide it with some sort of interest and mental stimulation. Just letting it loose in the garden, or even taking exactly the same walk each day, isn't very likely to do that, although any break from boredom is welcomed by a dog. Very active breeds, such as small terriers, require more exercise than their size alone would suggest, whereas some larger breeds intended primarily as guard dogs, such as Boxers and Mastiffs, are content with less. Probably the best guide as to whether your dog's walks are too long or too short is the length of time it needs to rest afterwards.

Ideally, a dog should be exercised where it can be let off the lead, and, within reason, allowed to run loose. If this can be done the dog will cover a distance of up to three times that walked by the owner (because of its running ahead and back again, and so on) and will derive interest and pleasure from investigating scents on the way. Younger dogs in particular will enjoy chasing and retrieving a ball or stick during periods of exercise and play, although because balls and sticks can be the cause of accidents solid rubber rings (quoits) are preferable to either (see page 296). However dogs *must* be kept under control near traffic or near livestock; sheep-worrying by dogs is responsible for many thousands of deaths each year, and in Britain farmers may legally shoot a dog behaving in this way. Don't let a dog roam further away than the distance at which you can control it.

Swimming also provides good exercise, and is beneficial provided that there is an easy route out of the water (which is usually not the case with canal locks, quarries or many domestic swimming pools) and that the water is not contaminated.

Dogs require more exercise when they are young adults (after six to nine months of age), and at this age a lack of exercise may encourage destructive behaviour. However, too much exercise before this age can be harmful, especially to the larger breeds such as Great Danes, causing permanent deformities of the joints and muscle tendons. Ideally young pups should not be allowed into areas which other dogs visit until at least two weeks after their vaccination course has been completed (see page 187); apart from the risk of infection, young dogs will not have received sufficient training for them to be easily controlled.

Q *Are there any occasions when dogs require less exercise than usual?*

A Bitches in the first half of pregnancy should be exercised as normal; later on less exercise is desirable, but the amount largely depends on the individual bitch's inclination. Elderly dogs can suffer from disorders that limit the amount of exercise which they can take (e.g. arthritis or heart conditions), and the rule should be to provide a number of short walks rather than one long, exhausting session. During hot weather the same goes for the flat-faced (brachycephalic) breeds, such as Boxers and Pugs, because of the difficulty they experience in breathing. And if a dog is ill, it is obviously wise to forgo exercise until its condition improves; just a gentle stroll outside to pass urine and motions is all that is required.

Q *Are running chains a good idea?*

A A running chain is a short length of chain attached at one end to the dog's collar and at the other to a ring or short tube (e. g. 'Liberty lead') which can run along a cable stretched taut between two anchor points. This arrangement allows the dog to have access to a greater area than it would if simply chained up, because it can run both along the length of the cable and for some distance either side of it. Also it does not have to drag a heavy length of chain after it, as it would if chained to a central post. (To ensure that most of the weight of a running chain is borne by the cable the anchor points of the cable should be fastened *above* the height of the dog.) Running chains are also less likely to get tangled or wound up, especially if a 'stop' is provided on the cable before an end which is fastened to a free-standing post or tree. A leather lead or rope can be used in place of a chain but chains have the advantage that they cannot be chewed through.

A running chain can be used in situations where a garden is inadequately fenced, so that the dog might escape, or where you want to allow a guard dog access to a particularly wide area. Being situated outdoors defecation and urination present no problems, but access to a kennel, or other sheltered area, should be available in case it is raining. There should be drinking water within reach and the length of the chain should be sufficient to allow the dog to lie down. The use of this device is definitely a second best to being allowed to roam around the garden at will, and certainly it is no substitute for proper exercise, but it may prove useful as a temporary measure while a gate or fence is being mended.

Unfortunately dogs kept on running chains for long periods become bored, and also tend to show exaggerated territorial aggression; a characteristic of any dog which is kept chained up. Such dogs will bark, lunge, and even try to bite at strangers, and great care should be taken to make sure that their collars, and the cable anchorages, are secure, because if a dog breaks free during this type of display a visitor is likely to be attacked.

Q *How can I train my dog to be safe in traffic?*

A This can only be done by never letting the dog out alone, and by teaching it to walk to heel and to stop when you do. This training is commonly begun around six months of age but there is no reason why simple training shouldn't be started after four months (although the dog shouldn't be taken out into public areas, such as the street or park, until at least two weeks after the last injection in its first vaccination course; (see page 187). For very young dogs 'training sessions' should be very short, only five to ten minutes, but frequent. There is no upper age limit,

How to put on a check chain (choke chain)

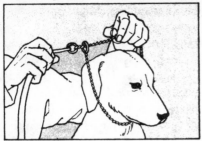

Right *When correctly applied the check chain should run from the lead, across the top of the neck, behind the left ear, and under the throat to the 'free' ring.*

Wrong *An incorrectly positioned chain, running in the opposite direction round the neck, will not slacken off when the lead is loosened, and may cause injuries.*

so if you do not happen to be the dog's first owner this is no reason why you shouldn't still embark upon training.

The first step usually recommended is to buy a check chain (otherwise called a choke chain, check collar or chain slip collar) with *large* links, and of the correct length; about 28 inches (70 cm) long for a large dog and about 18 inches (45 cm) for a small dog. Very small dogs require even shorter chains with smaller links. To establish the correct size measure the distance around the dog's head using a tape measure placed loosely under the throat and passing over the ears and across the top of the head; then add on a further 2 inches (5 cm). The check chain can easily be formed into a loop to pass over the dog's head, but because the larger rings on either end are of equal size one will not pass through the other. Instead, with the chain hanging vertically, hold one of the larger end rings in either hand and then by slowly lowering the upper ring allow the chain to drop down through the lower ring until both rings meet. A strong leather lead, 3–5 feet (90–150 cm) long should be attached to the upper ring and the chain loop then placed over the dog's head and around its neck.

It is customary for dogs to walk on their trainers' left side, and the loop of chain must be so positioned around the dog's neck that when the lead is not being pulled the loop will slacken. The correct way to fit it is shown in the illustration above. When correctly positioned the chain should run from the ring attached to the lead across the top of the dog's neck, behind the left ear, and beneath the throat to end at the free-running ring near to the dog's right ear. It is easily possible to put the chain on incorrectly so that it passes around the neck in the opposite direction, but if placed like this it will fail to slacken off when the lead is loosened and may easily injure the animal's neck.

The purpose of this loop of chain is to discourage the dog from pulling on the lead and dragging the owner around the streets. If the dog attempts to behave like this the chain will tighten around its throat producing discomfort, and as a result the dog soon learns not to pull.

Begin the training with the dog sitting on your left side, with you holding the lead in your right hand, so that it passes across the front of you and has only a little slack in it. The next stage is to walk forwards with the command 'Heel'. If the dog starts to *run* forward continue walking at the same steady pace (don't stop), but give the lead a short, sharp, backward jerk (*not* a slow pull) by using your left hand on the lead, and repeat the command 'Heel'. Similarly, if the dog tries to hold back, give the lead a jerk forwards with your left hand and again repeat the command. *Always remember* to praise your dog when it behaves as you want, and by frequent repetition the animal will soon learn that when you move it is required to walk alongside your left leg and not behind or in front of you.

The second stage is to teach the dog to sit every time you stop, and to start off again, walking to heel, when *you* begin to walk. When you stop use the command 'Sit', at the same time tightening the lead slightly by moving your right hand (which is holding the lead) further to your right, and simultaneously pushing the hindquarters down firmly with your left hand. When the dog is in the correct position don't forget to praise it, and when you recommence walking use 'Heel' again.

After a number of short sessions it should be possible to have the dog walk and sit without any commands or any jerking of the lead. This training alone will be invaluable in controlling it in traffic. However confident you may be it is wise always to have it on a properly fitting collar and lead whenever traffic is nearby. And don't permit the dog to stop use the command 'Sit', at the same time tightening the lead slightly itself while out, wait for a suitable occasion, then guide it to the gutter and give the appropriate command word.

It must be emphasized that great care should be exercised in the use of a check chain; the links should be broad and *not* narrow, it must be put on correctly and it should only be used to check the animal's progress, and *not* in a heavy-handed manner, especially on the neck of a young or small dog. Otherwise a variety of injuries can be caused, including bruising of the neck and ear, damage to the nerves and muscles and even to the blood supply to the brain (which may trigger off epileptic fits) and rupture of the trachea (windpipe). Because check chains are liable to be misused some trainers much prefer to recommend fitting the dog's normal leather collar (properly adjusted) and lead, and using these in the same way.

With further training a dog can be taught to remain in the sitting position (using the command 'Stay') while you walk away; initially just to circle around it, but later on going some considerable distance away. Then, with the command 'Come' and/or its name, it can be called back to you. Later still you might teach it to lie down and 'Stay', again until recalled.

Q *Is it possible to have a dog trained professionally?*

A It is certainly possible for a dog to be sent to a professional trainer but unfortunately the results are often disappointing, essentially because the dog learns to obey the trainer but not the owner. Ideally an owner should always be involved in the training process, as should other members of the family if they also want to be able to control the dog, for example when taking it for a walk. Because basically the dog wants to please the higher-ranking members of his 'pack', training by its owner is always likely to be more successful than by someone else.

Nevertheless the help and guidance of a professional trainer is generally invaluable in avoiding training faults. This type of instruction can be obtained at moderate cost by attending a dog training club. Training clubs exist in most urban centres; for example in Britain there are over 500 and their addresses can be obtained from either the Kennel Club or the National Dog Owners Association. Usually your local veterinarian will be able to assist in locating your nearest club. At such a club a number of dogs and their owners attend the training sessions, which are available at different degrees of severity, depending on previous experience and the standard of obedience training that you wish to achieve. As well as the basic procedures described earlier (which should be taught in about three months of training) dogs can be taught close heel work, jumping obstacles and the retrieving of dumb-bells and articles having the owner's scent. It is also possible to learn to control your dog at a distance using hand signals or a whistle.

Q *I have heard about 'shock' collars for training. What are these?*

A Shock collars are dog collars fitted with an electronic device which can be operated remotely by the owner, using radio waves, to give the dog an electric shock. They are used to deliver a painful stimulus as a punishment immediately after a dog has indulged in some undesirable behaviour, such as incessant barking, chasing cars or running away when called. Properly used they can be very effective in rapidly eliminating this type of bad behaviour. However, there is a real danger that they may be used indiscriminately and excessively. In some situations they will make matters worse; for example in a dog fight the application of pain merely reinforces the aggression of the participants.

If not properly adjusted, or if the dog's hair is wet, the electrodes of a shock collar may deliver more current or voltage than intended, causing burning of the skin. This seems less likely to occur with the remotely-operated collar described, which at least allows the owner to judge the dog's reaction to the shock, than with another type sometimes used to control barking. The so-called 'bark activated' shock collar is automatically activated by the noise of the dog barking. Unfortunately many models are technically unreliable. The intensity of the shock may vary, and the collar may also be triggered off by the barking of other dogs in the vicinity.

As a rule it would be advisable *not* to employ a shock collar for routine training but to reserve its use for dogs with behavioural problems that have failed to respond to more conventional corrective techniques. Even then it should only be used if there is a complete understanding of the training principles involved.

Q *Is it healthier for a dog to be provided with an outdoor kennel?*

A There is no evidence that this is so. Indeed, being outside during a cold night could, by lowering the dog's body temperature and the activity of its white blood cells, make it less able to mount a defence against infectious organisms, especially if it has previously suffered from a respiratory illness. However, dogs kept outside permanently do develop a thicker coat which provides better heat insulation.

Outdoor kennels are appropriate for working dogs, such as guard dogs, herding dogs and hunting dogs but inevitably a dog kept outside will have reduced human contact and be less of a pet. From the point of view of guarding the house it might be better to have the dog inside the premises;indeed the tendency to confine the dog to just one area of the house at night (often the kitchen) may reduce its effectiveness in deterring intruders.

If an outdoor kennel *is* provided, either as permanent accommodation or simply for daytime shelter and rest, it should be waterproof (with a floor raised off the ground and ideally with a sloping and overhanging roof) draught-proof and well insulated. Wood is often used and makes a warm kennel, though it can be difficult to disinfect; be careful not to use leadbased paints or poisonous wood preservatives in case the wood is chewed. Rendered brick is more easily cleaned but is often cold and damp as well as expensive to erect. Rendered composition blocks (such as breeze blocks) give better insulation.

Ideally two compartments should be provided, the one furthest from the entrance being the sleeping quarters, and this should be large enough for the dog to stretch out fully. Bedding in the form of straw, hay, or newspaper must be provided and changed regularly. If possible position the entrance so that it is sheltered from the prevailing wind and out of direct sunlight in summer.

Q *What sort of bed does my dog need?*

A A dog kept solely indoors should also have its *own* bed in a draught-free area, a piece of territory that it can regard as its own special sleeping area and in which it can keep its personal toys. Often part of the kitchen, away from food preparation areas, or the utility room is suitable. An old, folded blanket or rug can be adequate as a bed, or this can be placed inside a wooden or cardboard box of suitable size. Dog beds available in the shops include rigid plastic or fibreglass models, wickerwork baskets, 'bean bags' filled with polystyrene granules and metal-framed folding beds with a canvas or fur fabric cover. All should be thoroughly washed or scrubbed out from time to time. Bear in mind that porous materials (wood, wickerwork and cloth) will take longer to dry. Cardboard is cheap enough to be replaced if destroyed, because all beds are liable to be chewed, particularly by puppies. Children should be discouraged from interfering with dogs when they are in their own bed, particularly because some animals will object to this interference and may become snappy.

Q *Should I let my dog sleep on my bed if he wants to?*

A No, you should not, for a number of reasons. Firstly the dirt and natural grease which inevitably will be on the dog's coat will be transferred to your bedclothes, along with anything else which it may have rolled in or walked through. Unless all your bedclothes are washed fairly frequently they will acquire a distinctly 'doggy' smell. And of course the dog might not always have total control over its bowels or bladder.

Secondly, if the dog becomes infected with fleas, not an uncommon occurrence (see page 194), then so will your bed. If you are being bitten regularly it will be necessary to undertake a thorough de-fleaing treatment of all the parts of the bed. Indeed getting flea bites yourself may be the first indication that your dog is infected. Other parasites can also be more readily transferred from your dog to yourself if you share a sleeping area.

Finally, although it may be cute to have a small puppy sleeping on the bed, when it grows into a large dog it won't be quite so amusing, particularly if it begins to resent your presence (or if a bitch decides to have her pups there).

A dog should have its *own*, separate bed, ideally not in a bedroom although this is sometimes advocated for the first two to three weeks that a puppy is in a new home, in order to help it settle down. This arrangement will also allow you to detect when the puppy has woken up in the morning so that you can take it outside straight away and begin house-training.

It is best if a proper bed is provided from the very first day so that it becomes accepted by the puppy as its own individual sleeping area. Of course, it is the instinct of a pack animal to want to sleep with other members of the pack, particularly in the case of a puppy, which has been used to having the rest of the litter around it, but provided it is in a warm place (e. g. near the boiler) a puppy will readily settle down in its new bed. A hot (or strictly speaking warm) water bottle, if used, should be well wrapped up in case an inquisitive puppy chews through it. Another trick is to place an old clock beneath the bedding, so that the rhythmic tick simulates the heartbeat of a companion and enables the puppy to settle down. If it should start to cry in the night go and re-settle it if necessary, but you must indicate by your tone of voice that you do not like what is happening. Certainly resist the temptation to pick it up and nurse it, and certainly *do not* take it back into your bed; once this pattern of behaviour is rewarded it will tend to become perpetuated and can be very difficult to break.

Q *My two dogs used to get on well together, but now they often fight, although I am fairly sure this only happens when I am present. Why is this, and what can I do to stop it?*

A This situation usually arises when a new dog (often a puppy of a larger breed) is introduced into a household where there is an established dog, usually of some small breed. As long as the newcomer accepts that it is subordinate, and provided that the resident older dog continues to receive the owner's attention first, all will go smoothly. However, at some stage, and often without the owner being aware of it, the newcomer may challenge the older resident and, particularly if it is larger, establish itself as the new dominant personality.

Now if the owner persists in favouring the older dog when both are present the dominant animal will regard this as insubordination, because *it* expects to receive most of the owner's affection, and consequently will feel obliged to attack the other dog, even though the owner is present. If the owner should respond by punishing the aggressor this only makes matters worse; the dominant dog resents the other even more, and the subordinate realizes that while the owner is around it will be protected and is therefore encouraged to retaliate when the owner is present.

An owner's correct response is to establish clearly which dog is in fact the dominant partner. If this is uncertain it can be discovered by observing

126

the two dogs together when they are unaware of the fact, and noting which has first call on bones, toys, favourite sleeping areas, etc. This animal is the one which should receive the majority of attention *and* should receive it first. For example it should be put on to its lead (leash) and taken out first, fed first, and so on. If the subordinate dog still persists in threatening the dominant individual in the owner's presence it should receive no support from the owner. Indeed this behaviour can most quickly be stopped by the owner slapping the subordinate dog or simply ignoring it. Without the backing of the owner the inferior individual will quickly come to accept that the other dog is indeed dominant at all times; and with this stabilizing of their relative social positions the fighting will cease.

Q *How can I stop my dog from chasing after motorbikes and cars?*

A Fortunately, most dogs do not develop this habit, but of those that do many have a short life. It is of course instinctive for a dog to chase a moving object, which in the wild would be its prey required for food. For domesticated dogs, sticks, balls, cats and even moving vehicles have become substitutes. Greyhounds regularly chase a dummy hare around the track, though they are not meant to catch it (occasionally the mechanism breaks down and then they tear the 'hare' apart).

Because this chasing behaviour is instinctive, once it becomes established it can prove extremely difficult to eradicate. The most effective techniques involve something unpleasant happening to the dog when it acts in this way, and consequently throwing water or heavy objects at the dog from a slow-moving vehicle is recommended. Often two or three such 'treatments' provide sufficient discouragement for the behaviour to stop; if not this is one situation in which the proper use of a shock collar could be valuable.

You might consider that the most effective deterrent would be an injury received from a vehicle, and while this is probably true it could prove very distressing, and might even result in serious injury or death for the dog, driver, passenger, or some other road-user.

Q *My dog is very destructive when I am out. How can I curb this?*

A First of all let us be clear that we are not simply discussing the chewing habits of young puppies. All puppies go through a phase of chewing things, just as do young children, which is probably a combination of experimentation with different textures, flavours etc. and, especially around four to six months old, a means of relieving irritation when the permanent teeth begin to erupt. Obviously at this stage it is sensible to avoid leaving the puppy alone in a room with valuable items which it might damage.

Destructiveness by adult dogs in the absence of the owner occurs for different reasons; the most common combination of which is boredom, a fear of being abandoned (anxiety isolation), a surplus of energy and a craving for extra attention. It may take the form of chewing doors, furniture and rugs etc. or, if the dog is left outside, digging holes in the garden. Often it will be associated with other undesirable actions, such as barking or messing in the house.

There are unpleasant-tasting sprays which can be applied to the objects commonly attacked, or the dog could even be fitted with a muzzle for a short period, but in the long term training is more likely to be effective. As a step towards curbing this behaviour make sure that the dog receives adequate daily exercise in the form of long walks (see page 118) and also that it gets your undivided attention for at least five to ten minutes of each day in some positive activity, such as playing or obedience training. During these periods of interaction good behaviour, and correct responses to training, should be rewarded with tasty morsels of food and lavish praise, although later on praise alone is all the reward that will be required. This helps to establish both your dominance and your ability to reward or not depending upon the dog's behaviour, putting you in a position of authority.

Then you should embark upon a course of 'absences' from home which must appear to the dog as genuine absences. Consequently all the usual leaving ritual must be undertaken, i. e. putting on your hat and coat, locking up, turning out lights and even starting the car and driving away. However, it is suggested that one feature of your departure should be different; for example leaving on the radio in order to signify that this is a *new* kind of absence which will be unconnected with the previous ones when destruction took place. When you actually leave, merely give a cold, 'Goodbye', without any petting of the dog.

To reduce the dog's anxiety during your absence it can be given some object which it knows, from previous play sessions, it is allowed to chew on, such as a rawhide chew or nylon bone. Your absences should be of random length, but in the early stages averaging five minutes, and no longer than ten minutes. There can be any number of such absences each day. The average length of your absences should then gradually increase, although still keeping a random pattern, until after a while absences of half an hour length, and then even longer, can be introduced.

On each return, if there has been no destruction, you must amply reward the dog with affection, food and possibly a play session or a walk. If, on the other hand, the dog has misbehaved, you must show rejection by ignoring the animal for at least half an hour, and on the next occasion the dog must be left for a much shorter period. In other words you need to return to an earlier stage of the training programme.

In essence, the dog is to be rewarded or petted chiefly for its non-destructive behaviour during your absences. As with most training programmes progress may initially appear slow, but as the dog becomes conditioned it will be possible to leave it safely for longer and longer periods until eventually it can be left for as long as you wish; for example it should be possible to leave it eight hours or more after between thirty and sixty training absences. A similar pattern of training can be used for dogs that are destructive when left alone in a car.

Incidentally, the natural behaviour of some bitches at the end of pregnancy or pseudo-pregnancy (see pages 237 and 229) is to make a nest for the young, and to do this they may tear up whatever materials are handy, such as wallpaper and cushions. This type of behaviour, however, is merely transient and will not occur at other times.

Q *Is it possible to stop excessive barking?*

A Barking is a natural response of dogs to situations in which they become excited (see page 59), and because it requires little effort it may be overdone. Obviously barking is desirable if you want the dog to guard your house or car while you are away, and to warn you of the presence of prowlers or someone at the door. But although the dog should be praised for barking in these situations it should also be trained to *limit* its barking by being told after a while to be quiet, and if necessary being sent to its bed if it doesn't comply.

The dog that is let out of the house to relieve itself and then barks to come back indoors presents a problem. If ignored the barking is likely to continue and become louder, until eventually the owner lets the dog back inside. This conditions the dog to associate his loud and frequent barking with his re-entry. So inadvertently the owner is training the dog to behave in this way. Preferably the dog should be allowed back in before barking starts or during a lull of at least thirty seconds in the barking, and *never* during, or directly after, barking. In this way the dog learns that barking actually discourages the owner from allowing it back in.

Dogs that bark in the absence of their owner without good cause can become a great nuisance to neighbours and a cause for complaint. Essentially this problem should be tackled in the same way as that of destructiveness, i.e. by instituting a programme of planned 'absences' and rewarding the dog for its good behaviour during them. In addition, regular exercise and play training sessions must be provided. As a last resort a shock collar might prove a successful deterrent, but use a remote-control one rather than one activated by barking.

Solving this problem by training is much better than resorting to removal of the vocal cords (ventriculocordectomy), otherwise called debarking or muting. Only in very rare cases is this mutilating operation justified, one such being its use on army dogs during wartime to prevent them inadvertently giving away the position of troops to the enemy.

Q *How can I stop my dog from jumping up?*

A This behaviour may seem appealing when it starts during puppyhood, but later will become very annoying, especially when the dog has muddy paws or sharp claws. When a large dog jumps up at a child it can be very frightening and even dangerous, and the fear engendered may so encourage some dogs that they begin to adopt an aggressive attitude. The practice begins as an extrovert, dominant form of greeting and attention-getting, but should be discouraged *as soon as it appears*. To allow it initially and then punish it will lead to confusion in the dog's mind.

The owner should immediately and firmly say 'No' to show both dominance and displeasure, and then walk away ignoring the dog. Pushing the dog down, holding its legs, wrestling with it or other types of physical contact should be avoided because the dog will almost certainly find this pleasurable; in other words it will be rewarded, the behaviour will therefore be reinforced and it will continue. However if harsh words alone fail then a firm smack on the rump should be administered simultaneously. When the dog has calmed down it can be told to sit, and its compliance *then* should be rewarded with affection.

Q *It is very embarrassing when my male dog mounts my leg, especially in front of guests. How can I prevent this behaviour?*

A Sexual mounting is a normal part of play for male puppies, and masturbation is also a normal activity around the time of puberty. The dog will clasp objects or other dogs between his forelegs and indulge in pelvic thrusting. Normal adult males lose this behaviour and direct their sexual activity towards bitches in heat, although a few may continue to mount males or to mount people.

When people are the recipients of a dog's mounting it is generally considered to be the result of too early socialization with man, and restricted socialization with his own species, such as may happen if he has been removed from his mother and littermates at five weeks old or earlier. The dog becomes so strongly attracted towards humans that he comes to regard them as his normal sexual partners, and has little or no inclination, or ability, to breed with other dogs. Sometimes bitches will show similar mounting behaviour with people for the same reason. Such bitches are unwilling to accept any approach from a dog.

Punishment, as soon as the habit starts, may produce improvement, but often the dog welcomes any contact, especially physical, and consequently shouting, hitting or slapping the dog is gratifying to it and may only reinforce the behaviour.

Castration has been found to produce a rapid extinction of abnormal mounting in a third of cases, and a gradual reduction in the practice in a further third. But in the remaining third no improvement occurs. Administration of progestagens (progestins) such as medroxyprogesterone acetate to castrated males in which the behaviour persists (and also to bitches that show mounting) will often reduce its occurrence. Although in male dogs mounting activity is primed by male sex hormone, the behaviour becomes conditioned and part of the dog's repertoire. As a result it persists in some animals even after castration and progestagen therapy. In these cases training offers the only solution. The dog must be rejected by being taken to an unoccupied room as soon as it begins to show any sexual interest and left there on its own for at least three minutes, or if it barks, until the end of the first thirty seconds of silence after the three minutes have passed. This procedure is known to behaviourists as 'time-out'. In the first few days of this regime the dog's enforced departures will be numerous, but as a rule at the end of between seven and ten days real improvement will be apparent.

Q *How can I check my dog's tendency to wander?*

A Roaming, wandering or straying — whatever you call it — is instinctive behaviour for some male dogs, especially of certain breeds. Labrador Retrievers have a particular reputation for it.

Every effort should be made to deter the dog from wandering away from home, especially since it may cause road accidents and be injured in them. Fences and gates must be kept in good repair and be both high and low enough (see page 16) to confine the dog. Certainly never deliberately turn a dog into the street to relieve or exercise itself.

In general dogs that are well exercised and regularly trained show less tendency to roam, but they may still do so, especially if there is a bitch in heat nearby. Castration will cause roaming to decline in almost 95% of male dogs, and the administration of progestagens is also highly effective, both in males and in females who behave in this way.

Q *How should I arrange to board my dog while I am on holiday?*

A Like so many other things, the best boarding kennels are often recommended by word of mouth. Or you might ask your vet if there is a kennel he could recommend. You should then approach the kennel owners or manager to make the necessary arrangements. Do this as soon as you have decided on your holiday dates because the best kennels are always fully booked during the most popular holiday weeks (just like good hotels). And, like good hotels, good kennels tend to charge rather more. A good kennel will insist that your dog is fully and recently vaccinated, to protect both itself and the other boarders, and will demand proof in the form of vaccination certificates. You may thus need time to arrange for a vaccination course to be completed. Vaccination is generally required against distemper, infectious canine hepatitis, leptospirosis and parvovirus infection.

Of course a dog will miss its owners and its normal home, although most dogs are relatively unaffected by these changes for two or three weeks. Your dog will have the company of other dogs, but inevitably there will be little contact with people, and it may be reassured if it can take a familiar toy or blanket into kennels and if it can be fed on a familiar diet. A few dogs become extremely distressed and may refuse to eat (at least for several days), or may bark so frequently that when they are collected they have severe laryngitis and virtually no voice at all. Old dogs, like old people, don't adapt well to new surroundings and new ways of doing things, and so elderly animals are best not boarded.

If you have a dog that has to receive regular medication during your holiday period, the kennel should be informed as soon as possible; some are willing to give treatment or to arrange for their local vet to visit, but some are not. There are, however, some veterinary surgeons who run boarding kennels and who may be able to accept a sick dog for regular treatment while you are away.

Q *How can I judge whether a boarding kennel is a good one?*

A The way in which the establishment is managed is reflected in its general hygiene, e.g. the smell, the cleanliness of the kennels and the exercise runs, the condition of the food and water bowls, and the appearance of the attendants. The sleeping quarters should be dry and roomy with a raised sleeping bench (in the winter inquire about heating), and with a separate individual exercise run attached, which preferably should be roofed over. Security is important to prevent animals escaping; doors and fences should be sturdy and in good condition and the outdoor run should be of concrete to prevent tunnelling. Note whether the boarders look contented and well cared for. If the kennels look substandard and poorly run, try elsewhere. Even if you are satisfied, check that the accommodation you have seen is where your dog will be housed; sometimes second-rate accommodation is tucked out of sight.

8

Grooming Your Dog

Q *How often does my dog need bathing?*

A As a general rule a dog only needs a bath when its coat gets soiled, with mud, urine or diarrhoea for example, or as a result of that favourite canine pursuit, rolling in dung or some other unpleasant-smelling material. This is not to say that the dog does not need regular grooming, but actual bathing will be required less often.

To some extent the frequency of bathing will depend upon the breed and its housing; for instance you would expect to bath a toy dog allowed on to the best chairs more often than a sheepdog kept in an outside kennel. However, even outdoor dogs will benefit from the occasional bath, especially if they are covered in mud which they would otherwise lick in when grooming themselves.

Some breeds need to have their coats clipped or stripped at regular intervals to keep them looking their best, and bathing will generally form part of this special grooming process (see page 142). Even if no hair is normally removed, as with the silky-coated terriers (the Yorkshire, Maltese and Australian Silky) the Pekingese and the Afghan Hound, bathing will often follow a combing out and de-matting session. Of course, dogs that are being shown regularly will invariably have their coats attended to much more frequently, although in the case of some breeds (e.g. the Australian Terrier) repeated bathing will soften the coat and make it less suitable for show purposes.

Never bath any dog before the mats in its coat have been brushed or combed out (or if necessary cut away), otherwise they will become much more tangled and take correspondingly longer to remove. For this reason it is best *not* to bath your dog prior to taking it to a professional grooming parlour in the hope of saving time or money. It is better to let the experts carry out the entire grooming process in the usual sequence of rough grooming, shampooing and finishing.

Apart from the special circumstances alluded to above, most household pets should be bathed every two months or so. This helps to prevent

133

excess grease from the coat impregnating the carpets and giving a characteristic 'doggy' odour to the house. Indeed, long-haired breeds often smell better with *monthly* bathing and some owners prefer to bath a bitch after she has finished her heat period. Although bathing does remove the natural oils (sebum) from the coat, reducing to some degree its waterproofing, this is going to be of little consequence to a household pet.

Some dogs make a dreadful fuss about being bathed so it is a good idea to get the puppy used to it at an early age, i.e. soon after it is acquired.

Q *Are there any other reasons why bathing might be required?*

A Yes, there are sometimes medical reasons. Treatment for fleas may be given in the form of a shampoo containing an insecticide (see page 196), and bathing may be necessary to remove toxic or corrosive materials such as tar, paint and diesel oil from the coat. This may require the use of a liquid detergent. Vegetable oils or other solvents are often used to soften or dissolve these substances and then they themselves must be removed. In such circumstances veterinary attention should always be obtained as soon as possible. Many organic solvents, e. g. paint stripper, turpentine, paraffin (kerosene) and petrol (gasoline), are themselves irritant or corrosive and should never be used.

Some dogs, especially Spaniels, suffer from seborrhoea, the excessive production of the oily material, sebum, by the sebaceous glands of the skin. Sebum normally forms a thin layer over the skin and hair surfaces, keeping the skin soft and pliable by retaining moisture and also giving a natural sheen, or gloss, to the coat. Dogs with seborrhoea have greasy, scaly patches of skin and flakes of fatty material sticking to their hairs, which may be confused with the nits (eggs) of lice. The surplus sebum gives the dog a typical rancid smell. Although there are normally bacteria present on the skin their number greatly increases in seborrhoea and bacterial skin disorders (pyodermas) are more common. Although the condition cannot be cured, in the sense of preventing its recurrence, bathing every five to fourteen days with a medicated shampoo will keep seborrhoea under control. On the upper surface of the tail (and about 2 inches (5 cm) from its base in medium-sized breeds) there is an oval area of skin, known as the tail gland, which is rich in sebaceous glands and where the skin changes of seborrhoea are particularly obvious.

Many dogs with other skin disorders benefit from more frequent bathing than usual (hydrotherapy) because bacterial infections are reduced and healing is faster. Bathing before an operation is also valuable in limiting infection, provided that the health of the dog will permit it.

Q *What should I use to bath my dog?*

A As a rule, it is best to use a baby shampoo which will not irritate the eyes. However, the mild detergents in baby shampoos cannot remove heavy grime or grease, and if that is necessary a reputable non-medicated shampoo should be used. Shampoos are either soap- or detergent-based and may contain various additives. Soap shampoos often have lime-dispersing agents added, to avoid leaving a dull film on the hair when used in hard water. Detergent shampoos may incorporate lanolin, glycerine or various oils to make the hair glossier and easier to comb. Some shampoos contain substances to enhance the colour of a particular shade of coat.

In the absence of a shampoo, a tablet of ordinary unmedicated toilet soap such as you would use to wash your own skin, or even mild soap flakes, could be used, but these are often more difficult to apply and may sometimes irritate the skin. Soaps and shampoos should always be thoroughly rinsed from the dog's coat.

At times special medicated soaps or shampoos may be recommended or even provided by your vet, but otherwise medicated products, especially any containing cold tar or carbolic, are best avoided. Never use detergent liquids or powders intended for washing clothes, nor dishwashing liquids. However, when dogs are covered in oil or creosote, the application of diluted dishwashing liquid (50/50 with water), or of a detergent gel intended for removing grease from the hands (e. g. Swarfega), may be the only way to shift such tenacious materials.

With insecticidal shampoos, take care to dilute exactly according to the manufacturer's instructions so that the preparation isn't too concentrated. It is also best not to store already diluted mixtures, since some will lose their potency while others may be concentrated by evaporation (especially in very hot weather) and cause skin damage when eventually used.

Bath oils and protein-containing 'body-builders' (designed to coat each hair and thereby marginally increase its thickness), are usually of little value, though hair conditioners (creme rinses) can be useful after shampooing in preventing 'fly-away' hair. The positively-charged particles that conditioners contain neutralize the negative electric charges which dry hair picks up, especially after extensive brushing, and which cause adjacent hairs to repel each other. Other products provide 'fluffiness', e. g. for Poodles' coats.

Q *How should I go about shampooing my dog?*

A It is more convenient to carry out the bathing in a fixed sink or bath, and where a shower attachment is provided, or can be attached to the tap, it becomes much simpler to wet and rinse the coat. However, always be careful that the water used is only lukewarm. A warm utility room or bathroom is preferable to the kitchen, unless the sink and draining board can be thoroughly washed down afterwards, and in any case modern stainless steel sinks and draining boards are neither big enough nor strong enough to bath any dog much larger than one of the toy breeds. A large ceramic sink (which will take all but the largest breeds) will avoid you having to kneel or bend, but its shallow sides mean that if the dog shakes itself water will be splashed everywhere.

The possible objections to using the family bathroom are, firstly, hygienic (understandable if the dog has been rolling in cow pats!), secondly, the problem of getting a really dirty dog into the room without soiling yourself or the carpets, thirdly, the mess created if it shakes itself and, lastly, the fact that its nails may scratch the bath enamel. It is, however, possible to fit special rubber bath mats, with suckers to hold them in place and holes through which the water drains; these are a good idea anyway to prevent the dog slipping about.

Alternatively, the dog can be bathed in a separate zinc bath or plastic baby's bath placed in the kitchen or utility room or, in fine weather, outdoors (but preferably not on the lawn as wet paws become very muddy). Commercial grooming parlours, incidentally, prefer to use an old bath raised to about waist height, and fitted with a powerful spray attachment. If there is no shower available, have a one- or two-pint ($1/_{2}$–1 litre) plastic jug handy for the initial wetting or rinsing, and if you are bathing the dog away from any taps have the rinsing water handy nearby in plastic buckets.

Wherever you work you will need to have to hand the shampoo, preferably contained in a squeezee plastic bottle (e. g. an old dishwashing liquid bottle) so that its application can be controlled, a thick towel (or towelling bag) and/or a hair dryer (or fan heater) and a clean comb and brush. It is also a good idea to have someone to help you.   •

Ideally, the dog's ears should be plugged with small pieces of cotton wool to prevent water entering; but use pieces large enough to be easily pulled out with your fingers afterwards. If you believe that the shampoo may be irritant you can place a couple of drops of warm olive oil into each eye just beforehand (as described on page 258). Make sure that the dog is fitted with a strong and properly tightened collar to help you control any struggling. It is also advisable to wear a waterproof apron, coat or overall.

With the dog standing in the bath or sink, first wet its rear half with

136

warm water from the shower, or if a shower is unavailable, put 2 or 3 inches (5 — 8 cm) of warm water in the bath first and repeatedly ladle this over the dog with the plastic jug. Then pour on a little shampoo and work this into the coat to get a good lather. Lift up the feet to lather them. If you have too much water in the bath you won't be able to lather the legs or the underside of the body. Excessive rubbing should be avoided with long-haired breeds as the coat may mat up. Rinse off the shampoo from this area, using either the shower or clean warm water from the taps (or buckets). However, if you are using a medicated shampoo (e.g. insecticidal) you may need to leave it on for longer, in which case you should leave *all* the rinsing until later.

Repeat the whole procedure for the front half of the body, omitting the head. Then wet and shampoo the head and ears; place the shampoo first on top of the head, holding the nose upwards to stop it running into the eyes, then work it forwards into the muzzle and chin, and finally rinse it off. The main reason for using this sequence is that until their head is wet most dogs will not shake themselves; also, the rear end of the body is generally dirtier. If a dog is particularly dirty it may be necessary to shampoo the whole body again. (A medicated shampoo should be left in place for the recommended time — anything from fifteen to forty-five minutes — and only then rinsed off.)

Spray or rinse liberally to wash away all residues of lather from the coat, until the hair everywhere feels 'squeaky' when rubbed between fingers and thumb. After rinsing squeeze as much of the water as possible from the coat, then dry the face and ears, wrap the towel over the dog and lift him out or let him jump out, ideally before he has a chance to shake water all over the place. The alternative is to place him inside a bag made from towelling which fastens up with a zip or buttons, leaving only the head outside; such a device conserves body heat and can be obtained from pet stores or made at home.

Patting your hands over the towel helps it to soak up water. Dry the coat as quickly as possible and do not allow the dog to get chilled. By using a domestic hair dryer or sitting the dog in front of a fan heater, the final drying can be speeded up considerably, though it can be made even faster using a commercial variable-speed hand dryer. When using any dryer take care not to hold it over one area for too long or burning may result. Always keep the dryer moving. When grooming Poodles and terriers the area being dried should at the same time be thoroughly brushed (usually with a wire slicker brush), to separate the hairs properly and fluff up the coat. With other breeds the use of a stiff brush or comb against the natural run of the hair as it is being blown speeds up drying. After bathing the dog make sure that it doesn't immediately go and roll in some evil-smelling substance (see page 66).

Q *Are dry shampoos advisable for dogs?*

A Dry shampoos are essentially powders which are made to be dusted into the coat and then completely brushed out after fifteen to thirty minutes (brushing upwards and away from the body). A number of proprietary brands are available, composed of a mixture of absorbent materials such as talc (French chalk), boric acid and mild alkali, intended to remove both grease and dirt.

The effect can be pleasing if the application and removal is done thoroughly, for example in Pekingese. The use of powders avoids the softening of the hair that can be caused by bathing and also the difficulty of drying thoroughly the coat of a long-haired breed. However, if the coat is very dirty or greasy, these powders will not clean it effectively. The application and removal of the powder can be a tedious and messy process, and on black dogs any residual powder looks like dandruff. Powders also tend to make the coat dry and can irritate some dogs, making them sneeze and their eyes run. Finally, the extensive brushing necessary to remove the powder increases static electricity in the coat, making it 'fly away'.

All in all, dry shampooing is not very effective and not recommended for cleaning, even though it is often adopted for show purposes. Those who show dogs professionally often use talcum powder or a chalk block on the coat of dogs with white hair to enhance their appearance (e.g. Maltese Terriers, Bearded Collies, Smooth Fox Terriers and Old English Sheepdogs).

Q *Will bathing get rid of fleas?*

A Bathing a dog with a conventional shampoo, that is to say one which does not contain any specific antiparasitic agent, will not be sufficient to eliminate an existing flea problem. As is mentioned later (page 196), the successful removal of fleas depends upon treating both the infected animal(s) and the surroundings with an insecticidal preparation. At any one time there are usually far more fleas in the surroundings (e.g. the bedding and around the sleeping area) than on the animal.

Shampoos are available which contain insecticides and, provided these are used as directed, they should be safe. After the dog's coat has been soaked with water, the shampoo should be vigorously rubbed into it all over for five minutes, avoiding the mouth and eyes. Then, after the specified time interval (which varies with the active ingredient), the shampoo should be rinsed out with running water, e.g. from a shower attachment, for at least five minutes, so that no residue remains in the coat for the dog to ingest while cleaning its coat subsequently. Bathing with an insecticidal shampoo may sometimes be recommended prior to treatment with an antiparasitic powder or aerosol spray.

Insecticide-impregnated soap with which to lather the coat is also available. It is generally more difficult to use and, because to be effective the residue is best not completely rinsed out, it is more difficult to prevent the dog licking in the insecticide. This soap is generally less effective than a shampoo at getting rid of fleas.

Bathing alone, though, cannot be relied upon to drown the fleas. Many of them will simply hop off the animal as it is wetted, and can therefore hop on again later. Even if they did drown, there would be plenty of other fleas in the surroundings able to take their place. Also, because of their great mobility, combing the coat to get rid of fleas is likewise useless. The only advantage of combing is that by parting the hair it is easier to demonstrate the presence of fleas or flea dirts.

Bathing a dog in a disinfectant solution, and washing the surroundings with disinfectant, will likewise not remove fleas. Disinfectants are not formulated for this purpose and certainly flea eggs are able to withstand treatment with any of the disinfectants that you would be prepared to use on your floors und carpets. The ability of disinfectants to destroy organisms of all kinds is seriously overestimated by most people, largely as a result of misleading advertising. The pine-oil disinfectants, sold under many brand names for household use, have particularly low activity and are not taken seriously as disinfectants by experts in hospital hygiene. Other antiseptics (skin disinfectant solutions) sold for the bathing of wounds also have a disturbingly low activity against most organisms. Disinfectants are more likely to upset your dog by being licked from the coat, or even by causing a skin reaction, than to contribute to the successful removal of fleas.

Q *What types of brushes and combs should I buy for dog grooming?*

A Brushing is valuable for giving a sheen to the coat but in all except the very short-coated breeds combing is more effective for sorting out tangles and ensuring that all dead hairs are removed. A steel comb is less likely to break than one of plastic or bone, but the ends of the teeth should be rounded so as not to scratch the skin. In general two different spacings of teeth are required; a wider spacing for preliminary combing (especially in long-haired breeds) and a finer spacing for through combing and for use around the face. These different teeth spacings can be arranged at either end of a long comb. However, a comb with a handle is often easier to use, and may save your fingers being bitten if the dog snaps at the comb when a tangle is encountered, so that either two separate combs are needed or one which is double-sided. The teeth of the comb need to be inserted down to the skin for combing to be effective. So-called nit and flea combs are generally of no use in removing these parasites (see page 196).

Brushes made of natural (pig) bristles or, for very long coats, soft wire usually set in a pneumatic rubber pad, although more expensive, are preferable to those with nylon or other synthetic bristles. The latter can cause heavy charges of static electricity to build up and lead to breakage of the hair. Brushes are more convenient to use if they have either a handle or a strap which passes over the back of the hand. Rubber brushes (i.e. with tufts made of firm rubber) can be useful in removing dead hairs from the coat of short-haired breeds. Excessive brushing (especially with wire brushes) will break the hair or pull it out. Brushing should generally be done in the same direction as the 'lie' of the hair, though where the coat needs to stand away from the skin, as in Poodles, it is best done with short strokes in the opposite direction.

In contrast to the recommendations made regarding most long-haired breeds, a pure bristle brush and a coarse plastic comb (rather than a metal one) are usually recommended for dealing with Afghan Hounds. A carder, or slicker brush, which has a short handle and numerous fine-wire, angled teeth, is useful in removing dead hair and mats from long coats and for fluffing up the coats of Poodles and Bedlington Terriers after bathing. For short-coated dogs a hound glove or mitt, whose palm is covered with stiff hairs, bristles, fine wire pins or rubber studs is all that is required to remove dead hair and give a gloss to the coat.

Rake (or de-matting) combs with one or more rows of heavy metal teeth set at right angles to the handle are specifically designed to disentangle badly matted coats. They should *not* be used routinely as they will tend to pull out growing as well as dead hair and can inflict serious lacerations, particularly in areas of thin skin such as the inside of the thighs. Animals often need to be heavily sedated or anaesthetized before they can be used effectively.

Q *Do all breeds of dogs need grooming?*

A Yes, all breeds will benefit from frequent grooming, preferably daily, but at least twice a week. For all but the long-haired breeds (which need particular attention to prevent matting occurring) ten minutes a day should be adequate. As well as removing dirt, dead hairs and mats and generally improving the dog's appearance, grooming also provides an opportunity to examine the skin and haircoat for early evidence of such problems as parasites, foreign bodies, matted hairs, growths and wounds. It also acts like a massage, improving muscle tone and the circulation through the skin.

Breeds that have a smooth coat (such as retrievers, Boxers, Grey-hounds, Dachshunds and the smooth terriers) require the least grooming. Just the use of a hound glove or a rubber brush is enough. Breeds with a woolly coat that isn't shed (the Poodles, Bedlington Terrier and Kerry Blue Terrier) need daily combing out and brushing with a wire brush or slicker brush. Most of the other breeds also need daily brushing and combing. In general, either a wire brush or slicker brush may be used routinely on the wiry-coated terriers (both large and small) and a bristle brush on the remainder, although the occasional wire brushing of the latter (e.g. once a week) is often beneficial. The 'feather' on the legs of certain breeds like Irish Setters, Golden Retrievers and Spaniels should be regularly combed through, and a fine comb is needed for the hair around the face, under the chin and beneath the tail.

Always brush and comb systematically so that no area is missed, beginning with the head. Brush first with long firm strokes, and follow this with a more careful combing. Pay special attention to the feet, hind-quarters and to the ears of long-haired dogs (e.g. Spaniels). Grooming is simplified if the dog stands on a table (its height depending upon the size of dog) in an area where hairs can be tolerated. Breeds with woolly undercoats (like German Shepherd Dogs (Alsatians), Corgis and Collies) lose so much hair in the spring and autumn that as much as possible should be stripped out when the dog is outdoors. A helper may be needed to prevent the dog moving or jumping off the table or, using a hand under the abdomen, from sitting down. Some dogs will even develop the habit of leaning against you whilst being groomed, if you let them.

If an animal is snappy during grooming (often because its coat has not been attended to regularly) a tape-muzzle can be applied (see page 104). Mild sedatives are *not* a good idea; in general they make a dog, which might have hesitated before snapping, lose all inhibition. The use of a food treat and praise for behaving well will assist in training the dog to accept grooming. Whatever you do don't just abandon grooming because the dog doesn't like it.

Don't permit any mats to remain in a dog's coat. When these are small they can be pulled apart and combed out, but if neglected and allowed to grow larger they can only be removed by cutting the coat. To do this either cut into the mat with a special knife before teasing it apart, or slide a comb between the skin and the mat (to protect the skin) and then cut off the mat completely. It is all too easy to incise the skin when 'de-matting' and if a lot of the coat is affected it is best left for either a grooming specialist or a veterinarian to deal with. As mentioned earlier, heavy sedation or anaesthesia may be required in severe cases because of the pain involved.

Q *How often should my dog's coat be clipped?*

A The majority of breeds don't need to have their coats clipped. Those that require clipping most often (every six weeks) are the breeds that don't shed their hair (i.e. Poodles, and the Bedlington and Kerry Blue Terriers). Pet Poodles are usually trimmed in either the Lamb clip, the most popular, in which the entire coat is reduced to a uniform length (long or short according to preference) or the Dutch clip, in which the coat is left long on the legs to resemble a Dutchman's baggy trousers.

The wiry-coated terriers, whether large, like the Airedale, Wire Fox Terrier and Schnauzer or small, like the Scottish, Cairn and West Highland White Terriers (and also the Griffon) should have the dead hair stripped out of their coat at least twice a year (spring and autumn). Hand stripping using a stripping knife (stripping comb) is the ideal way of dealing with these breeds, and the only acceptable way for show purposes, but it is time consuming (an Airedale can take a whole day) and consequently expensive. Many owners simply require that their dog looks tidy and are satisfied if the coat is thinned out with thinning scissors and neatly clipped with electric clippers, which is faster and therefore cheaper, though it usually needs repeating more often (say every two months) because the dead hairs stay in place.

The American Cocker Spaniel has a more profuse coat than the English Cocker and should be trimmed every eight to ten weeks, very precisely if it is to be shown. The other Spaniel breeds benefit from stripping or clipping at slightly longer intervals (about every twelve to fourteen weeks). They need to have the inside of their ear flaps clipped, any surplus coat removed and any tufts of hair between the toes clipped away. Other breeds with a lot of 'feather' (long hairs) on the backs of their legs, such as Golden Retrievers, may also need the hair removed from between the toes. In hot weather, breeds with thick coats, such as the Old English Sheepdog, may find a clip advantageous.

Any materials which are stuck fast in the coat, such as paint and tar, are most readily removed by clipping. A particular problem may occur in long-haired dogs after a bout of diarrhoea. The liquid faeces can mat up the hair, forming a solid plug across the anus which then prevents the animal from passing any further motions. The matted hair needs to be carefully clipped away and then the whole region bathed and dried. The clipping of hair from the hindquarters of dogs (again, particularly long-haired individuals) suffering from faecal or urinary incontinence will greatly simplify the efficient cleaning of the soiled area.

As a rule, the small silky-coated breeds don't require any hair to be cut, unless it is to remove mats. The hair is usually parted on the head and along the back (e.g. Australian Silky Terrier and Lhasa Apso) and often finished off with a bow (e.g. Yorkshire and Maltese Terriers and the Shih Tzu).

With the correct grooming tools — electric clippers plus the correct size of blades, straight and thinning scissors and stripping knife (depending on the breed) — it is possible to clip your own dog, and courses in grooming, where all the necessary skills can be learned, are advertised in journals devoted to the breeding and showing of dogs.

Q *Is any special grooming done only for show purposes?*

A The Lion clip for poodles (reputedly designed by Marie Antoinette to complement her attendants' livery) is usually reserved for the show ring where it is obligatory, because it requires so much extra work both to execute and maintain. The coat is left long in front of the last ribs but the legs and tail are close-clipped except for pom-poms, which are left on all four 'ankles', halfway up the hind legs and on the tip of the tail. Most breeders adopt one of the other trims (Lamp clip or Dutch clip) for their Poodles when their show career is over.

All dogs generally receive a bath and extra grooming prior to a show, and the Yorkshire Terrier spends much of its time beforehand wearing curlers in preparation for the big day.

Also for show purposes, the sheen on the coat, especially of the short-haired breeds, is improved by a final smoothing over with a pad of velvet or silk, or a chamois leather, or — almost as good — a pad made from an old pair of nylon tights.

Q *When should I first start grooming a puppy?*

A A puppy should first be groomed as soon as you acquire it (usually at about eight weeks old) so that it becomes accustomed to the procedure. If a litter has been born to your own bitch the puppies can be gently brushed and combed, on a table, from five to six weeks old, even if there is very little hair to deal with. This early training is important in ensuring that dogs learn to accept grooming as an inevitable part of life and not something strange which, if they resist sufficiently, will be abandoned.

Until their first adult clip at about nine months old, Poodles are usually given a puppy trim beginning at about eight to twelve weeks old (often depending upon the completion of their vaccination course). However, they can be trained to accept the noise and vibration of electric clippers from an early age, if an electric razor is held near to them and the *back* of it rubbed up and down the coat at frequent 'training sessions'.

Q *Is it necessary to clean a dog's teeth?*

A Cleaning a dog's teeth is useful in preventing or minimizing the accumulation of tartar. The build-up of tartar (dental calculus) on the teeth is responsible for most of the dental problems of dogs; they seldom suffer from pitting of the tooth enamel (caries), the main problem for humans. The teeth most commonly affected with tartar are the upper and lower canines, the premolars and the molars.

Tartar forms naturally from the growth of oral bacteria on the teeth, from the trapping of food debris (plaque) and the precipitation of salts, principally calcium hydroxyapatite, from the saliva. In dogs who use their teeth a lot, frequent rubbing on the tooth surface minimizes tartar formation. Therefore dogs that regularly chew bones, hard biscuits and other dry food, or use 'dog chews', usually have little tartar. If a dog is fed soft foods, such as tinned pet foods, fish or finely chopped or minced meat, the teeth receive little wear, and dogs regularly fed this way soon accumulate tartar.

Tartar is deposited first where the tooth is rubbed least – where it meets the gum. This rough material traps more bacteria and food and irritates the gum, which eventually becomes inflamed (gingivitis) and causes a bright pink or red line above the teeth. The tartar at first looks like an orange-grey upper rim on the teeth, but in time large masses accumulate which, if not removed, can eventually completely hide a tooth. As more and more tartar is deposited, the inflammation gets worse. As the gum swells away from the tooth, the roots are exposed and bacteria are able to get into the tooth socket. Ultimately, this can result in massive infection, a loosening of the tooth and sometimes even abscess formation. This condition, known as periodontal disease, is very common in the toy breeds.

When a dog has periodontal disease it is depressed, has foul breath (halitosis) and salivates more than usual. A loose tooth can produce obvious pain on eating, so that the dog avoids hard foods and eats very gingerly.

To remove tartar properly (by cracking it with dental forceps and using a dental scraper or ultrasonic scaler), together with any loose teeth, requires the use of a general anaesthetic. This may need repeating annually or even more frequently. Some grooming parlours regularly attempt to remove accumulated tartar from the outer side of the teeth of *conscious* dogs, using a hook-shaped dental scraper but, even though they employ a downward action on the tooth, there is always the risk that a sudden movement by the dog will cause this metal instrument to cut the gum, causing pain and bleeding. Obviously, it would be better to *avoid* tartar accumulation, ideally by changing the diet and providing vinyl chew 'toys'; but it is also a good idea to clean your dog's teeth regularly yourself. Daily cleaning is preferable for preventing the recurrence of calculus, but weekly brushing is probably adequate.

A small, soft, child's toothbrush, moistened and dipped into tooth powder, or one of the special dog 'toothpastes' (dental creams), is probably best. Dogs seem to object more to human toothpaste because of the detergent content which makes it froth in the mouth. A good alternative is to use moistened sodium bicarbonate (baking soda) powder or cream of tartar or hydrogen peroxide. The noise of electric toothbrushes renders them unsuitable.

The dog should be held on a table, ideally in a sitting position with his feet held by a helper. The brush should be moved firmly, but not too vigorously, up and down and from side to side. Clean the outside and inside surfaces of both top and bottom teeth, paying particular attention to the teeth at the back of the mouth at the point where each tooth meets the gum, but stop if any bleeding occurs. If the dog will not permit the use of a brush, a cotton bud or a finger wrapped in soft rag may be used, though take care not to get bitten.

Q *How can I clean my dog's ears?*

A In breeds such as the Poodle excess hair should be routinely removed from the ear canal at the time of clipping, but in other breeds this is only required if the hair is causing a problem, such as the accumulation of wax. Take a few hairs at a time between your finger and thumb and pluck them out. Hair lower down the canal can only be removed successfully using artery forceps or epilation forceps, and this is best done by a vet.

Actually cleaning out the ear canal may be needed for one of three main reasons: to remove accumulated wax; to remove dust or water from the ear; or as part of the treatment for inflammation of the ear canal (otitis externa), as discussed on page 158. It is a good idea to check the inside of a dog's ears during grooming or if the dog is regularly seen to be shaking, rubbing or scratching its ears. At times the ears may be acutely inflamed, appearing reddened and painful when handled and may be full of moisture (exudate or pus). There might even be a foreign body in the ear canal (e.g. grass seed or a piece of twig). In these cases it is better to seek veterinary advice before attempting any cleaning. Bacteria and ear mites are two causes of irritation which require treatment with special ear drops and these are best obtained from your vet.

Before each application, it is important to clean as much debris as possible from the ear canal to allow the drops to penetrate. *Never* put any form of powder in the ear; it tends to set like concrete and completely blocks the canal. First, stand a small bottle of olive oil or liquid paraffin in a bowl of hot water until it is lukewarm. Do not heat it in a saucepan;

How to clean your dog's ears

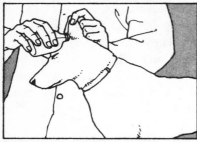

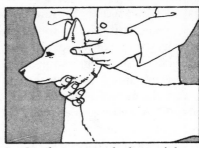

1. *Carefully fill the dog's ear canal with lukewarm oil, almost to the top. Do check that the oil is not too hot because it may cause severe scalding.*

2. *Gently massage the base of the dog's ear between your forefinger and thumb, so that the oil will soften accumulated ear wax and loosen any other debris.*

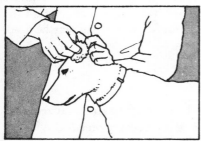

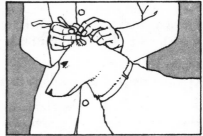

3. *Wrap a piece of cotton wool (known as cotton in North America) around your forefinger, and gently wipe out all surplus oil from the ear canal.*

4. *Using one or more flexible cotton buds, carefully clean all the folds of the ear canal. Then apply any eardrops that your veterinarian has recommended.*

it can get too hot and scald the ear. Have some cotton wool handy and some cotton buds. Place a small or medium-sized dog on a work surface and if possible have someone to help you restrain it. With your left hand (if right-handed) raise the ear flap (if necessary) and turn the dog's head so that its ear is uppermost. Sometimes you may need your helper to hold the dog's muzzle and turn its head for you. Fill up the ear canal almost to the top with warm oil, and then gently massage the base of the ear with your fore-finger and thumb to loosen the debris. Wipe away excess oil with a swab of cotton wool wrapped around your finger. Repeat as necessary. During the application or removal of the oil it is usual for the dog to shake its head violently, so perform this cleaning somewhere where oil splashes can be tolerated. Then clean out all the remaining oil and debris by carefully using one or more of the cotton buds. Clean around all the folds of the ear but don't push too hard. Finally, you should apply the eardrops and wipe any spilled oil from the dog's hair. If necessary repeat this procedure for the other ear.

Q *Should I ever clip my dog's claws?*

A Clipping a dog's claws is only necessary if they become overgrown, and this depends on the amount of wear they receive and to some extent on the weight of the dog. Medium-sized and large dogs that receive plenty of exercise, walking and running on hard ground or pavements, will seldom if ever need the four nails on each foot to be clipped. On the other hand, the smaller breeds, getting little exercise and spending most of their day on carpets, usually require frequent clipping (and in dog shows only the Chihuahua is allowed reasonably long nails). In Pekingese the nails seem to grow particularly rapidly. Likewise, elderly dogs which can only walk with difficulty, will usually develop overgrown claws requiring trimming. It is also not unusual to find that one or two claws on a foot are positioned at unusual angles so that they do not wear away as rapidly as the others.

If allowed to continue unchecked, a nail will grow round in a circle and sometimes penetrate the pad, causing pain and lameness, and sometimes forming a spiral which also causes discomfort when walking. This is most likely to happen with the dew-claws, situated on the inside of the leg a few inches above the ground and which never come into wear. It is a good idea to check the length of the claws at least once a month. If the claws are unpigmented (i.e. transparent), the pink quick which contains the blood vessels can be seen inside and normally reaches almost to the tip of the nail. If the nail extends well beyond the quick, it is too long and either yourself or your veterinary surgeon can clip away the surplus, taking care not to cut into the quick which will cause bleeding. (Make a cut about a quarter of an inch (5 mm) beyond the quick.) If the claw is pigmented (i.e. black), the quick cannot be seen and you will have to judge from experience where to cut. Remember that there is a slight increase in the length of the quick as the claw grows longer, so that to cut back a very long claw to a 'normal' length may damage the quick; it is better to leave the nail a bit longer than usual and then to file it regularly or to trim it again a fortnight later.

With the dog restrained by a helper, preferably on a table of suitable height, hold up each foot in turn with one hand and clip the nails with the other. Dogs don't much care for this procedure, particularly if the cut is made slowly, presumably because of the pressure on the sensitive quick. Use a large pair of nail clippers with spring handles, not the folding type used for cutting finger nails. The design with two separate side-cutting blades is often easier to position than the guillotine type. Never use scissors which will split and splinter the nail. Afterwards, any rough edges can be smoothed with a nail file or an emery board.

Make a clean cut straight across the nail, not one which slants. If by any chance some slight bleeding should occur, rapid clotting can be aided by holding a styptic pencil on the bleeding point; you could also apply a small piece of cotton wool or some inert powder, e.g. talcum powder or flour. Dabbing with friar's balsam, or pushing the nail into a bar of soap will often control slight bleeding too. If there is more severe bleeding a pressure pad should be applied (see page 274) and veterinary attention obtained.

The only other reason for clipping a claw is if it has been fractured and the broken end is dangling from the rest of the nail (which is especially likely with an overlong claw). Ideally, this part should be clipped off completely and any haemorrhage controlled as before.

Clipping the claws merely to blunt them and so prevent the dog from damaging the furniture is often futile; it is much better to train the dog to keep off the furniture altogether.

Q *Will my dog's eyes ever need to be cleaned?*

A A small amount of dried exudate ('matter') often accumulates at the inner corner of the eye and should be wiped away with a piece of moistened cotton wool; never use it dry because it will stick to the eye surface.

In some breeds e.g. Poodles and Pekingese, there is often an overflow of tears down the face. This can be bathed away with boric acid solution (two 5 ml teaspoonsful of crystals in half a tumbler of warm water), but the staining which can occur on a white coat is best controlled by administering tetracycline (as mentioned on page 163).

9

Signs of Illness

Q *What are the common signs of ill-health in dogs and what causes them?*

A Ten of the most common signs of ill-health in the dog, and some of the commoner causes of these, are presented in Table I on page 150. It must be emphasized that none of these signs is attributable to a specific illness with a single cause. As can be seen from the table each has a variety of causes which will usually require individual treatment. Obviously some causes of illness occur more frequently than others, although to some extent this depends on where the dog lives, i.e. whether in the town or country, and whether in a temperate or tropical climate. Other signs of illness, such as apparent anaemia and high temperature, are discussed later, in this and other chapters. Some causes, such as cancer, may affect the dog in a number of different ways. Only a few of the conditions listed in the table require further explanation here.

Tracheal collapse is a disorder which occasionally arises in middle-aged or elderly dogs of the miniature and toy breeds. Instead of remaining like a rigid tube the trachea, or windpipe, becomes flattened from top to bottom, especially at the point where it enters the chest. The effect of this is to cause the animal to make a harsh vibrating sound when it breathes, and often to cough when it exercises or becomes excited.

Intussusception is the telescoping of a short (tubular) section of the bowel into the adjoining section of bowel, thereby producing a treble thickness of bowel wall over this length. It is usually associated with the increased formation of gas or irritation in the intestines and can result in complete obstruction to the passage of food. Prompt surgery is required to correct the condition; if it is allowed to persist there follows a rapid decline and death within one to two weeks.

Cushing's syndrome and Addison's disease are complex metabolic disorders due to the over-production and under-production respectively of the hormones known as corticosteroids by the adrenal glands, which are situated one in front of each kidney. For different reasons both of

Table I   Causes of Common Signs of Illness

LACK OF APPETITE

Fever
* Canine distemper
* Infectious canine
     hepatitis
* Parvovirus infection
  Leptospirosis
  Septicaemia
  Autoimmune disease

* **Heatstroke**

Toxicity
* Food poisoning
* Renal failure
* Pyometra
  Abscess
  Diabetes mellitus
     (terminal)
  Poisoning
  Liver destruction

* **Cancer**

**Pain/shock/difficulty
in swallowing**
* Dental disease
  Burns & scalds
  Facial paralysis
  Trench mouth
  Rabies
  Traffic accidents
  Damage to
     mouth & throat
     (ulcers, foreign
     bodies, fractures)
  Meningitis
  'Slipped disc'

Obstruction
  Foreign bodies
  Intussusception

Neonatal
  Giving birth
  'Milk fever'
  'Fading puppies'

**INCREASED
THIRST**
Increased water loss
* Renal failure
     (including cancer)

* Pyometra
* Exercise
  Infectious canine hepatitis
  Diabetes mellitus
  Cushing's syndrome
  Liver disease
  Diabetes insipidus
  Addison's disease
  Dry or salty food
  Severe diarrhoea
     &/or vomiting
  Heatstroke

Psychogenic thirst

VOMITING
Infection
* Canine distemper
* Infectious canine hepatitis
* Parvovirus infection
  Leptospirosis

Toxicity/Irritation
* Food poisoning
* Renal failure
* Poisoning & drugs
* Pyometra
  Diabetes mellitus
     (terminal)
  Haemorrhagic
     gastro-enteritis
  Roundwormes (in
     puppies)
  Pharyngitis
  Over eating
  Dietary intolerance
  Peptic ulcers

Pain/Shock
  Accidents (fractures, etc)
  Burns & scalds
  Acute pancreatitis
  Peritonitis

* **Cancer**

Obstruction
  Foreign bodies or
     constriction in
     oesophagus
     stomach or
     intestines
  Dilated oesophagus
  Hernia
  Intussusception

Overstimulation
  Travel sickness
  Encephalitis

Neonatal
  Giving birth
  Nursing bitch
  'Fading puppies'

**INCREASED
SALIVATION**
Over-stimulation
  Heatstroke
  Poisoning (e. g.
     organophosporus)
  Snakebite
  Pseudorabies
  Toad venom
  Inflamed mouth
     or pharynx
  Hysteria
  Epilepsy

Nausea
* All causes of
     vomiting
  Travel sickness
  Dilated stomach

**Difficulty in
  swallowing**
* Dental disease
  Foreign bodies,
     ulcers or cancer
     (mouth & throat)
  Muscle paralysis
     or inflammation
     (face & tongue)
  Salivary cyst
  Fractured skull
  Rabies

DIARRHOEA
Infection
* Canine distemper
* Parvovirus infection
  Infectious canine
     hepatitis
  Leptospirosis
  Campylobacter
     infection

Toxicity/Irritation
* Food poisoning
  Roundworms (in puppi

150

Haemorrhagic
   gastro-enteritis
Whipworms
Dietary allergies
   & intolerances
Foreign bodies
Poisoning
Drugs (e. g. digitalis)
Colitis & ulcers

**Impaired digestion
or absorption**
Pancreatic insufficiency
Malabsorption
Cancer
Liver disease
Blocked bile duct

STRAINING
Intestinal obstruction
Enlarged prostate
Cancer
Fractured pelvis
Hernia
Foreign bodies

Irritation of intestine
* Food poisoning
Poisoning
Colitis
Haemorrhagic
   gastro-enteritis

Urinary obstruction
* Urinary calculi
* Cystitis
Enlarged prostate
Cancer

Giving birth
* Normal
Difficult (dystocia)

LOSS OF HAIR
Hormonal changes
Hypothyroidism
Cushing's syndrome
Ovarian imbalance
Femininisation

Parasites
Fleas (esp. allergy)

'Itch mite'
Follicular mite
Ringworm
Nematode larvae
Self trauma due to
   other parasites

Other causes
Persistent licking
Local damage (e. g. burns/
   tumours/infection)
Allergies (e. g.
   flea collar)
Thallium poisoning

DIFFICULTY IN
BREATHING
**Obstructed chest
movements**
Ruptured diaphragm
Fluid in chest
Pneumothorax
Abdominal pressure
   (tumour or fluid)

Obstructed airway
* Cancer
Tracheal collapse
Lungworm infection
Bronchitis
Abnormally long soft
   palate
Trauma (e. g. choke chain)
Cleft palate

* **Heatstroke**

Oxygen lack
* Heart disease
Heartworm infection
Pneumonia (e. g.
   distemper)
Anaemia
Poisoning (e. g. carbon
   monoxide, smoke,
   paraquat)
Parvovirus infection
   (in puppies)

COUGHING
Infection
* Canine distemper
* Kennel cough

Parvovirus infection
   (in puppies)
Roundworm (in puppies)
Lungworm infection
Tracheal worm infection
Tuberculosis

**Irritation or damage
to airway/lungs**
* Cancer
* Dental disease
Pneumonia
Bronchitis
Tracheal collapse
Tight collar or
   choke chain
Foreign bodies
Inefficient liquid
   dosing
Inhaling dust/fumes
Tuberculosis

Poor blood supply
* Heart disease
Heartworm infection

LAMENESS AND
PARALYSIS
Infection
Canine distemper
Tetanus
Rabies
Pseudorabies

Pain
* Bruising
* Foreign body in paw/leg
* Cut on paw
Arthritis
Interdigital 'cysts'
Warfarin poisoning
Snakebite

Other damage
* Accident (bone
   fracture/dislocation)
Tendon/ligament rupture
Hip dysplasia
Spinal disease
   (e. g. 'slipped disc')
Cancer
Severed nerve
Poisoning (e. g.
   warfarin/lead)
Aortic thrombosis

these disorders can be responsible for an increased consumption of water.

Q *What signs and symptoms are the most serious and require immediate professional attention?*

A In human medicine the term *symptoms* is usually reserved for sensations apparent only to the patient (i.e. which are purely subjective) such as feeling dizzy or having a painful knee; whereas *signs* are features which can be detected by an external observer, including the doctor. In veterinary medicine the inability of patients to communicate means that only signs are available for diagnosis; any sensations that are felt but produce no external manifestation remain hidden from us.

The following signs would indicate a real emergency that should receive immediate attention:

1 Severe bleeding.
2 Serious difficulty in breathing.
3 Collapse (i.e. being unable to stand).
4 Unconsciousness.
5 Fits (convulsions).
6 Shock (the signs of shock in dogs are essentially the same as in humans). There is rapid, shallow breathing (panting), the lips, gums and tongue appear pale, greyish and cold, the paws feel cold even in warm surroundings, and the animal often shivers and may vomit.

The necessary first-aid treatment when any of these extremely serious signs appears is described in Chapter 14, but professional help should be obtained as soon as possible.

Accidents often produce severe injuries that should receive attention with the minimum of delay, for example:

1 Penetrating fractures (where the broken bones have been forced through the skin).
2 Paralysis.
3 The protrusion of internal organs (either through a natural opening or through a wound).
4 Severe burns or scalds.

Swift action is necessary on other occasions:

1 If you know or strongly suspect that your dog may have eaten some poisonous substance.
2 If it has, or might have been, bitten by a poisonous snake.
3 If it strains continuously (which includes a bitch having difficulty giving birth).
4 If it is suffering from heatstroke (having been confined in an overheated area such as a car parked in direct sunlight), or from hypothermia.

Q *As animals can't communicate their feelings in words, how would I know if my dog was suffering?*

A In acutely painful conditions the dog resents being lifted and will flinch, cry, growl or even attempt to bite when the painful part (often an ear or limb) is handled. In many illnesses the dog does not experience any severe pain but nevertheless is obviously feeling unwell or uncomfortable.

The general signs of illness to watch for are as follows:

1 Lack of interest in what is happening in the household and even in going for a walk; the dog appears depressed, dejected and listless.

2 The dog lies in its bed and sleeps much more than usual.

3 Loss of appetite, with later a loss of weight and possibly increased shedding of hair.

4 Sometimes, increased restlessness. Inability to settle can be due to abdominal pain. Aimless wandering, especially obvious at night, is rare but can be due to excessive thyroid hormone production (hyperthyroidism) or brain damage (which sometimes causes animals to 'circle' continuously around the walls of a room).

There may also be other specific signs, often developing later in an illness:

1 Vomiting and/or diarrhoea.

2 Sneezing and/or coughing.

3 Discharges from the eyes and/or nose.

4 Difficulty in eating, e.g. dropping food from the mouth, gulping and drooling saliva.

5 Lack of skin elasticity, sunken eyes and even on occasion protrusion of the third eyelids (haws) indicating severe dehydration.

6 Repeated licking, biting, rubbing or scratching, especially at a particular part of the body.

7 Lameness.

8 Remaining in an unusual posture for long periods.

9 Laboured breathing.

10 Distension (i.e. swelling) of the abdomen.

Precisely what constitutes suffering is obviously open to individual interpretation, but an animal showing any of these signs must clearly be experiencing some discomfort. And the longer the signs persist then the more significant they become. It is worthwhile remembering, however, that vomiting without other signs may result simply from overeating, particularly if the dog has scavenged spoiled food.

Q *Should I always take my dog to the vet at the first sign of illness?*

A Generally speaking yes, and certainly if it is causing you anxiety. Most owners would prefer to know what, if anything, is wrong with their dog as soon as possible, and most vets would prefer owners to bring their animal for examination even for some trivial condition rather than to let a major illness go untreated.

Sometimes it is very clear from clinical signs that the animal is ill; for instance, when there is a sudden change in temperament from an alert dog, keen to exercise, to one that is listless and interested only in sleeping; *or* where blood is being passed (in the motions, urine, or vomit); *or* where there is a persistent discharge from the eyes or nose, or, in the case of a bitch, from the vulva when she is not in heat.

At other times, when the dog appears normal in all respects save one, it can be difficult to decide whether this indicates the start of an illness or not. An isolated bout of vomiting or coughing is not unusual, and sneezing may arise simply from inhaling dust. Temporary lameness may just be the result of minor bruising (e.g. following jumping). Even going off food for a day is not uncommon in dogs that are fussy eaters, and it is also possible that a dog that roams the district may have obtained food elsewhere.

If these signs persist, certainly for longer than twenty-four hours, it would be wise to obtain a professional opinion. The *more signs* of illness there are (from the list in the previous question), the *more severe* they are, and the *longer* they persist, the more likely it is that the condition is of significance and should receive attention. Sometimes serious injuries can produce few signs; for example, after a road accident there may be little to see except some dirt or oil on the coat, perhaps some missing hair, and pallor due to internal haemorrhage. Whenever you are in doubt about the importance of changes you notice always ask your vet for advice.

Q *What signs indicate good health in a dog?*

A The healthy dog should appear alert and interested in what is happening in its immediate vicinity, moving its eyes and ears in response to movements and sounds. It should be eager to exercise and play and to explore new territory with its owner, and it should not become tired easily. The dog should present a well-groomed appearance with a clean, glossy coat and bright, sparkling eyes which have no evidence of discharge at their corners. The skin should be pliable and unbroken, the nails not overgrown and the ears clean. The body should be firm and well-muscled and warm to the touch with no sensitive areas.

The animal should be neither thin nor overweight, and its movements should appear easy and supple without signs of pain or stiffness. Except when naturally pigmented the tongue and gums should be pale pink, and the teeth clean and white and the breath unobjectionable.

The dog's appetite should be good, but not ravenous, and its thirst should not be excessive. There should be no difficulty in picking up or swallowing its food. Urine and motions should be passed without straining, and be normal in appearance (i.e. no abnormal colours or blood, the stools formed rather than of a soft or liquid consistency). There should be no soiling of the coat or bedding and animals should not have to pass urine or motions frequently, e.g. should be able to go through the night without doing so.

Breathing should also be easy, without coughing, wheezing or exaggerated movements of the chest, and not unduly rapid (i.e. panting). Finally, the pulse rate and the temperature should be normal if taken; the pulse varies with body size from around 120 beats per minute in small breeds to seventy per minute in the largest, but the temperature is around 101.5 °F (38.5 °C) in all except the Mexican Hairless and Chinese Crested breeds in which it is 4 °F (2.2 °C) higher. Both pulse and temperature, though, are slightly raised in very young animals and in animals that are excited or have been exercised.

Of course, for a dog to be completely healthy there should be *no* deviation from normality. It is not unusual, however, to find dogs that appear healthy in all respects save one; very thin dogs who are still extremely active, or dogs with skin disorders whose appetite and other behaviour is perfectly normal. Nevertheless, even a single abnormal sign should be investigated.

Q *Should a healthy dog have a wet nose?*

A This certainly seems to be the case with most normal healthy dogs. However, there is no evidence that the skin on the nose contains any special moisture-producing glands. The moisture on the nose seems to come primarily from a large gland, the lateral nasal gland, at the back of each nasal chamber. The watery secretion from this gland passes down a narrow duct which opens about $^3/_4$ inch (2 cm) inside the nostril. The 'tears' (lacrimal fluid) from the surface of the eyeball drain into another duct (nasolacrimal duct) which opens a little in front of that coming from the lateral nasal gland. In addition, there are other glands in the lining of the nasal chambers. Licking (which dogs can only do upwards, towards the nose, never downwards, towards the chin) also serves to wet the nasal skin.

The function of a wet nose is to increase the moisture content of the air being inhaled and improve the animal's sense of smell. The lateral nasal gland also provides a large proportion of the water which is evaporated for cooling purposes in the panting dog (see page 45). In dogs, especially German Shepherd Dogs (Alsatians), which are in a stressful situation (i.e. feeling anxious) reflex stimulation of this gland can result in liquid dripping from the nose, sufficient even to form a puddle on the floor.

Dogs that are dehydrated as a result of illness or a lack of liquid to drink, particularly those with obviously high body temperatures (e.g. in fevers), characteristically have a dry nose. Two factors are involved:

1 Dehydrated dogs produce less secretions, including both saliva and nasal secretion.

2 An increased body temperature will increase the evaporation of moisture from the nose.

However, a dry nose is not reliable as a sign of illness; a dog that has been lying in front of a fire or radiator will also have a dry nose, and following recovery from canine distemper many dogs will have permanently hard, dry and cracked nasal skin. But if the dry nose is accompanied by other abnormal signs, such as listlessness and a lack of appetite, then it would be sensible to seek your vet's advice. Conversely, a wet nose can be found in an animal with fever if it has recently had its nose in the water bowl. (Incidentally, the ridges on the nose pad form a pattern as unique in each dog as a human fingerprint.)

Q *Do healthy dogs normally shed hair?*

A Yes, they do. Dog hairs undergo a cycle of growth, unlike the claws which grow continuously. In the first stage the hair grows by the multiplication of cells at the bottom of the hair follicle deep in the skin; this phase is called anagen. This is followed by a period when the growth stops and the hair is retained in the follicle; this phase is called telogen. These non-growing or dead hairs, called 'club' hairs, are less firmly anchored than the growing hairs and consequently are more easily removed. Removal may be by grooming or simply by friction from sitting or lying. Eventually the cells which produce the hair begin to multiply again and a new hair is formed. This new hair grows up the follicle, alongside the old club hair if this is still present, though as the new hair emerges at the surface the old hair becomes detached and is shed.

In the dog, as in the cat and man, the growth of hairs is not synchronized, i.e. they are not all at the same stage at the same time. Adjacent hairs can be at any stage in the growth cycle – the so-called mosaic pattern of growth. Although the length of the hair cycle varies between breeds the greatest activity (i.e. the most shedding of old hairs and growth of new ones) occurs during those periods of the year when there is a marked change in the number of hours of daylight, namely late spring and autumn. The periodicity of light influences hair growth in dogs more than the environmental temperature, though its effect is less in spayed bitches than in entire animals. More hair is shed in the spring and more hairs grow in the late autumn, with the result that the winter coat is denser than the summer one. However, many pet dogs kept indoors with artificial lighting will shed hair all the year round.

The maximum recorded rate at which canine hair grows varies from $1/_{60}$ inch (0.4 mm) per day in Beagles to half that in Greyhounds. Consequently with the alternation of growth and resting phases it usually takes about four months for a short coat to completely re-grow after shaving, but a long coat, such as that of an Afghan Hound, may take eighteen months.

However, in generalised disease or ill health the total number of hairs in the resting phase increases, so that the increased shedding of hair can be a sign of illness. Also, in some hormonal (endocrine) disorders, many hairs enter the resting stage at the same time and are therefore shed simultaneously, and the profuse shedding of hair by bitches in the weeks after giving birth is also due to a change in hormone levels. Severe damage to hairs, for example by ringworm, may cause them to break off, leaving a stubble.

Q *What does it mean if my dog is always scratching?*

A Scratching is the dog's response to an itch in the skin, otherwise called pruritus. Itching can have a number of causes: allergic reactions, impacted anal sacs, the bites of insects or mites, infection with bacteria and foreign bodies in the skin (see page 202). All of these cause the release of proteolytic enzymes which attack nerve endings in the skin and trigger the release of electrical impulses that then pass via nerves to the brain. In the dog, scratching is *most commonly* due either to the irritation of flea infestation (see page 194), or to ear mites (see page 158).

It is important to establish the true cause and to remove it if possible, so consult your veterinary surgeon at an early stage.

Scratching, and also biting and chewing, can result in extensive self-trauma, and while the cause is being brought under control it may be necessary to administer internally, or apply externally, drugs (often corticosteroids) to control the itch. On rare occasions an animal experiences such severe irritation due to inflammation of a peripheral nerve (neuritis) that in an attempt to obtain relief it will mutilate itself to the point of causing irreparable damage, e.g. chewing away its feet. This is seen in its most extreme form in the fatal disease known as pseudorabies (see page 165).

It may be necessary to protect the area which is being damaged by covering it, or, to prevent further biting, to fit a muzzle or an Elizabethan collar (see page 267). Self-mutilation is invariably made worse by boredom or depression, so that whenever possible a scatching dog should be distracted, for example by being fed, played with or taken for a walk.

Q *My dog keeps shaking his head. Is there anything wrong with him?*

A Yes, almost certainly the external ear canal of one or both of his ears is severely inflamed, a condition known as otitis externa but popularly referred to as 'canker'. (Incidentally, canker has nothing to do with cancer, despite the similarity of spelling.) A number of factors can contribute to this extremely common affliction.

It is normal for wax to be produced by glands in the skin lining the ear canal, and to stop an excessive build-up it is usual for the wax to dry out and be shed from the ear as flakes from time to time. However, the shape and structure of the ear in some breeds prevents efficient wax removal. The pendulous ears of the Cocker Spaniel and Bassett Hound severely restrict ventilation of the canal, and the narrow ear canal of the Miniature Poodle is easily blocked. In some breeds, such as the German Shepherd Dog and the Dachshund, too much wax is produced. Once the ear canal has been impacted with wax, and this is more likely if there is a lot of hair present, inflammation will commence. Bacteria and yeasts (fungal organisms), which are normally present in a passive role (see page 169), are now provided with suitable moist conditions in which to multiply and they intensify the inflammation.

Ear mites *(Otodectes cynotis)*, which are the most common cause of ear problems in cats, are less often the initiating factor in dogs. Nevertheless whenever they are present they invariably result in considerable head shaking and ear scratching. Ear mites do not penetrate the skin but live and breed on the surface, grazing on the dead skin cells and possibly sucking lymph from the skin vessels. They are so small that with the eye alone they can hardly be distinguished inside the ear canal. However, with a magnifying glass they can be seen as small, whitish specks moving slowly over the lining of the canal. Veterinarians usually use a combined magnifying glass and light source, an auriscope or otoscope, to view the ear. When some of the wax from the ear is placed under a microscope the mites can be easily identified.

At times foreign bodies in the canal (such as pieces of twig or grit, or grass seeds) are responsible for irritation; even the presence of soap or water can promote inflammation. On other occasions an allergic reaction or, rarely, obstruction of the canal by a tumour, is responsible. However, once the condition is established, the secondary bacterial infection and self-inflicted damage produced by head-shaking, scratching and rubbing, create a vicious circle which may have a number of unpleasant sequels:

1 Violent shaking of the head can lead to the ear flaps being struck on nearby objects, resulting in rupture of the blood vessels and the formation of a swelling in the flap (haematoma) due to an accumulation of the blood that leaks out under the skin. This needs to be drained surgically, otherwise the flap will distort into a 'cauliflower ear' in healing.

2 The ear drum, a thin sheet of tissue stretching across the bottom of the ear canal, may perforate, allowing infection to spread to the middle ear and even on rare occasions to the inner ear. Though it seldom produces deafness this can disturb the dog's balance so that it falls over when attempting to walk.

3 In long-standing cases the skin lining the canal becomes thickened and ulcerated, i.e. chronic inflammation supervenes.

To identify and treat the cause the dog is best examined by your veterinary surgeon and, because of the pain this produces, tranquillization or general anaesthesia may be required. Treatment involves thorough cleaning and flushing out of the ear canal, removal of any foreign bodies and the application of appropriate medication — usually in the form of ear drops applied frequently for several days. Usually such drops contain a combination of some of the following: corticosteroids to reduce inflammation, ceruminolytics to dissolve the wax, antibacterial and antifungal drugs, local anaesthetics to relieve the pain, and parasiticides to kill any ear mites. Where mites are involved both ears should be treated even if one appears unaffected, and, because mites are readily transmitted between animals, *all* the dogs and cats in the household should be treated simultaneously, whether they are showing signs yet or not. Mites can also travel to other parts of the body and so it is a good idea to treat the whole body with a parasiticidal spray or powder.

In chronic cases surgery is necessary to open up the canal to permit adequate ventilation, drainage and the removal of diseased tissue.

Q *If my dog has very pale gums and lips does it mean that he is suffering from anaemia?*

A Certainly this is likely if the pallor of these visible mucous membranes, together with that of the tongue and inner lining of the eyelids, is present continuously.

Apart from anaemia, the only other important cause of extreme pallor of these membranes is shock. This usually follows some form of injury and is accompanied by other signs which are so obvious (extreme weakness, panting, cold paws even in warm surroundings, trembling and often loss of consciousness) that it is easy to diagnose.

In anaemia there is a deficiency of red blood cells or of the red oxygen-carrying pigment (haemoglobin) which the cells contain. The lack of haemoglobin means that the blood is unable to carry sufficient oxygen to the tissues with the result that the animal tires easily and breathes rapidly even after mild exertion. In severe cases the heart beats rapidly even when the dog is resting.

Three main causes of anaemia are recognized. One is the severe loss of cells due to bleeding (haemorrhagic anaemia) which can occur suddenly if a major blood vessel is severed. Less obviously, a slow but persistent loss of blood can produce this type of anaemia, for example from a heavy infestation with blood-sucking parasites such as ticks or tropical hookworms, from the use of such drugs as aspirin and indomethacin, or from poisoning with an anti-coagulant poison (such as warfarin or difenacoum) which both damages the blood vessels and prevents the escaping blood from clotting.

Haemolytic anaemia arises from the destruction of red blood cells within the circulation. This may be caused by the organism *Leptospira icterohaemorrhagiae* (responsible for one type of leptospirosis) or, in certain parts of the world, by the blood parasite *Babesia canis*. Bacterial toxins, snake venom, long-term treatment with the anticonvulsant drug, phenytoin, and poisoning with phenols (e.g. creosote) and the non-selective weedkiller sodium chlorate can also be responsible. Another reported cause in dogs is eating a large quantity of onions! However, most cases of this type of anaemia in canines are due to the body forming antibodies which destroy its own red blood cells — autoimmune haemolytic anaemia. In Basenjis, and less often in Beagles, an inherited lack of the red blood cell enzyme pyruvate kinase can result in haemolytic anaemia, and another defect producing the same effect is transmitted in members of the Alaskan Malamute breed. The debilitation resulting from cancer is also usually accompanied by a mild anaemia of this type.

Finally, anaemia may be due to a failure of the red bone marrow contained within certain bones to produce sufficient replacement cells to keep pace with natural losses (hypoplastic anaemia). Because each red blood cell survives for about sixteen weeks it can take a long time for this defective production to result in discernible anaemia. It can develop if the dog is deprived of adequate amounts of the raw materials necessary for the production of red blood cells, such as iron, protein, and vitamin B, though true pernicious anaemia has not been detected in dogs.

Damage to the bone marrow can also be responsible for hypoplastic anaemia; rarely this is due to bone marrow tumours or excessive doses of radiation. The most likely causes are lead poisoning and drugs such as oestrogen (female sex hormone) though only in *large* doses, phenylbutazone (used in arthritis) and the antibiotic chloramphenicol.

How to find your dog's heartbeat

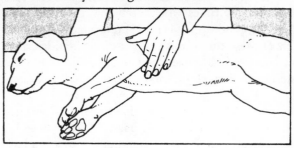

To detect the beat of your dog's heart, place your fingertips on the lower part of its chest wall, on the left side, just behind its front leg. In most non-obese animals the beat can be felt. If not, alter the position of the fingers slightly and try again.

Q *If my dog were to be involved in an accident, how would I know if he were dead or just unconscious?*

A The important distinguishing features are that in unconsciousness breathing and the beating of the heart are both present; in death both will have stopped.

An unconscious dog can resemble a dead animal in that there may be no movement for a long period, and during this time it may not respond to such stimuli as noise or pinching. (Dogs that remain unconscious for forty-eight hours after an accident rarely recover.) In both conditions, the muscles relax and become limp, and relaxation of the sphincters of the bladder and anus may permit urine and motions to be passed. Bear in mind that in death the eyes do not close automatically; they may remain open just as they might in unconsciousness, so this cannot be used as a distinguishing sign.

Two signs, however, are characteristic of death. First, the body *gradually* becomes colder (how cold depends on the temperature of the surroundings), and within three to seven hours the muscles go rigid (rigor mortis), a sure sign of death.

Q *My dog appears to have no control over her urination. What could be the cause of this?*

A The involuntary passage of urine producing constant or intermittent dribbling, of which the animal is often unaware, constitutes true urinary incontinence. It needs to be distinguished from conditions in which so much urine is produced that the animal's bladder is unable to retain it for any appreciable period, for example overnight (see Increased Thirst, Table I). In addition, dogs that have not been adequately house-trained, or in which training has broken down, or which urinate in submission (see page 66) may be confused with incontinent animals.

If the incontinence has been present since birth a congenital abnormality appears likely, possibly affecting the bladder or urethra (the tube which conveys urine from the bladder to the outside) but most often affecting the ureters (the narrow tubes which convey urine from each kidney to the bladder). In the condition of ectopic ureter (more common in bitches), one or both of these tubes opens not into the bladder, as is normal, but directly into the urethra or even the vagina, so that the urine (which is being formed continuously) cannot be retained and continuously trickles out.

Any alteration in the position of the bladder due to pressure from a tumour or following surgery, e.g. spaying (see page 30) can cause incontinence, and another reason why it may arise after spaying is a lack of female sex hormone.

Normal control of the bladder sphincter (the circular band of muscle which opens and closes to allow urine out) can be affected by damage to the pelvic nerves, spinal cord or brain, such as may occur in a road traffic accident. Nervous control may also become defective in elderly animals. If the muscle in the wall of the bladder is replaced by scar tissue after an injury the bladder will be unable to expand as usual, greatly reducing its capacity, so that the sphincter is likely to relax automatically under the pressure of only a small volume of urine.

However, most cases of incontinence in adult dogs occur because the sphincter becomes inflamed and is then unable to close properly. This is usually due either to bacterial infection, more likely in bitches because of their shorter urethra, or to the irritation of calculi (stones) formed in the bladder; sometimes the former will lead to the latter. In severe cases due to either of these causes the urine may appear blood-stained. In male dogs small calculi may pass down the urethra and then partially block it, which in turn leads to some degree of incontinence. In general, Corgis and Dachshunds are most likely to develop calculi, but some breeds have metabolic defects which predispose them to the formation of certain types, particularly Dalmatians (urate calculi) and Irish Terriers and Basset Hounds (cystine calculi).

Q *My dog seems healthy but has two wet streaks down his face. It looks as if he has been crying. Why is this?*

A Humans have the distinction of being the only species to display their emotions by crying (and incidentally by laughing as well), so although your dog will not be happy about this condition, it is not crying. However, these wet streaks *are* due to tears (lacrimal fluid) overflowing down the face. On white dogs this condition (epiphora) produces a characteristic ginger-brown stain.

Where this is a long-standing problem unassociated with any irritation or inflammation (such as with injuries, foreign bodies in the eye or rubbing by abnormal eyelashes), it usually arises because the nasolacri-mal ducts which normally drain the fluid from the surface of the eyes are unable to take all, or any, of the fluid.

Lacrimal fluid is continuously secreted by a gland above the eyeball for the purpose of washing away micro-organisms and dust from the surface of the eyeball, aided by the occasional wiper action of the eyelids in blinking. In normal dogs the fluid passes down the nasolacrimal duct into the nasal chamber, but if the duct becomes blocked, or if the bulging of the eyeball prevents the fluid reaching the duct opening, as in flat-faced dogs such as Pekingese, Pugs and Bulldogs, it has no alternative but to flow down the front of the face. Placing a drop of the green dye fluor-escein on to the eye and watching for its presence at the nostril is used to check for blockage.

In rare cases, usually involving Bedlington Terriers, the drainage holes into the ducts fail to develop. In Toy and Miniature Poodles, the most commonly affected breeds, and Maltese Terriers, a variety of factors can be responsible. The brown-on-white staining in these breeds appears to be due to the presence of porphyrins in the lacrimal fluid, and can be successfully controlled in most cases by the administration of the anti-biotic tetracycline which affects porphyrin binding. In general this is more successful than regular bathing or the use of 'tear-stain removers'.

Blocked ducts can sometimes be unblocked, but this is a time-consum-ing procedure necessitating a general anaesthetic; on rare occasions even complete surgical reconstruction of the drainage system has been per-formed.

Q *What could be the cause of my dog having diarrhoea?*

A The term diarrhoea includes both the excessively frequent passage of motions, and motions that are unusually soft or liquid. Some common causes are listed in Table I. Normal dogs pass motions between one and three times a day and the stools are formed; though on modern canned diets they are usually not completely solid.

A lot of water in the form of digestive juices is added to the food as it passes through the digestive tract, more than 2 pints for every 25 lb body weight (i.e. more than 1 litre per 10 kg), though almost all of this is later reabsorbed. However, if the gut is irritated (by viruses such as that causing distemper, or by irritant poisons, food poisoning or dietary allergies) material may be moved through so rapidly that much of the water cannot be removed. Usually material takes between five and ten hours to pass right through the digestive tract but where there is increased motility this can be reduced to only twenty or thirty minutes. If food cannot be properly digested or absorbed it remains in the intestine and holds water with it, just like a saline laxative (e.g. Epsom salts), so that the dog passes soft motions, remains hungry despite eating more, and gradually loses weight. Undigested materials can ferment in the bowel producing large amounts of gas which the animal subsequently passes.

A lot of fat in the diet can have an irritant effect because it is broken down to oleic acid which has a similar, though milder, effect to that of ricinoleic acid — the active ingredient of castor oil. Also, certain disease-producing bacteria can damage the cells lining the bowel so that water is lost from them into the bowel contents — just as it is in the human disease of cholera.

In general diarrhoea due to bacteria or food poisoning only lasts for a few days before clearing up spontaneously. Worms are seldom a cause of diarrhoea except in young puppies. In older dogs cancer must be considered as a possible cause, even though this is uncommon. Persistent or recurrent diarrhoea is almost always confined to the larger breeds, especially German Shepherd Dogs (Alsatians), and to a lesser extent Great Danes and Old English Sheepdogs, starting at an early age. There are three main causes for persistent diarrhoea: failure to digest food completely, failure to absorb it into the bloodstream once it has been digested, and, in very nervous dogs, a psychogenic diarrhoea such as also occurs in certain people, particularly at a time of stress.

If foods containing specific substances which the dog cannot effectively deal with, such as lactose in milk and gluten in flour-containing products, are omitted from the diet, a great improvement may result.

In all breeds of dogs, but especially the Collie breeds, and at any age, colitis may be responsible for diarrhoea. Since this disorder involves the large bowel, which is beyond the point where food absorption takes place, hunger and weight loss are not common features. The frequent passage of liquid motions with considerable straining and the presence of mucus (jelly-like material) and even blood (which signifies dysentery) are the tell-tale signs. Often this condition regularly disappears and reappears until eventually it is present continuously.

In all cases where diarrhoea persists, or the animal is passing blood, or is rapidly becoming weak, veterinary attention should be obtained as soon as possible.

10

Infectious Diseases and Vaccination

Q *What are the important infectious diseases of dogs?*

A Infectious diseases are, by definition, specific diseases caused by micro-organisms (viruses, bacteria, fungi and protozoa), popularly known as microbes or germs. All of them are far too small to see with the eye alone. The most important infectious diseases are indicated in Table II on page 167. The importance of the disease does not necessarily lie in the fact that it commonly occurs, although some do, but in the extreme severity of the illness or its public health significance, i.e. the danger of it being transmitted to human contacts. Aspects of these diseases are discussed later in this chapter.

The other diseases listed in the table (and the list is by no means exhaustive) are either less common, or else they produce less severe signs of ill health.

Most of the important infectious diseases are caused either by viruses or bacteria. With the exception of herpesvirus infection, all the diseases marked with an asterisk in Table II can be vaccinated against.

Viruses
Pseudorabies (Aujesky's disease) is occasionally seen in most countries of the world, particularly in areas where pigs are raised. It damages the brain of many species, but fortunately not humans. Dogs are usually infected by eating uncooked pork or, less often, rats that they have caught. The disease runs a short course with signs of excitement appearing within ten days of infection, followed by progressive paralysis and incoordination, dullness, coma and then death within a further two or three days. During the excitement phase the dog is very vocal, salivates copiously, and usually develops an intense itch, often around the head, that it rubs, scratches or chews at until the area is raw. This gives rise to the name 'mad itch'. In many respects the disease resembles rabies, though it runs a shorter course and aggression towards humans is not a feature of it.

In recent years coronavirus infection has been associated with cases of diarrhoea and vomiting in dogs, chiefly in the USA. In addition, although not listed, a rotavirus has been found to be the cause of some cases of enteritis in young dogs.

Rarely, dogs and humans (but not cats) become infected with a virus which is primarily harboured and shed by housemice. Usually the virus merely causes fever for about a week, although sometimes it is followed by inflammation of the brain and spinal cord (encephalomyelitis) or of the membranes covering them (meningitis). This disease has been called lymphocytic choriomeningitis, and even in its most severe form is seldom fatal.

Bacteria

Serious cases of the bacterial diseases listed in the table seldom occur nowadays, particularly since most dogs are routinely vaccinated against leptospirosis. In fact most bacterial disorders are caused by a small number of other species of bacteria, of which the most important are staphylococci, streptococci, pasteurellae, *E. coli*, *Proteus*, and *Pseudomonas*. These bacteria are responsible for a variety of conditions at different sites in the body (e.g. pyodermas, arthritis, enteritis, mastitis, otitis, etc.) and in terms of the total number of animals affected they are far and away more important. However, these conditions are *not* classed as *infectious* diseases, because the bacteria responsible are regarded as normal inhabitants of the body (especially on the skin and in the bowel) which only cause disease when the body's normal defence mechanisms are impaired.

Fusospirachaetal disease or trench mouth (so-called because the condition was common in soldiers in the trenches during World War I) is due to a combination of spirochaete and fusiform bacteria, and produces inflammation of the gums (gingivitis) and a painful mouth with halitosis. It is usually seen in debilitated animals and can give rise to ulceration, and occasionally may even spread to the lungs.

Tetanus (lockjaw) is an uncommon condition in the dog caused by a soil organism *Clostridium tetani* which enters through a wound and proceeds to produce a toxin (i.e. poison). As the amount of toxin increases, and spreads throughout the body, muscle spasms appear which cause difficulty in walking, standing, swallowing and even moving the eyes. If untreated the respiratory muscles are eventually paralysed, resulting in death. The disease seems more likely to occur in areas where horses are kept.

Tuberculosis (TB) is also uncommon in dogs in those countries where the general incidence of the disease in man and animals is low. Many of the canine cases which arise appear to have been contracted by in-

Table II — Infectious Diseases of Dogs

VIRAL DISEASES
* Canine distemper
* Infectious canine hepatitis (ICH) = canine adenovirus-1 (CAV-1) infection
  Canine respiratory disease (CRD) = kennel cough
  * Canine adenovirus-1 (CAV-1) infection
  * Canine adenovirus-2 (CAV-2) infection
  * Canine parainfluenza virus infection
    Canine reovirus infection
    Canine herpesvirus infection
* Canine parvovirus infection
* Rabies
  Pseudorabies (= Aujesky's disease)
* Neonatal canine herpesvirus infection
  Canine coronavirus infection
  Lymphocytic choriomeningitis

BACTERIAL DISEASES
* Leptospirosis
  * Leptospira canicola infection
  * Leptospira icterohaemmorrhagiae infection
  Canine respiratory disease (CRD) = kennel cough
  * Bordetella bronchiseptica infection
    Mycoplasmal infection
* Canine brucellosis
* Trench mouth (= fusospirochaetal disease)
  Tetanus
  Tuberculosis (TB)
  Nocardiosis
  Actinomycosis
  Campylobacter infection
  Salmonellosis
  Tularaemia
  Canine ehrilichiosis (= tropical canine pancytopenia)
  Salmon poisoning disease (SPD) complex

FUNGAL DISEASES
* Ringworm (= dermatomycosis)
  Histoplasmosis
  Blastomycosis
  Cryptococcosis
  Coccidioidomycosis (= valley fever)
  Sporotrichosis
  Candidiasis (= moniliasis)
  Phycomycosis (= mucormycosis)
  Maduromycosis
  Aspergillosis

PROTOZOAL DISEASES
* Toxoplasmosis
  Other forms of coccidiosis
  Babesiosis (= piroplasmosis)
  Leishmaniasis
  Giardiasis
  Entamoebiasis

* Asterisks denote most common or most serious diseases

halation from tuberculous owners or tuberculous cattle; a few arise from drinking infected, untreated milk. Nocardiosis and actinomycosis are also chronic diseases, which produce abscesses, ulcers and lung damage.

Bacteria of the groups *Campylobacter* and *Salmonella* have been recovered from dogs suffering from diarrhoea as well as from apparently normal (carrier) dogs. Because both organisms can cause disease in man such animals may represent a public health risk. Tularaemia is an uncommon disease that can also be transmitted to man. It is caught from eating infected rodents and produces swollen lymph nodes.

Canine ehrlichiosis (tropical canine pancytopenia) occurs in most tropical countries and is transmitted by tick bites. After a long period of fever some dogs, especially German Shepherd Dogs (Alsatians), develop haemorrhages and anaemia, and the disease terminates fatally. Salmon poisoning disease (SPD) complex, and an associated disease, Elokomin fluke fever, are well recognized canine diseases in North America which cause fever and diarrhoea. They occur in dogs that eat raw salmon or trout infected with flukes which in turn have been infected with the disease-producing bacteria.

Other diseases, such as listeriosis, haemobartonellosis, gas gangrene and anthrax are reported in dogs but so rarely that they have been excluded from the table. In general dogs possess a remarkable natural resistance to the anthrax organism.

Q *What about other types of organisms causing infectious diseases? How important are they?*

A Well, of the fungal and protozoal diseases of the dog undoubtedly the most common are ringworm, which affects the hair, skin and sometimes the nails, and toxoplasmosis. The other fungal diseases listed are seen less frequently but they are all well recognized in North America (blastomycosis is particularly common) and most occur worldwide. Generally the fungal organisms live in the soil and enter the body either through cuts in the skin, or by being inhaled or eaten. As a result lesions commonly arise in the skin, nasal chambers, lungs or mouth, though in some cases the disease spreads to involve other organs, often accompanied by fever.

Apart from *Toxoplasma* at least ten other species of coccidia can infect the dog. It is doubtful whether they can produce serious disease though outbreaks of diarrhoea have been reported. In Britain the *Sarcocystis* group have been found in a quarter of Greyhounds and over a third of sheepdogs. Canine babesiosis is a febrile disease resulting in anaemia and jaundice and is transmitted by ticks in southern Europe, Latin America and Asia. Leishmaniasis occurs in warm climates, including the Mediterranean region (though not the USA or Britain) and can produce intestinal damage and/or skin ulcers ('oriental sore'). Giardiasis and entamoebiasis occur worldwide, the former in about 10% of dogs in the USA, and occasionally cause dysentery. Other canine protozoal diseases not mentioned (trypanosomiasis, hepatozoonosis) are essentially tropical, though of course they may infect animals which are subsequently imported into more temperate regions.

Q *Can I clear up a point. When you speak of infection is this the same as a disease?*

A No, it is not, and it is very important to appreciate the difference. *Infection* merely denotes that the particular micro-organism has become established in, or on, the dog's body. However, this does not necessarily result in disease; indeed many micro-organisms (called commensals) normally live on the skin, throughout the alimentary tract, and in the outer parts of the respiratory, urinary and reproductive systems without causing disease. Only if the animal's normal defence mechanisms are damaged or weakened (e.g. due to starvation, cold or previous illness), thereby allowing these commensals to invade other areas, will they then produce disease. Even when known disease-producing organisms (pathogens) are present in the body they do not always cause disease. Individuals who can harbour pathogens without showing signs of the disease are known as carriers.

Carriers are of two types: first, there are those individuals who have had a disease and have shown the usual clinical signs (i.e. the signs typical of that disease). Even after recovery, however, they do not completely rid themselves of the organism responsible, retaining it either for a long time or, in some cases, permanently. These are called *convalescent carriers*. For instance, dogs that have recovered from infectious canine hepatitis or leptospirosis continue to harbour and excrete the virus in their urine for six months or more.

Secondly, there are some infected individuals who *never* show clinical signs of the disease. These are called *healthy carriers* or alternatively *immune carriers*. These animals have a natural resistance (innate immunity) to the particular pathogen and are not themselves affected by it. For example, some dogs infected with tuberculosis or salmonellosis show no signs of disease but will excrete bacteria, to the danger of others, for long periods.

The term *incubation period* used of an infectious disease refers to the time interval between the organisms responsible becoming established in the body (infection occurring) and signs of the disease appearing.

Q *My neighbour has advised me to have my dog vaccinated against distemper. How important is this disease?*

A Your neighbour is quite right in advising vaccination because, apart from rabies, this is still the most serious of canine diseases, and is frequently fatal. No part of the world is free from distemper, and its incidence amongst unvaccinated dogs (especially those under a year old) in urban areas remains high.

The virus is highly contagious and infection is usually by the inhalation of infected droplets (e.g. of nasal discharge, saliva or urine) during direct contact with an already infected individual. After multiplying in the tonsils and lymph nodes of the chest the virus spreads to the rest of the body. About 50% of dogs are able to produce antibodies to destroy the virus so quickly that either no signs of illness appear or there is only a mild fever and temporary loss of appetite. In the remainder more serious signs appear, usually within two or three weeks of becoming infected.

As is the case with all diseases not two individuals are affected the same way because some of the signs of illness will be more pronounced than others. In distemper this variation is particularly marked. Generally, however, there is a watery discharge from the eyes and nose which eventually becomes thick and yellow (purulent), coughing, vomiting, loss of appetite, diarrhoea and a fluctuating high temperature. Some dogs develop a severe pneumonia, complicated by secondary bacterial infection, from which they often do not recover. If teeth have not fully erupted their enamel may be damaged and discoloured producing a roughened, pitted, brown surface.

Nervous signs develop in about half of all generalized cases of distemper. These may appear early in the disease but can be delayed for several months after an animal's apparent recovery; the reason being that the viruses tend to persist in the brain and spinal cord and continue their damage, because the antibodies which would destroy them cannot easily penetrate those sites. A variety of nervous disorders can arise but the most common are fits, incoordination, paralysis, blindness and a characteristic muscle twitching, known as chorea, which, when it affects the jaw, gives the impression that the dog is chewing gum. In many instances the nervous damage is so severe and incapacitating that it is more humane for the dog to be put to sleep, although those affected only by chorea can live with this permanent disability, and anticonvulsant drugs may effectively control distemper fits in some individuals.

Incidentally, canine distemper not only affects dogs and other members of the dog family (such as foxes and wolves) but a variety of other species including ferrets, badgers, mink, raccoons and pandas.

Q *What sort of a disease is hardpad?*

A Hardpad is not a separate disease, as was believed at one time, but is a name that can be given to those cases of distemper in which there is a marked thickening of the horny (keratinized) layer of the skin on the pads. This occurs in approximately a quarter of dogs that develop obvious clinical signs. The pads have a hard rim to them and make a distinctive noise when the dog walks on hard surfaces; sometimes the pads crack open causing lameness. Many dogs with distemper also have hard, cracked noses, crusted with the typical yellow-green nasal discharge.

Q *Is it true that distemper only occurs in young dogs?*

A No, this is not so, though it is true that this age group is primarily affected. Dogs under a year old account for 80% of clinical cases and those under two years for 90%. The reason is the same as for many other diseases; *unless it has been vaccinated* a young dog has no protection (certainly not after three months old, as explained on page 186) and once infected it either quickly produces antibodies to destroy the virus or it develops the disease. Even if the latter happens it may eventually produce enough antibody to destroy the virus and recover. So the outcome is either that the young animal dies or it survives with an immunity. Of course if it survives it is quite likely (at least in an urban situation) to encounter the virus on several future occasions. But since it is now protected by antibody the dog will not develop the disease; in fact exposure to the virus will have the effect of stimulating the production of yet more antibody, and thereby reinforcing the animal's immunity. Consequently older animals are usually immune, either because they have been vaccinated or because they have survived a natural infection.

However, distemper can develop in older animals that have no immunity, or only a poor immunity, and then suddenly encounter the virus. This situation can arise in dogs that have never been vaccinated or at least not re-vaccinated for some time, and have also been isolated from natural sources of the virus (often in rural areas) so that they have either never developed a natural immunity or have not been able to maintain one.

Furthermore the efficiency of the immune systems may decrease with age. Alternatively the dog might be suffering from an immunological disease (e.g. leukaemia) or be receiving immuno-suppressant drugs, such as corticosteroids, all of which will adversely affect its immune status. Some dogs are twelve years of age or more before they first develop distemper.

As mentioned previously, a particular feature of distemper is that the virus at times remains in the brain for many months or years following an infection before it produces neurological signs. In many such cases no other evidence of distemper has ever been noted previously, indicating that when the dog became infected the virus was rapidly eliminated from all parts of the body *except* the nervous system. Such a dog may appear prematurely senile, showing torpor, a loss of training, trembling and progressive incoordination. The terms 'old dog distemper' or 'old dog encephalitis' are commonly used to describe this condition. The dogs affected are mostly mature, though not necessarily aged.

Q *I have heard of infectious hepatitis in people. How commonly does the disease occur in dogs and is it very serious?*

A Well, the virus responsible for human infectious hepatitis is not the same one. The virus responsible for infectious canine hepatitis (otherwise called Rubarth's disease) is known as canine adenovirus type 1 (CAV-1) and is distributed throughout the world. When it is taken in by mouth this disease can develop, although if inhaled the virus is more likely to cause kennel cough. Infection is common in unvaccinated dogs, but as with distemper, many cases are able to develop an immunity without showing signs or with only a slight, transient fever. Again, as with distemper, severe cases are most frequent in dogs under one year old.

The liver is the organ most extensively injured (hepatitis means inflammation of the liver) and the disease causes abdominal pain, which makes it difficult for the dog to lie down comfortably. Because of the liver damage approximately a third of the severe cases show jaundice (i.e. a yellow discoloration of the visible membranes). The virus also attacks the lining of blood vessels, which can result in internal haemorrhages and anaemia, and it causes fever and swelling of the lymph nodes throughout the body. Dogs seriously affected are extremely depressed and show intense thirst plus a complete loss of appetite. Sometimes dogs die suddenly, having shown few, if any, signs beforehand.

About one in five of dogs that are recovering from the disease develop a bluish opacity at the front of the eye (or cornea) — a sign known popularly as 'blue-eye'. It may involve one or both eyes, and although it occurs in all breeds Afghan Hounds appear to be particularly susceptible. Fortunately in most cases it disappears within a few days. There is some evidence that a more permanent after-effect of CAV-1 infection may be chronic kidney disease.

Current veterinary opinion is that infection with this virus (CAV-1) is commonplace, but that its importance is underestimated. This is due to the fact that many cases are mild or inapparent, and because many of the clinical signs it produces are not sufficiently distinctive and may be attributed to other diseases.

Q *Is kennel cough simply the result of barking a lot whilst in kennels?*

A No, it is not, although excessive barking will certainly contribute to the inflammation of the throat. Kennel cough, otherwise called canine respiratory disease (CRD) or infectious tracheobronchitis, is a highly contagious disease which can be produced by a number of infectious organisms acting singly or in combination. As its name suggests it is characterized by coughing, and commonly occurs in boarding kennels or indeed in any situation where a large number of dogs are brought into close contact, such as rescue shelters, dog shows or race tracks.

Probably the most important single pathogen is the bacterium *Bordetella bronchiseptica* which causes a severe inflammation of the nasal chambers, the trachea (windpipe) and the air passages which lead off the trachea (i.e. the bronchi). As well as a soft cough, sometimes becoming paroxysmal and leading to retching, there is usually a purulent nasal discharge. Any natural immunity to this organism, acquired as the result of previous infections, appears to last no longer than a year or eighteen months.

Inhalation of CAV-1 (the cause of infectious canine hepatitis), or of the related virus CAV-2 or of canine parainfluenza virus, will result in the onset of similar signs, although those due to CAV-2 appear to be more significant and those due to parainfluenza virus less intense. Canine herpesvirus, reovirus and mycoplasma are of minor significance on their own, although they undoubtedly increase the severity of the disease caused by the other agents.

On average the disease lasts for a period of around two or three weeks before an uneventful recovery, but because a number of organisms can be responsible, and the immunity to each is short-lived, it is possible for kennel cough to recur frequently in the same dog. Surprisingly few animals lose their appetite or show respiratory distress, but occasionally a dog (usually a very young or aged animal) will develop pneumonia and die, or be left with chronic bronchitis. There is also always the possibility that the cough may, at least in part, be due to canine distemper, which is also readily transmitted under kennel conditions and which will generally have far more serious consequences.

Nowadays it is possible for dogs to be vaccinated against the four major organisms that cause kennel cough, and this protection should certainly be provided if prolonged exposure to a group of other dogs is contemplated.

Q *I believe that exported dogs have to be tested for leptospirosis. Why is this?*

A Leptospirosis is caused by long, spiral bacteria, leptospires, belonging to the group known as spirochaetes (which incidentally includes the organism responsible for syphilis in humans). The two types (known as serotypes) of leptospires that are important in dogs are *Leptospira canicola*, which mainly causes kidney damage, and *Leptospira icterohaemorrhagiae*, which principally attacks the liver.

In fact the majority of countries do *not* require dogs to be tested for freedom from leptospirosis before they can be imported, only those in which dogs are currently free from infection with *L. canicola* (namely Australia, New Zealand, Hawaii, Norway, Sweden and Finland). This particular leptospire only causes a serious disease in dogs but will, though comparatively rarely, produce disease in humans (see page 217). Since the dog is the main reservoir host for *L. canicola* (i.e. responsible for carrying and disseminating the organism) the health authorities of those countries are anxious to avoid introducing carrier animals.

In the case of *L. icterohaemorrhagiae* the rat is the reservoir host, which makes it virtually impossible to free any country from infection. However, these same countries insist that imported dogs should also be free of *L. icterohaemorrhagiae* infection, again principally to avoid introducing carriers who will spread infection. This organism causes unpleasant diseases in both dog and man. A blood test on dogs has to be carried out within a specified time before departure from the country of origin and, because leptospiral vaccination can affect the results, a vaccination course should be completed two months before the date of testing.

These organisms are most often transmitted by infected urine, and dogs, and other animals, that recover from leptospirosis may continue to shed leptospires in their urine for months or years afterwards. A dog can become infected by consuming food or water contaminated by infected urine which may have come from rodents or dogs, or by licking the genital area of an infected dog, or even by sniffing and licking at infected urine scent-marks. Leptospires survive much longer in water, and because they can also enter the body through the skin (especially through broken skin), swimming in lakes and rivers contaminated with canine or rodent urine represents another important source of infection for dogs and humans.

Both organisms can cause fever, loss of appetite, vomiting and diarrhoea, plus abdominal pain in severe cases, and even death. Jaundice is more common in cases due to *Leptospira icterohaemorrhagiae*, and these may show pinpoint haemorrhages around the eyes and in the mouth.

Cases due to *L. canicola*, which occur more often, sometimes develop mouth ulcers. However, it would appear that many infected dogs only show very mild signs, if any at all. In fact between 10% and 40% of dogs in the USA are thought to have *L. canicola* infection *without* signs appearing.

It was believed for many years that a high proportion of the chronic renal disease in dogs was a sequel to earlier *L. canicola* infection. However because chronic renal disease is equally common in those countries from which *L. canicola* is absent it is obvious that there must be other causes of this complaint.

Q *Is it true that parvovirus infection is a new disease?*

A Yes, indeed it appears that canine parvovirus (CPV) infection is a genuinely new disease, and not just one that has been newly recognized. The testing of blood serum samples collected from dogs both before and after the first outbreaks occurred has produced no evidence (in the form of antibody against the virus) that the disease existed before 1978. In that year outbreaks were reported in North America, Australia, South Africa and Europe. Most countries can now be considered as infected.

The group known as parvoviruses consists of very small viruses (parvo simply means small), and includes the virus known as feline panleukopenia (FPL) virus, responsible for the important disease of that name (otherwise known as feline infectious enteritis) occurring in cats. It has been strongly suggested that the canine parvovirus is actually a new genetic variant, i.e. a mutation, of the FPL virus (two other variants are already known), and that this mutant may have been an unsuspected contaminant of some widely distributed biological product manufactured for use in dogs. Otherwise it is difficult to account for the sudden, dramatic appearance of CPV infection simultaneously in so many different parts of the world.

Q *Is parvovirus infection really a killer illness?*

A Despite its comparatively recent appearance CPV infection has established itself as one of the major life-threatening diseases of dogs. It is responsible for two distinct disease syndromes: the most common is an enteritis seen in dogs from weaning onwards, and the other is a heart condition of young pups.

Dogs older than five or six weeks show a typical enteritis which is often preceded by dullness and repeated vomiting. The diarrhoea may range from the passage of soft motions to blood-stained liquid (dysentery), and individuals severely affected rapidly become dehydrated and may die within two or three days. Such cases require intravenous fluid replacement but even with prompt treatment recovery is not assured, and can take several weeks. Around 10% of weaned puppies will die, though the mortality in previously healthy adult animals is no more than 1%.

Puppies infected soon after birth, or even during pregnancy (if the mother becomes infected whilst pregnant) suffer from damage to the heart muscle known as myocarditis. Fortunately, this condition is rare but on average it will kill 70% of an affected litter by eight weeks of age. Typically an apparently healthy pup of between three and six weeks of age will suddenly collapse and die. Over the next few weeks other members of the litter also die suddenly or develop acute heart failure with difficulty in breathing. Those puppies that survive beyond eight weeks probably all have some degree of heart damage, and some of these may subsequently show signs of heart failure which could prove fatal. The treatment of pups showing signs of myocarditis has been unsuccessful in preventing this outcome.

The virus is shed in large amounts in the motions of infected dogs and, like FPL virus, it is able to survive for over a year. It is resistant to most disinfectants, except aldehydes and hypochlorite bleach. Therefore indirect contact, that is contact with objects infected with the virus, plays a major role in the transmission of the disease. (Direct contact means contact with an already infected animal.) Dogs may encounter infected faeces, but in addition owners can bring the virus into premises on their shoes or clothes, and in kennels it can be transmitted via contaminated feeding bowls.

Although thorough cleaning and disinfection with bleach will reduce the level of infection, it is virtually impossible to remove the virus entirely. In other words, control based solely on hygienic measures is not effective. Fortunately, it is possible to vaccinate against this disease (see page 185), although the type of vaccine known as 'live' should not be given to pregnant bitches, in order to avoid the possibility of virus in the vaccine damaging the developing puppies.

Q *Are any canine diseases transmitted sexually?*

A The leptospiral organisms are occasionally transferred venereally, and there is a genital tumour of dogs (transmissible venereal tumour), common in southern France, Puerto Rico and the Orient, that is also spread this way. However, undoubtedly the most significant canine disease transmitted via mating is canine brucellosis, caused by the bacterium *Brucella canis*. Although fairly widespread in the USA and other parts of the world it is rare in Britain.

In both males and females it can cause infertility, and male dogs produce far fewer sperms, which show abnormalities and reduced motility. In infected bitches foetuses may die early in the pregnancy and be re-absorbed; since this is not easily detected it may be interpreted as a failure to conceive. In other cases puppies are stillborn or die soon after birth. The most frequent result of female infection, however, is abortion occurring in the last third of pregnancy. The accompanying discharge contains billions of organisms, and oral contact with this discharge is in fact a more common method of transmission than the venereal route. Infected animals may appear normal but continue to shed organisms for up to two years.

These bacteria have also, on rare occasions, infected people. However, the disease in humans is mild (fever, swollen lymph nodes and fatigue) compared with the more familiar form of brucellosis which they can contract from cattle or sheep.

Q *I have heard dog breeders speak about fading puppies. What sort of puppies are these?*

A The term 'fading puppies' is used to describe puppies that become ill, and often die, from the effects of infectious diseases soon after birth, that is to say within three or four weeks. Like canine respiratory disease (kennel cough) the fading puppy syndrome is not a single disease but includes conditions caused by a variety of micro-organisms, subdivided into 'puppy septicaemia', due to bacteria, and 'puppy viraemia', due to viruses. (Sometimes other disorders, e.g. congenital diseases and feeding problems, are also included in this syndrome.)

A number of different bacterial organisms have been implicated in puppy septicaemia where the illness is largely due to the toxins (poisons) which these bacteria produce. Those most commonly found to be the cause are *E. coli*, haemolytic streptococci and staphylococci. Although usually vigorous at birth, the puppies rapidly develop a bloated abdomen and low body temperature, and they are weak, cry and fail to suckle. Death occurs within two or three days of birth. Puppies are infected either from the surroundings, especially where hygiene is poor, or from their mothers who may be suffering from an infection of the uterus (womb) or mammary glands. At times the toxins of these bacteria may be transmitted to the puppies in the bitch's milk; this is known as 'toxic milk syndrome'.

As was mentioned previously the bacterium *Brucella canis*, which particularly affects canine reproduction, may also be a cause of infant puppy mortality in the USA, with most puppies becoming infected while still in a bitch's uterus. These may be stillborn or die within two days. Also the discharges from an infected bitch can affect pups from healthy litters if they are allowed to come into contact with them.

Puppy viraemia can result from infection with canine distemper virus (bitches infected whilst pregnant may produce dead or very sickly pups) although two other viruses are more frequently implicated; namely canine adenovirus type 1 (CAV-1) and canine herpesvirus. CAV-1 may infect the puppies during pregnancy, but probably most are infected after birth by carrier bitches, that is bitches who, whilst appearing healthy, continue to carry and excrete the virus. Canine herpesvirus differs from the other viruses mentioned in that it has never been recorded as causing serious, generalized disease in older dogs. It is however associated with a severe, and usually fatal illness in the first three weeks of life due to infection before, during, or soon after birth. Although recorded in Australia, North America and European countries (including Britain) this fatal disease is uncommon and no vaccine against it is currently available.

With both CAV-1 and herpesvirus infection pups may be born dead or very weak, but others that appear healthy when born gradually become depressed and unwilling to suckle. They show vomiting, abdominal pain and cry a lot. Death, usually of the whole litter, occurs after one or two weeks.

In the case of all of the neonatal infectious diseases referred to above an attempt should be made to limit the spread of the organisms responsible by isolating bitches that have produced 'fading puppies' and by thoroughly cleaning and disinfecting the areas where they have been housed. Obviously these measures are of particular importance in breeding kennels where several litters may be at risk.

Q Is it a fact that dogs acquire toxoplasmosis from cats?

A Yes, the cat is certainly the source of the minute protozoal parasite responsible for toxoplasmosis, called *Toxoplasma gondii,* which can infect the dog and many other species. In all of them some multiplication of the parasite occurs (called asexual reproduction) but only in the cat does it undergo sexual reproduction to produce a stage which the cat passes out in its faeces (an oocyst) and which, after about five days' development, is able to infect other animals. Because of this the cat is known as a final host of the parasite. The other species which become infected, but do not themselves produce infective stages, are called intermediate hosts. These intermediate hosts include most warm-blooded animals; for example, dogs, cattle, sheep, pigs, rodents, birds and humans.

Although a dog may become directly infected with *Toxoplasma* by eating an oocyst in, or derived from, cats' faeces the commonest route of infection for dogs is eating under-cooked meat or the flesh of prey animals which is infected. The parasite is not excreted by the intermediate host but it can pass from one intermediate host to another along a food chain. So a dog eating an infected mouse, or a man eating 'raw' steak or uncooked ham from an infected animal, will in turn become infected.

In pregnant bitches, as in other pregnant female intermediate hosts, *Toxoplasma* can transfer from the tissue of the mother to those of her offspring whilst they are in the womb and may damage them. In some species this congenital transmission of infection may continue for several generations.

In infected dogs (and other hosts) the parasites are generally present in the liver, lungs, brain, eye, heart and skeletal muscles. If the host has very little immunity, multiplication of the parasite occurs rapidly producing an acute phase (acute toxoplasmosis). After a time the host develops an immunity, with the result that the rate of multiplication slows down and the parasites become localized in cysts in the tissues. These cysts may remain intact throughout the life of the host and cause no harm. With time, however, the immunity will decline, and if the animal should then be exposed to stress the cysts can break down, releasing the parasites and causing another acute phase (i.e. a relapse). Infection with distemper virus is one event that can initiate reversion from the chronic to acute phase. Clinical signs of acute toxoplasmosis (e.g. fever, pneumonia, nervous signs) rarely appear but are more likely in young animals. Occasionally severe injury may be caused by the multiplying organisms destroying a significant number of cells in one of the vital organs, and infected bitches may produce stillborn or weak puppies.

Toxoplasmosis occurs worldwide and surveys to detect antibodies indicate that about a third of all dogs have been infected. Opportunities for infection can be reduced by feeding only canned, dried or adequately cooked foods (exposure to 155 °F (60 °C) kills the parasite), preventing hunting and scavenging and limiting contact with cat faeces by regularly emptying the litter tray of any cat in the household.

Toxoplasmosis is also an important human infection; around half a billion people are infected throughout the world. In the United States 50% of the population have been infected and 3000 congenitally infected infants are born each year. However, the dog, unlike the cat, does not represent a source of infection for man.

Q *Is ringworm really caused by a worm?*

A No, although in the past this was believed to be the case. In fact this skin condition has nothing to do with worms. It is due to the effect of parasitic fungi (dermatophytes) and the one which is most commonly responsible in the dog is called *Microsporum canis*. Despite its name this fungus is best adapted to the skin of the cat and adult cats may be infected without developing skin lesions. Cats represent an important reservoir of infection for both dogs and humans. Of lesser importance in dogs is the fungus *Trichophyton mentagrophytes* (carried by rodents), plus in warmer climes *Microsporum gypseum*, found in the soil.

These fungi grow on the 'dead' surface layer of the skin, including the hairs and very occasionally the nails. Young animals are more often affected because they have poor immunity and because of the lower fatty acid composition of the skin. Lesions are intensified if the animal is deficient in vitamin A.

The spores of the fungi (except *M. gypseum*) are transmitted between animals, and often to humans as well, by direct and indirect contact. Contaminated combs and brushes are important in spreading infection, and in the environment (e.g. on dog beds, leads and collars) spores can persist for over a year.

Ringworm is correctly classed as an infectious disease, although the signs typical of many other infectious diseases, for example a high temperature and loss of appetite, are absent. In most cases there are patches of baldness (alopecia) where the hairs have broken off, although only 10 % of lesions appear 'typically' circular. The head, feet and legs are most often affected, but sometimes large areas of the body are involved. Scaling and crusting of the skin can be severe, and the crusts may become secondarily infected with bacteria, producing pus. Gradually the lesions will enlarge and spread although, unless they are inflamed, itching and scratching does not occur. Some dogs show no very obvious lesions – only thinning of the coat or a few abnormal hairs.

In the majority of cases, though not always, hairs affected with *M. canis* will glow with a characteristic yellowish-green fluorescence (similar to that seen on luminous watch dials) when placed under ultra-violet light of a particular wavelength. This fluorescence does not occur with the other fungi mentioned. In all cases identification can be confirmed by examining affected hairs under a microscope, and by growing the fungus from them on special culture media.

Q *How should ringworm be treated?*

A In dealing with an infection, it is important to have all dogs *and cats* on the premises checked, and to isolate infected individuals. All contaminated articles should preferably be burned, and all surfaces should be disinfected. Efficient disinfectants include solutions of iodophors (e.g. Pevidine) or formalin (although this is unpleasant to use). For disinfecting small articles, alcohol may be used.

The diseased hairs on infected animals should be closely clipped away and burned; but always sterilize the clippers afterwards. Fungicidal shampoos or creams may then be applied. However, these measures should always be combined with between four and six weeks of oral dosing with the anti-fungal antibiotic griseofulvin (which strangely has no effect on bacteria). The drug becomes concentrated in the keratin of the new hairs (or the nails and skin) as they grow, rendering them resistant to fungal attack. Feeding oily food at the same time as griseofulvin is given enhances its absorption. However, it should not be given to pregnant dogs or cats because it can produce deformities in the developing offspring.

If any other animal or person within the household with a known infected pet develops itchy lesions on the skin, appropriate veterinary or medical attention should be sought.

Q *How could my dog get rabies?*

A Rabies is generally transmitted through the bite of an infected animal, by virus particles in the saliva of that animal being implanted in the bite wound. Other routes of infection are possible but much less common; for example infective saliva can enter through a scratch or an existing skin wound, or droplets of saliva may be inhaled. An animal may even eat the carcase of a rabies victim. In countries where rabies is established (enzootic) in the wild life, dogs frequently become infected by bites from rabid animals such as foxes, skunks, or bats. The proportion of cases in dogs attributable to bites from previously infected dogs and cats is related to the density of unvaccinated pets in that area. The incubation period in the dog is variable and though it is seldom longer than four months it *may* exceed six months. On average the clinical signs of rabies, which are the result of viral damage to the nervous system, appear between three and eight weeks after the bite.

Q *How would I know if my dog had rabies?*

A The disease characteristically has three phases. First, there is a prodromal stage, usually lasting less than two days (sometimes only a few hours) in which the dog shows a personality change. It may become more affectionate, or appear apprehensive and timid and want to hide away, or it may be agitated and bark excessively. This is followed in turn by a stage of excitability and irritability, and then a stage of paralysis. An animal is said to have 'furious' rabies or 'dumb' rabies depending on which of these two stages is encountered.

In dogs the stage of excitement usually lasts no more than two or three days and may be so short as to escape detection. In this stage affected animals are extremely restless and hypersensitive to light and noise, and will bite at inanimate objects as well as their owner and other animals. Dogs often develop a depraved appetite, chewing and swallowing such materials as wood, stones and straw, and they may chew at a restraining chain or kennel bars with such force as to break their teeth. If unconfined they may run for many miles, biting everything in their path. As paralysis begins to involve the muscles of the throat (larynx and pharynx) dogs develop a husky voice and drool saliva because of difficulty in swallowing. Some dogs die in a convulsion (fit) at the end of this stage; if not they become progressively paralysed. This paralytic or dumb phase is the stage in which rabid dogs are most often observed, and it may easily be confused with having a bone stuck in the throat, or with poisoning, or with an attack of distemper. Animals with generalized paralysis will die in a coma within four days. Hydrophobia, the fear of swallowing water (because of laryngeal paralysis) or even of seeing water, which triggers off violent muscular contractions and which is seen in about 50 % of human cases of rabies, is *not* a feature.

From the onset of clinical signs dogs rarely survive longer than ten days, and most die within five. During the time when signs are present, and for at least twenty-four hours beforehand, the dog's saliva is infected. Dog bites are the most frequent source of human infection.

Q *Why should a dog showing signs of rabies be destroyed?*

A In essence, once clinical signs of rabies are present in a dog, or in man, no treatment is effective and the disease is always fatal. (There *are* two recorded cases of humans recovering, one having received the extremely rare and expensive anti-viral drug interferon, though in both there was some doubt about the diagnosis, *and* there is also clear evidence that two experimentally infected Beagles recovered. Nevertheless, such cases *must* be regarded as extremely rare.)

Because rabid dogs cannot be cured, and represent such a source of danger to the human population, *in most countries their destruction is necessary as soon as possible.* However, in countries such as Britain, where the disease is not established, they may instead be isolated until they die naturally. But if a dog showing typical signs has bitten someone, it is important that its brain be examined as soon as can be arranged to enable the diagnosis to be confirmed, and thereby establish whether or not the bitten individual should undergo a course of rabies vaccination. Any suspected rabies case should *not* be handled but confined in an enclosed area from which it cannot escape and the public health authorities or police informed.

Because of the inherent dangers, those engaged in jobs where they are likely to encounter rabid animals, e.g. in quarantine kennels, are routinely vaccinated.

In some countries, such as the United States, what happens to a dog that has recently been bitten by another animal known to be rabid depends largely upon whether the dog has been previously vaccinated or not. In those instances, treatment with antiserum or vaccine *can* be given but the World Health Organization strongly recommends that all unvaccinated animals should be put to sleep immediately because of the risk they represent. If the owner is unwilling to allow this, the un-vaccinated animal, whether treated or not, must be isolated and observed for the onset of rabies signs for at least six months. Vaccinated dogs, however, are usually re-vaccinated and isolated for at least sixty, and preferably ninety days.

Q *If my dog has been vaccinated against rabies abroad, will it have to go into quarantine?*

A This depends upon the countries between which you intend to transfer your dog. As a general rule, countries where rabies is already well-estab-lished in the wildlife do not require dogs to be quarantined, e.g. the continental USA and India. On the other hand, countries which are rabies free *may* insist upon a period of quarantine for dogs entering the country, e.g. Australia, Great Britain and Hawaii (despite being a state of the USA). This requirement for compulsory quarantine may be waived if the dog comes directly from another rabies-free country without being off-loaded or otherwise coming into contact with other possibly infected animals *en route* (e.g. from Great Britain to Hawaii, or New Zealand to Australia).

However, Great Britain always requires six months' quarantine for dogs, regardless of the country of origin. Dogs entering Australia have to undergo sixty days' quarantine if they arrive on a ship and ninety if transported by air, though if the crates used for transport have had their seals broken this period is automatically extended to nine months. (In fact, Australia and New Zealand will in general only import animals from each other and from Great Britain and Ireland. Animals from other countries have to undergo six months' quarantine in Britain or Ireland and then a further six months' residence there *before* they can be exported to Australia or New Zealand.) Dogs entering Hawaii from the rest of the United States, whether vaccinated or not, have to undergo a minimum 120 days' quarantine.

Quarantine may appear a harsh measure, but those countries which are fortunate enough not to have reservoirs of rabies in their wild animals wish to avoid this happening, and many believe that a period of quarantine is the most effective method of prevention. The vaccination of dogs and cats against rabies will, in general, prevent them from acquiring the disease and thus from being a source of infection for man. However, with a disease which has such a long incubation as rabies there is always the risk that a vaccinated animal may in fact be incubating rabies at the time of vaccination. Once admitted to a country, such an animal could readily transfer it to the wildlife, such as foxes, which in Europe are believed to be the main reservoir of infection. Therefore, although a vaccination policy is the best one for countries infected by rabies, it is regarded as inferior to a quarantine policy for countries where rabies is *not* established.

Once there is a reservoir of rabies in the wild animals of a country, these constitute an important source of infection for man and for any unvaccinated domestic animals. Undoubtedly this alters many people's attitude towards wildlife conservation, and indeed avoidance of wild animals is recommended in infected countries. The periodic eradication of wildlife from various areas (by trapping, shooting, poisoning and gassing) may be required in an infected country to stop the spread of rabies. Inevitably rabies also causes a great deal of pain and suffering amongst the wild species themselves.

Q *Can I have my dog vaccinated against rabies?*

A In some countries, or parts of some countries where rabies is prevalent, canine vaccination against rabies is required by law. This is the case in all but seven states of the USA (the regulations for the vaccination of dogs and cats in the USA vary from state to state, and within a state between counties and even towns), and in north-eastern France if you wish to exercise your dog without a lead or to exhibit the dog. In most countries, such as Italy, Switzerland, Germany and Denmark, vaccination is voluntary. In some countries, such as Sweden and Britain, rabies vaccination is prohibited.

In Britain, rabies vaccination is only permitted for animals which are genuinely being exported to countries that require rabies vaccination to have been performed in advance, and for animals in quarantine kennels and catteries, largely to avoid the risk of infection being transferred between quarantined animals.

The reason for not allowing general vaccination in Britain is that the public would probably tend to rely upon vaccination for protection (even though this can never be 100 % protection), and therefore would be less likely to comply with the quarantine regulations and would delay in reporting clinical cases. For a voluntary vaccination policy to be effective, a minimum of 70% of the susceptible animals need to be vaccinated. Experience in European countries with a voluntary vaccination policy shows that usually only around 30% of animals are vaccinated. Finally, vaccination may also interfere with the confirmation of the diagnosis of rabies by producing changes in the brain which have a similar appearance to those occurring in cases of natural infection.

Q *I want to provide my dog with the best possible protection. What diseases should it be vaccinated against?*

A At present there are commercial vaccines specifically produced against eight important diseases of dogs. These are canine distemper, infectious canine hepatitis (ICH), canine parvovirus infection, rabies, leptospirosis (due to both of the common serotypes) and the three most important causes of kennel cough (or canine respiratory disease), namely the canine adenoviruses, canine parainfluenza virus and *Bordetella bronchiseptica* (see Table II). Although this appears a formidable list two points should be borne in mind.

1 It is common for vaccines against different diseases to be combined in *one injection*. For example vaccines against distemper, ICH and leptospirosis are frequently given simultaneously. (However, there is a limit to the number of vaccines that should be given *at the same time* because if too many are administered the antibody-producing cells may be overloaded and fail to respond fully to all the vaccines.)

2 The virus CAV-1 which is the cause of infectious canine hepatitis (see page 172) has been used to prepare both killed vaccines and live vaccines, either of which can be used to protect against this disease. (Killed, otherwise known as dead, or inactivated, vaccines contain materials from dead organisms to stimulate the production of immunity, whereas live vaccines contain *living* organisms for the same purpose. The live organisms will have been specially treated to weaken them so that they will *not* produce disease.) Live vaccines produce much greater immunity, i.e. which lasts for a much longer period of time. Unfortunately, whereas the killed CAV-1 vaccines are free from side-effects a small proportion of dogs which receive the live CAV-1 vaccines develop corneal oedema ('blue-eye') and some may develop mild kidney damage resulting in shedding of virus into the environment, which is undesirable.

In recent years live vaccines against ICH have been prepared using the related virus CAV-2 (because the two viruses are very similar CAV-2 vaccines also protect against ICH). A live CAV-2 vaccine has been recommended in preference to either type of CAV-1 vaccine because it combines long, solid immunity against ICH with the absence of ocular and renal side-effects. In addition, it provides optimal protection against kennel cough caused by both adenoviruses (there is no guarantee that dogs vaccinated with CAV-1 vaccines are protected against *respiratory disease* caused by CAV-1). Recently, however, the whole debate has been re-opened by evidence that certain live CAV-1 vaccines do not result in 'blue-eye' or virus shedding, and that a particular live CAV-2 vaccine *may* cause virus shedding plus microscopic lung damage.

Vaccines used against the bacterial disease leptospirosis are always killed, and those against distemper and parainfluenza virus infection are invariably live, but (as with the adenoviruses) both killed *and* live vaccines are available against rabies, kennel cough due to *Bordetella* and parvovirus infection. One injection of a live vaccine is sufficient to stimulate adequate antibody production, but with a dead vaccine two injections are normally required, about two or three weeks apart, to achieve reasonably effective levels of antibody. If pregnant bitches are vaccinated to boost their immunity, only killed vaccine should be used to avoid the possibility of live virus damaging the developing foetuses.

In most countries where rabies is known to be present it is clearly wise to have your dog protected against this disease, even though it may not be compulsory. Different types of rabies vaccines are available and some countries specify which one may be used. As has been mentioned, in some countries where rabies does not (at present) occur routine rabies vaccination is prohibited.

It is also possible, though not generally thought necessary, to immunize dogs against tetanus (lockjaw) using a tetanus toxoid (i.e. the toxin from the tetanus organisms chemically treated to render it non-poisonous). This acts in the same way as a killed vaccine.

Q *How old should my puppy be when it is first vaccinated?*

A Newborn puppies receive ready-made antibodies from the blood of their mother which are transferred to them in the first milk, or colostrum, which they suckle. These antibodies are not digested, but are absorbed intact from the young puppy's intestine into its blood stream during the first one or two days of life. (In the dog very little antibody is transferred from the blood of the mother to that of the foetus whilst the young are still in the womb, although this route is the only one used in man. In the dog 95 % of maternal antibodies are transferred in the colostrum.)

The transferred maternal antibodies provide protection for the young animal while its own immunity is developing, and those against distemper, ICH and leptospirosis persist for between eight and twelve weeks depending on how much colostrum a particular puppy has consumed. (About 45 % of the existing level of maternal antibody disappears with each passing week.) The antibody level in any particular individual cannot readily be established, although possibly as many as 50 % of pups will have lost all maternal antibodies soon after six weeks old.

If a puppy is vaccinated while these maternal antibodies are still present, the antibodies can react with and neutralize the vaccine leaving the puppy with no long-lasting immunity. Therefore, it is usually recommended that where there is no particular urgency to have a puppy vaccinated against the above diseases, the first injection should not be given until it is twelve weeks old, i.e. the longest period for which maternal antibodies *normally* persist. However, there is the possibility that the maternal antibodies might not last that long, and where there is a high risk of the puppy being exposed to infection during its early life, e.g. in an area where distemper is prevalent or where contact with many strange dogs is difficult to avoid, vaccination can be given earlier, usually at eight weeks old, and then again at twelve weeks old. Alternatively it is possible to circumvent the neutralizing effect of maternal antibodies on distemper vaccine by administering a dose of measles vaccine (see page 188).

Slightly different recommendations regarding timing are made in respect of *Bordetella* and parvovirus infections, and rabies. For protection against parvovirus infection the vaccine (regardless of whether it is of the killed or live type), should be given first at eight weeks old and again three or four weeks later. In the case of *Bordetella* there are two kinds of vaccine: one is an injectable product, first given after the animal has reached three weeks old and then repeated three or four weeks afterwards, and the second is an intranasal vaccine (i.e. administered as drops into the nasal chamber) which can be given from two weeks of age. Vaccination against *Bordetella* can start much earlier simply because not much maternal antibody against this organism is likely to be transferred and it will therefore cause little interference. Vaccination against both of these infections is comparatively new and therefore changes in the recommendations may well be made in the light of experience.

In general, rabies vaccine should not be given before three months of age. It can be injected on the same occasion as other vaccines but should be given independently, i.e. not mixed, and at a different site on the body.

As was mentioned in earlier chapters it is very important that before, and for two weeks after, the last injection of a vaccination course the young animal should be kept away from other dogs and places which they visit (ideally confined to its own garden) to avoid the possibility of infection occurring before an effective immunity has developed.

Q *You mentioned giving puppies a dose of measles vaccine? Surely dogs don't get measles, do they?*

A No, dogs don't get measles, but the viruses that cause canine distemper and measles in humans are very closely related. If a dog is given an injection of measles vaccine it will develop immunity to canine distemper — an example of 'heterotypic vaccination'. The immunity is not as complete as that conferred by a live distemper vaccine, but the administration of measles vaccine to puppies has one special benefit. The advantage is that in general measles vaccine will *not* be neutralized to any appreciable extent by any maternal antibody to distemper which may still be present in the puppy. Consequently a dose of measles vaccine can be given to puppies which are at particular risk from distemper (e.g. in breeding and boarding kennels, or petshops) at an early age (five or six weeks onwards), with the almost total certainty of providing immunity. The usual distemper vaccine should then be given between twelve and fourteen weeks old to provide longer-lasting protection.

This procedure overcomes the so-called 'immunity gap' which can arise if a puppy vaccinated at eight weeks old with distemper vaccine still has maternal antibody (so that the vaccine is neutralized) but the antibody disappears before the second distemper injection is given at twelve weeks; during the period without antibody and before *effective* vaccination the puppy is very vulnerable to infection. Recently it has been claimed that a combination of measles vaccine and distemper vaccine given at six weeks old will give even more certain protection.

Measles vaccination must be considered only as a temporary measure to provide protection until effective distemper vaccination can be given; it does not prevent infection with distemper virus but protects against development of the disease. There is no advantage in giving measles vaccine to older dogs, indeed its use should be avoided, especially in breeding bitches. This is to avoid the danger that a pregnant bitch might still have high levels of measles antibody which will be passed to her offspring and interfere with their measles vaccination. Measles vaccines intended for human use should not be used in dogs, and *vice versa*.

Q *If puppies are orphaned and don't get any natural protection from their mother's first milk, can they be vaccinated at birth?*

A If the puppies haven't received any substantial amount of maternal antibodies, because they never suckled after birth (for example in cases where the mother dies giving birth), then it would seem logical to vaccinate them as soon as possible. However, the value of vaccination depends upon the ability of the puppy's immune mechanisms to be able to respond to the vaccine, and in the first two weeks of life the production of antibodies following the administration of a vaccine is usually poor. This is because the body temperature of puppies during that period is often less than the 100.5–102.5 °F (38–39 °C) required to ensure the development of effective immunity. Indeed, giving a live vaccine during that time might even be harmful. Since there are hyperimmune sera available to give instant protection against distemper, ICH and leptospirosis, it is preferable at that age to give a dose of serum followed four weeks later by vaccination. Where vaccination is given at such an early age it is best to repeat it three or four weeks later.

Q *Does vaccination always work?*

A No, regrettably it does not. There is no vaccine which is capable of fully protecting 100 % of the animals inoculated with it. One important reason is that there is always a small proportion of animals whose immune systems do not respond in the normal manner to vaccines, or for that matter to natural infections. As a result, these individuals will not develop good immunity. This, however, is a fault of the animal's body and not of the vaccine. Unfortunately, unless their antibody levels are measured, which is difficult to arrange, such animals cannot be distinguished.

The vaccine itself must be administered within its stated expiry date and have been stored and administered in accordance with the manufacturer's instructions. Vaccines are stored under refrigeration, though not frozen, because they are inactivated more rapidly at higher temperatures. The entire dose must be given and not divided between dogs, and a clean syringe and needle must be used, uncontaminated by any disinfectant or antiseptic in which it may have been stored and which will inactivate the vaccine. Veterinary surgeons will invariably pay close attention to these important points; breeders and kennel owners have not always done so, with disastrous consequences.

Puppies should not be vaccinated if they still have maternal antibodies, as already discussed, otherwise the antibodies will neutralize the vaccines. Also vaccination should not take place if there is evidence of a disease already present (high body temperature, etc.). This is because the antibody-producing cells may already be fully occupied reacting to the disease and will not respond effectively to the vaccine. This is the reason for a dog receiving a clinical examination immediately prior to vaccination. However, as has already been mentioned, on rare occasions a dog may, at the time of examination, be incubating the disease against which it is being vaccinated so that although there are no clinical signs to indicate the fact, infection has already occurred. Clinical signs usually appear shortly afterwards.

Simply giving a vaccine does not always mean that the animal cannot become infected, but that it has increased protection against the disease. In some cases an infection can be so overwhelming as to swamp the animal's immunity. Certain drugs given internally will suppress a dog's immune responses (immuno-suppressive drugs) and in general vaccines should not be given during or for one month after treatment with them. Such drugs include corticosteroids, used to treat inflammatory conditions, and anti-cancer drugs, such as cyclophosphamide and azothiaprine.

In situations where the immune response is likely to be impaired, because of concurrent disease or drug administration, vaccination should be delayed. However, temporary protection can be given in the form of an injection of hyperimmune serum.

By way of reassurance, a survey of over 15,000 dogs vaccinated against distemper, in an area where it was common, showed that less than $1/2$% contracted the disease.

Q *Does vaccination ever cause the disease?*

A With modern vaccines this is extremely unlikely to occur and could only happen with live vaccines in which the viruses were not as weakened as was believed. Rare cases in which a dog develops the disease shortly after administration of a vaccine are almost always due to the animal having already been in the incubation stage of the disease (i.e. after infection but before signs appear) when vaccination was performed.

Occasionally a dog will show an allergic reaction to a vaccine, which requires treatment with adrenaline.

Q *How long will vaccination protect my dog? Will its immunity ever need to be boosted by re-vaccination?*

A Unless the dog comes into natural contact with the infectious organisms responsible for the various diseases described, the level of antibodies in its blood will gradually decline. Whether or not this has happened, however, cannot readily be ascertained. Therefore, in order to boost the level of antibodies and keep them at an effective level to combat the infections, it is advisable for repeat vaccinations to be performed.

The plasma cells which produce antibodies can 'remember' a particular bacterium or virus, and if that organism reappears in the body they can rapidly produce large amounts of the specific antibody against it. For maximum protection it is recommended that vaccination is repeated annually *as a general rule*, though the persistence of immunity does vary with the disease. Immunity conferred by killed vaccines wanes more rapidly than from live; for this reason leptospiral vaccines are always given annually. *Bordetella* and parvovirus vaccines are repeated at intervals of between six months and a year. Rabies vaccination is repeated annually with killed vaccines, but with live vaccines, following re-vaccination at the end of the first year, it is necessary only every third year thereafter.

The immunity provided by modern canine distemper and canine adenovirus live vaccines lasts for many years (perhaps even lifelong in the case of the latter), though because a few dogs have a much more rapid fall in antibody levels than is usual, many manufacturers play safe by advising annual re-vaccination with their products. Certainly over seven years old some dogs have a decreased ability to produce antibody and therefore after this age annual re-vaccination is a prudent precaution.

Vaccinations should be up to date before dogs are placed in situations where there is a high risk of exposure to infection, e.g. before going into kennels or to a dog show. If they are not up to date immunity should be boosted three or four weeks beforehand, though with the intranasal *Bordetella* vaccine a minimum of only five days is required.

Because great advances are currently being made in vaccine production, and the recommendations for the use of different products vary, this is a topic that should always be discussed with your veterinarian.

Q *I have just taken in a stray dog which, of course, I want to have vaccinated against all possible diseases. Will the vet be able to tell if it has already been vaccinated, and will it harm the dog to be vaccinated again?*

A First of all, a vet would not be able to tell from examining the dog whether or not it has been vaccinated against the usual infectious diseases; unless of course it is showing obvious signs of one of them which would strongly suggest that it has not been recently vaccinated.

It *is* possible to measure the level of antibody in the blood against a particular organism, although this will not tell you whether it is the result of vaccination or natural infection; not that this matters because the immunity would be the same. However, this type of test is not done routinely and would therefore be expensive and difficult to arrange, particularly since it would need to be done separately for each disease.

More importantly, it would be unnecessary to go to this trouble and expense since routine vaccination would be cheaper and would not be harmful even if it was not required.

11

Other Diseases and Operations

Q *Are the diseases of dogs similar to those of humans?*

A Well of course the organs of the dog are essentially the same, and serve the same purposes, as in humans and because they are likely to be damaged in similar ways (by micro-organisms, parasites, trauma, cancer and so on) there is a great deal of similarity between the diseases of both species. The differences that occur are largely a matter of degree, for example the most common type of heart disorder in man also occurs in dogs though much less frequently. Urinary calculi (stones) occur in both species but in man they generally form in the kidneys and in the dog almost always in the bladder.

In some instances a canine disease so closely resembles its human counterpart that it can be used as a 'model' for studying the disease in man. Examples are urinary tract infections, diabetes mellitus, colitis, hypertrophy (enlargement) of the prostate gland, epilepsy, Perthes disease (a hip condition in children and dogs), melanoma of the skin and carcinoma of the breast, the inherited blood-clotting disorder haemophilia, and duodenal ulcers. Congenital heart conditions, the disorders of the joints referred to as osteo-arthritis and rheumatoid arthritis, the muscle weakness known as myasthenia gravis, and certain types of glomerulonephritis (causing renal damage) and intestinal malabsorption (failure to absorb food from the intestine) also appear almost identical in the dog and in man. The effects of allergies, poisons and abnormal hormone levels also show many similarities.

Many orthopaedic injuries, from muscle damage in athletes and racing dogs to bone fractures, are very alike in both species, although different sites may be involved. However, the dog never suffers from a broken collar bone (clavicle) which humans commonly injure in falls, because this bone is poorly developed in the dog and appears merely as a fragment of bone surrounded by muscle near to the shoulder joint. Also, although the human ankle is very commonly injured the equivalent joint in the dog — the hock — is seldom the site of lameness. The so-called 'slipped disc' occurs in both dogs and humans (see page 213), though paralysis of the hind legs, common in the dog, is rare in man.

The major differences involve infectious diseases, many of which are not transferable; an example of the type of natural immunity called genetic immunity. Consequently people do not contract canine distemper or kennel cough, and dogs do not suffer from influenza or chicken pox. The dog has no appendix so dogs do not suffer from appendicitis. Nor do they suffer from haemorrhoids (piles) or varicose veins, disorders which clinicians attribute to the upright stance of humans.

Q *Do vets ever use homeopathic remedies?*

A Yes, at present there are a few veterinary surgeons who practise homeopathic medicine, and also some who treat pet animals by acupuncture. But, just as in human medicine, these constitute only a small minority of all practitioners. Many vets have expressed an interest in these relatively unknown forms of treatment for animal ills but before adopting them would require more substantial evidence of their efficacy.

Q *What parasites do dogs get?*

A Table III lists the common external parasites (ectoparasites) and internal parasites (endoparasites) of the dog. Those marked with an asterisk are the ones most commonly found, and those marked with a cross occur in North America, and Australia, but not in European countries, except in imported dogs. The table is by no means comprehensive because it excludes several parasites known to occur in the dog particularly in warmer climates, on the grounds that they cannot be considered common. For instance in many parts of the USA the skin of dogs kept on damp hay or straw bedding may be invaded by the normally free-living worm *Pelodera strongyloides*, producing intense itching and inflammation (rhabditic dermatitis).

Of the internal parasites in the table, the ascarids (roundworms), hookworms and tapeworms inhabit the dog's small intestine. Also occasionally found in the intestine of dogs (e.g. in the USA and Australia) is a strain of the minute threadworm *Strongyloides stercoralis*. Dogs are usually infected by the larvae penetrating the skin, and debilitated animals and puppies up to four months old can develop diarrhoea and difficulty in breathing. This worm is unique amongst the parasites of mammals in having some generations which are parasitic (composed exclusively of female worms) and others which are free-living in the soil. Dogs in the USA and Australia may also be infected with the oesophageal worm *(Spirocerca lupi)* which inhabits growths in the wall of the oesophagus (gullet) and with stomach worms (*Physaloptera* and *Gnathostoma*) which can cause vomiting.

Tapeworms which are found worldwide are listed in the table, but in particular areas dogs may become infected with *Diphyllobothrium latum* (principally in northern Europe) and *Spirometra erinacei*, the zipper worm (e.g. Australia and North America). Neither causes great concern to the dog but the developmental stages of *Spirometra* can produce painful subcutaneous swellings in humans (sparganosis). As well as the lung fluke which is included in the table, other flukes (flat, leaf-shaped parasites) are occasionally encountered, especially in the intestine. One example is *Nanophyetus salmincola*, responsible for the transmission of salmon poisoning disease organisms to dogs in the Pacific north-west of North America.

Q *Why is it so important to get rid of fleas on my dog?*

A Adult fleas are parasitic and survive by sucking the blood of their hosts. They are the most important single cause of skin disease in dogs. In many countries (e.g. England, Australia and the USA) the flea most commonly found on dogs is the cat flea *(Ctenocephalides felis)*, and paradoxically the dog flea *(Ctenocephalides canis)* is relatively uncommon. The dog flea predominates in Ireland, however, and in Greyhound kennels in England. A cat is often responsible for introducing cat fleas into a household, having acquired them from other cats which it meets outdoors. They will then readily transfer to dogs *and* to humans. Alternatively fleas may be acquired from other dogs or from infected surroundings, such as kennels. Occasionally dogs become infected with fleas from other species such as rabbits, birds, rats and hedgehogs; even at times human fleas! In a London survey 20% of dogs were harbouring fleas. (In North America and Australia smaller fleas, poultry sticktight fleas, are sometimes found firmly attached to the skin, especially around the face and between the toes, from which they are best removed with tweezers.) Interestingly, fleas are rare in mountain areas above 5000 feet (about 1500 metres) and in deserts where the humidity is low.

Fleas are important for five reasons:

1 Their bites can cause extreme irritation so that the dog may bite and scratch at itself.

2 Some dogs develop a severe allergic response to the saliva which the flea injects as it bites. Thereafter even a single bite will cause a flare-up of earlier lesions. The worst affected areas are generally the region spreading forwards from the base of the tail and the inside of the thighs; sometimes the lower abdomen. At these sites the skin appears reddened with several small swellings. As a result of the dog biting at itself to relieve

Table III   Parasites of the Dog

EXTERNAL PARASITES

* Fleas: Ctenocephalides felis
       Occasionally other species
Biting lice: Trichodectes canis
        + Heterodoxus species
Sucking louse, Linognathus setosus
'Itch mite', Sarcoptes scabiei canis
Follicular mite, Demodex canis
* Ear mite, Otodectes canis
Fur mite, Cheyletiella yasguri
Harvest mite, Trombicula autumnalis, and related species (North American chigger, heel bug, velvet mite, etc.)
Ticks: hard (ixodid) ticks
     + soft (argasid) ticks
Fly larvae: blow-fly maggots
       + Cuterebra (rodent botfly) larvae

INTERNAL PARASITES

Nematode worms
* Ascarids (roundworms): Toxacara canis
                 Toxascaris leonina
Hookworms: Uncinaria stenocephala
       *+ Ancylostoma species
Whipworm, Trichuris vulpis
Lungworm, Filaroides osleri
Tracheal worm, Capillaria aerophila
Heartworm, Dirofilaria immitis
+ Giant kidney worm, Dioctophyma renale
Bladderworm, Capillaria plica
+ Eyeworm, Thelazia californiensis

Tapeworms (Cestode worms)
* Dipylidium caninum
Taenia hydatigena
Taenia multiceps
Taenia ovis
Taenia pisiformis
Taenia serialis
* Echinococcus granulosus

Tongue worm
Linguatula serrata

Flukes
+ Lung fluke, Paragonimus kellicotti

---

* Asterisks denote most commonly occurring
+ Found in North America and/or Australia, but not in European countries
Parasitic protozoa, e.g. Toxoplasma gondii, have been included in the table of infectious diseases of the dog.

the irritation, hair is lost and moist, inflamed areas may appear. If allowed to persist the skin ultimately becomes totally hairless and arranged in thick, grey folds.

3 A heavy flea infestation in young puppies may result in so much blood being lost that anaemia develops.

4 As the flea bites, some of the blood taken from one dog may be transferred to the next. If the first dog was in a certain stage of an infectious disease, along with the blood there may also be transferred bacteria, such as *Francisella tularensis*, the cause of tularaemia, or viruses such as that responsible for lymphocytic choriomeningitis. The larvae of the filaroid worm *Dipetalonema reconditum* can also be transferred from the blood of one dog to that of another by flea bites.

5 Fleas can transmit the common tapeworm of the dog *(Dipylidium caninum)*. A dog infected with a tapeworm will from time to time shed from its anus segments of the worm containing eggs. If one of these tapeworm eggs happens to be eaten by a flea larva it eventually develops into a cystic form inside the adult flea. Then if this flea should subsequently be swallowed by a dog as it grooms itself, the cystic form develops into a new tapeworm in the dog's intestine. If the infected flea is eaten by a cat, or even a child, then the tapeworm will develop in the cat's or child's intestine.

Q *How can I get rid of fleas on my dog?*

A Adult fleas spend only short periods of time on a dog, just sufficient to obtain a meal of blood, and therefore may not be found when looked for on the coat. If they are present, they are easily seen with the naked eye as small, dark brown insects moving swiftly over the skin, particularly at the base of the tail. It is more common to find evidence of their presence in the form of flea dirts, looking like specks of dark grit, on the skin surface. These consist mainly of dried blood and can be distinguished from grit by the fact that if they are placed on a piece of damp cotton wool a red-brown stain spreads out from them over the dampened surface.

Fleas will be most numerous in the *environment* of the dog, which is where the female flea lays her eggs. This includes not only the dog's bed and bedding (including chairs and beds if the pet sleeps on them), but also between floor boards, tiles and sections of linoleum, in the pile of fitted carpets and even beneath skirting boards. Therefore, the successful removal of fleas requires a concerted attack; not only treatment of the dog itself, but also of other animals in the household, especially any cats, and of the surroundings.

Many proprietary parasiticidal powders or sprays are available for the treatment of your dog, either from your veterinary surgeon or from a pet shop. If a spray is used take care to follow the instructions *carefully*; it is very easy to over-do the treatment and if the animal licks off, or absorbs, an excessive amount of the spray it may be poisoned. Raise the hair by brushing it the 'wrong' way and spray against the lie of the coat from 6–8 inches (15–20 cm) away for between three and fifteen seconds (the smaller the animal, the shorter the time), avoiding the eyes and mouth. The hissing noise as the aerosol discharges often startles dogs, so keep a firm hold on the patient. If powders are used it is advisable to dust them thoroughly into the coat, again brushing the hair the 'wrong' way. Leave the powder in place for half an hour, during which time the animal should be watched carefully to prevent it licking its coat, and then brush out as much powder as possible. Taking the dog for a walk, playing with it or feeding it may help to distract it from grooming itself during this period.

It is possible to apply special insecticidal solutions, or suspensions, to the dog's coat, but because these are not washed off afterwards there is always a risk of the dog licking off toxic amounts. Insecticidal shampoos are also available and since they are completely rinsed out these are less likely to prove harmful; their use may sometimes be advised prior to treatment with a powder or spray. Tablet treatments are available as well; the drug in the tablets passes into the dog's blood and kills any fleas which suck blood later. Because these drugs in large amounts are toxic to the dog, the tablets should be used with care and not employed at the same time as sprays containing similar drugs. In general, they do not eliminate fleas as effectively as the powders or sprays. In the near future a newly developed group of chemicals, the pyrethroids, which have high insecticidal efficiency combined with low toxicity for mammals, seem destined to replace the older, more toxic drugs.

Where dogs are allergic to flea bites attempts have been made to reduce their sensitivity (hyposensitization) by giving a number of weekly injections of flea extract. Unfortunately with the type of extract generally available at present the chance of a long-lasting improvement is slight.

Q *Can I remove fleas from the environment?*

A Contrary to some people's belief fleas are not acquired from outdoor areas such as parks and gardens, but premises housing infected animals are likely to be extensively contaminated. On soft furnishings and carpets the same parasiticidal powders as used on animals can be applied, and vacuumed off after an hour (burn the contents of the vacuum cleaner afterwards). Alternatively, an ordinary fly spray or special environmental spray (e.g. Nuvan Staykil) can be used. These sprays are particularly useful for penetrating crevices, but they should not be used directly on dogs, and animals are best kept off treated areas for several days afterwards. Old bedding and baskets are best burned. In North America flea bombs, or 'foggers', are available which fill the atmosphere with insecticide. With really severe infestations it is advisable to call in professional exterminators. Most local authorities can offer help or advice.

After the initial treatment, further treatments of the dog and its bedding are advisable, varying from twice a week to once every two weeks (depending on the particular preparation used) to kill any fleas which have hatched out of eggs in the surroundings since the previous treatment.

Q *Are flea collars safe for dogs to wear?*

A Dogs are liable to acquire fresh flea infestations from time to time, particularly from any cats on the premises, and if repeated infestation is a problem a dog can be fitted with a flea collar. Flea collars are plastic collars impregnated with an insecticide (usually either dichlorvos or lindane) which is slowly released as a vapour to kill the fleas. However, in general they will not eliminate a heavy flea burden and are useful chiefly to control mild infestations. Usually the collar needs renewing every three months.

Unfortunately a tightly applied flea collar can produce a zone of acute inflammation around the neck of some dogs (flea-collar dermatitis) and in a few allergic individuals it will also cause dermatitis elsewhere on the body. Flea tags or medallions made of the same material can be attached to an ordinary dog collar, and work in a similar way. They are less likely to cause problems since they have less contact with the skin, though again where they do touch reddened patches may develop. (Some owners may also develop dermatitis after contact with these collars, especially when they are wet.)

If a flea collar is used, it is recommended that after being removed from the packaging material the collar should be allowed to air out for twenty-four hours, and then be fitted so that it is possible to insert two fingers between the collar and the neck. No other treatment for fleas (tablets, sprays, powders, etc.) should be given to the dog for five days before or after wearing a collar, in case poisoning results from their cumulative effects. The collar should be taken off if, or before, the dog gets wet and only replaced when the dog is dry, as water destroys the insecticide. It should also be removed if the dog develops signs of neck irritation, especially likely in the first week, or of poisoning (e.g. depression, vomiting, diarrhoea and staggering). Take care that when removed the collar is not chewed by the dog.

An effective alternative is to fasten a dichlorvos-impregnated fly strip above the dog's bed, but again this should not be used at the same time as a flea collar or any other de-fleaing treatment.

Q *Can dogs get mange?*

A Yes, there are two important microscopic mange mites which can afflict canine skin. The round-bodied itch mite *Sarcoptes scabiei canis* is the cause of canine scabies, otherwise called sarcoptic mange, a highly contagious disease spread between animals by direct contact. This mite cannot survive longer than a few days away from a host. The parasites burrow into the outer horny layer of the skin, between the hair follicles, causing intense irritation, especially when the skin is warm. Beginning usually at the edges of the ear flaps and on the elbows, the mites gradually spread across the rest of the body producing inflammation, thinning of the hair and small crusty lesions. This appearance is soon complicated by the extensive damage which the dog inflicts upon itself. It has been estimated that over 40,000 dogs in the United Kingdom are infected.

The mite will also transfer to humans and is capable of burrowing through clothing to reach the skin, chiefly those areas (lap, chest and forearms) which come into contact with a dog being carried or hugged. The skin reaction can range from an irritant rash to a severe allergic response. Since humans are an unnatural host the mites only stay on them for a few hours (the skin condition of *human* scabies is caused by a different, though related, mite — *Sarcoptes scabiei hominis*), but continued contact with an affected dog will result in persistent re-infection.

Demodectic mange (demodecosis) is caused by the cigar-shaped follicular mite *Demodex canis* which occurs in some of the hair follicles of almost *all* dogs. It is believed that most animals develop an immunity to the mites which restricts their spread, but where this does not develop the mites proliferate causing inflammation and hair loss starting at an early age (between three and twelve months old). The mites transfer from nursing bitches to their puppies by direct contact during the first few days of life, and lesions first appear on the muzzle, around the eyes and on the front legs, before spreading elsewhere. In the past, but less so nowadays, the short-haired breeds (e.g. Dachshunds, Boxers and Dobermanns) were more frequently affected. The lesions usually cause little or no itching and in most cases heal spontaneously within two months, though it can take years. Sometimes the condition progresses to produce generalized skin disease complicated by bacterial infection with pus production, and severely affected animals may die.

Diagnosis can be confirmed by finding the mites responsible in scrapings taken from the surface layers of the skin. Essentially treatment is with the same types of lotions and shampoos (following the clipping of affected areas) and tablets, that are used for controlling flea infestations. A new drug, amitraz, is particularly effective against *Demodex*. Since neither mite survives long away from the host, repeated treatment of the environment is unnecessary.

The condition sometimes referred to as ear mange, caused by the ear mite *Otodectes cynotis*, has already been described on page 158.

Q *What other skin parasites attack the dog?*

A The mite, *Cheyletiella yasguri*, is a similar size to the ear mite, i.e. just large enough to be seen with the naked eye. It can infect dogs of any age, though infestations are most severe in young puppies of the short-coated breeds. Some dogs show marked irritation, although older dogs in particular often demonstrate no signs apart from scurf on the coat, especially marked along the back. The white mites and their eggs give the appearance of extensive dandruff, though close observation with a magnifying glass reveals that it is moving — hence the popular name 'walking dandruff'.

Lice are flat, wingless insects which glue their eggs (nits) on to the dog's hairs. The nits will later hatch out into a new crop of lice and can be most easily removed by clipping off the affected hairs. Biting lice, chiefly *Trichodectes canis*, feed on skin debris, whereas the sucking louse *Linognathus setosus* (the most common dog louse) sucks blood and in large numbers can produce anaemia. Both types cause intense irritation and severe scratching. As a rule both these blue-grey lice are most numerous around the ears, neck and shoulders, especially in long-coated dogs such as Cocker Spaniels, though biting lice may congregate beneath the tail.

Both *Cheyletiella* and lice are transmitted by direct and indirect contact (for instance with contaminated grooming tools) and they are treated with similar preparations to those used for fleas. It is always worthwhile seeking veterinary advice about the correct preparation to be used because all of them are toxic to some extent and not all are equally suitable for every purpose. Any instructions and precautions should be carefully observed. As a general rule, special care should be taken with very young, very old, pregnant, nursing and ill dogs, and those which require repeated treatment. Unless advised otherwise, avoid using a number of preparations simultaneously because of the cumulative toxic effect.

The lice and all mites, except the harvest mite, differ from the flea in that they spend their entire life on the host. The harvest mite *(Trombicula autumnalis)* and the North American chigger *(Eutrombicula alfreddugesi)* are parasitic larvae which attach themselves to thin-skinned regions, usually the ears and between the toes, as the dog walks through vegetation. They need animal protein in order to develop further; after feeding they drop off and ultimately become adult mites which are non-parasitic and live on decaying vegetable matter. The larvae appear as small orange-red spots, and cause considerable irritation. As its name suggests, infestations with the harvest mite are associated primarily with the summer months. Parasiticidal preparations are required for treatment.

Calliphorid flies, otherwise called blow-flies (blue-bottles and green-bottles) may lay their eggs in open wounds or in the soiled coat of an ill or elderly animal. The maggots (larvae) which hatch from the eggs feed from the living animal just as they would from a carcase or piece of meat. They secrete enzymes which digest proteins in the skin producing craters on its surface. This condition (fly-strike) requires the area to be clipped thoroughly, cleaned and treated with insecticide; treatment for shock may also be necessary.

In the southern and western United States, during the third quarter of the year the fly *Cuterebra maculata* lays its eggs in soil. The larvae which hatch can attach themselves to the skin of dogs when they lie on the ground, usually puppies of breeds with dense coats, and eventually the larvae are able to penetrate the skin. Each larva then grows (inside a cyst-like cavity) to become $3/4$ inch (2 cm) long. An opening remains in the skin because this grub needs to breathe. Treatment requires removal of the grub with forceps (generally following enlargement of the opening by an incision made under local anaesthesia) and antibiotic treatment to combat secondary bacterial infection.

Q *Is it true that a tick should not be pulled from a dog's body?*

A Ticks are sometimes acquired by dogs, particularly in rural areas, and they attach themselves by their mouthparts, most often to the ears, head, neck, legs or flank. In the warmer parts of the world argasid (soft) ticks can infect dogs, but generally much more important are the ixodid (hard) ticks which suck blood and in large numbers may give rise to anaemia. The most common of these in Britain is the hedgehog tick *(Ixodes hexagonus)*. The tick appears as a small, dark swelling, fluctuating in size, which may be confused with a pigmented skin tumour, although the dog will often be seen scratching at it because its bite can be intensely irritating. In climates warmer than Britain, some species of hard ticks produce a toxin which progressively paralyses the dog, starting with its hind legs.

Simply pulling off a tick usually causes its deeply imbedded mouthparts to remain behind, and this may result in an abscess forming. Preferably the tick should be made to slacken its grip by applying a pad of alcohol, or ether, or by spraying it with an insecticidal aerosol spray, before carefully removing it with forceps. Any ticks removed should be burned.

Q *Apart from parasites are there any other causes of skin disease in dogs?*

A Yes indeed, there can be a number of other causes. Itching (pruritus) is one of the most obvious signs of skin disease, and although frequently caused by parasites (e.g. fleas — responsible for 90% of itchy dogs, lice, *Sarcoptes*, ear mites, harvest mites and some infestations with *Cheyletiella* or ticks), itching occurs whenever the skin is damaged or inflamed. For instance itching is one of the major signs of allergic skin diseases which develop when a *previously sensitized* individual encounters a particular allergy-provoking substance (an allergen). Important allergies in dogs are due to inhalation of pollens (particularly ragweed), moulds or house dust, insect bites and stings and direct skin contact with chemicals in soaps and detergents, carpets (usually the dyes), flea collars, plastics etc. Although foodstuffs are often blamed they are rarely responsible. Some dogs even develop an allergy to components of their own skin (an autoimmune disease) which frequently starts with reddening and ulceration of the mouth, lips and tongue.

Although healthy skin is very resistant to bacterial infection any damage or inflammation facilitates infection, chiefly by the pus-producing organisms staphylococci and, to a lesser extent, streptococci. Any area which is inflamed by an allergic reaction, lacerated by barbed wire or clipper blades, or which the dog bites or scratches at vigorously (e.g. following insect bites or impacted anal sacs) soon becomes infected, producing a moist, reddened area, popularly called wet eczema, that results in further itching, damage and infection. This is particularly common in breeds with a woolly undercoat.

Where the skin is thrown into folds the rubbing together of the folds and the higher moisture content within them encourages bacterial growth. Areas commonly involved are the lip folds (e.g. in Cocker Spaniels), folds on the face (e.g. in Pekingese and Pugs), screw-tail folds (e.g. in Boston Terriers and Bulldogs) and folds alongside the vulva (in obese bitches). Actual pus formation within the skin may be:
1 Superficial (= impetigo), with the formation of small pus-filled 'spots' (pustules), usually on the underside of the belly in puppies.
2 Deep (= furunculosis). Although this deep infection can occur in any region, favourite sites are the chin (acne, seen especially in short-coated breeds), the head (puppy-head disease, affecting short-coated pups under four months old), the nose (especially in Collies and German Shepherd Dogs), the pressure points on the elbows and hocks of large breeds,

around the anus (chiefly in German Shepherd Dogs) and between the toes of short-coated breeds. In the last-named condition, the delicate skin between the toes responds to being punctured by the coarse hairs by forming large fluid-filled swellings termed 'interdigital cysts' (something similar in humans is seen on hairdressers' hands). Severe cases are associated with minute cuts inflicted by sand, gravel, clinker or metal turnings (e.g. suffered by guard dogs in factory yards).

Although itching is common there are some skin disorders in which it is characteristically absent. In certain hormonal disorders there is a loss of hair, which is identical on both sides of the body (i.e. they appear as mirror images), occurring without any skin irritation. This is seen in hypothyroidism (lack of thyroid hormones, especially in Retrievers), Cushing's syndrome (excessive corticosteroid output – especially in small terriers, Poodles and Boxers), a markedly increased or decreased female sex hormone (oestrogen) output in bitches and oestrogen production in male dogs producing feminization. The usual cause of the last condition is an oestrogen-secreting tumour of the testicle, and it also results in enlargement of the nipples and makes the dog attractive to other males. These hormonal disturbances are not in any way contagious.

Skin can also be involved in the growth of tumours (some of which are cancerous; see page 210) and at times is affected by very bizarre conditions. Examples of the latter include cutaneous asthenia (rubber puppy disease) in which the skin can be stretched to extremes but also tears very easily, and canine icthyosis (fish-skin disease) where much of the body surface is covered with grey scales and feather-like projections.

Q *How does my dog get infected with roundworms and are they harmful?*

A Although most owners find the presence of even a single worm aesthetically distasteful roundworms usually only produce signs of infection when large numbers are present in puppies.

Strictly speaking all the nematode worms should be referred to as roundworms because they are all circular in cross-section. However, by popular usage this description is often reserved for the commonest members of the group – the ascarids.

Ascarid worms are white or beige, partially coiled (like a spring) and measure 2–6 inches (5–15 cm) long. They produce eggs in the intestine of the dog which pass out in its motions. An infective larva develops inside each egg and if this is eaten by a dog the larva develops into an adult worm in its intestine. (In the case of *Toxocara canis* this only happens after a complex 'migration' around the body of the dog, passing in turn through the liver, heart and lungs.) Alternatively, the egg may be eaten by another species, such as a rodent, and by eating this animal the dog in turn becomes infected. However, most puppies become infected with roundworms through their mother. In a bitch some larvae of *Toxocara canis* (though not of *Toxascaris leonina*) do not develop into adults but remain dormant in the body tissues. If the bitch should become pregnant these larvae are re-activated and some pass in the blood stream to the placenta and enter the foetus, lodging in the foetal liver and lungs. One week after birth they migrate to the puppy's intestine and become adult worms. This is an example of congenital infection and the majority of puppies already have roundworm larvae when they are born. Other re-activated larvae in the bitch pass to the mammary glands and out in the milk consumed by the newborn offspring — a further source of infection. Because these dormant larvae are not in the intestine they cannot be removed by conventional worming drugs, although drugs are being currently developed which *are* able to destroy larvae in the tissues.

Toxocara canis infection produces noisy breathing and coughing, especially during suckling in puppies under two weeks old. In older puppies, up to three months of age, there is persistent diarrhoea with vomiting, whining and a pot-bellied appearance. Adult worms may be vomited up, and infected animals have poor growth rates. A survey in suburban London showed 30 % of puppies to be infected; surveys elsewhere have found up to 70 % infection. In mature dogs clinical signs of ascarid infection are virtually non-existent.

Q *What is the significance of tapeworms in dogs?*

A The common tapeworms are long, flat worms (like white ribbons), attached to the lining of the intestine with hooks and suckers, and in general they cause no signs of ill health. In large numbers they may result in digestive upsets, anal irritation and a loss of condition. Tapeworms are hermaphrodite, segmented worms which grow continuously; the oldest segments, containing the eggs, are shed one or more at a time from the end of the worm furthest from its head. To complete their life cycle these eggs, after passing out at the anus, must then be eaten by a particular species of animal. In the case of *Dipylidium caninum*, the commonest dog tapeworm found in about a third of all dogs (though up to 75 % of Greyhounds) this 'intermediate host' must be the flea or louse. Some of the many *Taenia* species of tapeworm utilize the rabbit, and others the sheep, as intermediate hosts. An egg develops into a cyst-like structure in the intermediate host, and if this host is then eaten by a dog the cyst-like structure develops into a new tapeworm in its intestine. But if tapeworm eggs are eaten by a dog they do not develop further.

The tapeworm *Echinococcus granulosus* differs from the others in that it seldom exceeds $^1/_5$ inch (5 mm) in length whereas the other tapeworms may reach $1^1/_2$–9 feet (50 cm–3 metres) depending on the species. However, its small size is in direct contrast to its importance to its intermediate hosts (including sheep, cattle, pigs, horses and humans) in which a single egg can grow into a large cyst and cause severe illness and even death (see page 207). An infected dog can harbour several thousand adult *Echinococcus* worms with no ill effects.

Q *What other worms might infect my dog?*

A First there are a number of worms which commonly occur in dogs in kennel establishments but much less frequently in pet dogs; the hookworms, whipworm, lungworm, tracheal worm and bladder worm.

Although they also inhabit the small intestine hookworms have a more direct life cycle than roundworms or tapeworms. Eggs eliminated in the motions become larvae, which after being eaten by another dog pass to its intestines and there develop into adult worms. Larvae can also enter the body by burrowing through the skin, particularly of the feet, but whereas those of the tropical *Ancylostoma* hookworms complete their life cycle by being carried in the blood stream to the intestines, those of *Uncinaria* go no further. Large numbers of larvae entering the feet can produce severe dermatitis (skin inflammation) on the paws. *Ancylostoma* hookworms (very common in the southern USA and Australia) suck blood and in large numbers can cause severe anaemia and weakness, even death; *Uncinaria* hookworms are not blood suckers, but heavy burdens are likely to result in diarrhoea and/or poor growth. (In a pregnant bitch *Ancylostoma* larvae can infect puppies before birth and also accumulate in the mammary glands to infect them as they suckle.)

The whipworm *(Trichuris vulpis)* is so named because with its thicker rear part and more slender anterior section it resembles a whip. It inhabits the blind-ended part of the large bowel called the caecum and usually causes no signs, although some dogs show intermittent diarrhoea. After eggs produced by the worms are eliminated in the motions, an infective larva develops inside each of them so that if the infected eggs are eaten by a dog the larvae will develop into adult worms in the caecum. Around a third of racing Greyhounds have been found to be infected.

The lungworm *(Filaroides osleri)* inhabits the end of the trachea (windpipe) nearest to the lungs, and the worms reside in nodules up to $^3/_4$ inch (2 cm) across which protrude from the wall, like fingertips pushing into the airway. This partial blockage may cause a dry cough, particularly after exercise, which is most often seen in puppies of between four and six weeks old. Eggs passed out by the worm hatch almost immediately to larvae which are coughed up. When an infected bitch in breeding kennels licks her suckling pups the larvae are transferred to them. After being swallowed the larvae migrate to the puppy's windpipe and develop into adult worms. (In Australia and some other parts of the world, including recently Britain, another lungworm *Angiostrongylus vasorum*, transmitted via slugs and snails, is occasionally found causing respiratory distress in dogs.)

The tracheal worm *(Capillaria aerophila)* is in general responsible for similar, though milder, respiratory signs. It lives in the dog's windpipe and its eggs pass out by being coughed up and swallowed and traversing the intestine. Other dogs are infected by eating them.

The bladder worm *(Capillaria plica)* is a fine hair-like worm found in the bladder, usually among packs of hounds. Perhaps surprisingly it seldom causes any disability.

Secondly, other parasitic worms not normally found in Britain or northern Europe but of importance elsewhere may appear in dogs imported into those areas.

The heartworm *(Dirofilaria immitis)* infects dogs in the central and eastern parts of the United States, Australia and southern Europe. Microscopic larvae are taken from the blood stream of one animal and later injected into another by the bites of a mosquito, and they develop into adult worms in the heart and pulmonary artery. The damage and blockage caused by these worms can be severe, resulting in difficulty in breathing, liver and kidney disorders and even sudden death. In the same areas of the world a similar worm, *Dipetalonema reconditum*, the flesh worm, is found beneath the skin. This is transmitted from dog to dog by the bites of fleas or lice. It causes little in the way of disease but the larvae in the blood can be easily confused with those of the heartworm.

The giant kidney worm of the dog *Dioctophyma renale* deserves to be mentioned simply because it is the largest known nematode worm. It infects dogs in the Americas, Africa, the Orient, Russia and parts of Europe (though not Britain) through the eating of raw, or imperfectly cooked fish. The worms lie in the abdomen or right kidney (which they gradually destroy) and females, $1/4$ inch (6 mm) thick, can reach 3 feet (90 cm) or more in length.

In North America and South Africa the lung fluke *(Paragonimus kellicotti)*, which passes through stages in water snails and crayfish, can infect scavenger dogs causing intermittent coughing. Finally, in wooded areas of the western states of the USA, the small, slender worm *Thelazia californiensis* occasionally affects dogs following transmission by the deer fly. The worm lives beneath the third eyelid (or haw) causing an intensely irritant conjunctivitis, and has to be removed with forceps or a cotton bud after the eye has been desensitized with local anaesthetic.

Q *How can I tell if my dog has worms?*

A Ideally, at intervals throughout the dog's life, a sample of motions should be examined by a laboratory for evidence of worm eggs, though usually this is only performed if the dog is showing signs suggestive of worm infection. A laboratory examination *after* worming is a valuable way of assessing the efficacy of treatment, especially as most modern tapeworm treatments cause the worms to break up within the dog's intestine, so that worms are not passed intact, and are therefore not visible in the motions.

As was mentioned earlier, those segments of a tapeworm furthest from the head, which contain the eggs, are continually being shed and passing out of the dog's anus. With the exception of *Echinococcus* the segments are large enough to be seen with the naked eye, and they may be discovered in the motions, or sometimes seen around the dog's anus or in the bedding. For a time the segments retain the ability to contract the muscles in their walls, and though not capable of an independent existence, may be observed moving over the animal's coat or across the floor. They have the size and appearance of rice grains or cucumber seeds. The segments of *Echinococcus* are too small to be visible without magnification and can only be detected microscopically.

The eggs of other worms are also passed out in the motions, but individually, i.e. not contained within segments, and again these are so small that they can only be seen using a microscope.

Q *I have heard that children can get worms from dogs. Is this true?*

A In the case of a few worms, it *is* correct that they can infect humans; usually children because their immunity is less. The worm which has received most attention is the roundworm, *Toxocara canis.* This is *not* the same as the threadworm (pinworm or seatworm) which is common in children. In its life cycle the infective larva, still inside the egg shell in which it has developed, may be eaten by a dog or by another species, often a rodent, which in turn may be consumed by a dog. At times, however, these infective eggs (i.e. containing the larvae) may be eaten by children. A number of factors contribute:

1 The outside of the microscopic eggs is sticky, so that they readily adhere to a dog's coat, and to human fingers.

2 Young children, especially toddlers, have a habit of putting their hands and various objects, even contaminated soil, into their mouths.

3 The infective eggs can survive for two years or longer in the ground and will withstand all disinfectants, long-term freezing and even short periods in boiling water. Only the use of horticultural flame-guns on concrete runs effectively destroys the eggs.

4 The effects of wind, rain and human activity can spread the eggs over a wide area.

In humans the larvae hatch from the eggs, penetrate the wall of the intestine and disperse to the liver, kidneys, brain or eyes. They do not develop further but remain in those organs, and can cause damage leading sometimes to liver enlargement, blindness or convulsions. This disease, caused by migration or penetration of the larvae, is called visceral larva migrans, and it chiefly affects children between one and a half and three years old. It cannot be considered a common disease, although certainly more children become infected than ever show signs. Infection also seems to exacerbate existing illnesses such as asthma and paralytic poliomyelitis. At present there is no evidence that *Toxascaris leonina* can infect humans in a similar way.

It is also possible for a person, again usually a child, who swallows a flea infected with the intermediate stage of the tapeworm *Dipylidium caninum* to become infected with an adult tapeworm in the intestine, although this very rarely happens.

As previously mentioned, the extremely small tapeworm of the dog *Echinococcus granulosus* can infect a number of species, including man, which play the role of intermediate host. This parasite occurs in all the inhabited continents and the most common cycle is between farm dogs and sheep. Consequently most human infections are acquired in sheep-farming areas where the worms are prevalent amongst dogs, and derive from eating worm eggs picked up from the dog's coat or present on vegetables. In humans the eggs develop into slow-growing cystic structures (hydatid cysts) in the liver, lungs or other organs. These may eventually reach 6 inches (15 cm) or more in diameter, resulting in the severe, and sometimes fatal, illness hydatidosis. Rupture of the hydatid cyst may result in the numerous worm heads it contains being distributed all over the host's body, each one of which can then give rise to a further hydatid cyst.

Q *Is it a good idea to worm my dog, and if so, how often should I do it?*

A First of all it should be appreciated that most of the worms which affect dogs are not treated for unless they are believed to be present. *Routine* worming (or, more accurately, de-worming) is carried out primarily to control infection with the ascarid worms (roundworms) especially since they can be transmitted to man. The drug most commonly used is piperazine, which is relatively safe, cheap and reasonably effective. It is most definitely advisable to give this worming treatment routinely. However, this drug has no appreciable action against other types of worms, such as tapeworms. Recently even more effective drugs against ascarids have become available, some of which are also effective against tapeworms; they are, however, considerably more expensive.

It is generally recommended that puppies should be routinely wormed to remove ascarids at intervals of two or three weeks, beginning at three weeks of age until weaning, and then again at three months old and six months old. Subsequent worming at six-month intervals (or, though not so good, twelve-month intervals, e.g. at the time of the annual booster vaccination) probably provides adequate control. This routine worming is advisable because dogs can become re-infected at any age, particularly if they hunt rodents, and it is estimated that at any one time between 2 % and 60 % of *adult* dogs are infected (in Britain 12 % on average, but a higher percentage in city dogs).

Newly acquired dogs should always be wormed, and pregnant bitches should be wormed about a month before giving birth. This will not remove any worms dormant in the bitch's tissues but it will reduce the contamination of the puppy's environment.

In addition to this routine worming for roundworms, some veterinary surgeons also advise worming dogs every six to twelve months to eliminate tapeworms. Since tapeworms are less of a problem in puppies than in adults, any routine treatment is not usually started until six months of age. A number of effective drugs are available; currently bunamidine (e.g. Scolaban) is the most commonly used, but this drug is bitter and tablets should not be broken or crushed. Treatment to remove the tapeworm *Dipylidium caninum,* however, is usually a waste of time unless infestations of fleas (or lice) are removed simultaneously. To ensure control of hydatidosis in problem areas (e.g. mid-Wales) continual dosing of dogs with the drug praziquantel at eight- to twelve-week intervals is advisable.

When there is definite evidence of a worm infection, worming with the appropriate drug should be carried out as soon as possible and then repeated a month or so later to remove any remaining worms.

Q *Is it safe to use worming remedies bought at the pet shop?*

A In countries (for instance Britain and North America) where there are legal restrictions on what drugs can be sold for this purpose other than by a qualified pharmacist or veterinarian, the answer is probably yes. But it is subject to the proviso that these remedies are used strictly in accordance with the manufacturer's instructions.

Unfortunately, owners may misdiagnose their dog's illness as being due to worms and therefore delay getting proper advice and treatment. Or they may overdose their dog, particularly if the first treatment does not produce the expected improvement, which can have tragic consequences. Also, because of restrictions upon sale, several types of worming drugs (anthelmintics) are not sold from pet shops and similar retail outlets, and invariably this includes those most recently developed, and most effective.

In countries where there is no restriction on what remedies may be sold over the counter, a number of drastic purgative treatments and potentially toxic drugs may be on sale, so great care must be exercised.

As a general rule, to ensure that you receive the correct drug to treat your dog's condition, whether it is due to a worm infection or not, together with accurate advice about the dose to administer, it is always preferable in the long run to consult your local vet.

Q *What sort of a worm is the tongue worm?*

A This parasite *(Linguatula serrata)* gets its popular name from its appearance; it is long and worm-like and flattened like a tongue. But in reality it is not a worm at all but an unusual variety of mite which has no legs. The 'worms', which can be up to 5 inches (12 cm) long, attach themselves high up in the nasal chambers of the dog and the irritation they cause can at times result in nasal discharge, sneezing and difficulty in breathing. The eggs passed out by the females need to be eaten by an intermediate host (horse, sheep, cow or rabbit) before they can develop further. A dog acquires an early stage of the parasite by eating uncooked meat from one of these animals and after migration to the nasal chamber it develops into an adult 'worm'. The parasite is best removed by surgery. Like the nasal mites *(Pneumonyssus caninum)*, which in the USA, Australia and South Africa also infect the nasal chambers, unsuspected tongue worms may suddenly emerge from the nostrils of dogs undergoing inhalation anaesthesia.

Q *Do dogs get cancer?*

A Yes, cancer (or neoplasia, or tumour formation) is one of the most common conditions to affect dogs, and as in other animals, including man, it occurs increasingly frequently with age.

A tumour, or neoplasm (often popularly referred to as a 'growth') is a multiplying collection of cells whose growth cannot be controlled by the normal body mechanisms. As a rule, these cells lose their normal functions and concentrate solely on growing. Tumours can essentially be classified into two groups. Those termed benign grow slowly and are usually easily separated from adjacent tissues, so that complete surgical removal is generally possible. The problems that they cause are usually related to their site. A growing tumour can press on nearby structures interfering with their function, for example with the flow of blood or urine, or with breathing. Tumours on the skin can easily have their surface broken so that they bleed, or become infected by bacteria. Likewise, those in the mouth might be chewed upon, causing pain and bleeding.

Those tumours that are called malignant grow much more rapidly, and spread out into adjacent tissues (invasion and/or infiltration). After a period of growth, groups of malignant tumour cells often break off and are carried away in the blood stream or lymphatic circulation to lodge in other organs of the body, especially the lungs. This process is referred to as metastasis, and each group of cells can give rise to a new tumour (which is also called a metastasis, or secondary tumour) which will grow and spread in the same manner. Because of their invasive growth, complete surgical removal is more difficult and malignant tumours often recur after an operation. It is this malignant type of neoplasia which is generally called cancer (although some experts use the term cancer to refer to any type of tumour). Malignant tumours cause problems, not only because of the same type of local pressure effects, but by their rapid, progressive destruction of body tissues which inevitably leads to organs failing to function effectively.

The signs of cancer depend upon its site, the tissues involved, and the way in which normal body functions have been interfered with. The cause of neoplasia is still imperfectly understood, but essentially it seems that at some time during the repeated multiplication of the body cells, a mutation occurs in the genes responsible for controlling the growth and function of cells. All further cells derived from this 'mutant' will perpetuate the same defects of growth and activity. The genetic make-up of the species, of the breed and even of the individual all influence the likelihood of mutations occurring, but the longer the animal lives, the greater the chance of such a mutation appearing. Certain chemicals, e.g. tar compounds, viruses, and even parasites (e.g. *Spirocerca lupi* associated with canine oesophageal tumours) can stimulate the production of mutations and are therefore held responsible for certain types of neoplasia. Such cancer-producing agents are known as carcinogens.

Q *What kind of tumours do dogs get most commonly?*

A Each year about four dogs in every thousand develop a tumour. Of these about 40 % affect the skin, including 7 % which develop (chiefly in males) from the small glands encircling the anus, known as circumanal glands. Tumours of the mammary glands account for another 20 %, and since they only occur in bitches this means that two out of every five tumours in bitches are mammary tumours. A further 14 % of neoplasms (one in seven) affect one of the organs of the digestive tract, of which over a third derive from the gums in the mouth. Tumours of bones, lymph nodes and testicles each account for between 5 % and 7 % of the total.

Only just over a third of all canine tumours are malignant. The majority of skin tumours are benign (including all the circumanal tumours), while mammary tumours are just marginally more likely to be malignant, but almost all those involving the lymph nodes and bones are malignant. These last two types are interesting because whereas all other tumours occur more and more frequently with increasing age, these two are seen most commonly in dogs between seven and ten years old. This may be because they are caused by a virus which exists in the body for a long time before it is triggered off to produce cancer, although there is no definite proof of this. Since bone cancer is most common in large breeds of dogs, physical and genetic factors may provide this 'trigger'. (It is already established that many lymphosarcomas in the cat are due to a virus — feline leukaemia virus.)

Neoplasia often appears earlier in Boxers than in other breeds and is roughly four times as common. Neoplasia also occurs two or three times more frequently in Cocker Spaniels (especially circumanal tumours), Fox Terriers (particularly mammary tumours) and Boston Terriers. On the other hand Beagles have a very low incidence of tumour formation. Mammary tumours are 200 times less likely to occur in bitches spayed before their first heat.

Q *Is it possible to treat cancer in dogs?*

A Treatment of certain types of cancer (i.e. malignant neoplasia) by surgery, radiation therapy and drugs (chemotherapy), particularly if commenced in the early stages, *may* be successful in eliminating the tumour and preventing its recurrence. In particular, the early surgical removal of a potentially malignant skin tumour or mammary tumour usually results in a total cure. When internal organs are involved, however, the end result of treatment is often disappointing and the most that can be achieved is a slight increase in life expectancy. To prevent prolonged and unnecessary suffering in severely affected animals, euthanasia should be seriously considered as a humane alternative.

Q *What other dog diseases come with old age?*

A As well as cancer, there are a number of other conditions which become increasingly common as dogs grow older. One of the most significant is kidney failure. The kidneys have the important function of eliminating the waste products of metabolism, particularly those resulting from the breakdown of proteins in the body, and of regulating the composition of the blood plasma. With age, the number of functional units which comprise the kidneys gradually diminishes, and this may be accelerated by severe damage (e.g. from a road accident), bacterial or viral infection (e.g. leptospirosis or infectious canine hepatitis) or, rarely, neoplasia. When around 70 % of the kidney tissue has ceased to work, the waste products will accumulate in the blood and cause such toxic effects as a loss of appetite, listlessness, vomiting, increased thirst, dehydration, weight loss and, after a time, ulcers in the mouth. This condition, chronic renal failure, is not reversible, and to enable the dog to live with it the diet needs to contain less protein than normal, in order to reduce the production of these waste materials (see page 99). When cancer or some other progressive cause (e.g. amyloidosis) is responsible, euthanasia is advisable.

As in man heart disease occurs with increasing frequency as dogs grow older, although it is of a different type. Blockage of the pulmonary arteries with blood clots (coronary thrombosis) or with fatty deposits (atherosclerosis) is common in humans but very rare in dogs, and the major canine disorder is a progressive thickening and distortion of the mitral valve of the heart. Increasingly blood leaks back through the valve instead of being pumped around the body, a situation known as cardiac failure, so that fatigue, breathing difficulties and coughing become apparent, at first only after exercise but eventually even when resting.

As they get older dogs, especially bitches, are more likely to suffer from bacterial infections of the urine (urinary tract infection) which are the most common cause of cystitis (inflammation of the bladder). Enlargement of the prostate gland, causing interference with urination and defecation, is common in old male dogs, as it is in elderly human males.

The incidence of periodontal disease, the most frequent dental disorder of dogs (described on page 144) also increases with age in all breeds. Chronic ear conditions appear more frequently and there is deterioration of hearing and vision.

Osteoarthritis, due to a gradual degeneration of the cartilage lining the joints, occurs more frequently with age. The lameness it produces is shown particularly as stiffness and difficulty in rising, and becomes less obvious as the animal moves about.

'Slipped discs' are also due to degeneration, although in fact most cases become apparent in middle-aged rather than geriatric dogs. The intervertebral discs are the natural 'shock absorbers' between all the bones (vertebrae) of the spine. In reality a disc does not 'slip' anywhere, but with age the tough outer layer hardens and may rupture, allowing the soft inner core to bulge out and press on the spinal cord in either the neck or lower back regions. The result is severe pain, with complete or partial paralysis of the front or hind legs respectively. Short-legged, long-backed breeds are particularly at risk; in one survey Dachshunds accounted for 70 % of cases. Such dogs should be discouraged from jumping up, which often initiates the damage.

Other problems may include obesity due to overfeeding and lack of exercise, or under-nutrition — especially if the appetite is impaired. Constipation is not common in old dogs, compared with elderly cats, but if present it is usually associated with insufficient exercise. Lack of exercise can also result in the claws becoming overgrown. Inability to control the sphincters of the bladder and/or anus can result in urinary and/or faecal incontinence.

Q *Under what circumstances is it advisable to have a dog put to sleep?*

A Where it is known that a dog will have to endure continual or recurrent suffering, with little or no prospect of remission, then almost certainly the most humane course of action is to have it painlessly put to sleep. By suffering is meant not only acute or severe pain, but also the consequences of congenital malformations and serious injury, and those slowly progressive illnesses which inevitably can only terminate in death, such as paralysis, cancer and uncontrollable wasting diseases; in fact any disease where severe irreversible damage has been caused.

When an animal is clearly not able to enjoy its life any longer, it is unlikely that many owners would wish to prolong its suffering and would rather let it die with dignity. In law, the dog is the property of its owner and therefore the ultimate responsibility for the decision to have the dog humanely destroyed must be the owner's. This is why a veterinary surgeon often asks the owner to sign a formal request for euthanasia to be carried out. But naturally enough, faced with such a difficult decision, many owners will rely heavily on the advice and judgement of their veterinarian. Sometimes there is a legal requirement for a dog to be put to sleep because it represents a danger to the health of the general public and other animals, as with those suffering from rabies.

Vets themselves can face very difficult decisions regarding euthanasia — for instance where owners are unwilling or physically unable to give essential treatment or perhaps cannot afford it, or where owners wish to have a perfectly healthy animal put to sleep because they cannot, or will not, look after it. A recent survey in Scotland showed that just over half of the dogs put to sleep by veterinary surgeons were destroyed because of a serious illness or accident, 15 % because of a behavioural problem, and a quarter because their owners had moved, or died, or simply no longer wanted them. In many cases, although the veterinary surgeon finds the task distasteful, euthanasia is usually preferable to a lingering death from illness or to the owner devising his own method of destruction, or simply abandoning the dog.

Q *How do vets put dogs to sleep?*

A Nowadays the method usually adopted for canine euthanasia is for a veterinary surgeon to inject an overdose of a barbiturate anaesthetic, usually intravenously, but occasionally in very young, elderly or weak animals by another route. The dog goes to sleep as if being anaesthetized before an operation but does not recover. This method inflicts no pain and with an intravenous injection is extremely quick, since only a matter of seconds elapses before the animal becomes unconscious. With a very aggressive or nervous animal it may be necessary to administer a tranquillizer or other sedative drug beforehand in order that it can be calmed and adequately restrained for the injection. In general, it is preferable for euthanasia to be performed on a vet's premises since all the specialized equipment and trained assistance will be available there.

Animal welfare societies, faced with the unpleasant duty of having to destroy many unwanted animals, but with limited charitable resources, may be obliged to use a less expensive method. Reports suggest that the most suitable is to induce unconsciousness and then death by using nitrogen to flush all the vital oxygen out of a cabinet holding the animal.

Q *If my dog has to be put to sleep, how could I dispose of his body?*

A Some owners wish to have the body of their dog returned to them for burial at home, although most people prefer their vet to dispose of the body for them. (Subject to local laws, any grave should be made at least 3 feet (90 cm) deep.) Usually the vet will have an arrangement with the local authority to collect any bodies either for incineration or burial, whichever method of disposal is available in the area. There are also various pet cemeteries and crematoriums that can offer their services, and usually your vet will be able to give advice about the facilities which are available locally.

Q *The vet has told me that my dog is diabetic and would need an insulin injection every day. Is this going to be so distressing for the dog that it would be kinder to have her put to sleep?*

A Diabetes mellitus (sugar diabetes) is a condition that affects about six dogs in every thousand, three-quarters of them bitches. It is most common after middle age and Dachshunds are particularly likely to be affected.

The condition arises from the deficient production of the hormone insulin by the beta cells of the pancreas. As a result, glucose derived from the diet and from metabolism within the body cannot be stored for future use as an energy source and much of it is simply excreted in the urine. Diabetic dogs show the classic signs of an increasing loss of weight and weakness, despite a markedly increased appetite, together with an increased thirst and the passage of large volumes of urine. Approximately one quarter of them develop cataracts (opacity of the lens in the eye). Later, if no treatment is given, body fat is broken down to provide energy and at this stage the dog loses its appetite, becomes dehydrated, vomits and eventually goes into a coma (keto-acidotic coma), which if untreated would lead to death.

In humans the condition in elderly patients (maturity-onset diabetes) may be controlled simply by changing the diet to reduce the calorie intake, or in addition giving a hypoglycaemic drug to boost the output of insulin by the beta cells. Most of these patients, however, are either routinely diagnosed or feel unwell and visit their doctor *before* obvious signs develop. In contrast diabetes in a dog is closer to the type known in man as juvenile diabetes, and in general it needs to be very pronounced before the owner seeks veterinary advice. In this situation only insulin administration will provide adequate control. Insulin is not effective unless injected and long-term control requires daily subcutaneous injections of a long-acting preparation, plus daily urine testing and regular check-ups for the rest of the animal's life. If, as is usual, a fine, sharp needle is used for the injection (ideally a new disposable one each day) the discomfort for the dog will be very slight. But if you feel unwilling, or unable, to embark on such a disciplined course you would be better advised to have the animal put to sleep rather than to subject it to half-hearted attempts at treatment, however well intentioned.

Q *Are there likely to be any complications when treating a diabetic dog oneself?*

A The most frequent complication in the management of a diabetic dog is the inadvertent injection of an overdose of insulin, which causes the dog to show weakness, confused behaviour and staggering, followed eventually by convulsions and coma. Fortunately, the situation is rapidly reversed by dosing the dog *immediately* signs appear with one or more dessertspoonsful of honey or syrup, or a specially prepared glucose solution stored in the refrigerator against just such an eventuality.

Q *Can my dog pass on any diseases to me?*

A Diseases that can be transmitted from animals to man are known as zoonoses. Comparatively few of these are spread by the dog, although they do include some that can be extremely important, especially in children.

External parasites transmissible to man include fleas, the 'itch mite' *(Sarcoptes)*, the fur mite *(Cheyletiella)* and ringworm fungi. Cat fleas (the species most commonly found on dogs) often attack man and in some urban situations have even replaced the common human flea *(Pulex irritans)*. They generally come from the environment rather than from the dog itself, so that the first bites are usually on the ankles. In adult humans an itchy red rash is found, and in children irregularly inflamed weals which subside within forty-eight hours to leave small, red, raised papules which are intensely irritant. Later these lesions can occur anywhere on the body. Occasionally fleas may transmit the tapeworm *Dipylidium* to children.

Like *Sarcoptes*, mentioned earlier (see page 199), the fur mite is easily able to penetrate clothing and most frequently affects the forearms, trunk and buttocks of humans causing small red spots which itch furiously and develop into yellow, crusted lesions.

Ringworm fungi can also cause a marked inflammatory reaction in humans, with loss of hair if the head is involved. Human infestation with the ear mite is very rare, but has been reported to cause lesions on the trunk and legs.

Of the internal parasites *Toxocara canis* and *Echinococcus granulosus* are of greatest importance. *Toxocara* infection, primarily of children, results in passage of the larvae through the body (visceral larva migrans) and there may be damage to a vital organ. However in Britain the widely publicized ocular damage appears to affect only about one person in a million each year. *Echinococcus granulosus* is of greater significance, especially in sheep-rearing areas, and the infection of humans with the eggs of this minute tapeworm results in the unpleasant human disease of hydatidosis which at present can only be treated surgically and may prove fatal. Very rarely humans may be infected by the intermediate stages of other tapeworms (*Taenia* species, *Diphyllobothrium* and *Spirometra*) or with the canine whipworm or tongue worm.

If human skin comes into direct contact with soil containing the larval stage of those hookworms that infect dogs, the larvae may penetrate the skin, resulting in a dermatitis called cutaneous larva migrans or creeping eruption. This disorder is rare in temperate climates but in warmer regions, such as Florida, the migrating larvae are a considerable nuisance and may even progress to the lungs, causing a wheezing cough. In mosquito-infected regions the microscopic larvae of the heartworm (*Dirofilaria immitis*) may be transferred by a mosquito bite from the blood of the dog to that of man and become trapped in the lung, producing the usually symptomless condition of pulmonary dirofilariasis.

The transmission of rabies virus to the human population by the bites of dogs is of course of major concern, as is the role of dogs in spreading leptospirosis. Canicola fever caused by *Leptospira canicola* (whose main reservoir host is the dog) is a rare disorder in man, but Weil's disease due to *L. icterohaemorrhagiae* is much more common. The main reservoir for this organism is the rat, so that the disease, characterized by fever, headache, vomiting and jaundice, is most often associated with those working in rat-infested surroundings, e.g. canal and sewer workers, miners, and refuse operatives.

Bacteria may also be implanted in bite wounds, causing them to go septic and form abscesses. Salmonellosis (characterized by fever and diarrhoea containing blood), Campylobacter infection (causing abdominal pain and profuse diarrhoea) and tuberculosis are other bacterial diseases which the dog may, occasionally, communicate to man. Campylobacter infection has only recently been recognized and may be revealed to be a very significant zoonosis. Rarely the dog may act as a source of human infection with the virus of lymphocytic choriomeningitis, resulting in flu-like signs; but far more common sources of infection are housemice or hamsters. The suggestion has also been made, at present unsubstantiated, that human contact with canine distemper virus can lead to the development of the human disease multiple sclerosis.

Q *How can I minimize the chance of catching a disease from my dog?*

A The basic methods for controlling the spread of zoonoses to man are the same as for controlling the spread of disease between dogs, though, with the exception of vaccination against rabies, immunization is not available.

Dogs which are discovered to be infected should be treated as soon as possible, and/or isolated depending upon the dangers inherent in the transfer of the disease. With rabies, isolation on suspicion of infection and euthanasia if signs appear are advisable and in many countries mandatory. Where treatments are relatively innocuous, these may be carried out routinely as discussed previously.

Hygienic precautions are also of great importance to break the chain of transference at as many points as possible. The hands should be thoroughly washed after handling dogs and before putting the hands to the face or in the mouth, for example before eating. This applies particularly to young children. The kissing of pets should also be discouraged.

Dogs should not be allowed to lick the face, or sleep with humans or on their beds. Also dogs should not be allowed to lick plates and utensils used for human use, and their own feeding bowls should be washed separately from crockery and cutlery used by humans.

The dog's excreta should be collected and disposed of (preferably by burning) as soon as possible. Regular grooming and bathing of your dog, especially if long-haired, will reduce the risk of infection being spread by a contaminated coat. Although it is difficult to destroy the sticky roundworm eggs of dogs, they can be removed from the environment by thorough scrubbing of affected surfaces with hot detergent solution followed by a thorough rinsing down.

All food for animals should be stored well away from that for human consumption and prepared using different utensils and work surfaces. To reduce the risk of the dog acquiring an infection (e.g. with salmonellae) which could in turn be passed to man it is advisable to feed dogs only on dried, canned or cooked meat.

Q *What operations are commonly performed on dogs?*

A Comparatively minor procedures constitute some of the most commonly performed operations on dogs; in particular suturing wounds and arresting severe haemorrhage, especially after road accidents, and removing tumours from the skin, mammary glands or mouth. As dogs grow older their teeth, affected with periodontal disease, will often require cleaning or extraction. From time to time abscesses need to be opened and drained. The bacteria responsible may invade via natural orifices as with those involving the anal sacs or mammary glands, *or* through breaks in the skin, especially when implanted by a bite wound or carried by a small foreign body (often a grass seed tracking through the tissues). Less commonly an abscess may affect a root of one of the two largest teeth in the upper jaw (the fourth premolars), leading to a swelling and persistent discharge appearing on the face beneath the eye (dental fistula).

Opening into the abdomen in order to examine the abdominal organs, (exploratory laporotomy) is also a very common surgical technique undertaken when lesions that are suspected cannot be detected by radiography or other means. Laporotomy is, of course, a necessary preliminary to other abdominal procedures. The most frequently performed of these is probably spaying (ovariohysterectomy) — although not as frequently as in the cat. Removal of a bitch's womb is also necessary if it becomes infected, which generally occurs in bitches older than six years and between one and twelve weeks after they have been in season. In this condition, known as pyometra, the cervix (neck of the womb) may either open, allowing the pus to leak out and appear as a discharge, or it may remain closed, locking in the infection and resulting in greater severity of the clinical signs (i.e. depression, vomiting, loss of appetite and increased thirst).

Orthopaedic surgery to repair bone fractures, the majority of which occur in dogs less than three years old, is also common. In three-quarters of cases these are a result of road traffic accidents; the only other major cause is a fall from a height. Recent surveys show that the radius and ulna (in the lower part of the forelimb) are most likely to be involved, especially in small dogs (such as Papillons) carelessly dropped by their owners. The pelvis and the bones of the hind limb (femur, tibia and fibula) are fractured almost as often. The two halves of a long limb bone can be secured by a strong metal pin passing down the centre of each part; alternatively metal plates and screws can be used to fasten the pieces together while they heal. Fragments of bone can be wired into place.

Q *What other operations may need to be performed on dogs?*

A Well, sometimes it is necessary to carry out a Caesarian operation to remove puppies that cannot be born naturally — because of their size or the way they are presented in the birth canal, or because of some abnormality of the mother, such as a very narrow pelvic canal, possibly the result of a pelvic fracture. The operation involves opening into the abdominal cavity and then into the womb. The operation is so named because Julius Caesar was reputedly delivered in this way.

Opening into any hollow organ or body cavity is indicated by a medical term ending in '-otomy', such as laporotomy, already mentioned, referring to opening into the abdomen (strictly speaking the peritoneal cavity). Other common examples are: for the stomach — gastrotomy, intestines — enterotomy, bladder — cystotomy and thorax (chest cavity) — thoracotomy. These operations may be required to remove a foreign body or a tumour. Unfortunately it is not unusual for dogs to swallow foreign bodies which lodge in the intestines, stomach or oesophagus and have to be removed. Anything which is capable of being swallowed has been; balls, toys, rubber bones, pieces of shoes and clothing, string, stones, coins, cutlery and keys are all fairly common. There are also records of dogs having swallowed, variously, two choke chains, a 12-inch (30-cm) kitchen knife, and even a 3-foot (90-cm) steel poker! Large bladder stones, which in a bitch may occasionally grow to almost completely fill the bladder, can only be removed by cystotomy. Similarly the urethra of a male dog may need to be opened to remove calculi which have become lodged there.

The suffix '-ectomy' denotes removal of a part or organ, usually because it is diseased or cancerous, e.g. the kidney — nephrectomy, or spleen — splenectomy. Tonsillectomy is occasionally performed in dogs but much less frequently than in man. Occasionally it may be necessary to amputate a badly injured limb, tail or ear, or to remove a severely damaged eye.

Apart from fracture-repair a variety of other orthopaedic operations are carried out including the repair of ruptured joint ligaments, correcting repeated dislocation of the patella bone (knee-cap), the replacement of tendons using plaited carbon fibre, and disc fenestration to relieve pain caused by a bulging intervertebral disc (see page 213).

Dogs with chronic ear disorders often benefit from the improved ventilation provided by exposing more of the ear canal to the air, using the technique of aural resection.

Occasionally it is necessary to repair an abnormal opening in the wall of the abdominal cavity which allows part of the intestines to pass through, a fault known as a hernia. Quite often in road accidents the diaphragm is ruptured causing a diaphragmatic hernia. The passage of intestines into the chest cavity interferes with breathing and can have serious consequences. When some puppies are born, the abdominal muscles fail to close together at the umbilicus (the point where the umbilical cord is attached), with the result that a small bulge of protruding intestine can be seen or felt beneath the skin — an umbilical hernia. Usually this type is much less serious.

Operations on the eyelids are often required to correct such defects as distichiasis (where an extra row of eyelashes irritates the front of the eyeball) — seen in Pekingese, entropion (an inward curling of the eyelid margin which also irritates the eyeball) — seen in Chow Chows and Cocker Spaniels, and ectropion (where the lid rolls outwards exposing its lining and causing a watery eye) — seen in St Bernards and Bloodhounds. In some breeds (e.g. Chow Chows) individuals are treasured because their upper eyelids show entropion and their lower lids ectropion, producing what are called 'diamond eyes'. Operations on the eyeball itself require specialized techniques to treat such disorders as corneal ulcers, 'dry eye' (a lack of tears), cataract (opacity of the lens), displacement of the lens and glaucoma (increased fluid pressure in the eye). Dogs have even been fitted with hydrophilic contact lenses, not to improve their sight but to allow lesions on the front of their eyes to heal. An operation is also sometimes performed to correct blocked nasolacrimal ducts which cause tears to pour down the face; this defect is particularly obvious on white dogs such as Miniature Poodles as it causes brown, wet streaks below the eyes.

This is by no means an exhaustive list and many other specialized operations, usually requiring a high degree of technical skill, may be needed in particular circumstances.

Q *Are there any operations that ought not to be performed on dogs?*

A Some veterinary surgeons, especially in Britain, are unhappy about performing operations which will not benefit the animal but are carried out simply to gratify the whim of the owners or to enhance their social status. It is quite proper to describe such procedures as mutilations. The most commonly performed of these is tail docking which is generally carried out to conform to accepted 'breed standards'. In many European countries and in North America ear cropping is practised on certain breeds (e.g. on the Dobermann, Great Dane, Rottweiler and Boxer) to produce an alert appearance, but the practice is banned in Britain. The de-barking of dogs (ventriculocordectomy) is also practised in some countries, along with a variety of cosmetic operations, including the removal of areas of skin pigmentation that to the owner appear unsightly or interfere with the animal's suitability for showing. Other mutilating operations include inserting false testicles where they have not descended, capping discoloured teeth and, to be in fashion, inserting small gemstones in the canine teeth.

Q *I have heard my veterinarian talk about cryosurgery. What kind of surgery is that?*

A Cryosurgery, or cryotherapy, is a technique in which intense cold is applied in a controlled manner to kill diseased cells while producing the minimum of damage to healthy tissue. A rapid freeze followed by a slow thaw is required for greatest efficiency, so the use of liquid nitrogen is preferred, either sprayed over the lesion or to cool a probe placed in contact with it. To obtain the maximum destruction of abnormal cells two, or even three, freeze-thaw cycles are advisable.

The technique has been used in dogs primarily to remove superficial tumours (e.g. from the skin, nose, mouth and rectum) and grossly infected tissue around the anus (perianal fistula). As with other forms of surgery it is performed under general anaesthesia. Lesions heal with scarring, and on the skin hairs often grow back a different colour. An unpleasant smelling exudate may appear from the larger treated areas for up to two weeks afterwards.

Q *Do dogs ever get fitted with plaster casts?*

A Yes, fractures of the limbs below the elbow joint in the front limb and the stifle joint in the hind limb can be effectively treated with casts and splints. However, if plaster casts are applied too tightly they can cause pressure sores where they press on bony prominences and in extreme cases may lead to gangrene; if too loose they will not hold the bones together for healing to take place and may even slip off. They can also become soggy if allowed to get wet and the dog may chew at them. In recent years a number of materials which are lighter, easier to apply and more hard-wearing than Plaster of Paris have been introduced. These include fibreglass tape, plastic — as sheets or tape (Hexcelite) — and polyurethane (Neofrakt), which is also used to give durability to men's shirts. Despite their advantages, the newer materials have the major disadvantage of being two or three times more expensive.

Q *Why did my vet tell me not to give my dog any food or water before his operation?*

A Almost all surgical operations on dogs are performed under general anaesthesia (a generalized loss of sensation accompanied by unconsciousness). The use of a general anaesthetic is most important for humane reasons; it prevents fear and pain during the operation, and, by avoiding pain, greatly minimizes surgical shock which would otherwise frequently prove fatal. In addition, general anaesthesia relaxes the muscles and avoids the possibility of movement, which is an important prerequisite for successful surgery, particularly on delicate or complex structures.

Because of the use of general anaesthesia, the normal reflex movements (automatic responses) are temporarily abolished, including the coughing reflex. Normally any material which attempts to enter the larynx at the back of the throat provokes a violent bout of coughing to prevent its passing down any further, i.e. down the windpipe.

Under general anaesthesia vomiting can occur if there is food or water in the stomach, and this material will pass up to the back of the throat (pharynx), where the digestive and respiratory tracts cross each other. Because of the lack of an effective coughing reflex, there is then a grave risk that some of the material may pass through the larynx and down the windpipe to the lungs. Such vomited material, containing acid from the stomach, is very irritant and would provoke a severe pneumonia (inhalation pneumonia), which is invariably fatal.

Furthermore the pressure of a stomach distended with food on the abdominal side of the diaphragm can interfere with normal breathing while the dog is anaesthetized.

It is to avoid these potentially serious consequences that food and water must be restricted prior to general anaesthesia. Because food can be retained in the stomach for several hours, an overnight fast is usually advised, which means that an animal is not fed after its normal evening meal on the day before it is to be anaesthetized.

Water is removed from the stomach much more rapidly and it is therefore usually sufficient to prevent drinking on the actual day of anaesthesia. In all cases follow your veterinary surgeon's advice. Longer periods of deprivation are undesirable because they weaken the dog and reduce his chances of successfully withstanding the stress of surgery.

There are two other important points:

1 Do not feel sorry for the dog and give it a drink against your veterinary surgeon's instructions, because you may literally kill it with kindness.

2 Tell the vet, or his nurse or receptionist, when food and drink was last consumed. If you know, or suspect, that the animal has in fact eaten or drunk after it was supposed to, *say so*, do not conceal the fact. It is usually better to postpone the operation than to expose the animal to an unnecessary risk.

Q *Is general anaesthesia safe?*

A In the vast majority of cases, yes. Modern anaesthetic drugs are less toxic and have a greater margin of safety than previously, and in the hands of trained, experienced veterinary staff death from anaesthesia seldom occurs. However, it should be appreciated that, just as in human medicine, there are individuals who, quite unpredictably, may react unfavourably to a particular drug. Fortunately, such idiosyncratic reactions are few and far between.

Certain groups of animals are more at risk from the undesirable effects of anaesthetics — principally the very old, the very young, and severely ill, debilitated or weak animals, especially those suffering from shock. Whenever possible, it is better to delay anaesthesia and surgery until the animal is in a stronger condition to withstand it. But clearly in an emergency this is not possible.

Two general rules emerge therefore:

1 Postpone non-essential anaesthesia and operations (e.g. spaying) on sick animals until they have improved.

2 Perform any really essential anaesthesia and surgery immediately, before the dog's condition deteriorates further.

Q *Is a surgical operation the only reason for giving a general anaesthetic?*

A Although not undertaken lightly, general anaesthesia may be applied in other situations:

1 Where the dog's temperament makes it extremely difficult to handle — for example, with some animals it may be necessary in order to be able to examine wounds or remove skin parasites.

2 Where a long, painful procedure has to be performed which may unduly distress the dog, such as examining the bowel of a dog with colitis using an endoscope.

224

3 Where it is necessary for the dog to remain absolutely still — for example for radiographs to be taken. This is particularly necessary if such radiographs involve complex techniques, e.g. the injection of contrast media to show up certain tissues more clearly.

As with any type of 'photograph', movement produces blurring of the image so that it can be difficult to distinguish important details. For certain radiographic procedures it may be sufficient to keep the animal still by holding it, but this is usually unsatisfactory for complex procedures, as well as exposing the handlers to non-essential radiation. (Incidentally, radiography has no curative properties — it is used merely for diagnosis.)

Q *Couldn't the vet give my dog a local anaesthetic instead of a general one?*

A In most cases, local anaesthesia is used to remove sensation from a relatively restricted and superficial part of the body. The local anaesthetic (otherwise known as a local analgesic) in the form of a drug solution, is injected either around the sensory nerve endings of an area, or around the nerves which receive sensation from that area (the latter is referred to as nerve blocking). As a result, the transmission of sensations, including pain, from that area to the brain is temporarily prevented, and the animal is unaware of interference to that region of its body.

Spinal anaesthesia is seldom practised on dogs, but this technique results in complete blockage of the lower spinal nerves to produce a total lack of sensation, and paralysis in the posterior part of the body.

In all types of local anaesthesia, however, the animal still remains conscious and therefore subject to fear when it observes what is going on around it. It is also able to move. For these reasons, it is unsuitable for any surgical procedures which involve the deeper structures of the body, or where sudden movement could produce severe damage (e.g. near the eye). It is also not appropriate for lengthy procedures, or if the animal resents being restrained.

As a consequence, local anaesthesia in the dog is usually employed only for desensitization of the skin prior to the removal of small growths, or for injection into deeper structures to facilitate certain procedures. For example it is useful for desensitization of the skin before emergency drainage of the bladder, using a needle inserted through the abdominal wall, in cases of total urethral obstruction.

12
Mating
and Puppy Care

Q *How often do bitches come into heat?*

A All female animals undergo cycles of sexual activity called oestrous cycles. The overall regulation of these is performed by part of the brain, the hypothalamus, which responds both to changes taking place in the body, such as hormone levels, and to environmental changes, though these seem of less importance in dogs than in many other species. The role of the hypothalamus is to prepare the animal both physically and psychologically for mating, pregnancy and birth and to ensure the successful completion of these functions. It does this through its control of the hormonal output of the pituitary gland (at the base of the brain) which in turn affects the release of the sex hormones, oestrogen and progesterone, from the ovaries. The bitch, unlike the cat, only comes into heat once in every breeding season.

It is popularly supposed that the interval between 'heats' is six months (four months for the smaller breeds) and that these peaks of sexual activity each year are concentrated chiefly in the spring and autumn. However, careful investigation has revealed that none of these beliefs can be substantiated. There is actually a wide variation in the length of the inter-oestrus interval, from under two months to over fifteen months, with an average length of seven to eight months. Some clear breed differences emerge: German Shepherd Dogs (Alsatians) appear to have the shortest interval (averaging twenty-six weeks in a study performed in Britain but only twenty-one weeks in the USA), whereas most Basenjis come into heat only once a year. The smaller breeds (such as Toy Poodles, Yorkshire Terriers, Miniature Dachshunds and Boston Terriers), far from having shorter intervals between heats as was originally suggested in 1906, all show average intervals of eight months or more. As well as these differences between breeds, there is often so much variation in an individual dog as to make it difficult to predict the time of onset of heat on the basis of previous oestrous cycles. In one Greyhound the period between successive heats changed from five to seventeen months.

Records also indicate that the heat periods of most breeds are evenly distributed throughout the year, except for Basenjis in which most heats occur in the autumn. In general, however, most available records relate to permanently kennelled show dogs, and other evidence suggests that dogs allowed greater freedom do show some link, though only tenuous, between the season and the onset of heat, with marginally more bitches showing onset in late winter to early spring; this is certainly true of racing Greyhounds, and feral dogs also show more obvious seasonal links. The latitude and climate may also exert an influence.

Q *What signs would indicate that my bitch was coming into heat?*

A The oestrous cycle of a bitch may be considered to start with a preparatory stage (known as pro-oestrus) which is characterized by the vulva becoming increasingly swollen and turgid, and the appearance of a blood-stained discharge from the vagina which originates in the uterus (womb). The latter is the most reliable sign of heat, especially in a bitch kept isolated from males. Spots of blood can usually be seen, particularly on the animal's bedding, and the bitch frequently licks her vulva to clean herself. (Of course, injuries and illnesses may also be associated with a loss of blood in that region.)

Superficially this bleeding resembles menstruation in humans and other primates, although in fact the two states are quite different. Bleeding in the bitch *precedes* ovulation (see later), whereas menstruation *follows* ovulation in non-pregnant primates. No situation comparable to menstruation occurs in the bitch.

During pro-oestrus both sexes become increasingly interested in each other, with the male sniffing and licking at the bitch's genital area. The bitch may adopt a playful bowing posture, i.e. with her forelimbs lowered and her hind quarters raised, but will not permit mating and indeed will growl at, and even attack, males that attempt to mount. The bitch appears more restless than usual and urinates more frequently. On average this phase lasts for nine days, although it commonly varies between four and thirteen days; the recorded extremes are two and twenty-seven days.

Pro-oestrus is followed by the stage of oestrus or sexual receptivity, in which the bitch is prepared to mate, and the swollen vulva becomes softer to permit mating. Oestrus also lasts for about nine days on average, though again it usually varies between four and thirteen days, the extremes being three to twenty-one days.

It is the combination of these two stages, pro-oestrus and oestrus, lasting for approximately three weeks, that is popularly referred to as a bitch's 'heat' or 'season'. During oestrus the blood in the vaginal discharge gradually disappears, giving way to a clear discharge. In the

227

presence of a male with whom she is willing to mate, or even when stroked by the owner, the bitch stands quietly with her tail lifted and drawn to one side. However, a bitch will not permit mating unless she considers the male dominant to her. Some males or females (especially Afghan Hounds and Salukis) will not accept individuals of another breed as mates, particularly if they have been raised in kennels devoted to their particular breed.

It is the sex pheromones (scents) in the bitch's vaginal secretion (and perhaps also in her urine and anal gland secretions) which attract males, often from a considerable distance. Other sensory stimuli are much less important, and totally blind and deaf dogs have been mated and bred successfully. One chemical (methyl p-hydroxybenzoate) has been identified as responsible for triggering a strong mounting urge in male dogs. Throughout the remainder of oestrus the bitch's attractiveness to males gradually wanes.

The release of an egg, or eggs, from the ovaries (the process of ovulation) usually occurs within the first three days of oestrus when the bitch is most receptive. Ovulation is not associated with a slight rise in body temperature as it is in women, and therefore cannot be detected by taking the bitch's temperature. During the entire heat period and especially at the onset of oestrus, a bitch may try to escape, and she is best confined for the entire period if pregnancy is to be avoided.

A smear of cells collected from the vagina of the bitch with a cotton-wool-tipped swab is useful in determining the stage of the oestrus cycle, particularly in establishing the imminence of pro-oestrus and the optimum time for mating. To ensure a fertile mating professional breeders generally mate selected animals at least twice between the tenth and fourteenth day of heat (calculated from the onset of pro-oestrus), often presenting the male on alternate days from the tenth day onwards to check whether the bitch is receptive. It has been suggested that a mating early in oestrus results in a higher proportion of female puppies and a mating later in relatively more males, although there is no hard evidence to support this view. In general, it is preferable to take the bitch to the dog rather than *vice versa*, since it is important that the male dog should feel secure in familiar surroundings.

Mating in the dog is a lengthy affair due to the 'copulatory tie' described on page 51. The heat period will be followed by a period of either pregnancy (if the mating is fertile) or pseudo-pregnancy (if mating is unsuccessful or does not take place). There is then a much longer period of sexual inactivity (anoestrus) before the onset of the next heat — usually it lasts for four to five months.

There is no breeding season for male dogs and they are able to mate all the year round, although their libido peaks when bitches on heat are nearby. Because of the prolonged 'locking' they are capable of only a few ejaculations in a twenty-four-hour period.

Q *How can a bitch be pseudo-pregnant?*

A In all species of mammals a structure known as the corpus luteum (or yellow body) develops on the surface of the ovary, at each point from which an egg has been shed. If the female animal becomes pregnant these corpora lutea (in most species there are more than one) persist throughout pregnancy and continually produce the hormone progesterone. This hormone is essential for ensuring successful implantation of the embryo in the uterus, in preventing the mother's body rejecting the developing young during pregnancy, and in helping to trigger milk production at the time of birth. If, on the other hand, the female does not become pregnant the corpora lutea will in most species soon cease this production of hormone.

In the non-pregnant bitch, however, these structures persist and, inexplicably, continue to produce progesterone for between thirty and ninety days after ovulation has occurred. Consequently the uterus develops just as it would in early pregnancy, despite the fact that there are no embryos present; the uterus enlarges and the abdominal muscles may relax. Consequently, because this thirty-to-ninety-day period resembles pregnancy it is often spoken of as pseudo-pregnancy, false pregnancy, phantom pregnancy or pseudocyesis.

In many bitches there are no obvious external signs to indicate the existence of the condition, but in some bitches signs of varying degrees of intensity appear (overt pseudo-pregnancy), usually after six to ten weeks. The term *false pregnancy* is popularly applied to these external manifestations. Towards the end of the period there can be varying degrees of enlargement of the mammary glands, sometimes followed by milk production. If the bitch suckles herself, as some do, lactation will continue, and a many-tailed bandage or 'Elizabethan collar' (as illustrated in the following chapter) may need to be fitted to prevent her suckling. Some bitches also show marked psychological and behavioural changes such as nervousness and anxiety, building a 'nest' in preparation for whelping, and even a phantom labour followed by the adoption of objects (such as slippers, soft toys or even the household cat) as puppy substitutes, and the development of aggressive maternal behaviour.

It is often stated that bitches subject to repeated overt pseudo-pregnancies (i.e. following each heat period) are more likely to develop an infection of the uterus (pyometra), although there is no strong evidence to support this view. It may be possible to control the signs of false pregnancy with hot and cold packs applied to the mammary glands, reducing the intake of food and water for one or two days and by using drugs (e.g. tranquillizers and progestagens). The problem is not improved by the bitch having a litter of puppies; in fact, the signs often become more intense in the following heats. Where this is a frequent problem, and the bitch is not required for breeding purposes, spaying is the preferred long-term solution.

Q *At what age are dogs capable of breeding?*

A The age at which a dog becomes sexually mature and is able to reproduce is known as puberty. In the bitch this is evident by her coming into heat for the first time.

Most bitches first come into heat at between six and twelve months of age, though it can range from four to twenty-four months. As a general rule (though there are many exceptions) bitches of the smaller breeds reach sexual maturity earlier (six or seven months old) than those of larger breeds (ten to twelve months old, or more). Greyhound bitches may not come into heat until they are over two years old. It would seem that, in general, puberty does not occur until a bitch is past the stage of her most rapid growth.

There is evidence that puberty occurs earlier in warmer climates and in free-roaming, as opposed to kennelled, animals. Bitches housed together often 'synchronize' and come on heat at the same time. Sometimes young bitches will show a 'false heat' with bleeding (resembling pro-oestrus) about three months before the onset of the first true heat, which signals puberty.

Bitches do not attain their maximum potential for reproduction (i.e. full sexual maturity) until their second or third heat, and should not be mated until then. An animal which is still growing will find it very difficult to cope with the additional demands of developing puppies for adequate nutrition. This means that mating should not take place before a year old and, depending on the breed, might first occur between one-and-a-quarter and two-and-a-half years old.

A bitch should not be expected to produce two litters a year, even though this is biologically possible, because it imposes a great deal of stress upon her. If this happens there should then be an interval of at least twelve, and preferably eighteen, months before any further litter is conceived.

Male dogs reach puberty over a similar age range (six to twelve months old), though generally a few weeks later than bitches of the same breed. In some breeds (e.g. Chow Chows and Salukis) the male matures several months after the female, whereas in others (e.g. the Beagle) males may breed months before the female. As with bitches, adolescent males should not be mated. Stud dogs should be at least ten to twelve months old before serving a bitch, and ideally two years old before being used regularly.

Q *Can I give my bitch a contraceptive?*

A In many countries it is possible to obtain from veterinary surgeons contraceptive drugs for dogs which can be used either to postpone the onset of heat or to stop it (i.e. suppress or interrupt it) soon after it has started. They are used:

1 To avoid the inconvenience of heat, particularly the attraction of male dogs, in a bitch that is, for example, being taken on holiday or to a dog show, or in the case of Greyhounds, being raced. They are also of value where male and female dogs have to be housed together.

2 To avoid unwanted pregnancies; for instance in a bitch that it is intended to breed from at some later date but not at present (because she is immature or recovering from illness or the birth of a previous litter), or in a bitch that it is intended never to breed from but which, for health reasons, cannot undergo the spay operation.

The drugs most widely used for this purpose are oral or injectable hormone preparations; either progestagens (= progestins) or androgens.

Progestagens are synthetic progesterone-like substances which are less likely than progesterone to cause undesirable effects such as disorders of the uterus and mammary tumours. In most cases they should only be administered for comparatively short periods, but megestrol acetate and proligestone appear to be particularly safe and are effective in over 95 % of cases. After heat has been postponed with these drugs, three months will usually elapse before the next oestrus, but when mated at this next oestrus bitches will produce healthy puppies in litters of normal size with a normal sex ratio. Progestagens will, in general cause decreased activity, increased appetite and the retention of fluid, all contributing to an increase in weight, plus behavioural changes.

In contrast, androgens are masculinizing drugs. An oral synthetic androgen, mibolerone, has recently proved over 90 % effective and much less likely to have side-effects than the natural androgen testosterone (male sex hormone) which has been used in racing Greyhounds, and which causes enlargement of the clitoris, vaginal inflammation with discharge and difficulty in returning to normal cycles. With mibolerone most mature bitches attain normal fertility by their second heat even after continuous treatment for as long as two years. Treatment (given daily in the form of drops) should ideally be started at least a month before the next expected heat and must *not* be given during pregnancy because it will cause developmental abnormalities in female puppies.

Chemical spermicides, drugs to treat males and mechanical methods of contraception (intrauterine and intravaginal devices, caps and condoms) have rarely been used in dogs, because of various problems and unsatisfactory performance. Even 'chastity belts' for bitches (Petniks) have been tried and in some countries appear still to be available. And of course deodorant preparations are available to mask, with variable success, the odour of a bitch on heat. A recent development which may prove successful is the immunization of males to produce sterility for a period of six months or more.

Q *Do bitches always mate with the same partner?*

A No, an unsupervised bitch may mate with several different males during one period of oestrus. This makes it possible for two or more males to fertilize different eggs, so that puppies in the same litter can have different fathers. This phenomenon is known as superfecundation. Consequently, if you wish to obtain puppies from the breeding of two particular dogs it is important not to allow the bitch access to other males, either before or after the planned mating(s). The rules of the Kennel Club require that if a bitch is mated by two dogs during one heat period the names of both should be given as a possible father when the puppies are registered.

Q *Is a bitch ever too old to have puppies?*

A Ideally, bitches should not be used for breeding after they are six to eight years old, because there is a reduction in their fertility and an increasing risk of problems occurring during pregnancy or at the birth. The joint between the two halves of the pelvic bone undergoes some degree of separation at the time of whelping due to the dissolution of the fibrous tissue which binds them, but because there is a slow, progressive conversion of this tissue to bone such a separation is less likely to occur as bitches get older.

Likewise, if a bitch has not had a litter of puppies before she is four to five years old the opening of the pelvic canal will be narrower and, particularly in breeds with large heads, may give rise to difficulties in giving birth.

Male dogs are usually retired from stud work at around eight years old because of reduced fertility, though the indications are that many are still capable of fertile matings at twice that age.

Q *I've heard that if my pedigree bitch is mated by a 'mongrel' dog, this will affect all her future litters. Is this true?*

A No, this is merely a superstition. It may be disappointing to find out that an unscheduled mating has happened, especially if you were intending to mate her later with a pedigree dog to obtain a litter of pedigree puppies, but it will in no way taint the puppies of future litters. Each puppy is formed from the union of a mother's egg and a father's sperm. Egg and sperm both carry half the total number of chromosomes, and therefore genes, that will be found in the cells of the puppy and which will determine its characteristics, such as appearance, temperament, etc. The sperms do not survive any longer than seven days at the outside, so there is no possibility of any of a previous father's genes still being present at the next heat to influence the characteristics of subsequent puppies.

Q *My bitch has just got out and been mated. Can I stop her having puppies?*

A Yes, an injection of the hormone oestrogen given by your vet within two to three days of mating will prevent conception. However, under the influence of this hormone the heat period, including the attraction of males, will be prolonged and there is a slightly increased likelihood of pyometra (uterine infection) occurring. Alternatively, and this is probably preferable if it is not intended to breed from the bitch, she can be spayed within the succeeding month. Intravaginal douches are *not* effective at eliminating sperms because it only takes about twenty seconds or so for sperms to reach the Fallopian tubes (or oviducts) which lead from the uterus to the ovaries.

Q *Do you ever get homosexual dogs?*

A Following long deprivation of a bitch on heat, adult male dogs (particularly young adults) may mount other males and show the typical mating movements. This can also occur if another male is carrying the scent of a bitch on heat. Mounting behaviour should not be confused with the habit of dogs showing their dominance by standing with their forefeet on the back of a subordinate.

A bitch in oestrus is attractive not only to males but to other females, mostly those that are in the post-oestrus phase, i.e. that are pseudo-pregnant, and it is these that are most likely to mount her and simulate mating. This should be regarded as perfectly normal behaviour. Also, some bitches given androgenic drugs to prevent the onset of heat can develop mounting behaviour.

Both male and female puppies (especially the former) may show elements of sexual behaviour (e.g. mounting, pelvic clasping and thrusting) from as early as four weeks of age, but this is part of their normal play and development and is not accompanied by erection, penetration or the ejaculation of sperms. Such behaviour ceases at puberty and gives way to normal heterosexual activity.

Q *How can I tell if my bitch is pregnant?*

A The average length of pregnancy (gestation) in the bitch is around nine weeks (sixty-three days), but there is a good deal of variation depending on the breed; three days either side is quite common (e.g. sixty in the Beagle) and even a week either side is not unusual (from fifty-six to seventy days). Puppies born more than one week premature rarely survive.

During pregnancy the fertilized eggs (zygotes) pass down the oviducts to the uterus (womb). Whereas in humans the uterus is pear-shaped, consisting mainly of a large body and two very small horns, each of which connects with the corresponding oviduct (because usually only one baby is developing at a time), in the bitch the body of the uterus is very short and each of the horns comparatively long because there are usually a number of puppies. The fertilized eggs distribute themselves evenly along the horns.

Pregnancy consists of three major periods:

1 *The period of the egg,* lasting about nineteen days, in which the fertilized egg begins development but is not yet attached to the wall of the uterus and is nourished by uterine fluids, often referred to as 'uterine milk'.

2 *The period of the embryo,* lasting until about the thirty-third day, during which the major regions of the puppies' bodies become differentiated. An encircling placenta is formed which allows oxygen and nutrients to pass from the blood of the mother into that of the developing puppies, and for waste products to pass the other way. However, there is no mixing of the blood of the mother and the young animals; the blood of the foetus, like all its other tissues, is formed during the foetus's development.

3 *The period of the foetus,* from the thirty-third day to birth, in which the foetus and placenta grow to completion; 95 % of growth occurs in this phase.

There is little or no sign of pregnancy in the first month, though a very lively bitch may be quieter. From the fifth week progressive abdominal enlargement may be noticed. It is usually most apparent in lean bitches, those pregnant for the first time and those with a large litter. The bitch's weight will increase, eventually by 2–16 lb (1–7 kg) depending on the size of the breed and the number of developing pups, which may range from one, up to six in small breeds, fourteen in large breeds.

Changes in the mammary glands from the fifth week onwards are more noticeable in bitches having their first pregnancy. The teats are enlarged and protruberant and, if the skin is unpigmented, take on a bright pink colour. Later they become softer and from the sixth or seventh week (later in bitches that have had previous litters) the mammary glands begin to enlarge. With the first litter a watery secretion may be present a few days before the birth but actual milk may not appear until the pups are born; in subsequent pregnancies milk may be present two to three days before the birth. In the last week it may be possible to see the movements of the puppies when the bitch is resting, and the bitch may appear to be experiencing some discomfort.

There are no laboratory tests which will detect pregnancy in the bitch, because the typical hormonal changes of pregnancy are the same as those of pseudo-pregnancy which occurs in every bitch after heat. Pregnancy can be confirmed by careful expert palpation of the abdomen in the period between three-and-a-half to five weeks after a successful mating in almost 90 % of bitches (clumsy palpation, though, may damage the developing young). The embryos can be felt as small swellings resembling marbles. Difficulties are created by bitches that are fat, have well-developed abdominal muscles (e.g. Greyhounds) or tense their abdomen. After the fifth week so much fluid surrounds each of the foetuses that they cannot be distinguished from the other abdominal organs by palpation, until the seventh week, by which time their size has increased considerably. However, it may still be difficult at this stage to detect a *single* puppy.

Ultrasonic instruments of two types have been used to confirm pregnancy. A-mode instruments primarily detect the interface between foetal fluid and surrounding tissues and are 90 % successful at detecting pregnancy from four-and-a-half weeks onwards. Döppler instruments can detect the movement (but not the sound) of the foetal heart or a pulsating artery and become increasingly accurate from the fifth week; beyond the sixth week accuracy is 100 %.

From the seventh week onwards sufficient skeletal calcification has occurred for the foetuses to be clearly detectable on radiographs, — the only method of determining the number of foetuses. But unnecessary exposure to radiation is undesirable, especially during the first three weeks of pregnancy when it may cause abnormal development of the puppies.

Q *Our family bitch is pregnant. Should we give her any special treatment?*

A For most of the pregnancy she should be treated just as she is normally and not fussed over, though take care when lifting her not to put pressure on her abdomen (page 100). She should continue to receive daily exercise throughout the pregnancy, because this has the beneficial effect of maintaining muscle tone, though it should not be too vigorous, i.e. no jumping, especially in the last two or three weeks. Unnecessary medication (including flea powders and sprays) and radiography should be avoided.

A good, balanced diet should continue to be fed throughout the pregnancy, but during the last three weeks the amount should be increased so that she is given between a quarter and a half more food than usual (often the latter), chiefly in the form of extra protein, i.e. meat and fish products. The amount should ideally be related to the number of developing foetuses and can be judged by the bitch's appetite and the degree of abdominal distension. This extra quantity is best fed as a separate meal because, with an enlarged uterus, there is less room for the stomach to expand. However, take care not to overfeed and produce obesity. It's advisable to give routine treatment for roundworms (ascarids) a month before she is due to give birth to reduce contamination of the puppies' environment later, though this is a matter you can discuss with your vet.

Constipation may occur in the last few days of pregnancy and can be countered by giving one to three teaspoonsful (5–15 ml) of liquid paraffin, depending on her size. To increase the amount of maternal antibodies which will be passed on to the puppies, a booster vaccination can be given to the bitch before mating or during pregnancy, although in the latter case only *dead* vaccines should be used to avoid foetal damage.

About two weeks before the birth (whelping) is due, the bitch should be housed apart from other dogs in the household and provided with a whelping box in a quiet, warm area such as a corner of a relatively unused room. If necessary a screen can be placed around the box. Additional heating may be required because the ideal temperature should be at least 80 °F (27 °C). Although a wooden box is ideal, and is used by professional breeders, a stout cardboard box will be adequate for small breeds if it is large enough to allow the bitch to stretch out and can accommodate the puppies. Even a basket will be adequate for toy breeds. The sides should be high enough to keep out draughts (4–6 inches (10–15 cm)) but at least one side should be cut down to about 3 inches (7.5 cm) high for the bitch to step over easily and for you to be able to attend to her.

Some wooden whelping boxes have one removable side (to allow puppies to crawl out when they are old enough) and a horizontal shelf or rail fixed parallel to one or more sides, about 2—3 inches (5—8 cm) away from the side and at a similar height, to prevent the bitch lying right up against the side and possibly crushing a pup in the first two or three days after birth. Ideally, the box should be raised a few inches off the ground to avoid draughts. Place plenty of newspaper inside for her to tear up to make a nest; this is easily replaced if soiled and is therefore preferable to blankets. The bitch should become used to sleeping in the box for at least ten days before giving birth.

It may set your mind at rest if at this stage you take the bitch to your local vet for a check-up. It is also a good idea to clip the hair from around the vulva and mammary glands in a long-haired animal.

Q *How will I know when my bitch is about to give birth, and what should I do?*

A A few days before the end of pregnancy the bitch will become restless and nervous, often following her owner about, crying, whining, refusing to settle and perhaps failing to obey commands. Often she will be more wary of strangers, and there may be occasional vomiting. Whether or not she has been provided with a whelping box, she may seek out a suitable secluded spot for herself in which to give birth. In the place where she intends to whelp, the bitch will tear up her bedding, whether it is newspapers or other materials such as a bedspread or cushions, to create a 'nest'. It is better not to disturb her, even if the chosen spot is very inconvenient.

One or two days, sometimes more, beforehand, milk will be present in the mammary glands, or in the case of a maiden bitch (one pregnant for the first time) there will be a watery secretion first as the actual milk does not appear until the time of birth. The ligaments along the back relax, making the pelvic bones more prominent and giving a 'low-slung' appearance. In the last twenty-four hours or so the bitch usually goes off her food and her body temperature falls 2 °F (1 °C), down to 99.5 °F (37.5 °C). It returns to normal twelve to twenty-four hours after the birth. The vulva becomes larger and softer and a slight sticky discharge appears. It is advisable to take the bitch outdoors at this time to relieve herself. Keep the bitch calm and quiet, and make sure that other pets and children are kept well away from her.

If the bitch is more than three days overdue, it is wise to consult your veterinary surgeon.

Q *Should my vet be present when the puppies are born? I don't want to bother him if it is unnecessary.*

A You won't necessarily have to call your vet at all; most bitches can cope with birth perfectly adequately on their own, or with just a little help from their owners. Nevertheless, it is a good idea to inform your vet beforehand so that he or she can make arrangements to receive and deal with your bitch if an emergency arises.

Q *I have never seen puppies being born. What are the stages of labour in a bitch?*

A The irregular contractions of the uterus which occur during the first stage are not detectable by an observer, either visually or by feeling the abdomen, but they appear to cause the bitch some discomfort. She shivers, pants gently, moves frequently and glances nervously at her flanks and hindquarters. This stage usually takes between six and twelve hours, but can take up to thirty-six hours in a nervous bitch at her first whelping. Many bitches prefer to be alone and in dim lighting, although some are reassured by the presence of their owner. Some bitches will feed and drink during this time though others will not; it is a good idea to offer food and drink, nevertheless.

The onset of the second stage is shown by marked abdominal contractions, causing the bitch to strain (sometimes groaning as she does so) and to pant heavily. She usually licks her vulva from time to time. Within an hour, and after strong contractions, the first puppy, surrounded by the outer bag of fluid (the allanto-chorionic sac or 'water-bag') within which it has developed, passes down the birth canal. This fluid-filled sac appears at the vulva as a greyish balloonlike structure. It may burst spontaneously during the birth due to pressure, producing a flood of clear fluid, but generally the bitch licks at the sac vigorously when it appears, causing it to rupture.

The passage of the first puppy's head through the pelvic canal may prove difficult, especially if it is a first pregnancy, causing the bitch to cry out in pain and provoking very forceful contractions. However, once the head is out the rest of the puppy's body follows easily. In a proportion of cases (up to a third) the pup is presented rear end first, and in some the hind legs are still tucked up inside (a so-called breech birth); although most of these are born without problems it often takes a little longer. Bitches usually lie on their sides while giving birth, though some prefer to adopt a standing position, especially when straining hard. Some nervous bitches may cry or scream at this time.

Immediately after expulsion of the puppy, the bitch will bite through the membrane (amnion) which covers it, and vigorously lick it away from the puppy's head. This licking serves to stimulate the puppy's breathing and movements. If the membrane over the puppy is still intact and the bitch makes no attempt to break it straight away (as might happen with an inexperienced bitch) you should do so, otherwise the puppy will drown in the fluid which is inside. With a finger, rupture the membrane close to the puppy's mouth to allow it to breathe, then dry the puppy with a rough towel and try to make sure its air passages are clear by wiping the fluid from them. If necessary, the puppy can be held in the palm of your hand with its head nearest your fingers, and gently swung a few times to remove any remaining liquid. Brisk rubbing will normally stimulate breathing but if this doesn't work and the pup starts to go blue, *gently* blowing into its nostrils may start respiration. An alternative is to dip the puppy alternately in bowls of cold and warm water: the shock will often make it breathe. When breathing starts, dry the pup and return it to the bitch.

In most cases, after a few more contractions (generally within five to fifteen minutes) the placenta will be passed, looking like a piece of liver. This is called the third stage of labour. The appearance of some dark green fluid at this time is quite normal and does not indicate that anything untoward has taken place. At times a puppy may be born with the previous pup's placenta wrapped round it. A primitive instinct to hide the presence of new-born puppies from possible predators usually causes the mother to eat the placenta; if not, it should be removed and destroyed. Unless there are twins, the number of placentas passed should equal the number of puppies. Occasionally two or three placentas may be passed out together. Because a retained placenta can result in uterine infection, it is advisable to count how many have been expelled and if you believe there is any discrepancy to present her later for veterinary examination. In eating the placenta the bitch bites through the umbilical cord (the puppy's life-line attachment to the placenta when it was inside the womb). Again, if the bitch shows no interest in breaking the cord you should do so. Sever the cord about 1 to 2 inches (3–5 cm) away from the puppy's body, ideally tearing it (with clean fingers) because this will simultaneously seal the ends. Be careful not to pull on the cord because this might cause an umbilical hernia. If scissors are used to cut the cord they should preferably be sterile, and before making the cut it is advisable to tie a thread around the cord between the puppy and the cut to prevent any seepage of blood.

The interval between puppies is very variable, but is usually fifteen to thirty minutes. Sometimes they follow one another out in quick succession, but with a small litter the delays tend to be longer, with up to an hour between each. Generally the whole procedure is completed within two to six hours, though it may take up to ten hours with a large litter. In some bitches there is a perfectly normal interruption to parturition lasting two to three hours, or sometimes longer, during which contractions cease and the bitch lies quietly. Labour then starts again and the remaining puppies are delivered. The distinguishing feature between this and the presence of an obstruction to the birth is that when an obstruction is present straining will continue, to no effect.

The end of the birth process is signalled by the bitch settling down to mother the pups without further straining.

Q *During the birth of the puppies are there ever any emergencies when I should call my vet for help?*

A Very occasionally it is necessary to tranquillize a bitch that becomes almost hysterical in the first stage of labour. In some bitches labour soon ceases and does not re-start; this most often happens in large, overweight bitches where there are only one or two large foetuses, or in small breeds where the uterus is overdistended by a large litter. Do not allow this to go unattended.

Veterinary attention should also be obtained if at any stage (before, during or after parturition) the bitch produces a foul-smelling discharge, or collapses, or if profuse or continual haemorrhage occurs.

In general, however, the main indications for obtaining veterinary assistance are as follows:

1 Where the bitch has shown strong, forcible contractions for two hours without the first puppy appearing, or where there has been weak straining for six hours.

2 Where the bitch becomes exhausted with straining and the contractions get progressively weaker; referred to as uterine inertia.

3 Where more than an hour has passed since delivering the previous puppy and straining is still vigorous.

4 Where the puppy is partially delivered and cannot be dislodged. In this case no more than five minutes should elapse before attempts are made to get help. Fortunately, puppies often survive a protracted birth. In fact, their brains can withstand total oxygen lack for five to ten minutes, a situation which would produce permanent brain damage in a human.

A common cause of all four situations is some obstruction to the passage of the puppies, producing difficulty in giving birth (dystocia). The fault may be due to a narrow birth canal, commonly caused by a previous pelvic fracture but sometimes due to a breed peculiarity, as in the Scottish and Sealyham Terriers. Rarely, there may be some other obstruction, such as a tumour in the pelvic canal. Alternatively, the obstruction may be caused by the foetus being oversized or abnormally presented. Relative foetal enlargement is often met with in the toy breeds and in cases where there are only one or two puppies; abnormally-large heads are common in the brachycephalic breeds, e.g. Bulldog and Pekingese, and the Chihuahua. It may also arise from abnormal causes such as deformed puppies (monsters) or those that have become swollen following disease or death in the uterus. Problems of presentation may occur when the puppy is partially born (4 above), for example, in cases of breech birth (tail coming first with hind legs still inside), or where a puppy's head becomes turned to one side just before it passes through the vulva.

In cases where the head and front legs, or the hind legs, are already outside but there is difficulty in passing the remainder of the puppy, an attempt can be made to help the delivery (but don't interfere if all is going well). Carefully grasp the exposed part through a single thickness of clean towelling and gently but firmly pull it outwards and downwards, between the bitch's legs as she strains. In particular, prevent the puppy returning to its original position each time the bitch relaxes. If this approach fails, or if the presentation is more complicated, veterinary help must be obtained.

If it proves impossible for the vet to overcome the obstruction it will be necessary to perform a Caesarian operation to remove the puppies, i.e. through incisions in the abdominal wall and the uterus.

After the birth of the puppies has taken place, the following conditions make it advisable to consult your vet:

1 You believe a placenta or a foetus is retained, e.g. if a persistent green or brown vaginal discharge is present. Where there is doubt a radiograph can establish whether an unborn puppy remains.

2 If there was any problem with the delivery.

3 If you had to tie off the umbilical cord of one of the puppies.

4 If any pup looks or behaves abnormally, e.g. won't suckle or cries continuously.

5 If the bitch doesn't eat within twenty-four hours of the birth, or is obviously ill, or if these signs develop later.

6 If the bitch has had problems during or after having previous litters (e.g. the development of uterine infection).

7 If there is an unpleasant-smelling discharge or marked bleeding. However, a little reddish vaginal discharge is quite normal for up to three weeks after whelping *provided* that the bitch appears healthy.

Q *What should I do if the puppies appear abnormal or are unwanted?*

A In the case of grossly deformed puppies, it is much the kindest thing to have them humanely put to sleep immediately; indeed, they may very well not survive long in any case. The deformities include such things as spina bifida (where the spinal cord is exposed), gross umbilical hernia (where most of the intestines are outside the body, covered only by a pouch of skin) and hydrocephalus (the accumulation of fluid around the brain, causing a swollen cranium and abnormal behaviour). Probably the most common defect is a cleft palate (an opening between the mouth and the overlying nasal cavities, so that in suckling milk passes into the nasal chambers and drips from the nose). Other abnormalities such as extra dew-claws or shortened tails, however, will not present any danger to health. If there is any doubt it is always worth discussing with your vet the chances of successfully treating and rearing a particular puppy.

Unwanted puppies, i.e. those for which no homes can be found, are best put to sleep by your veterinarian as soon as possible, and not disposed of by inhumane methods such as drowning.

Q *Is it true that a bitch will sometimes eat her puppies?*

A 'Inadvertent cannibalism' occasionally occurs where a nervous, inexperienced bitch overdoes the biting through the umbilical cord and eating the foetal membranes, and chews into the abdominal wall of a puppy, causing complete or partial evisceration (disembowelling). Although severely damaged puppies will die, those with lesser lesions usually make a good recovery. At times this may lead to the puppy being eaten completely, although true cannibalism is relatively rare.

The sire of a litter, if known to be good-tempered, seldom poses a threat to the newborn pups, although in general it is preferable to allow only the bitch access to them.

Q *What attention will the bitch and puppies require after the birth?*

A Directly after whelping the mother can be given a warm drink and possibly some food before resting. In a small proportion of cases, the bitch may later suffer from infection and inflammation of the uterus (metritis) or the mammary glands (mastitis), or 'milk fever' (described later). Metritis can produce fever and severe illness. With mastitis the affected glands (usually only one or two) feel hot, hard and painful and the bitch refuses to allow suckling; eventually an abscess may form. In all these conditions a vet should be consulted immediately. Later, the teats can become sore from repeated suckling, particularly after the eruption of the puppies' milk teeth which starts at three weeks. The nipples should be examined daily and washed with warm water if there is a residue of dried milk. Any blocked nipples should be carefully bathed and massaged to stimulate the flow of milk. If the puppies' nails scratch the bitch they should be cut short.

Most newborn pups suckle immediately after they have been licked clean by the bitch, certainly within half an hour. The suckling reflex is most strong at birth, which is very important because most of the antibodies that provide immunity for the young animal are taken in from the colostrum or 'first milk' during the first one or two days of life. (At birth a puppy's gastrointestinal tract is sterile but within minutes is filled with micro-organisms acquired from the immediate environment, especially from its mother.) Usually the first pups in the litter will suckle in between the bitch giving birth to the others, but if the bitch is very restless they are best removed to a warm box until the whole process is complete, and then returned.

During the first three days the pups become increasingly proficient at suckling. For the first week feeding occurs roughly every two hours, and then the interval gradually lengthens to approximately every four hours. When suckling, puppies push with their hind legs while their forelimbs are used to 'knead' the breast until they are about seventeen days old (possibly to stimulate lactation and to improve the puppy's respiration by keeping the breast out of its face). They do not return consistently to the same teat as kittens do but, given a choice, tend to take a rear (inguinal) teat.

Newborn puppies cannot regulate their body temperature effectively (after birth it falls from 100.5 °F to 90 °F (38 °C to 32 °C)), and until they are a week old they cannot even shiver. As the environmental temperature falls so does that of the puppy. Therefore they are very dependent on external sources of heat, including warmth from the mother. The temperature of the surroundings should be at least 70 °F (21 °C) all the time, and many breeders use polyester fur or cellular blankets after the birth to help conserve heat. It is this need to conserve heat that makes week-old puppies sleep in a pile; at two weeks there is less heaping, at four weeks they sleep in groups, and at six weeks singly.

Puppies that are premature, weak or chilled are usually unable to suckle effectively, if at all. The bitch will lick and care for all her pups (including any stillborn pups) while they remain warm, but as their temperature falls any lethargic, dying pups will be ignored or deliberately pushed outside the nest by the bitch, despite their calls of distress. Contented puppies grunt occasionally but don't cry; this noise is a feature of those suffering from hunger or cold.

Q *How does development proceed later?*

A In the first few days of the puppies' life the bitch is extremely protective and often doesn't want to leave them, even to feed or relieve herself. Therefore don't interfere too much or bring strangers near. The bitch will stay with the puppies constantly for their first three weeks (gradually becoming less protective) and then the number of daily contacts with her pups decreases; in fact she often deliberately avoids contact and by the time they are six weeks old only spends short periods with them. The bitch will also begin to discipline the pups for any misbehaviour after three weeks. It is important for the pups to lead less secluded lives from three weeks on, because this is the start of the important period of socialization.

For the first two weeks after birth puppies are very immature and live in a sensory and emotional void, unable to see or hear and responding only to touch and temperature. Their taste sense is poor, although they obviously appear to like milk. Their faces are expressionless and they don't even wag their tails. However, they *are* able to crawl around slowly with their heads swaying until they locate their mother and can snuggle up to her; 90% of their time is spent sleeping and the rest feeding. The electrical activity of the brain, as measured by an E. E. G., is very weak.

At around two weeks old the eyes open and the pups can move about more effectively. They can stand to suckle or drink at three weeks and have learned to crawl backwards as well as forwards. During the first three weeks the puppies only pass urine or motions when stimulated by the bitch's licking (a simple involuntary reflex), and she consumes what they pass, thus keeping the nest clean. Then at three weeks old voluntary elimination starts. At the same time their ears open and their brain activity is greater, reaching the adult level at four to five weeks. At four weeks old they are able to tell from which direction a sound is coming. It is believed that some slight stress during the first five weeks of life is beneficial for avoiding later emotional or intellectual impairment.

Apart from possibly arranging for the removal of the hind dew-claws at three to five days old (page 43), there is little to do in the first three weeks except to feed the bitch and keep a watch on the general welfare of bitch and pups. The strain of feeding is most intense at three weeks old (the time of peak demand, i.e. just before weaning starts) and some shedding of the bitch's hair is quite common.

At birth a puppy of a medium-sized breed (e.g. a Beagle) weighs about 9 ounces (250 g) but weights range from 3 ounces (90 g) or less for a Chihuahua to 21 ounces (600 g) for a Great Dane. Puppies should gain at least 5–10% of their birth weight each day, thereby doubling it after eight to fourteen days. After four weeks they may be seven times their birth weight. To achieve this, the bitch of a large litter needs to produce more milk solids in proportion to its weight than a prize milking cow. The general recommendation is that one and a half times the bitch's normal ration (of a balanced diet) should be fed for the first week, twice as much in the second, and then rise to three times as much (three and a half times in the case of a large litter) in the third and fourth weeks. This should be fed as three or four meals per day. At the end of the fifth week the quantity can be reduced to double the normal amount, and then gradually restored to the normal ration by the time of weaning.

Q *What is 'milk fever'?*

A Occasionally, a bitch will show signs of a lack of calcium, a condition known as eclampsia (puerperal tetany or milk fever). It arises where there is a failure to replace the calcium lost from the blood both in forming the puppies' bones and in the continual production of milk. Consequently it is mostly seen in small dogs, especially those with large litters. Except for the German Pointer it is rare in large breeds. Generally it happens two to four weeks after the birth, although sometimes earlier, sometimes later. The bitch loses interest in the puppies and is restless, and whines or barks. She begins to walk stiffly, then staggers, and won't eat. Ultimately she will develop muscle spasms and convulsions, accompanied by a high temperature. Prompt veterinary treatment can rapidly reverse these signs but the puppies should be removed and fed artificially, at least temporarily.

It is difficult to prevent this condition occurring, and giving excessive calcium supplements during pregnancy can make matters worse.

Q *Is it possible to rear orphan puppies successfully?*

A If for some reason the bitch is unable to feed her puppies, it *is* possible to rear them artificially; for instance, if the bitch dies while giving birth, or soon after, or if she has had a Caesarian operation and is unable to feed the litter for a day or two. It may also be necessary to do this for a time if the bitch is ill, e.g. with mastitis or eclampsia, or has no milk. Also, some bitches reject one or more of their pups. And when there is a very large litter which the bitch would have difficulty in rearing, many breeders prefer to have some pups fostered rather than have them put to sleep.

Finding a foster mother or mothers for the puppies is always preferable to artificial feeding; choose one that is either feeding her own pups or lactating with a pseudo-pregnancy. Where one or two pups are added to a litter it should ideally be done when the bitch is absent but as soon after that litter's birth as possible, to minimize detection. Even so, the bitch *may* recognize and resent the additions, pushing them out of the nest or even killing them. To prevent this, it is recommended that new animals be rubbed with the foster mother's own puppies to give them all the same smell, or, alternatively, that their backs be dampened with sweetened milk to induce the bitch to lick them and thus accept them. It may be possible to discover suitable foster bitches through contacting your vet or local kennels.

Artificial feeding requires the puppies to be fed milk every two hours (including two feeds during the night) for about the first three weeks of life. After that the intervals can be lengthened and the night feeds dispensed with. A puppy's appetite (and its resultant weight gain) is the best guide to its requirements.

Compared with cows' milk, bitches' milk contains slightly less lactose (milk sugar), more than twice as much calcium and phosphorus and almost three times as much fat and protein. Even human baby milk replacements prepared at twice the concentration intended for babies (a substitute often recommended for puppies) have a very similar composition to cows' milk, except for a vastly increased level of lactose which may give rise to diarrhoea, and so are unsuitable except as a stopgap. Several commercial dog milk substitutes are available and there are also various formulae for preparing substitutes. Unfortunately, none of these entirely resembles bitches' milk and some are very different, though puppies seem to do reasonably well on many of them. The best simple recipe is to mix four parts evaporated milk with one part of water, and then add half a level teaspoonful of dicalcium phosphate (obtainable from a pharmacist) to each pint of the mixture (5 g per litre), plus twelve to fifteen drops of a liquid vitamin preparation (e.g. Abidec). However, this substitute is again high in lactose. An alternative which corrects this defect is more complex, namely one pint (570 ml) of cows' milk plus 6 fluid ounces (180 ml) of single cream, an egg yolk, seven drops (0.3 g) of cod liver oil, one level teaspoonful (4 g) of sterilized boneflour and half a level teaspoonful (2 g) of citric acid.

The proprietary milk foods can be made up freshly for each feed or, in the case of complex formulae, prepared every twenty-four hours and stored in the refrigerator. Make sure that all the ingredients are well whisked together so that there are no lumps of powder. This milk should be fed at blood heat (i.e. approximately 100 °F (38 °C)). Allow the puppy to take it in small amounts so that it can swallow easily, and avoid any going down the windpipe.

Feeding is best done using a special puppies' feeding bottle and teat (e.g. Catac) obtainable from pet stores or sometimes your veterinarian. If this is not available, a doll's bottle and teat or an eye dropper can be used, although the latter holds very little and, because of its larger opening, can give rise to choking. Feeding utensils must be thoroughly cleansed after use by being rinsed in cold water, washed in hot detergent water, then rinsed again and immersed in a hypochlorite bleach solution (e.g. Milton) as recommended for babies' bottles. Alternatively, a clean glass feeding bottle can be boiled for ten minutes immediately before use.

After feeding, the puppy's face should be wiped clean with a dampened piece of cotton wool and then the dog turned over and its abdomen and anal regions gently rubbed with this same swab to stimulate the passage of urine and motions. If its skin becomes dry, apply a little baby oil. It is also important to avoid hypothermia, keeping the puppies under an infra-red lamp, or on an electrically heated pad (thermostatically controlled) to produce a temperature of 85 °F (29.5 °C) in the first week, eventually reducing it by 5 °F (2.8 °C) each week, to 70 °F (21 °C). However, don't heat the *entire* area; have a cooler corner into which puppies can crawl if necessary. Artificially fed dogs can be weaned in the same way as any others.

Q *How should puppies be weaned?*

A Weaning refers to the process whereby puppies make the transition from an all-milk diet to a solid diet, and it is achieved by the gradual introduction of an increasing proportion of solids. It generally starts at three weeks old, when puppies become more inquisitive, and is usually completed at eight weeks old, though completion can be adjusted to be earlier or later, between six and twelve weeks. In the wild it is begun by a bitch regurgitating semi-solid food for her pups in response to them licking her face and mouth. The pups also often consume the bitch's faeces as a source of nutrition. When such behaviour occurs in domestic pets owners regard it as an unacceptable, although it is quite natural and not a cause for concern. Puppies may also begin to sample food from their mother's feeding bowl.

Breeders have traditionally begun weaning at three weeks, first offering small amounts of scraped raw meat (a mushy substance obtained by scraping a sharp knife backwards and forwards over raw meat), and if necessary putting some into the puppy's mouth to give it a taste for the new food. Within a few days a teaspoonful can be given twice a day, and later supplemented with a gruel made from baby food (e.g. Farex) and milk. Nowadays, balanced meat-based puppy foods are available which can be offered well mashed up with milk or water two or three times a day, usually when the bitch is absent. Puppies should also be given some cows' milk in a dish so that they can learn to lap.

Gradually the puppies consume more of the meat food and take less of the bitch's milk. In fact, the bitch may begin to stand up when the pups approach to limit their suckling, and when they have grown so much that they can reach her teats even when she stands, she may run away or growl to deter them.

At five weeks the mother's milk supply will slacken off, and as the pups suckle less it will gradually be further reduced. If milk production continues long after weaning, the mammary glands can become swollen and painful, but the application of hot towels, combined with massage and the complete withdrawal of all food and water for a day, generally results in a rapid decline in milk production. The application of a tight binder such as a many-tailed bandage (page 265) may also be helpful. To stop this occurring, give the bitch no food and only a little water on the actual day when you intend weaning to be completed. The following day provide only a quarter of her normal ration, and on the next a half and the next three-quarters, and then put her back on to the amount of food she was receiving prior to breeding.

When weaning is complete, puppies are usually fed four meals a day. Traditionally, two of these (on waking and at bedtime) have been feeds of milk plus cereal, and the other two (midday and early evening) of meat supplemented with puppy meal, one or more teaspoonsful of cod liver oil, yeast tablets and the occasional scrambled egg. Gradually the milky feeds are cut out so that the pup receives three meals a day at four months old, two a day at six months, and possibly only one when it is nine months old. When a balanced commercial puppy diet is fed, no vitamin supplements are required, and it can be fed for all of the meals. As the number of meals is reduced, the quantity of food at each is steadily increased, its consistency becoming firmer (i.e. no longer mixed with water or milk) and biscuit meal being added according to the manufacturer's recommendations. Having regard to the puppies' weight, approximately twice as much should be fed as for an adult dog (see page 84) until it is half-grown.

If at any stage of weaning diarrhoea occurs regularly or the puppy won't feed, consult your vet.

248

13
Nursing the Sick Dog

Q *I dread having to give my dog a tablet as he struggles so much. Is there a proper way to give him a tablet or capsule?*

A Quite often dogs will accept a tablet or capsule concealed in a titbit of minced meat or softened chocolate, especially if they are hungry. Consequently, if you intend to use this method give the titbit *before* your dog has its main meal. Some dogs will even take a tablet out of your hand quite voluntarily, especially if it has no unpleasant odour and is among a few yeast tablets presented all together on your outstretched palm.

Simply placing the tablet in a dish of food usually results in the food being eaten and the tablet being left. Crushing a tablet and mixing the powder in with the food might be a successful way of administering it, unless the medication has an unappetizing taste, although sometimes this can be disguised by adding a strongly flavoured substance such as sardine oil or yeast extract (e.g. Marmite). There is however always a risk that the animal will not eat the medicated food or not all of it, so that the dog remains untreated and the dose is wasted. Furthermore, of course, this method of administration is least likely to work with dogs that have lost their appetite, which is a feature of many illnesses. At times a dog may be 'persuaded' to lick in powdered medication that has been mixed with jam or honey and smeared on to its teeth; although regular administration in this way becomes tedious and messy. Some tablets should *not* be broken or crushed (for example certain worming tablets) because they contain a very bitter drug surrounded by an inert coating. If the drug contacts the mouth it provokes profuse salivation. Therefore if your vet tells you *not* to crush or break a tablet before giving it *do* follow this advice.

Unless the dog will take the tablet from your hand or in a titbit (and *swallow* it, not spit it out later) it is preferable to open the dog's mouth, place the tablet at the back and *ensure* that it is swallowed. If the dog is reasonably good-tempered you can do this single-handed although someone else's assistance in holding the dog is often useful. Where the

How to give your dog a tablet

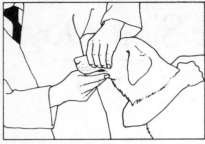

1. *Position the dog in a good light, ideally with someone holding it. Place fingers and thumb at either side of the upper jaw.*

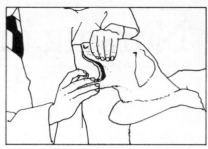

2. *Press just behind the upper canine teeth while pulling the jaw upwards and the lower jaw down with the hand holding the tablet.*

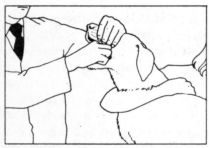

3. *Place the tablet as far back in the throat as possible. Use your fingers or the flat end of a pencil to push it over the back of the tongue.*

4. *Then close the dog's mouth and, with its head inclined upwards, gently stroke its throat until it gulps and licks its nose.*

dog is difficult to handle some assistance is essential. With small dogs in particular it is useful to have them held to prevent struggling. The procedure will be much easier if the dog is made to sit where there is a good source of light, and if its mouth is at the height of your elbow. For a large dog this means sitting on the floor; for smaller dogs sitting on a table, chair or bench, the exact height of which depends upon the dog's size. Some dogs prefer to lie down; this is all right, especially if you can still arrange to have its mouth at elbow height.

If you are right-handed hold the tablet or capsule ready between the thumb and index finger of your right hand. Then place the index finger and thumb of your left hand on either side of the upper jaw, just behind the prominent canine teeth, and simultaneously press the lips inwards and pull the jaw upwards. The second finger (and if necessary the other fingers also) of the right hand should be used to push downwards on the front teeth of the lower jaw to open the mouth wide. If you are left-handed reverse these instructions.

Having opened the dog's mouth, place the tablet or capsule as far back in the throat as possible. It can be quickly pushed over the back of the tongue either with your fingers, or, in a small dog, by using the *flat* end of a pencil or ballpoint pen. Immediately close the jaws together and gently hold them closed with the dog's nose pointing obliquely upwards until it gulps and licks its nose, indicating that the medication has been swallowed. Stroking its throat will encourage this; alternatively a sharp tap under the chin often startles a dog into swallowing. Do not let the dog put its nose down before swallowing; often it will spit the tablet out again.

There are other ways to place the tablet right at the back of the throat, especially with little dogs; one which is very simple is to hold the tablet in a pair of artery forceps. This is a specialized instrument, but easily ordered from a pharmacist, and it renders tablet administration as easy as it ever could be. Another is to use a plastic 'pill giver', sold in pet shops, which will both hold and eject the tablet.

The aim is to be firm, quick and efficient. With successive attempts the animal will become more restless and the job more difficult, so try to get it right the first time. Watch the dog afterwards to check that the tablet is not spat out; if it has been, the procedure will need to be repeated.

Giving a tablet is much simpler than giving a capsule. The outer gelatine shell of a capsule becomes sticky on contact with moisture so usually, unless it is put down the throat at the first attempt, the capsule will stick to your fingers or to the inside of the dog's mouth, and successive attempts will become progressively much more difficult.

Occasionally owners attempt to put powdered drugs directly into their animal's mouth. This is almost impossible to do successfully and should not be attempted.

Q *How can I give my dog liquid medicine?*

A Giving liquid medicine to a dog is not much more difficult than giving a tablet but it takes a little longer. Puppies, in particular, are often dosed with antibiotics in the form of palatable paediatric syrups (i.e. intended for children) rather than tablets or capsules.

Have the animal restrained, ideally in the sitting position, by another family member or a friend. As with tablet administration arrange for the dog's mouth to be at the height of your elbow.

Have the medicine already measured out into a small plastic bottle, or a vial of the type used for dispensing liquids or tablets, or (best) contained in a 5-ml disposable plastic syringe. A syringe is preferable because it is much easier to handle and avoids any spilling of the

How to give your dog liquid medicine

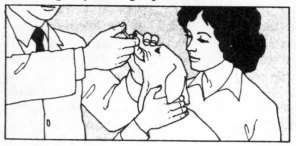

Hold the dog's head so that its mouth is shut and its nose is pointed slightly upwards. Place the end of a 5 ml syringe between its lips at the side of the mouth and then very slowly squirt, the liquid out.

medicine; if a spoon is knocked or you cannot pour it easily some of the liquid gets spilled. If a spoon has to be used, remember some useful tips: half-fill two spoons rather than try to manipulate one which is completely full (or else pour a teaspoonful of liquid into a dessertspoon); put a small book or similar object under the tip of the handle to keep the top of the bowl horizontal — this will avoid spilling and facilitate picking the spoon up. (If it seems likely there will be spillage and a syringe is not available the liquid can even be poured out through the spout of a small teapot.) A plastic eye dropper can be substituted for a syringe, though it will not hold very much, but a *glass* eye dropper is best avoided in case it gets chewed on and splinters.

If you are right-handed hold the dog's jaws firmly shut with your left hand, having the fingers above and thumb below, and give the medicine using your right hand. If left-handed reverse these instructions. Incline the dog's nose very slightly upwards, place the end of the vial, syringe or spoon between the lips at the *side* of the mouth and slowly pour, or squirt, the liquid out. The aim is to encourage the dog to swallow, but without coughing or spluttering. If the dog begins to splutter stop giving the liquid and let it put its head down to recover (though still holding it) before giving the remainder. (If the head is tipped upwards too far choking will occur frequently because liquid will trickle into the larynx each time it is given.)

It is not necessary to place the dosing implement between the teeth, although this is possible with the syringe or eye dropper and will usually speed up administration. In general let the liquid slowly trickle between the teeth. Certainly *do not* attempt to open the jaws and place a spoon or bottle between them, either at the side of the mouth or at the front, because this invariably provokes a struggle, resulting in only partially successful dosing and great distress to all parties.

Afterwards it is often valuable to make a fuss of your dog, or to give it some favourite titbit, to reassure it that you are not intending to be unkind. Certainly praise your dog if it has been co-operative.

Q *Does it matter at what time my dog has his medicine?*

A The instructions from your vet (written or verbal) might indicate precisely when a particular medicine should be administered; for example, before or after meals. Many drugs which influence the digestion or absorption of food need to be given just before meals. Of the remaining drugs, most will be absorbed faster and more completely if they are not given at the same time as food.

When the instructions state that the medicine (tablets, capsules or liquid) should be given a certain number of times a day, the intention is for the times of administration to be as equally spaced as possible. In other words, twice a day means every twelve hours, and three times a day every eight hours, insofar as this is feasible. Obviously, it is not usually necessary to get up in the middle of the night to give medicine, and times of administration may have to be fitted around working hours, but as far as possible the doses should be evenly spaced.

Q *The vet has given me an inhalant for my dog. What is it and how can I administer it?*

A Inhalants are volatile substances which are mildly irritant to the respiratory tract — such as oil of eucalyptus, friar's balsam and Vick. In order to work, the inhalant must first be converted to a vapour which can be breathed in. Body heat can do this and so a little inhalant can be applied directly to the dog's chest or chin. However, vaporization is best achieved by adding a little of the inhalant to very hot water. Then both the water vapour and the vaporized inhalant are inhaled. The mild irritant effect of the inhalant on the respiratory membranes causes a runny nose — in other words it increases the volume and decreases the thickness (viscosity) of respiratory secretions. This has the very beneficial effect of washing away the thick sticky mucus which otherwise will block the nasal passages. The water vapour also helps in this and moisturizes the dry membranes. In fact water vapour alone often has a very beneficial effect.

It is unusual for a dog to cooperate by holding its head over a steaming bowl, but this is not unknown. However, there is a danger of the bowl being upset and the hot water scalding the dog. Possibly the best procedure is as follows. First, apply a smear of petroleum jelly (e.g. Vaseline) to the upper and lower eyelids and around the nostrils to avoid undue smarting. Half-fill a small basin or bowl with boiling water and add to it a *little* of the inhalant (i.e. six drops of liquid or a quarter teaspoonful of solid medicament). Then place this on the windowsill of a small room, such as the bathroom or toilet, with any windows closed, place the dog inside and close the door. If there is serious risk of the dog jumping up and upsetting the bowl or scratching the door or otherwise not readily accepting the treatment it is advisable for the owner to stay in the room with the animal. After five minutes the animal should be allowed out and the strings of mucus cleaned from around its nose. Most dogs appear to find real relief from this treatment and if this is the case it can be repeated two or three times a day.

Q *Although I don't like the idea, are there any occasions when I should force-feed my dog?*

A As a general rule, of course, it is quite unnecessary, but where a dog has lost its appetite, and it has proved impossible to persuade it to eat, so-called 'force-feeding' may be resorted to. There should *not* be much emphasis on the force; indeed to cram an animal's throat with food or liquid that it cannot, or will not, swallow is likely to lead to some of the food passing down the windpipe (trachea). This usually results in an inhalation pneumonia developing, which is frequently fatal.

The term force-feeding really means using a spoon, an invalid feeding cup or (best) a 5-ml or 10-ml disposable plastic syringe to feed the dog milk, soup or foods which have the consistency of a paste or cream. Foods of this consistency can be prepared by using a home liquidizer, or by mashing up minced meat, fish or grated cheese with honey or syrup. Alternatively, hydrolyzed protein products (from your vet or pharmacist) can be fed.

Very liquid foods can be administered using the same technique as for liquid medicine (see page 251), holding the head with the nose pointing *slightly* upwards and slowly trickling the liquid between the parted lips at the side of the mouth. Help may be required to hold the dog and it must be given a rest between each mouthful to allow it to breathe properly, especially if its nose is blocked. Do not pour in too much liquid at a time, and, if the dog begins to cough and splutter, stop immediately and allow it to lower its head. It is best not to hold the mouth open and spray the liquid on to the back of the throat because this readily leads to choking.

With more solid food of a paste-like consistency, the mouth can be opened, as described for tablet administration, and the paste either scraped on to the upper or lower front teeth from a finger, or from the *handle* of a spoon, or squeezed on to the tongue from a syringe. If the paste is sufficiently stiff, it can be made into a small ball, placed at the back of the throat and administered in the same way as a tablet (see page 249).

Because it is usually not possible to persuade the dog to take very much at a time, it will be necessary to give food frequently, every two hours for example. Force-feeding requires great perseverance to ensure that the dog receives an adequate amount of food. It should not be carried out if the animal is not fully conscious; the normal cough reflex will be absent and, as mentioned before, inhalation pneumonia may result.

Where there is prolonged appetite loss, it may be necessary for your vet to inject drugs to stimulate the appetite, or, as with unconscious animals, to feed the dog artificially. This can be done either through a tube which is inserted at the side of the neck and passes down into the stomach, or by using a special solution given intravenously (i.e. into the blood stream). Unfortunately, even these artificial methods are not practicable for really long-term use, and therefore it is important to try to get the dog feeding normally as soon as possible.

Q *How should I clean a wound?*

A A wound recently inflicted (especially of the irregular type known as lacerated wounds) may be dirty. An older wound may be infected with bacteria and discharging pus. Both will require cleaning before being dressed or re-dressed. In the first six hours the multiplication of bacteria within a wound is only slight. In this time, known as the 'golden period', thorough cleaning will effectively de-contaminate the wound. Any large foreign bodies (e.g. pieces of grit) should be picked out and any soil washed away. Clay soil and organic materials, such as manure, will introduce more bacteria than sand or silt. In the *next* six hours there is considerable bacterial multiplication so that after this time the wound should be considered significantly infected.

Cleaning will be made easier, especially in a long-haired dog, if the hair around the wound is first clipped. Before clipping, the wound must be covered or plugged with a piece of moistened, clean cotton wool to stop any hairs straying in. When clipping hair from the margin of a wound it also helps to smear the scissor blades with petroleum jelly (e.g. Vaseline) so that the hairs will adhere to them.

Then clean the wound using a pad of clean gauze, cotton wool or lint, or even, in an emergency, paper towels. Soak the pad first in tepid water; cleaning will be made easier if it contains a small amount of a detergent antiseptic such as cetrimide (found, for example, in Savlon). This is used primarily because of its detergent effect, not for its limited antibacterial action. Other non-detergent antiseptics should not be used because most of them are poor at killing bacteria and some may cause skin reactions or delay healing. Certainly do not use any household disinfectants. An alternative is to rub the wet pad on to a tablet of toilet soap, though not carbolic or coal tar soaps. Washing is much the most effective way of removing bacteria.

Lightly wring out the pad and with it gently dab and wipe away the dirt and/or pus. Alternatively a spray (e.g. shower attachment) is very effective at removing contamination from irregular wounds or abrasions (see page 271). If you are too vigorous in cleaning you may damage the exposed blood vessels and cause bleeding; if this happens, *immediately stop* further cleaning. The continual oozing of blood can be controlled by holding in place for a few minutes a pad soaked in *cold* water. Dab the wound dry with clean pieces of gauze, lint or paper towels.

To keep the wound clean and to prevent it from being interfered with, apply a pad of gauze or lint (preferably not cotton wool, which tends to stick to raw areas), securing it in place either with a crêpe bandage or adhesive tape. If adhesive tape is used, cut a piece long enough to overlap itself when in place.

Q *If my dog is ill would it be a good idea to give him a hot-water bottle?*

A This is a useful way of supplying heat to an ill or cold animal, but attention should be paid to the following points:

1 The hot-water bottle should never be filled with very hot water, and certainly *not* boiling water. It must always be well wrapped-up in a towel, or else placed in a special hot-water bottle cover which totally encloses it. This is to avoid causing burning of the skin which can be extensive and may result in the loss of skin over a large area of the body.

2 Animals which are seriously ill, or even unconscious, will be quite unable to move away from a hot-water bottle, so that they are even more at risk from one which is excessively hot.

3 Severely shocked animals (e.g. victims of a road accident) will suffer if their body temperature is suddenly raised much higher than that of their surroundings. So again, the hot-water bottle should be kept only warm.

4 After filling, check that the bottle is watertight and, at intervals during its use, check that the cover is still in place and that the bottle is not leaking.

An infra-red heater (preferably a short-wave generator) securely fastened at least 3 feet (90 cm) *above* the dog's bed (higher if the dog is able to stand) could be used instead. It will supply radiant heat continuously and from time to time you should check that the dog is not too warm, especially in summer. Special electric blankets and heating panels can also be obtained, preferably fitted with a thermostat so that the heat output can be controlled. However, if the dog is not in *very* cold surroundings providing it with a heavy cloth coat may be adequate.

Q *Do dogs suffer from bedsores?*

A Yes, bedsores (decubital ulcers) do occur in dogs which are recumbent and unable to move, especially those which are paralysed. They are caused by prolonged, localized pressure which interferes with the blood supply, and therefore the nutrition, of the skin. Although bedsores can occur almost anywhere they are most common over the bony prominences (elbows, hocks and along the limb bones) especially in large, heavy dogs.

To prevent their occurrence a recumbent dog should be given soft bedding, ideally a 3—4-inch (7—10-cm) thick foam rubber mat; alternatively a sack well-stuffed with hay, straw or cedar-wood shavings can be used, or a polystyrene-filled 'bean bag'. Pillows may be used to prop up the dog so that he is resting on his breast bone for some of the time. Care should be taken to keep the dog off hard surfaces such as floor tiles and paving slabs by boxing him in with furniture or fireguards, or even placing the dog inside a child's playpen. The dog should be turned so that he is lying on a different part of the body every two hours during the day (and ideally at least once or twice during the night). The skin over the bony prominences, particularly on the limbs, should be gently massaged regularly and a little alcohol (e.g. surgical spirit or rubbing alcohol) should be gently rubbed over any areas of damaged skin and allowed to evaporate. Actual ulcers should receive veterinary attention.

Paraplegic animals (i.e. suffering from paralysis of the hindquarters — usually following spinal damage) are very prone to bedsores. These animals are also incontinent and require frequent cleaning. They can however be given limited exercise, if the veterinary surgeon agrees. The dog is allowed to walk just ahead of the owner using its front legs normally, while its paralysed hind parts are supported and carried by the owner in a sling made from a towel or similar strong material.

The formation of hard, thickened areas of skin (callouses) over the elbows and hocks of the large breeds of dog is very common even though they are not permanently recumbent, especially when they spend a lot of time resting on hard surfaces. A similar lesion called a sternal callous may appear on the chest of those breeds with deep, pointed chests (such as Dachshunds or Pointers). Callouses may become infected and cystic swellings (known as hygromas) may develop beneath them but usually they do not ulcerate.

Q *What is the best method of bathing a dog's eye?*

A Bathing a dog's eye is useful as a first-aid measure to help flush pieces of grit or grass seed, etc., out of the eye, or where the eyelids have become gummed together by discharges.

Either a patent human eye lotion can be prepared as directed by the manufacturer, or a warm *(not hot)* boric (boracic) acid lotion can be made by dissolving two level teaspoonsful of boric acid crystals in half a tumbler of lukewarm water. In an emergency, or if nothing else is available, just use warm water. *Do not* add salt to it; if too much is added the resultant brine will be very irritant and damaging.

With someone else restraining the dog, soak a small pad of cotton wool or lint in the water or eye lotion, and squeeze the liquid out on to the lids (if stuck together), or on to the surface of the eyeball.

Wet cotton wool, twisted into a spiral, can be used gently to brush away any foreign body from the surface of the eyeball, provided that this is not repeated too often. With eyelids which are stuck together, the wet pad should be gently wiped over the outer surface, mainly using an outward movement (i.e. from the nose towards the side of the face), until the lids gradually become free. Then the surface of the eyeball should be bathed. Repeated re-soaking of the pad may be necessary. Finally, the surrounding skin area should be dried.

If there is obvious infection beneath the lids, or a foreign body cannot be removed, veterinary help must be obtained. If pain persists in the eye and the animal tries to rub it, place between one and three drops of warm (not hot) olive oil into the eye with an eye dropper or, in an emergency, drop the oil from the *blunt* end of a pencil. Try to prevent the dog from rubbing the eye unduly until the vet can attend to it.

Eye baths, as used by humans, are the wrong size and shape for use with dog's eyes, so don't bother trying to find one. Finally, a word of warning: never let any dry material (cotton wool, lint, etc.) contact the surface of the eye; it will stick to the moist surface and, when pulled off, will remove the outer layer of cells.

Q *How can I put eye drops, or eye ointment, into my dog's eye?*

A Unless your dog is unusually cooperative it is advisable to have help to avoid his struggling or scratching while you apply the medication. There will be less sudden shock associated with the application if the tube of ointment or bottle of drops is warmed to blood heat first, for example by standing it in a cup of warm water.

When applying either drops or ointment it is necessary to raise the nose and turn the head slightly, so that the affected eye is uppermost. Eye drops are simpler to apply than ointment. Nowadays, drops are usually supplied in a small plastic squeezee bottle. Holding the nozzle of the bottle about $1/2$ inch (1 cm) above the eye, squeeze out two or three drops on to its surface. If an eye dropper is being used have the dropper ready filled, and then press the rubber or plastic bulb. The dog will then blink, spreading the drops all over the eye surface. Do *not* get any applicator too near the eye surface in case the dog suddenly moves, bringing it into contact with the eye and causing damage.

Eye ointment (ophthalmic ointment) is more difficult to apply, but it will remain in the eye for much longer than drops. If warmed beforehand it will flow more easily. Remove the cap from the tube and use the index finger and thumb of one hand to part the eyelids by placing one above the eye, and the other below, and then moving them slowly apart. If necessary someone should hold the dog's head still. Use your other hand to squeeze the small tube of ointment, placing a length of about $1/8$ inch (3 mm) on the inside of the lower lid, near to the inner corner of the eye (i.e. the corner nearest to the other eye). Take care *not* to touch the eye itself. As the animal blinks, the melted ointment will be spread across all of the eye surface. After application, try to prevent the animal from repeatedly rubbing or pawing at the affected eye, for example by taking it out for a walk.

Incidentally, *don't* use drops or ointment unless your veterinary surgeon has advised it because certain preparations can be quite unsuitable. For instance, many preparations contain corticosteroids, which if applied to an eye ulcer may *prevent* it from healing. Also some proprietary preparations sold for human use are unsuitable for conditions affecting the dog's eye. It is far preferable to seek early advice from your veterinarian about any eye problem.

Q *My vet has suggested that I use hot fomentations to treat an abscess on my dog. What does this mean?*

A A hot fomentation is the application of heat from a pad of lint, gauze, linen or cotton wool soaked in hot water or a hot lotion. It may seem a rather old-fashioned treatment, but it is in fact extremely effective and widely employed. In treating an abscess, the intention is primarily to increase the blood supply to the area by enlarging (dilating) the blood vessels. Consequently, the skin in the heated area looks redder because of the increased amount of blood. Immediately after infection has been implanted in the tissues, after a bite wound for example, hot fomentations *may* prevent an abscess developing. The increase in the supply of white blood cells will destroy the bacteria in the area. If the infection is not discovered until the bacteria are making the area hot and painful, hot fomentation speeds up the formation of the abscess so that it can be drained and healing can begin. Hot fomentations *after* an abscess has been opened surgically, or has burst naturally, promote healing of the wound and ensure that the site is inspected and cleaned regularly.

Also, particularly in racing dogs, hot fomentations may be applied to strains and sprains (i.e. torn muscles, tendons and ligaments). In these cases the heat relieves pain and helps to speed up healing. (Liniments are also used for this purpose, but are *not* suitable for the treatment of an abscess.)

Hot water alone may be used, or a level teaspoonful of table salt (sodium chloride) may be added to a tumbler of hot water to produce what is called a 'normal' saline solution, a solution with the same tonicity as the body fluids. Even better, if you want a developing abscess to 'ripen' (or 'point') or are bathing a discharging abscess, is to use a tumbler of hot water containing a level dessertspoonful of Epsom salts (magnesium sulphate). This exerts considerable osmotic pressure and produces a 'drawing' effect which is valuable in removing toxic products.

How hot should the water be? Well, obviously not so hot as to scald the skin or produce discomfort, but tepid water is not hot enough. If it is just bearable to your fingers, that is about right.

Put the liquid into a small bowl and soak in it the pad of material, which should be at least 3 inches (7.5 cm) square. Partially wring out the pad and apply it immediately to the affected part, holding it in contact with the skin. If the abscess has already burst or been opened (e.g. an anal abscess, see page 43), gentle squeezing will help remove any infected discharges. It will certainly be necessary for someone to restrain the dog while you do this. As soon as the pad has cooled appreciably, remove it, re-soak, squeeze and re-apply. Continue in this way for at least five minutes. The more often you can perform a hot fomentation, the better, but three to four times a day, spaced as evenly as possible, is the minimum.

If the abscess site is on the foot (as with so-called interdigital 'cysts'), it is usually simpler to make up a double quantity of lotion in a small bowl and place the animal's leg alternately into the lotion and out again, at short intervals for a total of about five minutes.

Poultices are used for a similar effect but these are more difficult to apply and are less often employed.

Q *Most dogs seem to hate bandages. Is it always better to let a wound heal on its own rather than to cover it up?*

A Whether a wound is produced accidentally or following surgery, there can be a number of reasons for dressing or bandaging it:
1 To stop any bleeding by applying pressure (pressure bandage), though this is usually only a temporary measure.
2 To prevent the wound becoming contaminated by bacteria and other micro-organisms, inert materials such as grit, dirt, loose hair, and even,

in hot weather, by blowflies laying their eggs in the wound.

3 To prevent the dog interfering with the wound. Repeated licking will delay healing, may introduce infection and may give rise to a thick mass of shiny tissue known as a lick granuloma. Sometimes the stitches may even be removed causing the edges of the wound to pull apart before healing is complete (wound breakdown).

4 To provide support, for instance where there is also a sprain or strain (i.e. tearing of a ligament or a muscle, respectively), or where there may be undue tension on surgical stitches. In dogs with fractures the bandages may hold a supporting splint in place.

5 To immobilize a part of the body (a limb or the tail, for example). This will prevent further damage which could be caused by the dog putting weight on a wounded limb, dragging a paralysed limb or banging a damaged tail. A temporary immobilizing bandage is used to avoid a dislocated hip being re-dislocated after treatment.

In general, wounds do seem to heal faster if they can be kept open to the air rather than covered. However this presupposes that some other way can be found to deal with the problems described above. Unfortunately, in many cases some form of dressing is essential; the extensive wounds caused by burns, for example, are almost certain to become infected if they are exposed.

The disadvantage of wound dressings is that they may stick to the wound surface. They can also become wet and then rub and chafe the wound. Both of these occurrences will delay healing. Dressings can be wetted by the serum which inevitably exudes from wounds, by exposure to rain, dew on the ground, or puddles, and by excessive licking or even sweating. Serum, or discharge from a wound, can be absorbed by surrounding it with a lot of cotton wool or similar material, but this can make the wound very hot and irritating. If it is possible for the wound to be left open, the liquid will evaporate leaving the wound dry.

Some types of wound are best never bandaged, mainly infected wounds with small openings. These include the frequently encountered puncture wounds caused by bites, or discharging channels from abscesses. Such wounds should be left open for drainage and regular treatment. Small wounds requiring only one or two skin sutures are often not dressed. Larger surgical wounds may have a pad of gauze stitched on top of the skin sutures to hide them and reduce interference by the dog.

It may sometimes be necessary to fit a muzzle or 'Elizabethan collar' (see page 267) to prevent a dog from interfering with an exposed wound. In the United States injections of diluted cobra venom around a lesion which is being licked excessively have proved to be very successful in stopping the behaviour — presumably by reducing sensation in that area.

Q *The vet has bandaged my dog's leg. How can I try to keep the dressing dry?*

A If you find your dog spends an excessive amount of time licking the bandage, do your best to prevent it, if necessary by the methods described later (see page 266).

As far as possible the dog should be kept indoors during wet weather, because a bandage which becomes wet will have to be replaced with a dry one to prevent chafing of the wound; often, however, this is just not feasible.

It is possible to cover the bandage completely with waterproof adhesive tape. A number of separate short strips, passing in different directions, should be applied to cover the paw, and then the tape wound in a spiral up the leg, with each turn overlapping the previous one. However, this arrangement can be very difficult to remove again and a simpler method is to place the bandaged limb inside an appropriately sized polythene bag or sponge bag (the sturdier the better). Any spare width of the bag should be wrapped around the leg and the whole thing secured in place at a number of points with pieces of adhesive tape which pass completely around the limb to overlap themselves. Have one of these pieces of tape right at the top so that half of its width sticks to the bag and half to the dog's hair and skin; this stops the bag working loose and dropping off.

Dry the bag when the dog returns from outdoors and if it becomes punctured remove it and replace it. If the bandage has become wet, it also will need renewing.

Q *How should I apply a bandage to my dog?*

A As a general rule bandaging by an owner is most likely to be a first-aid procedure used to stop severe haemorrhage, seal a penetrating chest wound or to provide support, and limit movement, in the case of a fractured limb or tail.

Most of the familiar rolled bandages (called roller bandages) employed by doctors and vets are made from rigid open-weave cotton, which is cut to the required length and discarded after being used once. However for those unused to bandaging, a crêpe bandage (elastic bandage) is much easier to apply and has a better chance of staying in place. Crêpe bandages are made from a stretch cotton which is much less likely to work loose. They are fastened with a safety pin. Because of their cost, they are usually not cut and are reused after washing and drying. Those of 2 inches (5 cm), $2^{1}/_{2}$ inches (6.25 cm) or 3 inches (7.5 cm) widths are most suitable for use on dogs, depending on their size. (Of course, in an emergency, any

How to bandage your dog

A Limbs and tail

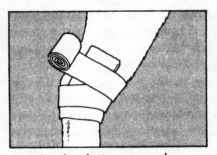

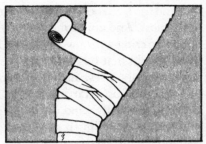

1. *When bandaging a wound on a limb or the tail, start a few inches away from the dressing and gradually work towards the body. Unroll the bandage as you go.*

2. *Each turn of a crêpe bandage should overlap two-thirds of the previous turn. Twist the bandage every 2 or 3 turns to keep it tight. Fasten with a safety pin.*

B Chest and abdomen

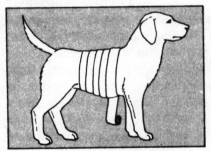

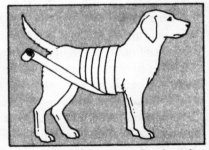

1. *When bandaging the chest or abdomen each turn passes right around the body.*

2. *Bandage towards the head, and after covering the wound go back to the tail.*

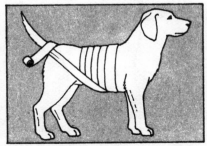

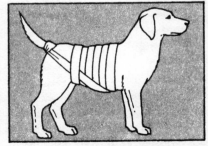

3. *Passing the bandage around the base of the tail helps to anchor it securely.*

4. *Bring the bandage forwards again and, after one last turn, pin it in position.*

material, e.g. handkerchief, dress belt, scarf, tie, strips of rag, etc., may have to be used instead of a proper bandage.)

Unless the dog is unconscious, it will need to be restrained on a table or on the floor by a helper while you apply the bandage. If a limb is to be bandaged, the job is simpler if the dog lies on its side with that limb uppermost. And unless the bandage is being applied solely to prevent the dog interfering with a wound, a pad of lint or cotton wool ¹/₂ inch (1 cm) thick should first be placed on the surface of the body.

Unroll only a few inches of bandage before you start; have the rest tightly rolled up. Starting a few inches to one side of the area to be covered, gradually wind the bandage round and round the affected part of the body, unrolling it as you go. In the case of a limb or the tail, begin to bandage furthest away from the rest of the body and gradually work towards it. The second turn of the bandage should completely overlap the first; after that each turn should overlap two-thirds of the previous one. If the bandage has to go around the chest or abdomen it will need to be pushed under the body on each turn.

Generally a moderate degree of tension should be retained in the bandage to prevent it becoming slack, though if a pressure bandage is being applied to stop haemorrhage this may need to be slightly tighter in order to be effective. Take care though not to have the bandage too tight or it might act as a tourniquet and stop the circulation of blood; around the neck, it might also interfere with the dog's breathing.

It helps to secure the bandage more firmly if, after every two or three turns, the bandage, while it is still under tension, is twisted, so that the inside surface now becomes the outside and *vice versa*; this is called a spiral bandage with reverses. Whether you bandage in a clockwise or an anti-clockwise direction is immaterial and is largely a matter of convenience, depending on whether you are right- or left-handed.

Using a many-tailed bandage

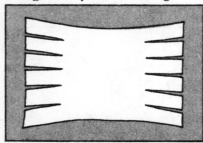

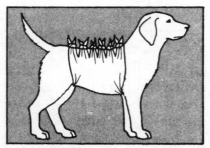

A many-tailed bandage is made from a rectangular piece of linen or muslin. Deep cuts, about 1¹/₂ in (3 cm) apart, are made along each of the shorter sides.

The bandage is used to cover wounds on the lower chest or abdomen. After the wound has been dressed, each pair of tails is tied together above the back.

After covering the affected area, and going a few inches beyond it, the bandage can be cut and pinned in place. But to preserve the entire bandage intact, it is often preferable to work back over the first set of bandaging until the bandage runs out, and then to pin it securely with the safety pin provided. Take care not to accidentally pin the skin as well.

Check the end of a bandaged limb, or tail, from time to time for any sign of swelling, which would indicate that the bandage is too tight. Then it must be removed immediately and re-applied with less tension. If it works loose, or is interfered with, it should also be removed straight away and reapplied a little more tightly. But bandaging will usually be required only in an emergency; if you are to change dressings on a regular basis your veterinary surgeon will tell you how often to do this.

Q *What is a many-tailed bandage, and is it suitable for a dog?*

A A many-tailed bandage is a rectangular binder which covers the lower part of the chest and abdomen and is used to protect wounds in those areas. It is not a type of bandage that is often used on a dog, probably because suitable sizes are not made commercially. But it can prove useful, for example in protecting a spay wound if a bitch has a tendency to interfere with it. It can be made of linen or muslin, or any reasonably strong, closely woven material.

Because dogs vary so much in size it is necessary to do a little measuring with a tape measure beforehand. The rectangle should be as *wide* as the distance between the dog's shoulder and hip and as *long* as the distance around the widest part of the dog's trunk plus an extra 6–8 inches (15–20 cm). Straight cuts are made about every $1^1/_2$ inches (4 cm) along each of the short sides. These cuts should run for about one-third of the material's width, thus producing a number of 'tails' along each of these sides; the number on each side must be equal.

If necessary, a dressing of cotton wool or lint is first applied to the wound and then (with the dog restrained) the bandage is placed beneath the chest and abdomen with the tails protruding on either side. Each pair of tails (right and left) is in turn brought up the sides of the animal and the tails are tied together over the dog's back.

As an alternative an even wider piece of material can be used with four holes cut in it, the correct distance apart, for the dog's legs to pass through. This is then pulled up in a similar manner and fastened along the dog's back either with tapes sewn on to the edges of the material or with press-studs.

Q *How can I stop my dog from chewing at its bandage?*

A Some dogs seem unable to leave a bandage or other dressing alone, and they will repeatedly chew, suck or lick at it. A check should be made that the bandage is not too tight and that the wound beneath it is clean and dry. Having ruled out such causes of irritation, there are three basic ways to tackle this problem.

The first is to cover the bandage with some very strong, waterproof material. This provides additional protection, and hopefully will prove so difficult to remove that the dog will give up trying. Very strong adhesive tape (made for sealing cardboard cartons) can be used as a complete covering. Materials like vinyl sheeting or leather have also been employed, either wrapped around a limb and secured with tape, or made up into booties (available at pet stores), laced to fit securely around the foot. However, these coverings are heavy and rigid, and a really determined dog can still chew through them.

The second method is to cover the outside of the bandage in some material that is non-poisonous but tastes so unpleasant that the dog will leave it alone. Again, this is by no means foolproof but can at times be successful. The substances employed are usually those with an acid or bitter taste, or which produce a burning sensation, for example aromatic bitters, white vinegar, lemon juice, Tabasco sauce, or curry paste. Probably the best, though expensive for repeated application, are preparations intended to stop humans from chewing their fingernails.

The third and usually the most successful technique is either to fit a muzzle, or to enclose the sides of the head, so that the dog cannot bring its mouth into contact with the wound. If a muzzle is employed it is important that it should fit snugly. Often a kind, well-meaning owner buys a muzzle which is so absurdly loose that the dog can stick its nose out between the straps and easily chew through them if it feels like it. To obtain the correct fit it is important to take the animal to the pet store and try on one or two different sizes. Special models are made for flat-

Fitting a protective 'bucket'

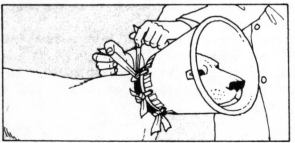

The base of the plastic bucket is cut away and holes are punched around this cut edge. Pad the edge with strips of adhesive tape. Then, with lengths of tape, string or bandage, the bucket is tied to the collar.

Making an 'Elizabethan collar'

1. *Using a piece of string, measure the distance from the dog's collar to its nose. Also measure the distance around its collar, divide by 3 and add ³/₄ in (1.5 cm).*

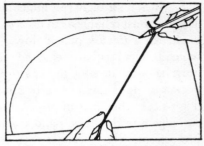

2. *Draw two half-circles, having these distances as their radii, on a piece of stiff material, starting at exactly the same point and using a pencil and string.*

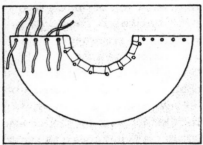

3. *Cut out the collar and punch holes along the straight sides. Try it on the dog, and if it is too tight, trim the inner curve. Punch more holes round the curve.*

4. *Using strips of sticking plaster, pad the inside edge. Finally, put it around the dog's neck, lace up the side holes and fasten to the collar with string.*

nosed dogs. There should be very little, if any, slack in a well-fitting muzzle. Even so with the conventional style made of a number of leather straps many dogs can still stick their tongue out and lick at a bandage or wound. To prevent this, wind adhesive tape around the lower part of the muzzle before it is put on.

To enclose the dog's head a cone-shaped ruff (often referred to as an 'Elizabethan collar') is placed around it and attached to the dog's existing collar. It may only be necessary for either of these devices to be fitted when the owner is unable to be present (e.g. at night) and obviously either type will have to be removed for the dog to eat or drink.

Q *Can you tell me how I can fit an 'Elizabethan collar' to my dog?*

A It is possible to buy so-called 'anti-lick collars' from your pet store, already riveted to a leather strap collar. Other types (which you may be able to obtain from your vet) are made of flexible plastic which fasten around the neck and are adjustable for different sizes of dog. An alternative, which is strongly recommended and adopted by many veterinarians as being most reliable, is to use a small plastic bucket, child's plastic sand bucket or a *flexible* plastic flower pot (depending on the animal's size) which has had its base removed with a sharp knife. The opened-up base must be just wide enough to pass over the dog's head and the depth of the bucket or pot should be sufficient for it to extend a little in front of the dog's nose when it is in position. Holes should be punched around the cut edge and this edge padded with adhesive tape to cover any rough projections. The bucket is then securely fastened to the dog's normal (well-fitting) collar with a number of lengths of tape or string, each passing through one of the holes.

Whatever device is used should cover the dog's head and prevent it reaching the wound or dressing but should not stop it from lying down and sleeping. It will also prevent dogs from scratching or rubbing at their ears or face, and will stop a bitch from suckling herself. The animal will probably not care for it initially and may even try to push it off with its hind legs although most dogs become accustomed to it very quickly.

If you want to *make* an Elizabethan collar you can either create a pattern first, using newspaper or wrapping paper, or draw it directly on to the material you intend using. This should be strong and sturdy, such as vinyl or stiff cardboard. Measure the distance from the dog's collar to the tip of its nose and using that length as the radius draw a half circle from the edge of the material. Then measure the distance around the dog's collar (properly fitted), divide it by three and add on $^3/_4$ inch (1.5 cm). Using *that* length as the radius draw a second half circle from the *same* centre point. Now by cutting along the line of the two half circles you will be left with a C-shaped piece of material.

A series of holes must now be punched along the two straight sides, a little way in from the edge. These holes must be about $^1/_2$ inch (1 cm) apart and can be made with a stationery punch or sharp tool (even a red-hot metal knitting needle). Now fold the material into a cone-like shape around the dog's neck so that it encloses the head. The two straight sides should overlap by about $^3/_4$ inch (2 cm) and the holes line up. If it is much too tight and digs into the neck, trim off a little material around the edge of the smaller curve and try it again. Then punch holes at $^1/_2$-inch (1-cm) intervals all around this lesser curve. Pad the edge with strips of sticking plaster, so it will not damage the neck.

After the final adjustment of the collar's size, place it around the dog's head again and fasten the two sides together by lacing through the holes with a shoelace or a piece of string — or even fasten the holes together with paper fasteners (with the metal prongs opening out on the outside). Then fasten the device on to the dog's collar as described previously.

———————— 14 ————————
First Aid for Dogs

Q *Is it useful for owners to have some knowledge of first aid for dogs? Wouldn't it be better to wait until the vet sees the animal?*

A First aid is the term for the care and treatment given to an individual in an emergency *before* professional help is available — following a serious injury or the sudden onset of illness. Just as in man and other animals, the principal aim of first aid in the dog is to preserve the life of the animal. The other objectives of first aid are to reduce pain and discomfort, and to lessen the likelihood of the injury resulting in some permanent disability or disfigurement by preventing further damage to already injured tissues.

To be successful in these aims usually requires treatment to be given promptly after the incident. There are signs (described here in order of priority) which necessitate *immediate* treatment to save the dog's life: the absence of breathing (or severe difficulty in breathing), severe bleeding and signs of severe shock (weakness to the point of collapse, panting, pale lips and gums, coldness and trembling). Signs which may have equally serious consequences are unconsciousness with or without convulsions and signs indicating poisoning (see page 285).

It is imperative that the treatment of these life-threatening signs receives priority; always leave the cleaning of wounds and other non-essential procedures until later and concentrate on saving the animal's life.

As we have seen in the section on handling, a vital preliminary to the first aid treatment of a dog is the approach to, and restraint of, the injured animal (see page 103), although animals which are very seriously injured are usually those least likely, or able, to offer any serious resistance.

In virtually all emergencies the help and advice of a veterinarian is essential, and his assistance should be obtained as soon as possible. Make the initial contact with your vet by telephone to avoid any possible confusion about the reception of the injured animal (see page 11).

The first aid measures described on the following pages are therefore designed to precede, not to replace, proper veterinary attention. Even though a vet might later advise that euthanasia (putting to sleep) of an injured dog would be the most humane course of action, it is not for the first-aider to make this decision, and all efforts should be directed towards keeping the animal alive until a professional opinion can be obtained.

Q *What is the most common emergency for which a dog would require first aid?*

A There is no doubt that road accidents are the most common emergencies in which dogs are involved, especially in urban areas. Many different types of injury. Of those that die all but 5 % have suffered damage to in every eight dogs dies from them, usually either immediately or within twenty-four hours; the highest mortality rate for any of the common types of injury. Of those that die all but 5 % have suffered damage to their chest or abdomen. These accidents are the inevitable consequence of allowing dogs to wander at will and most could be avoided if dogs were properly trained and not allowed to exercise unaccompanied.

The animal may be struck a direct or glancing blow, not only from the front bumper or a wheel, but also from a low-slung part of the chassis, transmission or exhaust system as the vehicle passes above the dog. It may suffer crush injuries, with rupture of internal organs, as a wheel passes over part of its body, and it may at times be dragged behind the vehicle for a distance. In addition to shock, a road accident can produce a variety of external and internal wounds with varying degrees of hae-morrhage, fractures, dislocations, concussion or paralysis. Head and pelvic injuries are very common, and sometimes there is a diaphragmatic hernia (passage of the abdominal organs into the chest cavity through a ruptured diaphragm) which causes great difficulty in breathing. The only external evidence of a dog's involvement in a road accident may be some loss of hair, oil and dirt on the coat (occasionally tyre marks), and sometimes one or more broken toes. Despite the minimal external signs there is often serious internal bleeding.

The animal might remain at the scene of the accident, often dazed or unconscious, or it may run away in a blind panic, only to return home, if at all, several hours later.

First-aid treatment for road accidents consists primarily of treatment for shock, plus attention for whatever other serious sign(s) might be present (e.g. severe haemorrhage, difficulty in breathing, fracture, paraly-sis, etc.) before obtaining veterinary attention. It is of course imperative that if the animal is still in a dangerous position in the roadway it should first be removed to a safer, and preferably sheltered, position.

Q *On what other occasions might my dog require first aid?*

A Cuts and wounds, with a variety of causes, are common. The majority are 'clean' cuts (incised wounds), resulting for instance from stepping on broken glass or sharp metal concealed in long grass or in a stream, jumping through a garden frame, window or glass door, or even from licking out cans with a sharp edge. These wounds can be deep and usually bleed profusely. Cutting wounds can also be produced by wire nooses in animal snares and by rubber bands placed around the neck, limbs or tail, usually by children. Because of its continual tension, a rubber band gradually cuts through the skin and deep into the underlying tissues, sometimes even down to the bone or through the windpipe.

Irregular, torn wounds (lacerated wounds) can arise from a dog being bitten by another, being caught on barbed wire or getting its feet trapped in an escalator; this type bleed less but are more likely to become contaminated. Puncture wounds have only a small surface opening caused by the entry of a sharp, pointed object such as a nail, thorn or canine tooth (especially that of a male cat). They bleed very little and soon heal, though often infection is left deep in the tissues and subsequently there develops a painful swelling, an abscess, which later bursts. Where one dog has been shaken by another in a fight the small puncture wounds in the skin may overlie massive tissue damage and bruising beneath.

Penetrating wounds (i.e. penetrating the chest or abdomen) are fortunately rare. They may result from the protrusion of a fractured rib after a road accident, from being impaled on a spike (e.g. on a railing after a fall) or from a malicious act such as stabbing or shooting. Typical firearm wounds have a small entry wound, and a large, ragged exit wound for the projectile, though sometimes, as with air-gun pellets, the projectile remains in the tissues. The explosive release of stored-up energy can cause extensive internal damage.

As well as being caused by road accidents, fractures and dislocations can result from being trodden on or kicked, having a tail or a limb

How to give artificial respiration

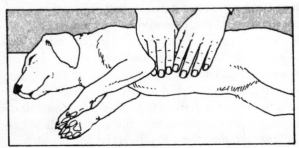

Remove any collar and, with the dog lying on its side, stretch the head and neck forwards. Place both hands over the rib-cage and press down firmly every five seconds, releasing the pressure immediately afterwards.

slammed in a door, or from an over-ambitious jump or a fall. In urban situations dogs can fall considerable heights, for example from windows, parapets, and into stairwells, which can result in unconsciousness, fractures (particularly of the forelimbs, chest and jaws) and internal injuries. 5% die from their injuries.

A new hazard has recently appeared with the introduction of front-loading video cassette recorders; a dog accidentally inserts the tip of its tail into the loading mechanism and the animal's attempts to withdraw cause the entrance flap to tighten and amputate the tail tip.

Burns and scalds are also not uncommon in dogs and many of these arise in the kitchen. Usually the animal is splashed with boiling water or hot fat, although often this is not recognized at the time. Sometimes the mouth is burned trying to eat hot food or dried pet food mixed with very hot water or from licking barbecue grills. Burns on the feet can arise from stepping on to the embers of bonfires or the hot charcoal discarded from a barbecue. So-called chemical burns are due to the effect of corrosive liquids on the skin; at times dogs may walk through such substances as warm tar, creosote or battery acid. Electrical burns and electrocution usually result from a puppy, under six months of age, chewing through a live electrical flex or cable.

Q *How can I administer artificial respiration to a dog?*

A Artificial respiration is required in all circumstances where a dog has stopped breathing, or is breathing irregularly or with difficulty. When breathing ceases, all the body organs, including the brain and the heart, are deprived of the normal continuous flow of oxygen. After a few minutes they will be unable to function and then the animal will become unconscious and die. In an emergency therefore artificial respiration should take precedence over every other procedure. Once it is being performed successfully, attention can then be directed towards other problems.

The cessation or impairment of breathing may in fact be caused by an existing lack of oxygen to the brain (asphyxia), as occurs if the animal is enclosed in an unventilated space, has a plastic bag put over its head or is obliged to breathe smoke or carbon monoxide. An oxygen lack can also result from obstruction of the air passage by a foreign body in the throat (e.g. a ball) or by water in the lungs (as in drowning), or by compression of the airway (as with an incorrectly applied check chain). The respiratory muscles might be paralysed following electrocution or the lungs may have collapsed after a penetrating chest wound. In all of these situations the prompt administration of artificial respiration can be vitally important in ensuring that the animal survives.

If there is any foreign material in the air passage or in the lungs, it must first be removed. If the dog has drowned (usually because steep walls prevent it escaping from the water, e.g. in a swimming pool, canal lock, or even a rainwater butt) it is important first to wipe away any oil or mud from the mouth and nostrils, and then to allow as much water as possible to drain from the lungs by holding the dog upside down by its thighs. Obstructions in the throat usually produce choking, coughing or gulping. Foreign bodies, such as bones or needles, should if possible be quickly removed with fingers or a pair of pliers, and any vomit or blood at the back of the throat should be carefully wiped away. After opening the jaws and pulling the tongue forward the mouth and throat can be checked with a torch.

Artificial respiration will not be effective if there is a penetrating chest wound; air can usually be heard passing through the opening and blood coming from the wound appears frothy. Bloodstained froth is also coughed up and appears at the mouth and nostrils. Such a wound must be quickly sealed by plugging the opening with a clean (preferably sterile) piece of gauze, lint or cotton wool, or in an emergency any other clean piece of material. Ideally, this plug should be covered by a further thick pad which is then bandaged in place. The immediate aim, however, is to obtain an airtight seal.

Now with the dog lying flat on its side (with the head preferably lower than the rest of the body in the case of a drowned animal) and any wound uppermost, remove its collar, make sure that the head and neck are stretched well forward and place your two hands on the chest wall over the ribs. Now press down firmly to expel the air from the lungs, but *don't exert too much weight* on a small dog because you can easily produce crush injuries. Immediately release the pressure allowing the chest wall to expand again and to fill the lungs with air. This procedure should be repeated at approximately five-second intervals. Pressing too rapidly will not allow the oxygen to remain in the lungs for a sufficient time to diffuse into the blood.

Once artificial respiration is under way, attention can be paid to other problems; provided that the heart continues to beat, artificial respiration can keep the animal alive almost indefinitely, certainly long enough for veterinary attention to be obtained. If the animal is being transported to the vet's premises and it has not yet begun to breathe on its own, it will be necessary to continue this procedure during the journey. At intervals a check should be made that the air passage is still clear and that there is still a heartbeat. The heartbeat can be checked by placing the fingertips on the lower part of the chest wall on the left side, just behind the front leg. In the case of a very small dog the beat can be detected with a hand around the lower part of the chest between, or just behind, the forelegs. If the fingers and thumb are on opposite sides of the chest, the heartbeat can be felt between them. (Try this *now* on a healthy dog so that you will know where to feel in an emergency.)

If the animal begins to breathe regularly and at a steady rate, artificial respiration can be stopped, but regular checks should be made on the dog to ensure that it is continuing to breathe properly.

Q *Is it true that flat-nosed breeds of dog are more likely to need artificial respiration?*

A The abnormally long, soft palate of the flat-nosed (brachycephalic) breeds commonly interferes with breathing and *may* at times lead to a dog collapsing, particularly after exercise. If this should occur pull the dog's tongue forward out of the mouth. If this does not result in improved breathing carefully place a finger down its throat to lift the end of the soft palate out of contact with the larynx, and if necessary apply artificial respiration.

Occasionally a dog (of any breed but especially a Bull Terrier) may suddenly develop distressed respiration in which breathing-in requires considerable effort and breathing-out causes flapping of the lips. Usually collapse does not occur and relief can be provided by either pulling the dog's tongue forward or sharply compressing its chest.

Q *Can I give my dog the 'kiss of life'?*

A Mouth to mouth resuscitation has been attempted but, because of the shape and size of a dog's mouth, it is usually not very effective. It is better to close the animal's mouth with your hands and to blow firmly and regularly into its nose with your lips closely applied to its nostrils. As described before, it is important to ensure first that the air passage is clear. Blowing should occupy about three seconds, followed by a two-second pause, and this should be repeated continuously.

This technique may prove more valuable in providing oxygen than the pressure on the chest method of artificial respiration for those animals with a penetrating wound into the chest cavity.

Q *How is it possible to control severe bleeding in a dog?*

A Minor haemorrhage will stop on its own after a while due to a narrowing of the end of the damaged blood vessel(s) and the formation of a blood clot which effectively blocks the cut end. Consequently, clots which have already formed should not be disturbed because this will allow bleeding to begin again.

However, when a large blood vessel is severed, the flow of blood is so considerable that any clot which begins to form is soon washed away. This is particularly likely to occur when an artery is damaged since it carries blood under higher pressure; indeed, a separate spurt of blood is seen with each beat of the heart.

The best method for controlling severe bleeding is to apply pressure to the damaged blood vessel with a pressure bandage. A $^{1}/_{2}$-inch (13-mm) thick pad of clean and preferably sterile absorbent material such as cotton wool or lint (or in an emergency a handkerchief) is placed over the end of the blood vessel and firmly bandaged in place with a crêpe bandage (or in an emergency a scarf, dress belt, handkerchief, etc.). The rough surface of the material facilitates clot formation.

While such materials for a pressure bandage are being assembled, pressure can be applied to the blood vessel with fingertips, preferably covered with a clean handkerchief (or rubber gloves if these are handy). Alternatively, the sides of a large wound can be tightly pressed together. As far as is possible in the circumstances, try to avoid pushing fragments of foreign bodies such as glass further into the wound. Any obvious and easily detached pieces should be quickly removed before bandaging. (With wounds on the neck it may be preferable to hold a pad tightly in position rather than to apply a bandage which can interfere with breathing). If the pad rapidly becomes soaked with blood, a further pad and bandage should be applied more tightly on top of the first.

The animal, if still conscious, should be restrained by a helper during this procedure, and if necessary later treated for shock.

The application of pressure to the artery supplying the injured area may be attempted, but only if a pressure bandage is clearly unable to control serious haemorrhaging. Either really hard pressure can be applied with the fingers at the pressure points (where a superficial artery passes over a bone) or a tourniquet can be applied.

The three major pressure points are located as follows:
1 On the inside of the thigh where the femoral artery crosses the bone (femur) — to control bleeding from the lower half of the hind limb.
2 On the inside of the forelimb just above the elbow joint where the brachial artery crosses the bone (humerus) — to control bleeding from the lower half of the forelimb.
3 On the underside of the tail near to the body where the coccygeal artery passes beneath the vertebrae — to control bleeding from the tail.

Pressure can also be applied to the carotid artery in a groove at the lower part of the neck just in front of the forelimb, to control bleeding from the head and neck, although in practice this point is difficult to find and the control of bleeding is often not very satisfactory.

In an emergency a tourniquet can be made from a narrow strip of cloth

1–2 inches (2.5–5 cm) wide, a handkerchief, tie, dress belt, supple dog lead or a thick rubber band, firmly tied or clipped into position around the limb or tail. *The tourniquet should be between the body and the wound.* Its efficiency can be improved by using the remaining ends of the material to tie a short stick (or even a ballpoint pen) on top of the first knot, and then twisting the stick around several times until the bleeding stops.

Today, however, the use of pressure on an artery (especially with a tourniquet) is *not* recommended for routine use because totally cutting off the blood supply to the tissues can result in their death. Consequently, pressure should never be applied continuously for more than fifteen minutes, and a tourniquet must never be applied around the neck or covered with a bandage, in case it is forgotten. *Pressure bandaging generally produces more reliable control of bleeding as well as being safer and quicker.* If a tourniquet is used in the treatment of snake bite (see page 293) it only need be tight enough to interfere with the lymphatic circulation and not the blood supply.

Bleeding from sites around the head can require special first aid treatment, although in all cases the dog should be effectively but quietly restrained lying down, usually with the site of haemorrhage uppermost.

To control bleeding from the eyeball, hold a pad of lint or cotton wool soaked in clean cold water (never dry) over the eyeball. Do not attempt to bandage it in place and prevent the dog from rubbing the eye.

With bleeding from the nostrils, apply a similar pad soaked in cold water over the nose, but do not attempt to cover the nostrils or to poke anything up the nose.

With severe bleeding from the ear flap, first place a pad of cotton wool either side of the flap, like a sandwich. Then fold the ear flap flat across the head with the ear tip pointing towards the opposite side of the head, and bandage it firmly in that position using a crêpe bandage. Do the same in cases of bleeding from the ear canal but first place a small piece of cotton wool down the canal to assist clotting. Always stop the dog from scratching or rubbing at the ear, and from shaking its head.

With bleeding from the tongue, lips or mouth, keep the dog's head low to prevent clots forming at the back of the throat. When there is haemorrhage from the *inside* of the lips or cheek squeeze the part between your fingers and thumb. If the dog is unconscious, blood and clots must be wiped from the mouth and throat to ensure that the airway remains unobstructed.

And, of course, it is essential to arrange for the dog to receive veterinary attention as soon as possible.

How to control severe bleeding

1. *With the dog well restrained in a suitable position, a thick pad of absorbent material, such as lint or cotton wool (cotton), or a clean handkerchief in an emergency, is held over the bleeding point.*

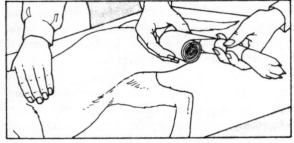

2. *Then firmly bandage the pad in place with a crêpe bandage, or a scarf or a dress belt. If the pad should become soaked apply another pad, tightly bandaged on top of the first.*

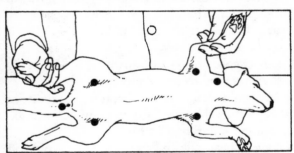

3. *Temporary control of severe haemorrhage can be obtained by pressing with the fingers at the points illustrated, i.e. when there is bleeding from the tail, hindleg, foreleg and the head region.*

Q *What can I do about internal haemorrhage?*

A Internal bleeding refers to bleeding into internal organs or into the chest or abdominal cavities. It usually follows crushing or a severe impact injury such as a fall or kick (e.g. by horses or cattle) or from involvement in a road accident. The fact that haemorrhage is occurring may not be evident until signs of shock appear; this is usually because blood cannot reach the exterior. However, at times blood may be seen. Frothy blood appearing at the mouth or nostrils suggests bleeding from the lungs or air passages (a trickle of blood is usually due to wounds actually in the mouth or nose). Vomited blood usually comes from the stomach and appears dark brown because of the action of stomach acid (converting it to acid haematin). Extensive bleeding from deep within the ear canal strongly suggests an injury inside the skull. Sometimes blood may be apparent in the urine or motions after an accident.

Regrettably, it is not possible to stop an internal haemorrhage with first-aid treatment. The best that can be done is to treat the animal for shock (see below), wipe any frothy blood from the mouth and nose to keep the airway clear, and to obtain the assistance of a veterinarian as soon as possible.

Q *How will I know if my dog is suffering from shock? How should he be treated?*

A Shock is a clinical state in which there is a fall in blood pressure and in the volume of blood in the circulation. The blood flow to the body tissues is poor and the cells, including those of the brain, suffer from a lack of oxygen. Many different types of injury will cause shock but the signs and the treatment are similar in all cases. Shock can result from severe blood loss or a loss of other body fluids (after persistent vomiting or diarrhoea, for example), serious pain and tissue damage (from severe wounds and fractures, electrocution and the effects of burns, scalds, and poisons − especially corrosive poisons) and the effect of bee and wasp stings (anaphylactic shock). Internal bleeding can result in 'secondary shock' occurring some time (four to six hours) after an injury.

The tell-tale signs of shock are as follows:

1 The animal is weak and almost always lies down. It is often only semi-conscious and does not respond to stimulation.

2 Breathing is rapid (more than fifteen to twenty breaths per minute in the case of a large dog, more than thirty to forty per minute for a toy breed) and shallow (i.e. panting respiration).

3 The lips, gums and tongue appear pale and greyish and feel cold and clammy.

4 The paws feel cold, even though the animal may be in warm surroundings, and it often trembles or shivers. The temperature, if taken, is found to be below normal.

5 The heart beats more rapidly (i.e. more than eighty beats per minute for a large breed, for a small one more than 140 beats per minute).

6 The pupils are dilated and the eyes appear glazed.

7 The dog *may* vomit.

These signs may already be present when the injured animal is discovered or they may develop later.

First, artificial respiration should be given to any animal whose breathing is irregular, and any serious haemorrhage should be controlled. The dog should be kept warm, preferably indoors, by covering it with a blanket. It is important to prevent heat loss, so that if the animal is wet it should be dried, and it should not be allowed to lie directly on a cold or wet surface. Put some insulating material, such as a blanket, coat or newspaper, beneath it. However, because shock is made worse by raising the animal's temperature above that of its surroundings, the dog should not be placed directly in front of a fire or radiator, or given a hot water bottle. The animal should be kept as quiet and undisturbed as possible. If a journey to the vet is required, sudden changes in position (i.e. sudden lifting, turning and jolting) should be avoided because this can cause a rapid deterioration in condition which might prove fatal.

If the animal is sufficiently conscious to drink, and wishes to do so, a small amount of warm milk or water with added glucose can be beneficial. However, withhold liquids if the animal begins to vomit, never force liquids down its throat, and avoid giving any form of alcohol (e.g. brandy). Alcohol can prove beneficial in some types of shock but it is also harmful in others. Because the nature of the shock may not be immediately apparent, the safest rule is to avoid alcohol altogether. Keep the animal lying down, ideally with the hindquarters a little higher than the head, and try to avoid causing pain and fear. Speak calmly to the dog and try to reassure it.

Shock is a serious condition and veterinary attention should be obtained with the minimum of delay. An important part of treatment is the administration of fluid therapy to restore the circulating blood volume and, in some cases, the use of specialized stimulant drugs.

Q *What signs would indicate that my dog had a fracture?*

A A fracture is a break or crack in a bone caused by the application of physical force. Most fractures are the result of road accidents, and the bones most often fractured are the radius and ulna (two bones which run alongside each other in the lower part of the forelimb) and the femur (thigh bone). Almost as common are fractures of the pelvis and of the tibia and fibula (the two bones of the lower hind limb).

Fractures are termed open or closed depending on whether or not the skin surface is also disrupted by the injury. Sometimes the broken end of the bone is even pushed out through the skin. Open fractures are, as one would expect, more likely to become infected. Other classifications of fractures are based on the number of breaks, fragments of bone, or on the amount of damage done to the surrounding tissues. However, from the point of view of first aid, such classification is unimportant. The only type which is popularly referred to is a 'greenstick fracture' in which the bone is not completely broken but merely cracked and bent. This type usually occurs in young animals where the bones are still flexible.

There are six main signs of fracture, though not all need be present:

1 Pain around the fracture site, which makes the animal resent handling and can lead to shock.

2 Swelling around the fracture due to bleeding and bruising.

3 An unnatural degree of movement. The lower part of the limb, or end of the tail, may swing freely or even be dragged along.

4 A loss of function. The dog is not able to move or use the fractured part normally. It may appear lame, because it cannot put weight on to a limb.

5 There may be some deformity such as a lump or sharp edge which can be felt somewhere along the bone. A limb may appear shorter or abnormally twisted, or the skull appear sunken.

6 A grating noise (crepitus) may be heard when the animal moves or the part is handled. This is due to the rough, broken ends of the bones moving against each other (and of course is absent in a greenstick fracture).

If, when you examine your dog, you are doubtful about the shape of a bone, or the degree of movement, it is useful to compare the same part on the other side of the body.

Q *How would I know if my dog had suffered a dislocation?*

A A dislocation (also known as a luxation) occurs when one of the bones which form a joint moves out of place. The bones are usually separated by force; dislocation of the hip joint is the most common example, frequently following a road accident. In general, the thigh bone (femur) moves forward making the hind limb appear shorter. The lower jaw is also often dislocated and then the mouth will not close properly.

In some dogs a congenital defect of the stifle joint allows the knee-cap (patella) to dislocate very easily without undue force especially in small breeds (e.g. Miniature Poodles). In other dogs the same thing can happen when they turn suddenly while running at high speed. The patella is normally held in front of the joint and when dislocated it usually slips to the inside of the leg, causing pain and making the animal hold its foot up off the ground. This defect accounts for 20% of all dislocations.

Many signs of dislocation are similar to those of fracture — pain, swelling, deformity and loss of function, but there are useful distinguishing features:

1 Pain and swelling is confined to the region of the joint.

2 Movement is more restricted than usual, not increased.

3 There is usually no grating sound.

4 Bones never penetrate the skin.

It can, however, be difficult to distinguish between a fracture and dislocation, particularly if the fracture is near a joint; occasionally they will occur together.

Q *What first-aid treatment should I give a dog with a fracture or dislocation?*

A The general first-aid treatment for both fractures and dislocations is very similar. After an accident the dog should be carefully approached and restrained (see page 103) and then taken to a place of safety and warmth. If the animal is small enough you may be able to carry it in your arms, supporting any obviously injured part, or in a large cardboard box if one is handy. A large dog which can walk, even if limping, can be slowly led a short distance to shelter while held by its scruff. A large dog which is unable to walk (because it is unconscious, collapsed, very weak or paralysed) should be lifted and/or pulled with the help of at least one other person, on to an old coat, blanket or rug. The animal should be moved on to this makeshift stretcher body first, with its legs trailing and without bending the spine. Then the animal can be lifted by two people holding opposite ends of this stretcher. If there is a need for artificial respiration, or treatment for haemorrhage or shock, this must receive priority. Then the dog should be put in a confined area to limit its movements — in a dog basket, its own bed or a small room, hemmed in by furniture, depending on its size (ideally lying down with the affected part or limb uppermost) — until a vet can examine and treat it. This is to minimize pain and, in the case of a fracture, to prevent further damage to surrounding tissues. Make the animal as comfortable as possible and do not handle the area of fracture or dislocation more than is necessary.

In general, do not attempt to correct the dislocation because this often can only be achieved after using a general anaesthetic to relax the muscles. There is, however, one possible exception. If the patella has shifted from its normal position in front of the stifle joint to the inside of the leg, causing the animal to raise its leg, it may be possible to slide it back again without causing too much discomfort. If you are able to feel the small patella bone on the inside of the joint proceed as follows. With someone restraining the dog grasp the limb below the joint with one hand and pull on the limb to straighten the leg as with the fingers of the other hand you move the patella round to the front of the joint. However, if this manoeuvre does not produce correction after two attempts, or if the patella soon slips back again, or if too much pain is produced, *do not continue* but obtain the assistance of a veterinarian.

A fractured limb can be well supported and immobilized with a firm bandage. But if there is any possibility that you are dealing with a dislocation and not a fracture, it is best omitted. The procedure is to apply a thick pad of cotton wool, 4—6 inches (10—15 cm) long, over the area of the fracture (usually this will be a limb but occasionally a fractured rib) and then to bandage the pad tightly in place with a crêpe bandage.

As a general rule attempts to secure splints to the limbs do more harm than good and are best avoided. If the lower jaw is hanging free it can be supported by applying a crêpe bandage fairly loosely around the head, but check that the animal can breathe satisfactorily, especially if there is bleeding in the mouth.

Spinal fractures and dislocations may result in paralysis of the hind-quarters, shown by the dog's inability to move its hind legs, and, to avoid further damage, it is important that when such an animal is lifted its spine is kept perfectly straight. If possible the dog should be lifted on a flat board, and an ironing board can be useful. Unfortunately, the outlook for such cases is poor and the victims often have to be put to sleep.

Q *Because dogs race around so much do they suffer from sprains and strains?*

A Yes, certainly these can occur. A sprain is the tearing or over-stretching of the ligaments surrounding a joint, and the joints most likely to be affected are the shoulder, stifle, carpus and tarsus (hock joint). The affected joint is swollen and painful so that the animal appears lame. A common problem is rupture of the anterior cruciate ligament in the stifle joint (particularly in Scottish Terriers, Boxers, Newfoundlands and Rottweilers) and unattended the injury can lead to the development of osteoarthritis.

A strain is the same type of injury (tearing or overstretching) affecting a muscle or one of its tendons (which anchor the muscle to bone). It generally occurs suddenly during vigorous exercise (e.g. racing or jumping), or in a road accident. The swelling and pain can cause lameness. The Achilles tendon passing down the back of the hind leg is most likely to be torn and as a result the dog may walk with all the lower part of the limb (below the hock) in contact with the ground.

Often it may be difficult to distinguish between these two conditions and to differentiate them from fractures and dislocations. Consequently it is wise to obtain veterinary attention as soon as possible and in the interim to restrict the dog's movements and make it rest. If the swelling is severe, a towel soaked in cold water should be applied.

Q *What should I do if my dog has convulsions?*

A A convulsion, or fit, is a series of violent, uncontrolled seizures (or spasms) of the muscles, accompanied by partial or complete loss of consciousness. It begins with a series of muscle tremors followed by muscle contractions; the animal falls to the ground and shows 'paddling' movements and champing of the jaws. Often the dog will salivate and pass motions and urine. Upon recovery, it may be dazed, confused and unable to see properly. Most convulsions last between one and three minutes, but at times the convulsions become continuous (status epilepticus).

Causes include convulsive poisons (e.g. organochlorines, anti-freeze, lead and metaldehyde), brain tumours, head injuries, meningitis and encephalitis (inflammation of the brain and its covering membranes — e.g. the result of infection with distemper, rabies or pseudorabies), tetanus, diseases of the liver and kidney (due to the accumulation of waste substances in the body) and a low level of sugar or of calcium in the blood. The last-named condition (hypocalcaemia) may occur in the nursing bitch and is then called eclampsia (see page 245).

The condition popularly known as epilepsy is believed to be due to an inherited defect in the metabolism of nerve cells in the brain and is particularly common in Miniature and Toy Poodles and Spaniels. The recurrent convulsions are triggered by excitement (e.g. company, or thunderstorms) and first appear between the ages of six and eighteen months. They may be so short, mild or infrequent as not to justify continuous drug treatment. Hydrocephalus (water on the brain) is another inherited cause, most common in Chihuahuas and the flat-nosed breeds.

It is best to leave the convulsing animal where it has collapsed, unless it is in a dangerous situation (e.g. in a roadway, or near to a fire). If it is in danger, try to carefully lift or pull the animal to safety, but avoid getting bitten in the process (throw a blanket or coat over the dog first). Keep the animal as quiet and undisturbed as possible; at home move nearby furniture and objects quietly away from the animal, draw the curtains, turn off nearby electric or gas fires, turn off the radio, television or hi-fi, and, if necessary, arrange cushions or rugs to protect the animal from projections on which it might strike its head. Ask onlookers to leave. Always interfere with the dog as little as possible during the fit; certainly do not attempt to hold it or give it anything by mouth.

Arrange for veterinary treatment as soon as possible. If the fit is continuous, the need for treatment is urgent, but only if there is no alternative should an attempt be made to transport an animal that is still having convulsions. (It is best done by picking the dog up in a blanket and, still covered, restraining it as best you can on the back seat of a car.)

The fit will usually end spontaneously but still keep the dog confined in the same cool darkened room until it is sufficiently recovered to be transported, or until the veterinary surgeon arrives. Any froth around the mouth, and any urine and faeces on the coat, can then be gently cleaned up. The dog will usually sleep afterwards.

Often a warning that a dog is about to have a fit is given by the presence of a staring expression, salivation and licking of the lips, twitching, restlessness, jumping when handled or in response to a noise, and either hiding or seeking affection.

Q *What should I do if my dog becomes hysterical?*

A The condition popularly referred to as hysteria is a phase of excitement and personality change caused by a certain type of brain lesion, and which usually precedes a fit. The dog suddenly begins violent howling or barking, runs wildly about in a semi-conscious state banging into objects, and urine and motions may be passed. Outdoors the animal may run a considerable distance; indoors it often attempts to hide in a dark place, such as in a cupboard or under a bed. This behaviour may last between a few minutes and several hours before the dog goes into convulsions; alternatively the exhausted animal may go to sleep.

Great care should be taken in approaching the animal because it is frightened and does not recognize people and therefore may easily bite. It should be confined to a quiet, darkened room or similar area such as a garage or shed where it will do the minimum of damage until the attack of hysteria is over. Onlookers should be removed and as far as possible not allowed to panic or try to restrain the animal. The animal should not be allowed to run free as it may easily become involved in a road accident. A veterinary surgeon should be contacted as soon as possible; in the meantime if the animal goes into a fit it should be dealt with as described earlier. If it happens to go to sleep it should not be disturbed.

Q *How might my dog be poisoned?*

A It is estimated that about one dog in 2500 is poisoned at some time in its life, most often before two years old, and that between one in eight and one in five cases end fatally. Most poisons are taken orally by dogs. Occasionally, a poisonous gas or vapour may be inhaled, such as carbon monoxide from a motor vehicle exhaust or a solid fuel- or oil-burning appliance (though not from natural gas). Also toxic are the vapours of organic solvents (e.g. in glues, dry cleaning fluids or fire extinguishers) used in poorly ventilated areas, and the smoke and fumes from burning materials, especially plastic foam. Very rarely may a poison be absorbed through the skin.

The evidence of poisoning may be beyond dispute. You might actually see the dog consuming material which you know, or subsequently discover, is poisonous. Or there may be strong circumstantial evidence if the dog develops signs of poisoning and could have had access to a poison

— a toxic spray might have been used in the neighbourhood or a rat bait laid. It may be that the dog has been dosed with a drug or its coat treated with an insecticide, or drugs used by members of the household may have been interfered with. Examination of the dog may show signs consistent with poisoning, such as the burning and blistering around the lips caused by a corrosive, a strange smell on the breath, a residue of material around the mouth and, especially, the dribbling of coloured saliva. Many rat and slug baits are coloured and this observation may actually help to indentify the poison.

Deliberate malicious poisoning of pets occurs from time to time, often as a series of cases in an area. The dog usually consumes far more poison (disguised in some tasty morsel) than could be ingested accidentally, so that signs appear much earlier and are of greater intensity. In Britain dogs may also eat poisoned bait laid illegally to kill birds of prey, crows and other wildlife. The practice is widespread, with alphachloralose, mevinphos and strychnine being the poisons most commonly used. In Britain, where strychnine is intended to be limited to the destruction of moles by farmers, its sale is restricted. But in those countries (e.g. France, Netherlands and the USA) where it is freely available as a rodenticide, it is far and away the most important single cause of poisoning in dogs.

Q *What are the signs of poisoning in dogs?*

A Corrosive poisons are usually ingested out of curiosity (especially by puppies) or by being licked from the paws or coat. This type of poison kills by producing shock from the enormous amount of tissue damage and pain created. Corrosive poisons include such substances as acids, alkalis (e.g. ammonia, quicklime, and oven-cleaning sticks), phenolic compounds (creosote, lysol and the Jeyes' Fluid type of disinfectant) and petroleum products (petrol (gasoline), paraffin (kerosene), diesel oil, and white spirit (paint thinners)).

Other types of poison damage the dog's health, and may even cause death, because they interfere with some essential metabolic function. This type generally produces one of four types of signs:
1 Digestive signs such as abdominal pain, vomiting and diarrhoea.
2 Difficulty in breathing.
3 Nervous signs, which can vary in their intensity from staggering, excitement and muscular tremors (twitching), to convulsions, paralysis, coma and apparent blindness.
4 Depression, including a loss of appetite.
The last-named often follows the other signs and precedes death in the case of slow-acting poisons. Some rat poisons produce other signs; warfarin and other anticoagulant poisons cause internal haemorrhages

and anaemia; thallium (seldom used now) can produce hair loss, and alphachloralose has an anaesthetic effect and causes the animal to become very cold.

It should be emphasized that *all* these signs can be produced by conditions *other than* poisoning, and there are many instances of dog owners suspecting that their animal is being deliberately poisoned by someone bearing a grudge when in fact the animal is suffering from a disease, often the early stage of some infectious condition. This should be borne in mind before requesting toxicological analyses; testing for any common poison is not cheap, and a blanket test for all possible poisons would almost certainly be prohibitively expensive. Furthermore, the unavoidable delay involved in obtaining analytical test results means that they usually contribute little to treatment, though a positive finding may assist in treating, or preventing, the poisoning of other animals.

Q *If I think my dog has been poisoned, what should I do?*

A The treatment for oral corrosive poisoning is quite different from that for other types of poisoning, so the first thing to do is to look at the animal's mouth for the tell-tale signs — burning and blistering (with yellow-grey areas on the lips, gums and tongue), pawing at the mouth and often a characteristic odour (e.g. of creosote or disinfectant). If these signs are present, and the dog is not collapsed or unconscious, wash away as much of the chemical as possible from around and inside the mouth. In a conscious animal wipe around the mouth with a pad soaked in water and trickle water into the mouth through a disposable syringe, as for dosing with liquid medicine (see page 251). It will be beneficial whether the dog splutters the water out or swallows it. Indeed, rather than attempt to neutralize such poisons, the best policy is usually to dilute them in the stomach with plenty of water. The one real danger is of liquid passing down into the lungs and causing an inhalation pneumonia. If the animal is already unconscious and is perhaps showing difficulty in breathing, treat as for shock and administer artificial respiration. Obtain the help of a veterinary surgeon as soon as you possibly can.

In the case of all other consumed poisons, providing that the animal is still conscious and not having convulsions, the first thing to do is to administer a substance to make the animal vomit. This should ideally be done within half an hour of the poison being taken. And then get the animal to a vet without delay. (Vomiting is *not* used in cases of corrosive poisoning because further tissue destruction and shock will be caused as the poison passes back from the stomach.) The most reliable method of making a dog vomit at home is to administer a crystal of washing soda (sodium carbonate) the size of a hazel nut. This should be administered in the same way as a tablet (see page 249). An alternative is to give a large crystal of rock salt. Giving liquids to cause vomiting is often less successful but the following might be tried if they are available and washing soda is not:

1 Hydrogen peroxide: 2.5 ml (half a 5-ml teaspoonful) of the usual 6% (20 vol.) solution; or one 5-ml teaspoonful of a 3% (10 vol.) solution.

2 A strong salt solution: half a level tablespoonful of salt in as little warm water as will dissolve it.

3 English mustard: half a level tablespoonful as a powder mixed in half a teacupful of warm water.

These doses are adequate for a medium-sized dog.

In all cases administration will be simpler using a disposable syringe. If vomiting is going to occur it usually does so within ten to fifteen minutes. If nothing happens do not give further amounts. If the vet is unable to visit and you have to take the animal to his premises, it could be that vomiting will take place on the journey. If the animal is unconscious you may need to give artificial respiration and/or treatment for shock; and if it is having a fit it should be dealt with as described earlier. Do *not* try to give an unconscious or convulsing animal *anything* by mouth. If you know the name of the poison taken tell the vet, and if you have the packet take that along with you. Otherwise, take a sample of the poison (or suspected poison); possibly it can be identified.

At the vet's the animal might be given an injection of apomorphine or xylazine to stimulate vomiting if this has not already occurred, and/or have its stomach washed out. It could also be given supportive treatment in the form of fluid therapy and drugs to counteract the particular signs that may have developed. In some cases of poisoning, though by no means all, there may be a specific antidote which can be administered to assist in reversing the effects of the poison. In the case of warfarin, an injection of vitamin K counteracts its anticoagulant effect; with alpha-chloralose simply keeping the animal warm until its anaesthetic effect wears off is usually all that is required (though initially this poison *may* have an excitement phase).

If the dog has been poisoned by inhaling toxic fumes or gases, the essential action is to move it immediately into fresh air and if necessary to give artificial respiration while waiting for veterinary attention. Do take care, however, that you are not also overcome by the same toxic vapours.

Small areas of hair covered with oil-based paints or with tar can be cut off (allow the paint to dry first) but more extensive deposits of tar need to be softened first with vegetable oil, lard or margarine for several hours before being washed out with detergent and lukewarm water. While this softening process is going on, it is advisable to cover the area with a pad of gauze and bandage it in place. Diesel oil, creosote and phenolic disinfectants are corrosive and should be removed quickly. While waiting for veterinary assistance, as much of the material as possible should be wiped away with rags or absorbent paper towels and the area washed with warm water. If the eye or mouth is involved, wash these areas with plenty of water. On no account use liquids such as paint stripper or turpentine on the skin because these are themselves corrosive and will cause further damage.

Q *How can I prevent my dog from being poisoned?*

A To minimize the risk of a dog being poisoned the following points should be observed.

1 Do not administer any drug which has not been supplied, prescribed, recommended or approved by your veterinary surgeon. Cases are known of owners sharing addictive drugs with their pets, sometimes with disastrous consequences. All preparations for human use (e.g. sleeping pills, aspirins) should be kept out of the animal's reach.

2 Keep dogs away from poisonous substances. The slug bait metaldehyde appears to be particularly attractive to some dogs and animals that get a taste for it may actually seek it out, despite the fact that in Britain repellants have been added to all metaldehyde slug baits since August 1980. Access to rodent and slug poisons should be prevented by siting the poison carefully or covering it. Placing it in the middle of a length of thin drainpipe or under a heavy paving stone raised a couple of inches above the ground is often effective. Remove any dead or dying rodents or pigeons before the dog finds and eats them. Keep the dog off areas of the garden and other land during and after treatment with weed killers, and clean up spilled liquids such as creosote, paraffin (kerosene) and disinfectant which the dog might walk in and subsequently lick off.

Avoid spraying dogs with horticultural sprays and make sure that they do not have access to open containers of spray liquid. Since diluted solutions of most pesticides deteriorate on storage it is officially recommended that any surplus spray solution (or any unwanted undiluted solution) should be disposed of by pouring it down an outside drain. However dogs eating grass sprayed with paraquat (a poison which causes concern since there is no effective treatment) are stated not to be at risk since the chemical becomes so tightly bound to plant tissue that it is not removed during digestion. Most casualties among dogs due to this poison result from their eating of illegal poison baits intended for foxes and prepared with concentrated agricultural paraquat.

3 Do not apply an excessive amount of any preparation in the form of powders or sprays to kill parasites. Try to avoid the animal licking the

coat while these are in place; powders should be brushed out after thirty minutes. Never apply DDT or fly sprays to a dog's coat.

Any antiseptic solution applied to the mammary gland of a suckling bitch should be rinsed off before the puppies feed again. Hexachlorophene poisoning has followed failure to do so.

4 Ensure that the dog always has drinking water available to it, otherwise it may resort to drinking from buckets containing disinfectant solution or garden sprays or even water containing ethylene glycol anti-freeze drained from a car radiator. As little as 1 fluid ounce (30 ml) of anti-freeze may prove fatal to a 15-lb (7-kg) dog, although signs (depression, vomiting, staggering and convulsions) will not appear until at least half an hour after consumption.

5 Do not treat any wooden kennels, or beds, or wickerwork baskets for dogs with wood preservative, or paint them with lead-based paint. All dogs, particularly puppies, are likely to chew at painted woodwork and the sweet taste of lead may encourage them in the habit.

6 Discourage dogs from eating houseplants or plants in the garden because many of them are poisonous, for example daffodil bulbs, laburnum, rhododendron, poinsettia and mistletoe. Overall, however, plant poisoning is not a great problem in dogs.

Q *What is the difference between the treatment of burns and scalds on a dog?*

A Strictly speaking, a burn is caused by dry heat (a flame or hot surface) and a scald by moist heat (boiling water, hot fat or steam). But this distinction has no practical value and the first-aid treatment for any thermal injury is the same — the immediate application of cold water to the area to remove all residual heat from the tissues. If the animal is actually on fire (occasionally this does happen — sometimes as a result of a malicious act), the flames must be smothered immediately by covering the dog with a blanket, rug or coat. Then water should be applied as soon as possible for five to ten minutes with a spray attachment or hose, or simply poured or sponged on.

Don't try to apply grease to the burn, to prick any blisters, *or* try to pull away any burned material (like a blanket or collar) which is stuck to the skin. If any such adherent material is part of a large mass, the rest can be detached by cutting through it three to four inches away from the skin surface.

All burns and scalds should be examined by a veterinary surgeon unless the total area of skin involved is smaller than the palm of your hand and shows no obvious scorching of the hair, or blistering and swelling of the skin. Even so, if the eye or mouth is involved, or the dog is in a state of shock, veterinary attention is required.

Burns can arise from seemingly trivial causes: holding a hot hair-clipper close to the skin, the malfunctioning of a hair dryer or contact with a hot water bottle — especially if the animal is unable to move. A temperature of 158 °F (70 °C) for one minute will destroy skin cells.

Classically, burns are described as first, second or third degree. First-degree burns produce only redness, slight swelling and pain. Second-degree burns result in blistering with considerably more swelling and pain. Third-degree burns are those where the complete thickness of the skin is destroyed, even exposing the underlying tissues; with these severe burns, pain is absent, shock is severe and healing takes a considerable length of time. If the hair can be easily detached the injury is deep. A major burn is a second- or third-degree burn involving more than 20 % of the total body area. Very extensive burning will usually prove fatal and in survivors extreme scarring will produce disfigurement and often difficulty in eating and walking. If a burn involves more than 50 % of the body surface, euthanasia is advisable because the chances of survival are slight; dogs rarely survive more than ten days.

Shock and sepsis are the two major consequences of a burn. First-aid treatment for shock is often necessary, otherwise it may lead to other problems such as a failure of kidney function. Burns can go septic because the protective outer layer of the skin has been destroyed, permitting the entry of pus-producing bacteria. For this reason it is essential that burns should be kept clean.

With a mild burn or scald (i. e. involving a small area and showing only slight redness, swelling and pain), it may be sufficient, after bathing in cold water, to clip the hair, wash the area with toilet soap and then to apply an antihistamine cream. Then a pad of sterile gauze should be used as a dressing and kept in place with a crêpe bandage. The area should be re-dressed (washed, creamed and a fresh pad applied) each day for one to three days, but if a blister or any pus develops a veterinarian should be consulted.

Quite often hot liquids are splashed on to a dog in the kitchen, and the resultant scalds are not detected until, in stroking the animal a day or so later, one or more scabs are felt. These may be oozing with serum or pus which is matting the hair. This type of lesion should be referred to your vet, but if some delay is inevitable clean away any pus by washing with mild toilet soap, rinsing and dabbing dry. But do not try to remove the scab.

Skin contact with very cold surfaces produces lesions similar to thermal burns, known as freezer burns, though here cold water treatment is not required. Nor is it needed with electrical burns arising from chewing through a live flex (usually by puppies under six months old), or falling on to an electric railway conductor rail. Here the important points are to separate the animal from the live surface, *after* the current has been switched off, and then to apply treatment for shock and, if necessary, artificial respiration. If it is difficult to cut off the domestic electricity supply, the dog can be pulled away from the live surface after first being covered with a dry coat, blanket or rug for insulation. However, do not attempt this with a high-voltage supply that is still functioning, (e.g. a conductor rail or overhead cable), because you may be electrocuted yourself.

Q Do dogs get sunburn?

A In general sunburn is rare in dogs though in sunny climates (e.g. Australia and the southern states of the USA) it can affect unpigmented (i.e. white) nasal skin of long-nosed dogs, principally at the junction of the hairy and hairless regions. It is particularly common in the collie breeds, giving rise to the popular name 'collie nose' for the condition (canine nasal solar dermatitis). There is reddening and crusting of the skin with a gradual loss of hair, and in successive years the lesion spreads and the damage becomes worse. Neglected cases may eventually develop skin cancer. Affected dogs should be kept indoors during the hours of strongest sunlight (10 a. m. to 4 p. m.) and a sunscreen cream, containing paraminobenzoic acid, applied thirty minutes before it *has* to go outside, to urinate, etc. As a temporary measure additional pigmentation can be provided by covering the affected area with shoe polish or a black felt marker pen. For enduring protection tattooing with black ink has proved effective.

Q What is a frictional burn?

A Frictional burns arise when a dog is dragged behind a moving vehicle or contacts a revolving wheel. They comprise abrasions (a type of closed wound), plus burning due to the heat of friction, and are usually extensive, very painful, ooze blood and are easily contaminated. As a first aid measure they require bathing (see page 255), dressing with gauze and bandaging; otherwise sepsis of the area is a very common sequel.

Q How should I deal with heatstroke in a dog?

A Dogs, like all animals, will be affected by heatstroke if kept for long in extremely hot, poorly ventilated surroundings, especially if they are without water. The flat-faced breeds (e.g. Boxers) are more likely to be affected because they have more difficulty in increasing the volume of air breathed in and out to cool themselves. Heatstroke most commonly affects animals left in cars parked in the sun during the summer months, but dogs chained up in direct sunlight, or in enclosed rooms or small buildings (sheds and outhouses) in hot weather, will also suffer. It should be borne in mind that areas initially in the shade may later be in the full glare of the sun.

The temperature-regulating mechanism of the body cannot maintain the normal temperature and this gradually rises (hyperthermia). An animal with heatstroke becomes distressed and weak, it pants rapidly, drools saliva and the tongue and lips look very red (later even taking on a bluish tinge). If its temperature continues to climb, the animal will collapse, go into a coma and eventually die.

Immediate treatment is required. The dog must be removed from the hot surroundings and its temperature lowered by applying cold water to the skin. If the animal is unconscious, it can be carefully placed in a bath or a paddling pool filled with cold water, or even carried into the sea, with its head kept above the surface. Alternatively water can be sprayed from a hose or simply poured or sponged over the dog. Usually there is an obvious improvement in the dog's breathing and an increased awareness of its surroundings within five to ten minutes. Care has to be taken not to overdo the lowering of temperature because the disturbance of the brain's usual temperature-regulating mechanism impairs its normal function. Often the body temperature continues to fall for some time after the application of cold water has ceased. In short, there is a danger of lowering the dog's temperature too much. If you have a rectal thermometer and are able to take the temperature it is wise to stop when the temperature falls to 102.5 °F (39.2 °C). A dog's normal body temperature is around 101.5 °F (38.5 °C). It often helps to stimulate the circulation by massaging the animal's legs during this procedure. If necessary, apply artificial respiration.

Dry the dog and let it rest in a cool place with plenty of drinking water. In some cases the temperature begins to rise again although recovery may appear to be complete, and so it is always advisable to seek veterinary attention.

Q Do dogs ever get bitten by snakes?

A It is not uncommon for a dog to suffer a snake bite, usually on the head or neck as dog and snake face each other, but also on the legs. In most countries there are one or more poisonous snakes (and the venom which they inject during a bite varies in its virulence). In Great Britain there is only one, the common adder *(Vipera berus);* in North America there are several, belonging to two sub-families, the pit vipers (including the rattlesnakes, water moccasin and copperhead) and the brightly coloured coral snakes. It is useful to be able to distinguish between the bites of poisonous and non-poisonous snakes. With poisonous snakes the venom causes a severe swelling in the centre of which are two small puncture wounds where the fangs have penetrated the skin; with non-poisonous snakes the bite appears as a U-shaped or semilunar row of tiny punctures with minimal swelling and pain.

Q If my dog is bitten by a snake what should I do?

A With a non-poisonous snake bite, cleaning of the wound, and possibly applying some hydrogen peroxide, is all that is required. With a poisonous bite wound, the prime concern should be to obtain veterinary attention quickly so that an injection of anti-venom can be given. In the meantime, the dog should be kept as calm as possible and its movements restricted to limit the amount of venom absorbed from the injection site. Cleaning the wound is useful, though not immediately essential.

If there is likely to be a considerable delay before a vet can examine the animal or if the venom is known to be extremely toxic (as with many American species of snake), the absorption of venom can be further reduced by applying a light tourniquet and an ice pack. However, a tourniquet can only really be applied to bites on the limbs or (improbably) the tail. Most venom is absorbed through the lymphatic system and so the tourniquet does not need to be so tight as to stop the circulation of blood. A broad rubber band or piece of elastic placed around the limb (between the body and the bite) and clipped in place with a bulldog clip is very effective. Alternatively, a handkerchief or piece of rag could be tied around the limb. It should still be possible to slip a finger under the tourniquet when it is in place. After each forty-five-minute period the tourniquet should be removed for five minutes and then re-applied.

An ice pack can be prepared by placing ice cubes in an old sock, tying up the open end and then crushing the cubes. The pack should then be lightly bandaged in place over the bite. Colder material from a deep freeze should first be wrapped in towels to avoid freezing the body tissues.

Although the removal of venom by sucking from the wound is valuable, there are practical difficulties about performing this successfully on a dog. It involves incising the tissues between the two fang marks with a razor blade to a depth of about $1/5$ inch (5 mm — the thickness of two matchsticks), applying your mouth to the incision and sucking. Any fluid thus removed should be spat out and rinsed away. Be careful not to cut into a major blood vessel and not to get bitten.

Apply artificial respiration if the dog's breathing becomes laboured.

In North America and Australia, though fortunately not Great Britain, bites may also be inflicted by spiders (widow spiders, funnel-web spiders, and brown spiders), ticks and fire ants, as well as stings by scorpions. The venom or other injected material can produce severe local swelling and pain, and in many instances nervous signs. Treatment should be along the same lines as for snake bites, with veterinary attention a priority.

Q *Do dogs ever suffer from hypothermia?*

A Yes, it occurs in dogs poisoned with the rat poison alphachloralose (see page 285), and also in those suffering from exposure after long periods in very cold, wet or windy conditions. If the animal cannot maintain its normal body temperature, despite shivering, its body activity slows down so that it becomes lethargic and then unconscious. At body temperatures below 90 °F (32 °C) shivering stops. The animal feels cold to the touch, its breathing is slow and shallow, and eventually it will die. Newborn animals and old animals are particularly vulnerable to low temperatures, as are immobile individuals (i.e. through injury or being caught in a trap).

The dog should be dried quickly if wet and brought into warm surroundings as soon as possible. However, it should not be subjected to local heat, e.g. by being placed in front of a fire or on a hot water bottle or electric blanket, because the sudden increase in blood flow may cause the animal to collapse. In cases where the animal is comatose, it should be placed in a bath of water at blood heat for ten to fifteen minutes, dried and wrapped in blankets. If the dog is able to drink, it can be given warm milk, but do not give it alcohol or attempt to force feed it. The vet may inject warm fluid directly into the abdominal cavity — a 'core-warming' technique.

Q *Do dogs ever get frostbite?*

A Frostbite may affect the ear tips of erect-eared breeds exposed for a long time to sub-zero temperatures and the scrotum of male dogs in contact with the snow. The dog has no sensation in the skin, which appears pale and very cold to the touch. If frostbite is suspected, gently apply *warm* water with a pad, but *do not* rub vigorously or apply intense heat suddenly. Later, affected areas may appear red, or, in severe cases, black. It is sensible to obtain veterinary advice. *White* hair usually regrows on the ear margins.

Q *Is it ever necessary to deal with wasp and bee stings in dogs?*

A Yes, occasionally it is. Dogs who try to catch these insects may get bitten inside or around the mouth. This will result in pawing at the mouth and increased salivation. Attention is usually drawn to stings on the skin by a cry of pain followed by continual licking of the site. Multiple stings can result in severe illness, but the most serious consequences occur if either the tongue is stung (because it can swell so much that it blocks the passage of air through the throat) or if the individual animal is allergic to the sting and goes into a state of severe shock and collapse (anaphylactic shock). Both of these latter conditions demand immediate veterinary attention.

If the sting is still present at the site looking like a large black splinter (as is often the case with bee stings but usually not with wasp or hornet stings), it should be carefully removed with a pair of tweezers. Then antihistamine cream should be applied to the stung area. If that is not available, or if the sting is in the mouth, the area should be bathed with a 2% sodium bicarbonate solution (one level teaspoonful bicarbonate of soda in a tumbler of warm water). This solution can be introduced into the mouth in the same way as for a liquid medicine (see page 251) and the dog allowed to spit it out.

If there is considerable swelling in the mouth and breathing proves difficult, the dog should be laid on its side and the tongue pulled well forward out of the mouth. Artificial respiration should be applied if necessary and treatment for shock given. Unfortunately, where there is severe obstruction at the back of the throat, artificial respiration will not be sufficient to overcome the blockage and it is imperative to get the dog to a veterinarian as soon as possible.

Q *What is meant by a 'foreign body'?*

A A foreign body is any solid object or fragment which enters part of an animal's body (e.g. a needle, grass seed, piece of bone or glass).

Young dogs are more likely than older ones to swallow objects. Some foreign bodies penetrate the body tissues, either passing through the skin or through the wall of the digestive tract. Others merely become lodged in a part of the body, usually part of the digestive tract, e.g. mouth, stomach or intestines, but sometimes in the ear or nose, beneath the eyelids or between the pads. A foreign body usually causes distress, pain and interference with normal body functions, and a penetrating foreign body can spread infection.

Wherever possible, the foreign body should be removed; this is obviously of vital importance where it is interfering with breathing or causing great distress. The dog will need to be well restrained, preferably on a table in a good light, for you to do this successfully. If necessary, a torch can be used to examine the mouth, nose or ear. Then supportive measures such as artificial respiration and treatment for shock and/or haemorrhage can be applied.

Q *What signs would indicate that a foreign body is troubling my dog? What should I do?*

A Foreign bodies in the mouth cause profuse salivation, often gulping, frantic rubbing and pawing at the mouth, movements of the tongue and jaws and, if the airway is blocked, choking and gasping. If, after opening the mouth (as for the administration of a tablet, see page 249) the foreign body can be seen, it should be firmly grasped with fine-nosed pliers and removed. If there is a thread attached to a needle, it should not be detached because it will serve as a useful guide to the needle's position. Occasionally, a toffee (if the dog is given sweets) or a small cooked bone, such as a vertebra, may be speared by a canine tooth, or a piece of bone may become wedged between the teeth, across the roof of the mouth. Again it may be possible to remove these with pliers. A dog chasing a stick may run into it so that it passes through the roof of the mouth or the soft tissue alongside the tongue; this requires veterinary attention.

Barbed fish hooks which have penetrated the lips or tongue cannot, because of the barbs, be drawn out the same way as they went in. These hooks need to be pushed all the way through, with the animal under a general anaesthetic, and then the barbs cut off with wire cutters so that the shank can be withdrawn.

A foreign body lodged in the larynx (voice box) or trachea (windpipe) may be forced back by lying the dog on its side on a firm surface and applying a sudden sharp downward push on the abdomen, just behind the last rib, with both hands. If the animal's mouth is open it may prove possible for a helper to grasp the foreign body as it is forced up and to prevent it passing back down the throat again. The usual foreign body causing this problem is a small rubber ball which the dog swallows during play, usually by catching it at speed while chasing after it.

Foreign bodies (often grass seeds) up the nose or in the eye or ear should be removed, if protruding, with tweezers. In each instance the affected part will be rubbed by the animal; foreign bodies in the nose also cause sneezing and those in the eye result in increased tear production. (Children may even push beads or beans into the nostrils of good-tempered dogs provoking considerable rubbing, sneezing and snorting which can end in a nose bleed.) If they cannot be removed a vet should be consulted and in the interim a little warm olive oil or liquid paraffin can be dropped into the eye or ear. Do not attempt to put anything up the nose.

Foreign bodies which have been swallowed may cause vomiting, and if they penetrate the wall of the digestive tract blood may be visible in the vomit. If you *know* that your dog has swallowed some sharp object, veterinary attention should be sought immediately. In the interval before the vet can treat the animal, it may prove helpful to feed small pieces of cotton wool soaked in milk or a solution of yeast extract (e.g. Marmite) to make them palatable, in order to form an inert packing around the object. Foreign bodies such as needles can at times pass right through the digestive tract only to turn just before passing out of the anus, thereby lodging in the rectum. The animal licks at the anus and strains, and there may be bleeding. Sometimes string may be seen protruding from the anus. In these cases do not attempt to remove the foreign body but consult your vet. The common billet-hook type of dog-lead clip, fitted with a springy strip of metal, can when detached become tightly clipped around the 'web' of a dog's foot, that is the skin between the toes. It usually proves quite impossible to remove the clip; neither pushing forwards nor backwards will loosen it. In general this type of clip can only be removed by sawing apart with a hacksaw, preferably with the animal tranquillized or anaesthetized. (For this reason dog leads fitted with a trigger hook or pressed scissor hook are preferred.)

Foreign bodies in the paws and skin, such as glass fragments, drawing pins and pieces of tar-covered grit from roads, should be pulled out using fingers, tweezers or pliers wherever possible. If the foreign body has temporarily to remain in a wound, because it is impossible to remove, covering the wound with a thick pad of cotton wool, lightly bandaged in place, can help to limit further trauma. In the summer grass seeds should be removed from the coat, especially the ears, by combing after a walk and in long-haired dogs clipping the hair between the toes at that time of year minimizes the possibility of acquiring grass seeds in the feet.

Q *Is it worthwhile assembling a first-aid kit in case an emergency occurs?*

A This is a very wise precaution and it will certainly enable you to deal speedily and effectively with commonly encountered emergencies. Table IV on page 298 shows what could be usefully included.

Table IV Contents of a First Aid Cabinet

ESSENTIALS

A pair of 5-inch (12.5-cm) flat scissors with rounded (not pointed) ends. These can be proper surgical scissors or an all-purpose pair.

A pair of tweezers with flat (not pointed) ends.

A standard 5-ml teaspoon; (3 teaspoonsful = 1 tablespoonful).

One or two 5-ml size disposable plastic syringes to administer drugs orally.

Two or three 2-inch (5-cm) wide crêpe bandages and a selection of safety pins.

One 100-g box of cotton wool.

One box of sterilized white absorbent gauze.

One 100-g box of absorbent lint.

One roll of l-inch (2.5-cm) wide adhesive plaster (preferably elasticated).

Two or three 2- or 3-inch (5- or 7.5-cm) wide open-weave bandages (to make tape muzzles) or two 3- or 4-foot (90- or 120-cm) lengths of 1½-inch (4-cm) wide tape for the same purpose.

A small bottle of detergent antiseptic such as Savlon, for cleaning wounds.

A small packet of boric acid crystals for bathing eyes.

A tube of antihistamine cream (for application to burns and scalds).

A bottle (100 ml) of 20 vol. (6%) or 10 vol. (3%) hydrogen peroxide (for producing vomiting and cleaning wounds).

A small clearly labelled bottle containing large crystals of washing soda (for the treatment of poisoning).

A small (75- to 100-ml) bottle of olive oil or liquid paraffin (for the cleaning of ears).

A packet of flexible cotton buds.

A styptic pencil (to stop minor bleeding).

A small (25- to 50-g) packet of sodium bicarbonate (for bathing stings).

OTHER USEFUL ITEMS

A pair of nail clippers.

A broad rubber band, or length of wide elastic, plus a bulldog clip, to act as a tourniquet.

A pair of fine-nosed pliers (for the removal of foreign bodies).

A rectal clinical thermometer.

An 'Elizabethan collar', which can be bought or made (see page 267).

A well-fitting muzzle.

A cat basket or some other reliable carrying container, lined with newspaper or blanket – invaluable for a small dog.

Finally, it is useful in an emergency to be able to lay hands an a sturdy lead, about 40 inches (1 m) long, to act as a slip lead (see page 104), *and* an old blanket or rug to act as a stretcher.

Index

302